MOON HAN

GRAND CANYON

© BILL WEIR

Coyote Buttes North

Legend

Divided Highway		Point of Interest	★
Primary Road		Accommodation	●
Secondary Road		Other Location	■
Unpaved Road		Unique Natural Feature	✚
Trails		Mountain	▲
U.S. Interstate		Point	△
U.S. Highway		Ski Area	⚡
State Route		Airstrip	✕
County Road		Campground	⋀
Reservation Road		Dry Lake	
City	○	National Park/Rec. Area	
Town	○	National Forest	
Intermittent Stream		Indian Reservation	
Waterfall		Wilderness Area	

© AVALON TRAVEL PUBLISHING, INC.

GRAND CANYON AND VICINITY

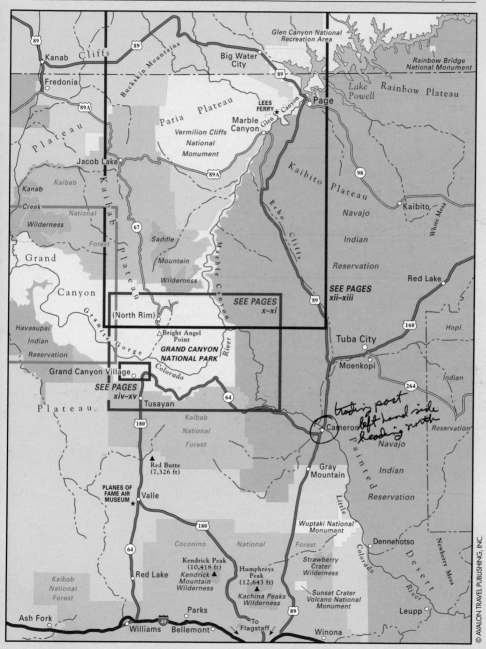

© AVALON TRAVEL PUBLISHING, INC.

GRAND CANYON AND THE
COLORADO RIVER

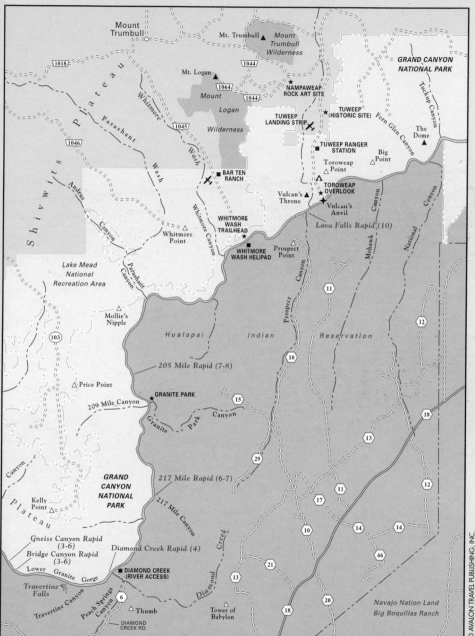

Mount Trumbull

Mt. Trumbull ▲ Mount Trumbull Wilderness

GRAND CANYON NATIONAL PARK

Tuckup Canyon

1018

1044

Mt. Logan ▲

1064

Mount Logan

1045

Wilderness

1044

★ NAMPAWEAP ROCK ART SITE

★ TUWEEP (HISTORIC SITE)

Fern Glen Canyon

The Dome ▲

Whitmore Wash

Parashant Wash

TUWEEP LANDING STRIP

■ TUWEEP RANGER STATION

1046

S h i v w i t s   P l a t e a u

Andrus Canyon

■ BAR TEN RANCH

Whitmore Canyon

WHITMORE WASH TRAILHEAD

Toroweap Point △

Big Point △

Vulcan's Throne ▲

★ TOROWEAP OVERLOOK

★ Vulcan's Anvil

Mohawk Canyon

National Canyon

Lake Mead National Recreation Area

Parashant Canyon

△ Whitmore Point

△ Mollie's Nipple

▓ WHITMORE WASH HELIPAD

Prospect Point △

Lava Falls Rapid (10)

Prospect Canyon

⑪

103

H u a l a p a i   I n d i a n   R e s e r v a t i o n

⑫

205 Mile Rapid (7-8)

⑩

△ Price Point

★ GRANITE PARK

209 Mile Canyon

⑮

Granite Park Canyon

⑱

Canyon

⑬

⑫

�29

GRAND CANYON NATIONAL PARK

217 Mile Rapid (6-7)

217 Mile Canyon

⑪

⑰

Canyon

△ Kelly Point

P l a t e a u

Gneiss Canyon Rapid (3-6)

Bridge Canyon Rapid (3-6)

Diamond Creek

⑩

⑭

⑭

⑭

⑳46

Diamond Creek Rapid (4)

Lower Granite Gorge

Travertine Falls

Travertine Canyon

■ DIAMOND CREEK (RIVER ACCESS)

Peach Springs Canyon

6

△ Thumb

DIAMOND CREEK RD.

Diamond Creek

⑬

㉑

Tower of Babylon △

⑱

⑳

Navajo Nation Land
Big Boquillas Ranch

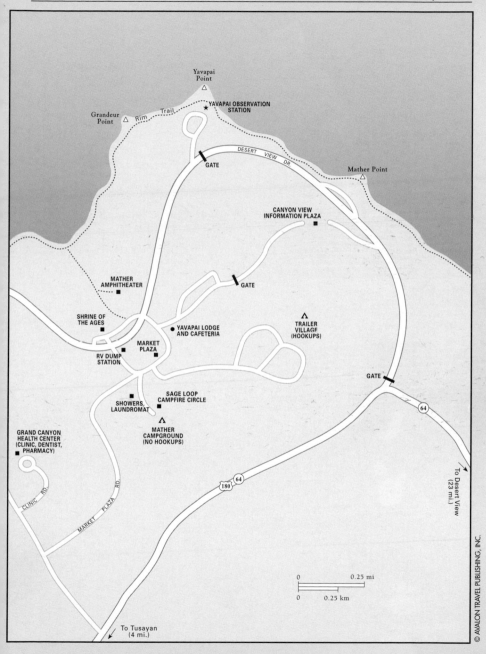

Yavapai
Point

YAVAPAI OBSERVATION
STATION

Grandeur
Point

Rim   Trail

DESERT   VIEW   DR.

GATE

Mather Point

CANYON VIEW
INFORMATION PLAZA

MATHER
AMPHITHEATER

GATE

SHRINE OF
THE AGES

YAVAPAI LODGE
AND CAFETERIA

TRAILER
VILLAGE
(HOOKUPS)

MARKET
PLAZA

RV DUMP
STATION

GATE

64

SHOWERS,
LAUNDROMAT

SAGE LOOP
CAMPFIRE CIRCLE

GRAND CANYON
HEALTH CENTER
(CLINIC, DENTIST,
PHARMACY)

MATHER
CAMPGROUND
(NO HOOKUPS)

CLINIC   RD.

MARKET   PLAZA   RD.

180   64

To Desert View
(23 mi.)

0   0.25 mi

0   0.25 km

To Tusayan
(4 mi.)

Upper Antelope Canyon

© BILL WEIR

MOON HANDBOOKS
GRAND CANYON

SECOND EDITION

BILL WEIR

AVALON
TRAVEL

Moon Handbooks: Grand Canyon
Second Edition

Bill Weir

Published by
Avalon Travel Publishing
5855 Beaudry St.
Emeryville, CA 94608, USA

Please send all comments, corrections,
additions, amendments, and critiques to:

Moon Handbooks: GRAND CANYON
AVALON TRAVEL PUBLISHING
5855 BEAUDRY ST.
EMERYVILLE, CA 94608, USA
email: atpfeedback@avalonpub.com
www.travelmatters.com

Printing History
1st edition—1999
2nd edition—January 2002
5 4 3 2 1

ISBN: 1-56691-371-3
ISSN: 1522-3485

Editor: Angelique S. Clarke
Series Manager: Erin Van Rheenen
Copy Editor: Vera Gross
Graphics Coordinator: Susan Mira Snyder
Production Coordinator: Jacob Goolkasian
Map Editors: Naomi Dancis, Olivia Solis
Cartographers: Mike Morgenfeld, Chris Folks, Allen Leech
Proofreader and Indexer: J.L. Trizzino

Front cover photo: © John Elk III

Distributed by Publishers Group West

Printed in The United States by R.R. Donnelley

ABOUT THE AUTHOR
Bill Weir

Back in school, Bill Weir always figured he'd settle down to a career job and live happily ever after. Then he discovered traveling. After graduating with a B.A. degree in physics from Berea College in 1972, Bill found employment as an electronic technician, but the short vacation breaks didn't provide enough time for the trips he dreamed of.

So in 1976 he took off on his trusty bicycle, Bessie, riding across the United States with Bikecentennial '76. The following year he took off on an even longer bicycle trip—from Alaska to Baja California. Then came the ultimate journey—a bicycle cruise around the world. When Bill returned home to Arizona, he set to work researching and writing *Moon Handbooks: Arizona.*

Bill continues to explore Arizona and beyond, always discovering new places and learning more about the old. During 1994, for example, he visited the amazing cultures and landscapes of Tibet and Nepal. Then, in the following year, he dusted off ol' Bessie the Bicycle for the final leg of the round-the-world trip started 19 years ago. Poor Bessie, however, was put out to pasture, so Bill got his new "Bessie Too the Bicycle" and explored more of the Himalayas—riding from Bangladesh to Nepal via Sikkim—and more of Europe, pedaling north from Greece until the road ran out at Nordkapp in the Norwegian arctic. Bill's most recent cycling adventure crossed the "Rooftop of the World" on a ride from Lhasa in Tibet to Katmandu in Nepal, then west across the Himalayan foothills of India and into northern Pakistan, ending in the alpine valley of Swat.

Visit www.arizonahandbook.com for the latest updates, web links, photo galleries, and booklists. You'll also find news and photos of Bill's latest cycling and trekking adventures.

Contents

Abbreviations

4WD—four-wheel drive
a/c—air-conditioning
ATV—all-terrain vehicle
AZ—Arizona highway
B&B—bed-and-breakfast
BLM—Bureau of Land Management
CCC—Civilian Conservation Corps
d—double
elev.—elevation

F—Fahrenheit
hp—horsepower
RV—recreational vehicle
s—single
tel.—telephone
topo—topographical map
US—federal highway
U.S.G.S.—United States Geological Survey
UT—Utah highway

Keeping Current

Nothing stays the same, it seems. Although this book has been carefully researched, the Grand Canyon and its surrounding areas will continue to grow and change. New sights and services will open while others change hands or close. Your comments and ideas on making *Moon Handbooks: Grand Canyon* more useful to other readers will be highly valued. If you find something new, discontinued, or changed, please let me know so that the information can be included in the next edition. Please send emails with your thoughts and experiences to atpfeedback@avalonpub.com or you can reach me directly through my website www.arizonahandbook.com.

If you have a question about an order or other business transaction, always contact Avalon Travel Publishing directly—as I may be off at some remote monastery or mountain! Address your letters to:

Moon Handbooks: Grand Canyon
Avalon Travel Publishing
5855 Beaudry St.
Emeryville, CA 94608, USA
email:atpfeedback@avalonpub.com

Map Contents

MAP SYMBOLS

Divided Highway	County or Forest Road	Ski Resort
Primary Road	Point of Interest	Airfield/Airstrip
Secondary Road	Accommodation	State Park
Trail	Restaurant/Bar	Campground
Railroad	Other Location	Waterfall
U.S. Interstate	Unique Natural Feature	Mountain
U.S. Highway	State Capital	Point
State Highway	City	Golf Course
Indian Route	Town	

Preface

As one of the Seven Natural Wonders of the World, the Grand Canyon certainly lives up to its billing! The many rim viewpoints help you get the big picture. You'll also find that the Grand Canyon contains countless canyons within canyons, each a little world of its own with distinct geology, plants, and animals. Trails and routes inside will lead to discovery of some of these canyon realms. A river trip down the Colorado rates as one of the world's greatest adventures, opening up even more areas to appreciation and exploration.

Fascinating areas surround the Grand Canyon. Travels on the lands of the Havasupai, Hualapai, Navajo, and Hopi provide cultural insights and spectacular scenery. Arizona's highest summit, Humphrey's Peak, soars from the San Francisco Volcanic Field south of the Grand Canyon. The high Kaibab Plateau north of the Grand Canyon offers not only beautiful forests of spruce, fir, ponderosa pine, and aspen, but some of the best Canyon viewpoints. If you're looking for grand scenery and solitude, then you've got it on the remote Arizona Strip between the Grand Canyon and the Utah border. Very few visitors travel the wilderness trails and back roads here.

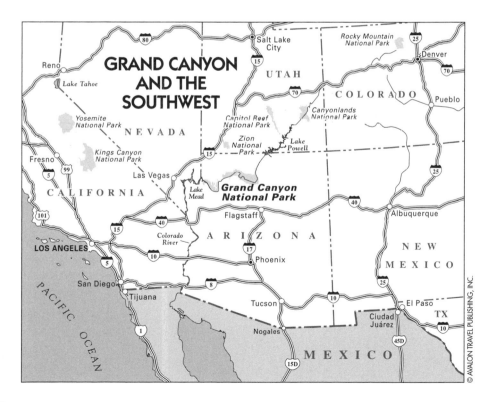

Introduction

Two mighty but opposing forces—uplifting of the massive Colorado Plateau and vigorous downcutting by the Colorado River—occurring millions of years apart, created the awe-inspiring Grand Canyon and its many tributaries. Neither pictures nor words can fully describe the sight. You have to experience the Canyon by traveling along the rim, descending into the depths, riding the waves of the Colorado River, and watching the continuous show of colors and patterns as the sun moves across the sky.

The Canyon's grandeur stretches for 277 miles across northern Arizona; it's as much as 18 miles wide—10 miles on average—and one mile deep. Roads provide access to developed areas and viewpoints on both rims. Trails allow hikers and mule riders to descend the precipitous cliffs to the Colorado River. Yet most of the park remains as remote as ever, rarely visited by humans.

The Land

This is a land of time. Massive cliffs expose limestone composed of animals that lived in long-departed seas, sandstone of ancient desert sand dunes, and shale beds made of silt from now-vanished rivers and shores. Volcanic eruptions deposited layers of ash, cinders, and lava. Deeper in the Canyon lie the roots of mountain ranges whose peaks towered over a primitive land two billion years ago. Time continues to flow in the Canyon with the cycles of the plants and animals that live here, and with the erosive forces of water ever widening and deepening the chasm.

GEOGRAPHY

Colorado Plateau

This giant uplifted landmass in northern Arizona also extends across much of adjacent Utah, Colorado, and New Mexico. Rivers have cut deeply into the plateau, creating the Grand Canyon of the Colorado and other vast gorges. Volcanoes breaking through the surface have left hundreds of cinder cones, such as multicolored Sunset Crater, and larger volcanic complexes, such as the San Francisco Peaks. The most recent burst of volcanic activity in Arizona took place near Sunset Crater about 800 years ago. Most elevations on the plateau range from 5,000 to 8,000 feet. The most dramatic boundaries of the Plateau lie to the south at the Mogollon (MUGGY-own) Rim and west at the Grand Wash Cliffs.

Forming of the Grand Canyon

Geologists have a difficult time pinpointing the age of the Grand Canyon itself, though it is far younger than even the most recent rock layers—those on the rim, which are about 250 million years old. These lay near sea level 70

© BILL WEIR

Angels Window at Cape Royal on the North Rim

million years ago, when the earth's crust began a slow uplift. Some time after that the ancestral Colorado River settled on its present course and began to carve the Canyon. The big question is when! Too much of the geologic record is missing to provide a conclusive answer yet. Studies of river deposits have led to conflicting theories of the birth of the Grand Canyon: any time between 5 and 70 million years ago. Even the direction of the ancestral Colorado is in dispute—some geologists think that the Little Colorado and upper Colorado once drained northward; a look at a map of Marble Canyon supports this view because the tributaries suggest a tilt of the land to the north. Or perhaps the Colorado River followed its present course but in the opposite direction, later to be reversed by tilting of the Colorado Plateau. Other theories claim that the Colorado and Little Colorado flowed southward either into a giant lake or into the Rio Grande to the Gulf of Mexico. A second, younger river could have carved the lower Grand Canyon and eventually captured the upper river near the present junction of the Colorado and Little Colorado Rivers. Or perhaps the lake had filled to overflowing from other sources, then broken through and carved the Little Colorado and Colorado Rivers in a catastrophic flood about 5 million years ago. Still other geologists stick with John Wesley Powell's theory that the Colorado has always followed its present course after the uplift began about 70 million years ago. The problem with this idea is that no river deposits older than 5 million years have been found near the lower end of the Grand Canyon.

No matter how the Grand Canyon did form, gradual uplift continued, giving the waters a steeper gradient and thus greater power. Today, the South Rim reaches elevations of 7,000–7,500 feet, while the North Rim towers about 1,000 feet higher. The Colorado River drops through the Canyon at an average gradient of 7.8 feet per mile, 25 times that of the lower Mississippi.

CLIMATE

In the Grand Canyon, as on a mountainside, temperatures change with elevation, but with added canyon peculiarities. Year-round, the bottom of the canyon stays 20–30 degrees warmer than along the rims. In winter, the sun's low angle allows only a few hours of sunlight a day to reach the Inner Gorge, creating a cooling effect. The situation reverses during the summer, when the sun's high angle turns the Canyon into an oven. At night, temperatures often drop lower than you'd expect, when cold, dense air on the rims pours over the edge into the depths.

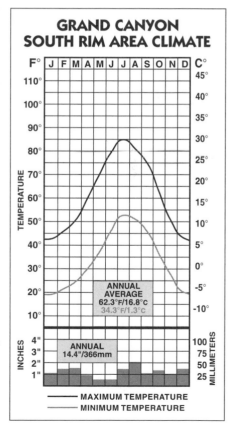

GRAND CANYON SOUTH RIM AREA CLIMATE

ANNUAL AVERAGE
62.3°F/16.8°C
34.3°F/1.3°C

ANNUAL
14.4"/366mm

——— MAXIMUM TEMPERATURE
——— MINIMUM TEMPERATURE

The Seasons

In one day, a hiker can travel from the cold fir and aspen forests of the North Rim to the hot cactus country of the Canyon bottom—a climate change equal to that between Canada and Mexico. In the Inner Gorge (elev. 2,480 feet at Phantom Ranch), summer temperatures soar, with average highs over 100°F; the thermometer commonly tops 115°F in early July. Spring and autumn offer pleasantly warm weather and are the best times to visit. Winter down by the river can be fine too; even in January, days warm up to the 50s or low 60s and

it rarely freezes. Only 9.4 inches of precipitation makes it to the bottom in an average year; snow and rain often evaporate completely while falling through the mile of warm Canyon air.

The South Rim enjoys pleasant weather most of the year. Summer highs reach the mid-80s, cooling during winter to highs in the upper 30s and lower 40s. Winter campers need warm sleeping bags to combat frosty nights when temperatures plunge into the teens. Yearly precipitation at the South Rim's Grand Canyon Village (elev. 6,950 feet) is

14.4 inches, with snow accumulations seldom exceeding 2 feet.

Although averaging only 1,000 feet higher, the North Rim in the Bright Angel Point area really gets socked in by winter storms. Snow piles up to depths of 6–10 feet in an average season, and the National Park Service doesn't even try to keep the roads open there from early November–mid-May. Summers can be a joy in the cool, fresh air; highs then run in the 60s and 70s. Bright Angel Ranger Station (elev. 8,400 feet) on the North Rim receives 25.6 inches of annual precipitation.

Most moisture falls during the winter and late summer (mid-July–mid-September). Summer rains often arrive in spectacular afternoon thunderstorms, soaking one spot in the Canyon and leaving another bone dry only a short distance away. The storms put on a great show from the rim viewpoints, but you should take cover if lightning gets close (less than seven seconds between the flash and the thunder) and especially if the hair on your head stands on end or if you smell ozone. As in mountain areas, the Grand Canyon's weather can change rapidly. Always carry water and raingear when heading down a trail.

Storm Hazards
Rainwater runs quickly off the rocky desert surfaces and into gullies and canyons. Flash floods can sweep away anything in their paths, including boulders, cars, and campsites. Take care not to camp or park in potential flash-flood areas. If you come to a section of flooded roadway, a common occurrence on desert roads after storms, just wait until the water goes down—usually only an hour or so. Summer lightning causes forest and brush fires and poses a danger to hikers foolish enough to be exposed when storms threaten.

Flora and Fauna

The seemingly endless variations of elevation, exposure, and moisture allow for an astonishing range of plant and animal communities. The Canyon also acts as a barrier to many nonflying creatures who live on just one side of the Colorado River or only in the Inner Gorge. Some mammals, such as Abert's (on the South Rim) and Kaibab (on the North Rim) squirrels, spotted skunk, cliff chipmunk, and common pocket gopher, evolved into separate subspecies on each rim.

VEGETATION ZONES AND WILDLIFE

Spruce-Fir Forest
You'll find dense forests of spruce and fir and groves of quaking aspen on the Kaibab Plateau of the North Rim, mostly above 8,200 feet. Common trees include Engelmann and blue spruce, Douglas fir (not a true fir), white and subalpine fir, aspen, and mountain ash. Lush meadows, dotted with wildflowers in summer, spread out in shallow valleys at the higher elevations.

Animals of the spruce-fir forest include mule deer, mountain lion, porcupine, red and Kaibab squirrels, Uinta chipmunk, long-tailed vole, and northern pocket gopher. Birds you might see include turkey, great horned owl, saw-whet owl, broad-tailed hummingbird, hairy woodpecker, hermit thrush, Clark's nutcracker, Steller's jay, and mountain bluebird.

Ponderosa Pine Forest
Stands of tall ponderosas grow between elevations of 7,000–8,000 feet on both rims. Mature forests tend to be open, allowing in sunlight for Gambel oak, New Mexican locust, mountain mahogany, greenleaf manzanita, cliffrose, wildflowers, and grasses.

Animals and birds found here include most of those resident in the spruce-fir forests. The Abert's squirrel, though common in the Southwest, lives within the park only on the South Rim. This squirrel has tufted ears and a body and tail that are mostly gray with white undersides. The shy Kaibab squirrel, easily identified by an all-white tail and tufted ears, lives only on the North Rim. It probably evolved from Abert's squirrels that crossed the Colorado River long ago, perhaps during the Pleistocene epoch.

Pinyon-Juniper Woodland

These smaller trees abound in drier and more exposed places between elevations of 4,000–8,000 feet. Their neighbors commonly include broadleaf yucca, cliffrose, rabbit brush, Mormon tea, sagebrush, fernbrush, serviceberry, and Apache plume.

Mule deer, mountain lion, coyote, gray fox, desert cottontail, Stephen's woodrat, pinyon mouse, rock squirrel, cliff chipmunk, lizards, and snakes (including rattlesnakes) make their homes here. Birds include mourning dove, plain titmouse, Bewick's wren, black-throated gray warbler, and pinyon and scrub jays.

Desert Scrub

Except near permanent water, the low-desert country below 4,500 feet cannot support trees. Instead, you'll find such hardy plants as blackbrush, Utah agave, narrowleaf yucca, various cacti, desert thorn, Mormon tea, four-wing saltbush, and snakeweed.

Animals include bighorn sheep, black-tailed jackrabbit, spotted skunk, desert woodrat, antelope ground squirrel, and canyon mouse. Most reptiles hole up during the day, though lizards seem to tolerate higher temperatures

common raven *(Corvus corax)*

BOB RACE

than snakes. Chuckwalla, spiny and collared lizards, common king snake, whipsnake, and the Grand Canyon rattlesnake live in this part of the Canyon. The shy Grand Canyon or pink rattlesnake, a subspecies of the western rattlesnake, lives nowhere else. Birds of the desert scrub have to either look elsewhere for nesting trees or choose a spot in cliffs or on the ground. Species you might see include common raven, turkey vulture, golden eagle, red-tailed hawk, rock and canyon wrens, and black-throated sparrow. You'll probably hear the song of the water-loving canyon wren without ever seeing him; he sings in an unforgettable descending scale.

Riparian Woodlands

Until 1963, seasonal floods of the Colorado River ripped away most vegetation below the high-water mark. Then, when the Glen Canyon Dam was completed upstream, tamarisk (an exotic species originally from the Arabian deserts) speeded up its takeover of formerly barren beaches. Native cattail, coyote willow, and arrowweed now thrive too. Seeps and springs support luxuriant plant growth and supply water for desert wildlife.

Beaver, river otter, ringtail cat, raccoon, deer mouse, spotted sandpiper, blue grosbeak, Lucy's warbler, Woodhouse's toad, and the tree lizard make their homes near the streams. Fremont cottonwood trees in the tributaries provide welcome shade for overheated hikers. The cold, clear waters that flow from Glen Canyon Dam have upset breeding patterns of the eight native fish species (only four now survive); they now spawn in warmer waters at the mouths of the Little Colorado River and Havasu Creek. Rainbow trout and at least 16 other species have been introduced.

OLD-GROWTH FORESTS

Only 5 percent of Arizona's old-growth forest remains. It survives in remote canyons and on a few mountains, some under federal protection. Scientists find the old-growth forests an amazingly complex interaction of life and decay. Hundreds of species of fungi, insects, birds, animals, and plants feed or protect one another in ways still being discovered. We've also learned about forest management from these old systems. Checks and balances in these forests limit damage of insect and mistletoe infestations, an advantage that managed forests of uniformly aged trees don't share. Fires in the old growths burn cool and close to the ground and do little harm, because the shade from mature trees prevents excessive growth of brush and thickets of small trees; also, the branches of mature trees lie above the reach of most fires. Natural fires move through every 5–7 years, clearing the underbrush and fertilizing the soil with ash. Even in death, a large tree can stand 50 years, providing a home for generations of birds and insects. Foresters once removed these old snags as fire hazards, but now we know that many birds depend on them.

History

PREHISTORY

The First Peoples

Native Americans knew of this land and its canyons centuries before White people arrived. At least 4,000 years ago, a hunting and gathering society stalked the plateaus and canyons of northern Arizona, leaving behind stone spear points and some small split-twig figures resembling deer or sheep. Preserved in caves in the Grand Canyon, these figurines date from approximately 2000 B.C.

The Ancestral Puebloans Arrive

Ancestors of today's Pueblo tribes came to the Grand Canyon area in about A.D. 500. Like their predecessors, they hunted deer, bighorn sheep, jackrabbits, and other animals, while gathering such wild plant foods as pinyon nuts and agave. The ancestral Puebloans also fashioned fine baskets and sandals. At their peak, between 1050 and 1150, they grew crops, crafted pottery, and lived in aboveground masonry villages. Toward the end of this period,

drought hit the region. By 1150 nearly all the ancestral Puebloans had departed from the Grand Canyon, leaving more than 2,000 sites behind. It's likely that their migrations eventually took them to the Hopi mesas, and farther east to the Rio Grande Valley.

Archaeologists have used the term Anasazi for this culture, but the Navajo word means "ancient enemies"—not a phrase that modern-day Pueblo tribes care to use in reference to their ancestors! So this book uses the more respectful phrase "ancestral Puebloans."

Other Tribes Come to the Canyon

While the ancestral Puebloans kept mostly to the east half of the Grand Canyon (east of today's Grand Canyon Village), another group of hunter-gatherers and farmers, the Cohonina, lived downstream between A.D. 600 and 1150. They adopted many of the agricultural and building techniques and crafts of their neighbors to the east. In 1300, the Cerbat, probable ancestors of the modern Havasupai and Hualapai, migrated onto the Grand Canyon's South Rim from the west. They lived in caves or brush shelters and ranged as far upstream as the Little Colorado River in search of game and wild plant foods. The Cerbat also planted crops in areas of fertile soil or permanent springs. It's possible that the Cerbat had cultural ties with the earlier Cohonina.

Paiute living north of the Grand Canyon made seasonal trips to the North Rim, occasionally clashing with the Cerbat. The Paiute lived in brush shelters and relied almost entirely on hunting and gathering. They spent their summers in high country such as the Kaibab Plateau, then moved to lower elevations for the winter. Hopi knew of the Grand Canyon too; they came on religious pilgrimages to collect salt.

EXPLORATION

Spanish and American Explorers

In 1540, when Francisco Vásquez de Coronado led an expedition in search of the Seven Cities of Cíbola, Hopi villagers told a detachment of soldiers about a great canyon to the west. Hopi guides later took a party of Coronado's men, led by García López de Cárdenas, to the South Rim but kept secret the routes into the depths. The immensity of the Grand Canyon impressed the Spaniards, who failed in their attempt to find a way to the river. Franciscan priest Francisco Tomás Garcés, looking for souls to save, visited the Havasupai and Hualapai in 1776 and was well received. Historians credit Garcés with naming the Río Colorado ("Red River"). James Ohio Pattie and other American fur trappers probably found the Grand Canyon in the late 1820s, but they provided only sketchy accounts of their visits.

Exploring the Grand Canyon

Lieutenant Joseph Ives led the first real exploration of the Colorado River. He chugged 350

Triangulation Station

© THE EXPLORATION OF THE COLORADO RIVER AND ITS CANYONS

miles by steamboat upstream from the river's mouth in 1857–58 before crashing into a rock in Black Canyon. The party then continued overland to the Diamond Creek area in the western Grand Canyon. Ives thought the region worthless and doubted that people would come again.

Most of the Canyon remained a dark and forbidding unknown until Major John Wesley Powell bravely led a boat expedition through the chasm in 1869. On this trip and on a second journey in 1871–72, he and his men made detailed drawings and took notes on geology, flora and fauna, and prehistoric ruins. Powell recorded his experiences in *Canyons of the Colorado,* now published as *The Exploration of the Colorado River and Its Canyons.*

SETTLING IN

Ranching on the Arizona Strip

Not many pioneers took an interest in the prairie here—the ground proved nearly impossible to plow and water for irrigation was lacking. Determined Mormons began ranching in the 1860s despite the isolation and occasional Navajo raids. They built Winsor Castle, a fortified ranch, in 1870 as a base for a large church-owned cattle herd. Mormons also founded the towns of Fredonia, Short Creek (now Colorado City), and Littlefield.

Some of these settlers had fled Utah to escape federal laws prohibiting polygamy. About 3,000 members of a polygamous excommunicated Mormon sect still live in Colorado City and neighboring Hildale, Utah. Federal and state officials have raided Colorado City several times, most recently in 1953, when 27 arrests were made—those charged received one year of probation. Now government policy seems to be mostly "live and let live."

Miners and Tourists

After about 1880, prospectors entered the Grand Canyon to search for copper, asbestos, silver, and lead deposits. Their trails, many following old Indian routes, are still used by modern hikers.

In 1883, stagecoaches began bringing tourists to the Western Canyon at Diamond Creek, where J.H. Farlee opened a four-room hotel the following year. Prospectors Peter Berry and Ralph and Niles Cameron built the Grandview Hotel in 1895 at Grandview Point and led tourists down a trail to Horseshoe Mesa. Other prospectors, such as John Hance and William Bass, also found guiding visitors more profitable than mining. Tourism began on a large scale soon after the railroad reached the South Rim in 1901. The Fred Harvey Company bought Bright Angel Lodge, built the deluxe El Tovar Hotel, and took over from the smaller operators.

The Park Is Born

As the Canyon became better known, President Theodore Roosevelt and others pushed for greater federal protection. First a forest reserve in 1893, the Grand Canyon became a national monument in 1908 and a national park in 1919. The park's size doubled in 1975 when legislation extended the boundaries west to Grand Wash and northeast to Lees Ferry. Grand Canyon National Park now includes 1,892 square miles and receives about five million visitors annually.

The People

NATIVE AMERICANS OF THE GRAND CANYON AREA

Havasupai

Long before the first White people arrived, this tribe farmed the fertile Havasu Canyon floor in the Grand Canyon during the summer, moving to the plateau after harvest to gather abundant wild foods and firewood during winter. Spanish missionary Francisco Garcés visited the Havasupai in 1776, finding them a happy and industrious people. Though a peaceful tribe, the Havasupai ("people of the blue-green water") suffered the usual fate of Native Americans—confinement to a tiny reservation while White people grabbed their lands. The Havasupai protested, but it wasn't until 1975 that the tribe's winter homelands were returned. The Havasupai Reservation now spans 188,077 acres; most of the 500–600 tribal members on the reservation live in Supai village.

Supai lies 35 air miles northwest of Grand Canyon Village in Havasu Canyon, a major Grand Canyon tributary. The waterfalls, travertine pools, and greenery of the remote canyon have earned it fame as a Shangri-La.

Hualapai

The "Pine Tree People" once occupied a large area of northwestern Arizona. In language and culture, they're closely tied to the Havasupai and Yavapai tribes. Early White visitors enjoyed friendly relations with the Hualapai, but land seizures and murders by the newcomers led to warfare. Army troops defeated the Hualapai and herded them south onto the Colorado River Reservation, where many died. Survivors fled back to their traditional lands, part of which later became the Hualapai Indian Reservation. About half of the 1,500 tribal members live on the 993,000-acre reservation, which includes much of the lower Grand Canyon's South Rim. Highlights for visitors include the drive into the Grand Canyon to Diamond Creek, Colorado River rafting trips, and spectacular viewpoints from the rim of the western Grand Canyon. Peach Springs, a small town 54 miles northeast of Kingman on US 66, is the only town on the reservation.

Paiute

A small band of Paiute lives on the Kaibab-Paiute Indian Reservation, west of Fredonia in far northern Arizona. In earlier times they used this area as a winter home and spent summers in the forests of the Kaibab Plateau to the east. About 250 Paiute, who speak a Uto-Aztecan

Navajo ready for a journey, circa late 1800s

language, live on the reservation. The tribe arrived sometime after 1300, though members believe themselves related to the ancestral Puebloans who once lived on this land. The adjacent Pipe Spring National Monument preserves pioneer and tribal traditions.

Navajo

The semi-nomadic Navajo, relatives of the Athabaskans of western Canada, wandered into the area east of the Grand Canyon between A.D. 1300 and 1600. This adaptable tribe learned agriculture, weaving, pottery, and other skills from its Pueblo neighbors and became skilled horsemen and sheepherders with livestock obtained from the Spanish.

The Navajo habit of raiding neighboring tribes—this time, White people—almost caused the tribe's downfall. In 1863–64 the U.S. Army rounded up all the Navajo it could find and forced them to make "The Long Walk" from Fort Defiance in eastern Arizona to a bleak camp at Fort Sumner in eastern New Mexico. This attempt at forced domestication failed dismally, and the surviving Navajo were released four years later to return to their homeland. The colorful velveteen blouses and long, flowing skirts worn by some Navajo women date back in style to this period; it was what U.S. Army wives were then wearing!

Hopi

Legends and long-abandoned pueblos indicate that the tribe has lived in the region for more than a thousand years. Old Oraibi, a Hopi village dating from at least A.D. 1150, is thought to be the oldest continuously inhab-

Navajo petroglyph in lower Canyon de Chelly

ited settlement in the United States, and some Hopi identify even older village sites as the homes of their ancestors, whom they call *Hisatsinom*.

Spanish explorers entered the region in the 1500s, looking for gold and treasure, but they left empty-handed. Desiring to save Hopi souls, Spanish friars arrived about 1630 and had some success until traditional Hopi leaders, fearing the loss of their own culture, joined with the New Mexico Pueblo tribes in a revolt against the Spanish in 1680. Hopi killed any foreigner unable to escape, massacred many of their own people who were Christians, and tore down the mission buildings. During the 1800s, American frontiersmen arrived seeking mineral wealth and fertile lands, but they too usually met with disappointment.

The Hopi still devote themselves to their ancient religion and continue to raise traditional crops of corn, squash, and beans. Modern educational and job opportunities have enabled the tribe to improve its living conditions. Curious tourists overwhelm the villages at times, but the Hopi welcome visitors who respect local culture and regulations. Highlights of a visit on the reservation include Walpi, a traditional stone village that seems to grow out of its spectacular ridge-top setting on First Mesa; the museum at the Cultural Center on Second Mesa; and the kachina and other dances performed on many weekends (not all dances are open to the public).

Visiting the Tribal Lands

Privacy of the residents needs to be respected; permits are required for sightseeing or other activities off the main roads. Native Americans prefer *not* to be treated as anthropological subjects, so it's important to ask permission before taking photos. The Hopi generally forbid photography, so don't even think of pulling out a camera on the reservation!

You'll find at least one motel and campground on all of the reservations noted above except for the Kaibab-Paiute, which has only a campground. The Navajo and Hopi Reservations have good tribal museums.

Two other museums of Native American cultures, the Heard in Phoenix and the Museum of Northern Arizona in Flagstaff, provide especially good introductions to the tribes and their crafts.

On the Road

Outdoor Recreation

Hiking

Entering the Grand Canyon under your own power gives you the best feel for its size, grandeur, and details. Easy paths follow sections of the rims, a few wide and well-graded trails enter the depths, narrower and more difficult trails extend farther out into the backcountry, and some very difficult routes go to places rarely visited. Because of the Grand Canyon's immensity and potential hazards, hikers need to give some thought to what they wish to do, then carry sufficient water, food, maps, and supplies for the trip.

The region also has fine hiking in tributaries of the Colorado River, such as Paria Canyon north of Lees Ferry and Havasu Canyon farther downstream. The hike to Rainbow Bridge on the Navajo Indian Reservation offers many awe-inspiring views. Near Page, you can wander into the cave-like passages of Antelope Canyon, also on Navajo lands. Mountains of the Arizona Strip north of the Grand Canyon have some great little climbs, as do the many peaks of the San Francisco Volcanic Field to the south.

Whitewater

The Colorado River through the Grand Canyon has it all—big-water rapids, serene passages of smooth water, and gorgeous canyons, and it provides an amazing tour of the Earth's geology. The 280 river miles from Lees Ferry to the end of the Grand Canyon at Lake Mead requires a big commitment in time and gear, so you'll want to plan carefully. You can go either on your own—if suitably equipped and experienced—or with a river company. See the "Running the Colorado River" section.

© BILL WEIR

Sunset from Mather Point

Bicycling

To be fully alive to the land, skies, sounds, plants, and birds of Arizona, consider touring on a bicycle. Gliding across the desert or topping out on a mountain pass are experiences beyond words. Some effort, a lightweight touring or mountain bicycle, and awareness of your surroundings are all that's required.

In Grand Canyon National Park, cyclists have the big advantage of being able to ride the Hermit road and the road to Yaki Point even when they're closed to cars. Although hiking trails in the park are closed to bicycles, the Kaibab National Forest on both rims features some excellent mountain biking through the forest and to Canyon overlooks. The North Rim offers the most possibilities, including the road out to Point Sublime for perhaps the very best views in the entire park. The regions surrounding the Grand Canyon have good riding too, both for mountain biking and long-distance touring.

Start with short rides if you're new to bicycle touring, then work up to longer cross-country trips. By learning to maintain and repair your steed, you'll seldom have trouble on the road. An extra-low gear of 30 inches or less will take the strain out of long mountain grades. The performance of mountain bikes for touring can be improved by using road tires (no knobs) and handlebar extenders (for a variety of riding positions). Bookstores and bicycle shops provide good publications on bicycle touring. As when hiking, always carry rain and wind gear and plenty of water. Also, don't forget to wear a bicycling helmet.

Fishing

Rainbow trout thrive in the cold water that flows from Glen Canyon Dam, upstream of the Grand Canyon. Lees Ferry offers the easiest fishing access, either from the shore or on a boat. Fishing downstream from here requires the effort of hiking into the Grand Canyon or taking a river-rafting trip. Trout also lurk in permanent tributaries such as Bright Angel Creek. Other popular fishing areas in the region include vast Lake Powell above the Grand Canyon and Lake Mead below it.

The trout could not have survived before the dam was in place. Before the early 1960s, the warm river water had so much silt and such irregular flows that only a handful of specially adapted fish and some hardy exotic species swam in the Colorado. The native Colorado pikeminnow, humpback chub, bonytail chub, and humpback or razorback sucker are now endangered; anglers should know what they look like and return any they catch to the water.

Skiing

Grand Canyon National Park doesn't have developed ski areas or trails, but the North Rim area offers limitless backcountry skiing. On the South Rim, cross-country ski loops lie just a few miles south of Grandview Point in the Kaibab National Forest. Flagstaff features the best downhill facilities of the region and a large Nordic center. Williams offers a smaller downhill area and a couple of cross-country areas too.

KEEPING THE "WILD" IN WILDERNESS—KNOW BEFORE YOU GO

As more people seek relief from the confusion and stress of urban life, the use of wilderness areas increases. Fortunately, the Grand Canyon area contains an abundance of this fragile and precious resource. Most of the park's trails and the many designated wilderness areas nearby are closed to mechanized vehicles—including mountain bikes—to protect the environment and enhance the experience of solitude. Hikers need to purchase camping permits for the backcountry of Grand Canyon National Park, for any recreation on tribal lands, for day or overnight visits in the Bureau of Land Management's Paria, Buckskin, or Wire Pass Canyons, or for day use in the nearby Coyote Buttes area. You're generally free to visit the other designated wilderness areas on Kaibab National Forest and BLM lands anytime without a permit.

Spectacular and memorable hiking and camping await the prepared outdoors enthusiast. But because Arizona's deserts and canyons are very different from most other parts of the country, even expert hikers can get into trouble. If you're new to these outdoors, read up on hiking conditions and talk to rangers and local hikers. Backpacking stores and the Internet are good sources of information. Start with easy trips and gradually work up to long hikes.

Suggestions for backcountry travel and camping include these wilderness guidelines:
• Before heading into the backcountry, check with a knowledgeable person about weather, water sources, fire danger, trail conditions, and regulations, secure hiking permits if required.
• Tell a reliable person where you're going and when you expect to return.
• Travel in small groups for the best experience; group size may also be regulated.
• Try not to camp on meadows, as the grass is easily damaged.
• Do not dig tent trenches or cut vegetation.
• Use a camp stove or fire pan to prevent marring the land with fire.
• Camp at least 300 feet away from springs, creeks, and trails. State law prohibits camping within a quarter mile of a sole water source so that wildlife and stock won't be scared away.
• Wash away from streams and lakes.
• Don't drink untreated water in the wilderness, no matter how clean the water appears. It may contain the parasitic protozoan *Giardia lamblia,* which causes the unpleasant disease giardiasis. Boiling your water for several minutes will kill *Giardia* and other bacterial or viral pathogens. Filtering and iodine treatments usually work, too, although they're not

as reliable as boiling (see the special topic *"Giardia"*).
• Bring a trowel for personal sanitation and dig 4–6 inches deep. In desert areas it's best to bag and carry out toilet paper because the stuff lasts for years and years in a dry climate; backcountry visitors in the Grand Canyon and Paria Canyon *must* pack it out.
• Carry plenty of feed for horses and mules.
• Leave dogs at home; they foul campsites and disturb wildlife and other hikers. If you do bring one, keep it under physical control at all times. They're not allowed in the Grand Canyon National Park backcountry.
• Take home all your trash, so animals can't dig it up and scatter it.
• Help preserve prehistoric and historic ruins.
• A survival kit and small flashlight can make the difference if you're caught in a storm or are out longer than expected. A pocket-sized container can hold what you need for the three essentials: **fire building** (matches in a waterproof container and a candle), **shelter** (space blanket, knife, and rope), and **signaling** (mirror and whistle).
• If you get lost, *realize it,* then find shelter and stay in one place. If you're sure of a way to civilization and plan to walk out, leave a note of your departure time and planned route.

STAYING HEALTHY

Hypothermia

Although the Grand Canyon has a well-deserved reputation for intense summer heat below the rims, another danger in the cooler months or at high elevations can sneak up and kill with very little warning. Hypothermia, a drop in the body's temperature below 95°F, causes disorientation, uncontrollable shivering, slurred speech, and drowsiness. The victim may not even realize what's wrong. Unless corrective action is taken immediately, hypothermia can lead to death. That's why hikers should travel with companions and always carry wind

ON THE ROAD

GIARDIA

It can be tough to resist: You're hiking in a beautiful area by the banks of a crystal clear stream. The water in your canteen tastes stale, hot, and plastic; the nearby stream looks so inviting that you can't resist a cautious sip. It tastes delicious, clean, and cold, and for the rest of your hike you refresh yourself with water straight from the stream.

Days pass and you forget about drinking untreated water. Suddenly one evening after your meal you become terribly sick to your stomach. You develop an awful case of cramps and feel diarrhea beginning to set in. Food poisoning?

Well, it could be the effects of *Giardia*, a protozoan that has become common in even the remotest of mountain streams. *Giardia* is carried in animal or human waste that is deposited or washed into natural waters. When ingested, it begins to reproduce, causing a sickness that can become very serious and may not be cured without medical attention.

You can take precautions against *Giardia* with a variety of chemical purifying and filtering methods or by boiling water before drinking it. Directions for chemical and filtering methods need to be followed carefully to be effective against the protozoan in its cyst stage of life, when it encases itself in a hard shell. The most effective way to eliminate such threats is to boil all suspect water for a few minutes.

and rain protection; close-fitting raingear works better than ponchos.

Remember that temperatures can plummet rapidly in Arizona's dry climate—a drop of 40°F between day and night is common. Be especially careful at high elevations, where summer sunshine can quickly change into freezing rain or a blizzard.

If you get cold and tired, don't waste time. Seek shelter and build a fire; change into dry clothes and drink warm liquids. A victim not fully conscious should be warmed by skin-to-skin contact with another person in a sleeping bag. Try to keep the victim awake and drinking warm liquids.

Coping with the Heat

We can take cues from desert wildlife on how best to live in a potentially hostile environment such as the Grand Canyon. In summer, early morning and late afternoon offer the most pleasant temperatures to be out and

about. Photographers also have the incentive of these times having the best light for photography. When you're captivated by the grand scenery, you can easily forget to drink enough water, but at the end of the day you'll be glad you did drink enough! For maximum efficiency, the body also needs food when hiking—salty snacks will increase endurance and prevent water intoxication, caused by sufficient water but too little salt to go with it. (See more on how to beat the heat in the "Fun on the trail Checklist" in the Inner Canyon Hiking section.)

Medical Services

In emergencies, dial 911. Hospital emergency rooms offer the quickest help, but cost more than a visit to a doctor's office or clinic. Hospital care is very expensive—having medical insurance is recommended. In Grand Canyon National Park, a clinic on the South Rim provides medical care.

Entertainment and Events

Staff at Grand Canyon National Park on both rims offer a wide range of programs, such as walks, presentations, campfire talks, and children's activities. Music concerts are held occasionally too. Art exhibits appear in the Kolb Studio on the South Rim and at other venues. The towns of Flagstaff, Williams, Page, and Kanab offer a full schedule of rodeos, parades, art festivals, historic celebrations, gem and mineral shows, and sporting events; call or stop by a tourist office to see what's coming up.

Major Holidays

Even though not always mentioned in the text, many museums, tourist attractions, and services close on such holidays as Thanksgiving, Christmas, and New Year's Day; call ahead to check. Most places stay open on Easter, as it's observed mainly in churches.

New Year's Day: January 1
Martin Luther King Jr.'s Birthday: January 15; observed on the third Monday in January
Presidents' Day: third Monday in February; honors Washington and Lincoln
Easter Sunday: late March or early April
Cinco de Mayo: May 5; a Mexican festival celebrated in many Southwest communities
Memorial Day: last Monday in May
Independence Day: July 4
Labor Day: first Monday in September
Columbus Day: second Monday in October
Veterans Day: November 11
Thanksgiving Day: fourth Thursday in November
Christmas Day: December 25

ON THE ROAD

Accommodations

This book has been written to assist travelers of all budgets! You'll rarely need to spend more than $35 for a room except right at the Grand Canyon, on tribal lands, and during peak travel times elsewhere, when camping will be a good option. If you have the funds and the desire to be pampered, top-notch hotels and resorts will do just that. And you'll have plenty of midrange accommodations choices most everywhere. Expect a sales tax of about 10 percent to be added to quoted rates at most places. You're sure to find seasonal and long-term price changes, however, so *please* don't use what's listed in this book to argue with staff at businesses. Prices quoted here reflect those charged in summer, which is the high season for northern Arizona and adjacent Utah. Reservations come in handy then and are essential at the Grand Canyon's North Rim. Off-season prices can be a great value, especially in the "gateway towns" of Flagstaff and Williams. You'll find the major hotel and motel chains well represented in northern Arizona. Some of the region's restored historic hotels offer the elegance and romance of the old days.

Bed and Breakfasts

These private homes or small inns offer a personal touch. Rates range $45–275 d, with most around $75–125. Always call or write for reservations. Although the author didn't find any B&Bs at the Grand Canyon, surrounding towns often have a good selection. Local visitor centers provide listings. **Mi Casa Su Casa/Old Pueblo Homestays** can book many B&Bs at Box 950, Tempe, AZ 85280-0950, tel. 480/990-0682 or 800/456-0682; website: www.azres.com.

MOTEL AND HOTEL CHAINS

By Stephen Metzger

If you've been on the road at all in the United States in the last few years, you've noticed the amazing proliferation of chain lodging—from Motel 6s to Super 8s to all the Inns (Holiday, Ramada, Comfort, Days. . .). Even many of the ol' Best Westerns have been upgraded and re-marketed in recent years; the familiar yellow-crown signs that once rose comfortably into the low skylines of twilight have been replaced by modern deep-blue signs with stylized red crowns and electronic marquees advertising sports bars and exercise rooms. Most of these lodges offer competitive rates; clean, quiet rooms; and a known quantity in terms of price, amenities, and general quality. Unfortunately, they've also helped further the depersonalization of small-town America; the colorful little mom-and-pop places can't compete.

Following is a list of some of the common hotel and motel chains and what you can expect them to provide. In general, you can count on a swimming pool, laundry, television with a movie channel, free local phone calls, free morning coffee, and a choice of smoking or no-smoking rooms; most places have a few handicapped-accessible rooms too. Many offer discounts to members of various groups and clubs: the American Automobile Association, American Association of Retired Persons, military employees, and others. Always ask.

Refer to this information when you come across a listing for one of the chains described below.

Best Western, tel. 800/528-1234; website: www.bestwestern.com. Best Westerns are individually owned and range considerably in size and appearance—from roadside motels to down-town high-rises. They all must meet strict standards, however, and you are generally assured of quality and comfort. I stay at them frequently, as I know they'll be clean and quiet and the service dependable and friendly. Most have pools; many have restaurants on the premises.

Days Inn, tel. 800/DAYS INN (329-7466); website: www.daysinn.com. Consistently comfortable and clean, though without much personality. Most have pools; no restaurants.

Holiday Inn, tel. 800/HOLIDAY (465-4329); website: www.holiday-inn.com. Generally the most upscale of the lodges listed here. Each has a restaurant, lounge, pool, and meeting rooms.

Holiday Inn Express (same telephone and Internet) is a scaled-down version of Holiday Inns. These lodges offer continental breakfasts, and most have pools.

Motel 6, tel. 800/4-MOTEL-6 (466-8356); website: www.motel6.com. Cookie cutter, but comfortable and less expensive than the other chains. Each may have a small pool and bathrooms with shower stall but no tub. This chain is extremely popular, and rooms fill up quickly. Often times the No Vacancy sign goes up well before nightfall.

Ramada Inn, tel. 800/2-RAMADA (272-6232); website: www.ramada.com. Ranging from urban high-rises to smaller-town motels, Ramadas all offer restaurants, lounges, and meeting rooms and are reliably comfortable and clean.

Super 8, tel. 800/800-8000; website: www.super8.com. These are consistently clean, quiet, and inexpensive.

A Word about Hotel Rates

The more I travel the more I realize how capricious hotel rates are, how the rate you get depends on so many variables—whether you phone in your reservation or walk in off the street, whether it's two in the afternoon or 10 at night, whether you asked for a "discount" or not. Keep in mind hotels, and to some degree motels, have widely fluctuating rates, and that above all they don't want empty rooms. True story: I pulled into Fort Collins, Colorado, one afternoon and walked into the lobby of a major hotel chain. Since it was packed with tour groupers, and waiting 10 minutes at the counter got me no closer to a clerk, I walked outside to a pay phone and called the front desk. "Rates are $79 a night," I was told, "but sorry, no rooms available tonight." So I walked next door, where I was told there was one room available, a smoking room. Nope, wouldn't do. So I walked back to the lobby of the first hotel, worked my way to the counter, and asked for a room. "Yes, we do have a room, Sir. For $69."

"Do you offer any corporate discounts?" I asked.

"Let's see. . . Yes, we can give you a room for $59."

Now, this is backward from how it usually works (though it does go to show how arbitrary it can all be). Often you can get a better rate by phone, even if you're calling from just outside the door, as they figure you're not committed yet, and they *want* you. Once you're in the door they figure you're less likely to go somewhere else.

Another true story: One night in Raton, New Mexico, I stopped for the night at dusk at a small independent motel. A man in front of me was talking with the desk clerk.

"How much for a room?"

"Do you qualify for any discounts?" the woman asked.

Shrugging and giving her a blank look, he said, "What do you mean?"

"Triple A, corporate, AARP, you know. . . "

"Uh, I guess not. . . "

"Sixty-four dollars for a single."

He said he'd take it, filled out the registration form, and left with his key.

My turn: "Do you have a nonsmoking single available for this evening?"

"Do you qualify for any discounts?"

"Yes, I do."

"Fifty-four dollars for a single."

"I'll take it."

Is there a lesson here? If there is it's that, like I said, rates are not as fixed as you might think. Some things to keep in mind: The later in the day the better your chance of getting a cut rate. The owners want their rooms full, and, if it looks as if they might not be, they'll offer incentives, in the form of a few bucks off the "standard" rate. (Of course, you also risk not finding a vacancy, and that risk might not be worth it to you.) Also, *ask* about discounts. Most hotels offer at least American Automobile Association, American Association of Retired Persons, and corporate discounts, and you might qualify. Finally, in the case of chain and franchise lodging, I've had better luck phoning the hotel directly than calling the 800 number and talking to an operator who might be booking a room in a town 3,000 miles away from the switchboard.

Bottom line: Phone around, and talk like you do it all the time. You might be surprised at the results.

Stephen Metzger is the author of Moon Handbooks to Colorado, New Mexico, and Santa Fe–Taos.

COURTESY OF AISLINN RACE

Hance's Camp in the late 19th century

Hostels

The towns of Flagstaff, Williams, Tuba City, and Kanab have hostels at a cost of about $15 per night for a bed in shared rooms. Only the hostel in Tuba City requires a hostel card. Some hostels will accept phone reservations made with a credit card. Check out their website, website: www.hostels.com for news and listings.

Hostel directories can come in handy if you'll be traveling this way. The *Hostel Handbook* lists both Hostelling International places and independents; contact Jim Williams at 722 St. Nicholas Ave., New York, NY 10031; tel. 212/926-7030; website: www.hostelhandbook.com. *Hostels U.S.A.* by The Globe Pequot Press provides a comprehensive guide to Hostelling International members and the independents with descriptions of atmosphere and features; it's sold in bookstores. Both publications cover the United States and Canada.

Guest Ranch

Bar 10 Ranch lies in a remote area of the Arizona Strip just north of the Grand Canyon, where you can really "get away from it all." It offers miles of open country, cowboy-style meals, and an informal Western atmosphere. Activities include horseback riding, pack trips, hiking, scenic flights, river trips, and entertainment. Many visitors spend a day here when shuttling in or out from a river trip by helicopter and flying by small plane to Las Vegas or other destinations. You can also drive here, though high-clearance vehicles are recommended. Make the required reservations with Bar 10 at Box 910088, St. George, UT 84791-0088, tel. 435/628-4010 or 800/582-4139; website: www.bar10.com.

Campgrounds

The best parts of northern Arizona lie outdoors, where you can choose among hundreds of campgrounds—federal, state, tribal, or private. Federal government sites, the most common, are offered by the Forest Service, National Park Service, and Bureau of Land Management (BLM); sites commonly feature tables, toilets, and drinking water, with fees ranging from free to $15 per night. The Havasupai, Hualapai, Paiute, Navajo, and Hopi tribes offer campgrounds, too. Commercial campgrounds provide the most frills—showers, laundromats, hookups, stores, game rooms—some even have swimming pools. Rates at these average $15–20 per night; most accept both tents and RVs.

Dispersed Camping
You're welcome to camp almost anywhere in the national forests, BLM areas, and the back-country of the Lake Mead National Recreation Area. This dispersed style of camping costs nothing and, for seasoned campers, provides the best outdoor experience. Because there are no facilities, it's up to you to leave the forest in its natural state. Be very careful with fire—try to use a camp stove rather than leave a fire scar. Sometimes high fire danger closes the forests in early summer. The Kaibab National Forest covers much of both the South and North Rims of the Grand Canyon on vast expanses of forested plateaus. BLM lands and the Lake Mead National Recreation Area extend across much of the Arizona Strip north of the Grand Canyon and west of the Kaibab Plateau. Stop at a national forest office or BLM office for maps and information on camping, hiking, fishing, and back-road travel.

Food and Drink

People debate whether Arizona actually has a native cuisine. Either way, you'll find a wide selection of appetizing dishes here. South-of-the-border food is popular, and every town has a Mexican restaurant. Western-style restaurants dish out cowboy food—beef, beans, and biscuits. You can sample Native American fry bread and the Navajo taco—beans, lettuce, tomatoes, and cheese on fry bread—on or off the reservations. The larger towns offer a cosmopolitan array of ethnic and fine-dining restaurants.

Only the sales tax is added to your bill; you're expected to leave a tip of at least 15 percent for table service.

Restaurants within Grand Canyon National Park are nonsmoking and Flagstaff and Utah have laws prohibiting smoking in most restaurants. Nonsmoking sections elsewhere are voluntary, although it's likely that more communities will adopt clean-air policies.

Alcohol
The legal drinking age in Arizona is 21. No alcohol is permitted on the Navajo or Hopi Reservations.

If you choose to drink, don't get behind the wheel of a car. Arizona has strict laws forbidding driving under the influence of alcohol or drugs. A first offense can bring a mandatory jail term, fine, license suspension, and education or treatment.

Getting There and Around

The parking facilities at Grand Canyon National Park have been overwhelmed by the sheer numbers of visitors with cars. Shuttle buses have already replaced private vehicles on the Hermit Road and Yaki Point/S. Kaibab Trailhead areas near Grand Canyon Village. In the future, visitors to the Grand Canyon Village area will leave their cars just outside the park in Tusayan and use public transport to get around. You can reach the South Rim by scheduled bus service from Flagstaff, by train from Williams, and by plane from Las Vegas. A shuttle vehicle connects the South and North Rims during the summer season.

By Car

Most people choose their own cars as the most convenient and economical way to get around. High-clearance 4WD vehicles will come in handy if you plan extensive travel on back roads. Phoenix and Las Vegas have the largest selection of car and RV rentals in the region, as well as the best air connections if you're flying in. See the Driving Tips special topic for advice on travel in the Grand Canyon area.

Driveaways

These are autos scheduled for delivery to another city. If the auto's destination is a place

DRIVING TIPS

Summer heat puts an extra strain on both car and driver. Make sure the cooling system, engine oil, transmission fluid, fan belts, and tires are in top condition. Carry several gallons of water in case of breakdown or radiator trouble. Never leave children or pets in a parked car during warm weather—temperatures inside can cause fatal heatstroke in just minutes. Radiator caps must not be opened when the engine is hot, because the escaping steam can cause severe burns.

At times the desert has *too much water*—late-summer storms frequently flood low spots in the road. Wait for the water to go down, until you can see bottom, before crossing. If the car begins to hydroplane after a rainstorm, it's best to remove your foot from the accelerator, avoid braking, and keep the steering straight until the tires grip the road again. Drive in the "footsteps" of the car ahead, if you can.

Dust storms also tend to be short-lived but can completely block visibility. Treat them like dense fog: pull completely off the road and stop, turning off your lights so as not to confuse other drivers.

Radio stations carry frequent updates when weather hazards exist. With a VHF radio (between 162.4 and 162.55 MHz), you can pick up continuous weather forecasts in the Flagstaff, Lake Powell, St. George, and Las Vegas areas.

If stranded in the backcountry, whether on the desert or in the mountains, stay with the vehicle unless you're *positive* of the way out; then leave a note detailing your route and departure time. Airplanes can easily spot a car—leave your hood and trunk up and tie a piece of cloth to the antenna—but a person trying to walk out is difficult to see. If you're stranded, emergency supplies can definitely help: blankets or sleeping bags, raingear, gloves, first-aid kit, tools, jumper cables, motor oil, shovel, rope, traction mats or chains, flashlight, flares, fire extinguisher, maps, water, food, and a can opener.

School crossings and buses require extra care. You must stop if someone is using a crosswalk. Crossings in use by school children have you intend to visit, a driveaway can be like getting a free car rental. You have to be at least 21 years old and pay a refundable deposit of $75–150. There will be time and mileage limits. Ask for an economy car if you want the lowest driving costs. In a large city—Phoenix or Tucson in Arizona—look in the Yellow Pages under "Automobile Transporters and Driveaways."

By Bus

Greyhound, tel. 800/231-2222, offers frequent service on its transcontinental bus routes across northern Arizona and between Flagstaff and Phoenix. Greyhound often has special deals on bus passes and "one-way anywhere" tickets; website: www.greyhound.com. Overseas residents may buy a Greyhound Ameripass at a discount outside North America.

Nava-Hopi Tours, tel. 928/774-5003 or 800/892-8687, connects Grand Canyon National Park (South Rim) with Flagstaff and offers a Flagstaff-Phoenix-Sky Harbor Airport (Phoenix) run; website: www.navahopitours.com. **Navajo Transit System,** tel. 928/729-4002, traverses the Navajo and Hopi Indian reservations, but it provides no connections with other bus lines in Arizona.

Local bus services are available at Grand Canyon National Park (South Rim) and Flagstaff; shuttles within the park are free, but there's a charge for ones to Tusayan or the North Rim.

a 15 mph posted speed; police have ticketed drivers going 20 mph in them! When you see a school bus stopped with red lights flashing and a stop sign arm extended, you must stop in *both* directions until the lights and arm are turned off, unless there is a *physical* barrier dividing the roadway and you're traveling in the opposite direction.

Unless posted otherwise, speed limits are 15 mph when you're approaching a school crossing, 25 mph in business and residential districts, and 55 mph on open highways and city freeways. Although it's tempting to let loose on long, empty highways, they haven't all been designed for extreme speeds—a speeding car could top a small rise and suddenly find itself bearing down on a flock of sheep crossing the road. Deer, elk, and other stray animals can pose a danger too, especially at night.

You can make right turns from the right lane on a red light, unless prohibited by a sign, after coming to a complete stop and yielding to other traffic. Left turns on a red light can similarly be made if you're in the far left lane of a one-way street and turning onto another one-way street and there's no sign prohibiting the turn.

Reversible lanes in Phoenix and some other cities have signs designating the lane for certain hours for "Through Traffic," "Do Not Use," and "Other times 2 way left."

Seat belts must be worn by all front-seat passengers. Child safety seats are required for those younger than five years or less than 40 pounds.

Arizona has very strict laws against driving under the influence of drugs or drink. Penalties for the first offense include mandatory jail term, fine, license suspension, and screening, education, and/or treatment.

The *Arizona Driver License Manual* contains a good review of driving knowledge and road rules. It's available free in most large towns at the state Motor Vehicle Division office.

By Train

Amtrak, 800/872-7245, runs the luxury Southwest Chief daily in each direction across northern Arizona with stops at Kingman, Williams, Flagstaff, and Winslow. It connects Los Angeles with New Orleans, Orlando, Chicago, and other destinations to the east. Amtrak usually charges more than buses but has far roomier seating, as well as parlor cars and sleepers. The cost depends on availability, so advance planning, off-season travel, and luck will get you the lowest fare. Ask about "All Aboard" roundtrips, flight and train packages, and other deals. Travel agents outside North America sell USA Railpasses. Check the excellent website at website: www.amtrak.com.

By Air

Nearly all scheduled flights to the Grand Canyon originate in Las Vegas. They arrive at the Grand Canyon Airport in Tusayan, just a short drive south of Grand Canyon Village on the South Rim. No flights land on the North Rim. Passengers have the bonus of a grand overview and may also receive a narrated tour.

More than a dozen major airlines fly to Phoenix and Las Vegas. Fares and schedules tend to change frequently—a travel agent can help you find the best flights. You can also "do it yourself" on the Internet. Big-city newspapers usually run advertisements of discount fares and tours in their Sunday travel sections. You'll have the best chance of getting low fares by planning a week or more ahead and staying over a Saturday night (or any night with Southwest Airlines); roundtrip fares will almost always be a much better value than oneways, though changes may be costly.

TOURS

See your travel agent for the latest on package tours to Arizona. Within the state, local operators offer everything from quick bus jaunts to rafting trips through the Grand Canyon. Gray Line offers the largest selection of bus excursions; tours leave from Phoenix, Tucson, and Flagstaff. Smaller companies offer jeep trips to scenic spots inaccessible to passenger vehicles; you'll find jeep tours available in Tusayan, Flagstaff, Monument Valley, Page, and Canyon de Chelly. You can also take "flightseeing" trips from many airports, especially at the Grand Canyon. The "Tours" sections in each chapter list tour operators; local chambers of commerce will help you, too.

Grand Canyon Field Institute

Small groups explore the Grand Canyon with day hikes, backpacking, river-running trips, van tours, and classroom instruction. You can pick up a schedule at Grand Canyon Association bookstores in the park or write the institute at Box 399, Grand Canyon, AZ 86023, tel. 928/638-2485, website: www.grandcanyon.org/fieldinstitute.

Elderhostel

This nonprofit organization offers educational adventures for people 55 and over (spouses can be younger). Many of the programs take place in Arizona, exploring archaeology, history, cultures, crafts, nature, and other topics. Participants join small groups for short-term studies and stay in simple accommodations, which helps keep costs low. For a catalog, write Elderhostel, 11 Avenue de Lafayette, Boston, MA 02111-1746, tel. 978/323-4141 or toll-free 877/426-8056, website: www.elderhostel.org.

Money Matters

National Park Passes

With the Grand Canyon National Park charging a stiff $20 per vehicle entry fee (good for seven days), you may be best off buying the $50 **National Parks Pass,** which will get you and others in your vehicle into this or any other national park, monument, or historic site in the United States for a 12-month period. You can purchase the pass at entrance stations, some sales outlets, online at website: www.nationalparks.org, or by calling 888/GO-PARKS. Seniors age 62 and older who are U.S. citizens can take advantage of the $10 **Golden Age Pass,** good for a lifetime; it additionally gives a discount at many campgrounds on federal lands. Individuals who receive government benefits because of permanent disabilities should look into the lifetime **Golden Access Pass.** Drop by any national park or regional office to obtain these cards.

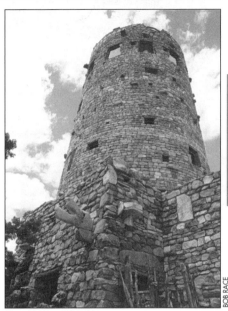

Desert View Watchtower

Taxes and Tips

The state sales tax in Arizona is 5 percent, but city and/or county taxes may be tacked onto that amount. Expect roughly 10 percent to be added to quoted prices for accommodations, meals, and some tours. There's no tax on groceries in Arizona. Plan to leave a 15–20 percent tip for table service at restaurants.

Foreign Currency Exchange

No foreign currency exchange is available in northern Arizona. Instead, use the ATM machines found at Grand Canyon National Park and in almost every town. Most businesses gladly accept traveler's checks in U.S. dollars.

ON THE ROAD

BOB RACE

VISITING GRAND CANYON NATIONAL PARK ON A SHOESTRING

The steep prices charged for park admission and services can be daunting, yet the Grand Canyon can easily be seen for little more than a song. Getting a small group together will slice costs on the entry, camping, and lodging. A $50 Golden Eagle pass will give unlimited entry to the park and all other National Park Service areas in the country for 12 months, a much better deal than forking out $20 every seven days to visit the Grand Canyon. You can camp free in the Kaibab National Forest that adjoins both the South and North Rims, though you'll need your own wheels to do this. Backpackers and cyclists can stay in cheap walk-in campgrounds at both rims. The cafeterias at Yavapai and Maswik Lodges in Grand Canyon Village offer good deals, or you can fix your own meals. And the best things—the views, sunsets, day-hikes, and interpretive programs—are free.

Communications

Telephone

All of northern Arizona has a **928 area code;** adjacent Utah uses a **435 area code.** Use the area code when dialing 1+ or 0+ numbers to other area codes. To obtain a local number from Information, dial 1-411; for a number elsewhere, dial 1-(the area code)-555-1212. Many airlines, auto rental firms, and motel chains have toll-free 800, 866, 877, or 888 numbers; if you don't have the number, just dial 1-800/555-1212. Pre-paid telephone cards provide much lower costs for long-distance calls than plunking in coins or using a telephone company credit card; discount stores often have the lowest prices for the pre-paid cards.

Postal Services

You'll find **post offices** in most every town; Flagstaff supports several branches. Normal post office hours are Mon.–Fri. 8:30 A.M.–5 P.M. and sometimes Saturday 8:30 A.M.–noon. You can get a variety of postal information at tel. 800/275-8777 (ASK-USPS) or at website: www.usps.gov.

The mail service stores in many towns offer one-stop services for packing materials and delivery services. **Federal Express,** tel. 800/463-3339, and **United Parcel Service,** tel. 800/742-5877, will pick up packages and also maintain a network of drop-off centers; call for directions to the nearest one.

Photocopying, Faxes, Internet, and Email

Copy shops and stores specializing in mailing services have photocopying and fax services; in out-of-the way places, try asking at a motel. Nearly all public libraries offer computers with Internet access at no charge, though you may need to sign up for a machine. You'll need your own email account to send or receive messages; library staff can tell you how to set one up on the Internet. Tourist offices often know of other places offering Internet access. Beware of commercial Internet computers at the Grand Canyon that charge exorbitant rates of $10 per hour or more. Campgrounds sometimes have a telephone jack in the office so laptop owners can check their email.

Information

MAPS

The *Guide to Indian Country* map published by the Automobile Club of Southern California provides superb coverage of the Four Corners region, including the Grand Canyon and the Navajo and Hopi Indian reservations. The map is sold in stores, and AAA members can get it free from AAA offices. The *Arizona Road & Recreation Atlas* by Benchmark Maps covers the state with exceptionally beautiful and easy-to-read maps at a 1:400,000 scale; it's sold in stores. The National Forest Service maps will be handy when traveling in the Kaibab Forest (separate maps for south and north of the Grand Canyon) and Coconino Forest (Flagstaff area); the scale is 1:126,720; they're cheapest from forest service offices, but stores also have them. For exploring the lonely Arizona Strip, the *Arizona Strip District Visitor Map* will prove essential for navigation; its scale is 1:168,960 and it is published by the Bureau of Land Management and sold at their offices and in stores. Hikers and mountain bikers will appreciate the detailed U.S.G.S. topographic maps of the region, available in a variety of scales and formats from outdoors stores. You can also download topo maps for free from Internet sites such as website: www.topo.zone.

Arizona Office of Tourism

Staff offer information on every region of the state. You can find most of their literature at other tourist offices, but this one in Phoenix has the best selection. It's on the fourth floor, set back from the street at 2702 N. Third St., Suite 4015 (Phoenix, AZ 85004); open Mon.–Fri. 8 A.M.–5 P.M.; tel. 602/230-7733, fax 240-5475. Staff also offer information toll free at tel. 888/928-3434 and at the Painted Cliffs Welcome Center,

I-40 Exit 359 near the New Mexico border, daily 8 A.M.–5 P.M. The excellent website: www.arizonaguide.com hosts many chamber of commerce sites and contains travel tips and event listings.

Grand Canyon

Staff at the visitor centers on both the South and North Rim can make suggestions for exploring the park and tell you about scheduled events. *The Guide* newspaper comes in both South and North Rim editions and list choices for sightseeing, hiking, and programs; it's free at entrance stations or visitor centers. The park's mailing address is Box 129, Grand Canyon, AZ 86023; website: www.nps.gov/grca.

You can obtain a **weather forecast** and other recordings and reach all park offices through the **automated switchboard,** tel. 928/638-7888. **Hearing-impaired** people can use the TDD number for park information, tel. 928/638-7804.

For trail information and backcountry camping permits, drop by the **Backcountry Office** in the Maswik Transportation Center on the South Rim, tel. 928/638-7875, open daily 8 A.M.–noon and 1–5 P.M. Call between 1–5 P.M. to speak with someone in person. The North Rim Backcountry Information Center near Bright Angel Point, tel. 928/638-7870, is open daily 8 A.M.–noon and 1–5 P.M. May 15–Oct. 15, weather permitting.

Kaibab National Forest

The forest extends both south and north from Grand Canyon National Park, offering scenic vistas, hiking, mountain biking, developed campgrounds, and primitive camping. The Kaibab National Forest maps show the trails and back roads; ask for the one subtitled

ON THE ROAD

Williams and Tusayan Districts for the South Rim; for the North Rim, the subtitle is North Kaibab District. On the South Rim, stop by the **Tusayan Ranger Station,** open Mon.–Fri. 8 A.M.–4:30 P.M., in the Tusayan Administrative Site, across from and 0.2 mile south of Moqui Lodge just outside the South Entrance Station; contact Box 3088, Grand Canyon, AZ 86023, tel. 928/638-2443; website: www.fs.fed.us/r3/kai.

For the North Rim, staff of the **Kaibab Visitor Center** at Jacob Lake provide information on the many viewpoints, trails, campgrounds, and historic sites in the Kaibab National Forest along the North Rim; they can also issue backcountry permits for many areas of Grand Canyon National Park. Exhibits include a 3-D model of the Grand Canyon and wildlife displays. You can purchase books and maps. It's open daily 8 A.M.–5 P.M. from about mid-May–mid-Oct. and possibly later in the year with a shorter schedule; tel. 928/643-7298. The **North Kaibab Ranger District** office has year-round North Rim information, open Mon.–Fri. 7 A.M.–5 P.M., at 430 S. Main St. in Fredonia (Box 248, Fredonia, AZ 86022), tel. 928/643-7395; website: www.fs.fed.us/r3/kai.

Bureau of Land Management

For hiking and access information on BLM and Lake Mead National Recreation Area land on the Arizona Strip, contact the **Interagency Visitor Center,** 345 E. Riverside Dr., St. George, UT 84790, tel. 435/688-3246; website: www.az.blm.gov. It's open Mon.–Fri. 7:45 A.M.–5 P.M. (best times for reaching someone with first-hand travel experience) and Saturday and holidays 9 A.M.–5 P.M. Take I-15 Bluff St. Exit 6 and turn southeast one-third mile; the office is on your left.

The BLM **Kanab Resource Area** office takes care of the Paria Canyon-Vermilion Cliffs Wilderness at 318 N. 100 East, Kanab, UT 84741, tel. 435/644-2672; open Mon.–Fri. 7:45 A.M.–4:30 P.M.; website: www.ut.blm.gov.

Internet Sites

These offer a great deal of information. The **National Park Service** site contains visiting information and lists of rules and regulations important for backcountry hikers and river runners at website: www.nps.gov/grca. The **"Unofficial Grand Canyon National Park Home Page"** is a very good source at website: www.kaibab.org. The **Grand Canyon Chamber of Commerce** offers an introduction to the park and links to surrounding towns at website: www.thecanyon.com. Over at Page and Glen Canyon National Recreation Area, website: www.pagelakepowellchamber.org lets you know about things to do in town and out on Lake Powell. In north-central Arizona, the **Flagstaff Chamber of Commerce** at website: www.flagstaff.az.us and **flagstaff.com** at website: www.flagguide.com will fill you in on the sights and services there with links to nearby towns and recreation areas.

Arizona Highways at website: www.arizonahighways.com offers some of the same beautiful photos, travel information, hikes, and entertaining stories found in its magazine pages. You'll find lots of hiking and other outdoor information at **Great Outdoor Recreation Pages** site website: www.gorp.com/gorp/location/az/az.htm, including national forests and wilderness areas. If you're interested in learning about the desert, check **Desert USA**'s website: www.desertusa.com for places to visit and what plants and animals you might meet there. **Adventure in Hiking** at website: www.swlink.net/~ttidyman/hiking features trails, hiking news, links, clubs, and Grand Canyon information.

Weights and Measures

The Metric System

National Park Service literature uses both English and metric units, but otherwise the metric system is just about nonexistent in the United States. For help in converting from the modified English measuring system used in the United States, consult the conversion table at the back of this book.

Time

Travelers in Arizona should remember that the state stays on Mountain Standard Time all year, except for the Navajo Reservation, which goes on daylight saving time by adding one hour from April–October to keep in step with its Utah and New Mexico sections. Note that the Hopi Reservation, completely within Arizona and surrounded by the Navajo Reservation, stays on standard time year-round along with the rest of the state. In summer, Arizona runs on the same time as California and Nevada, and one hour behind Utah, Colorado, and New Mexico. In winter, Arizona is one hour ahead of California and Nevada, and on the same time as Utah, Colorado, and New Mexico.

Electricity

Electric current in the United States is 110–120 volts, 60-cycle; appliances manufactured for use in other countries may need a transformer, as well as a plug adapter for the flat two-pin style of the U.S. plug.

ON THE ROAD

Grand Canyon National Park

Most people head first to the South Rim, entering at either the South Entrance Station near Grand Canyon Village or the East Entrance Station near Desert View. A 25-mile scenic drive along the rim connects these entrances.

The South Rim features great views, a full range of accommodations and restaurants, and easy access—it's just 58 miles north of I-40 from Williams. Roads and most facilities stay open all year. Attractions include views from Yavapai Observation Station and other points near Grand Canyon Village and the scenic drives of Hermit Road to Hermits Rest (8 miles) and Desert View Drive to Desert View (25 miles). Some remarkable architecture lines the South Rim, including a series of unique stone structures designed by Mary Colter. The South Rim also features most of the Canyon's easily accessible viewpoints and trails. It's not surprising, then, that large crowds of visitors, especially in summer, are the main drawback of this part of the Canyon. Park staff have big plans to relieve the congestion by adding more shuttles, bike paths, and foot trails; see the Special Topic "Shuttling Out to the South Rim."

The Colorado River

GRAND CANYON HIGHLIGHTS

Dramatic Views: Many easily accessible viewpoints line both rims of the Grand Canyon.
Amazing Hiking: Trails on the rims and into the depths draw people of all abilities.
Mule Trips: You can descend into the Canyon just as the first tourists did, letting the animals do most of the work.
Grand Canyon Railway: Passenger trains once again steam into the Grand Canyon depot on a nostalgic ride from Williams.

Kaibab Plateau: Alpine meadows and forests with summer wildflowers lie just back from the North Rim.
Toroweap: Dizzying views of the Colorado River from cliffs nearly 3,000 feet high lie at the end of a long, unpaved road on the North Rim.
River Running: The mighty Colorado River will sweep you through the heart of the Grand Canyon on one of the world's greatest adventures.

The park collects an admission fee of $20 per private vehicle ($10 per pedestrian or bicyclist) that's good for seven days at the south and east entrances of the South Rim and at the main entrance of the North Rim. You'll get a park brochure and a copy of *The Guide,* which lists programs and sightseeing suggestions. Once you're in the park, visitor centers, exhibits, programs, and day hiking are free. Budget travelers can save money by stocking up on gas, groceries, and camping supplies at Flagstaff, Williams, or other towns away from the Canyon; prices at Tusayan and within the park can run substantially higher.

Only about one in 10 visitors makes it to the North Rim, but that visitor is rewarded with pristine forests, rolling meadows, splendid wildflower displays, and superb panoramas. Viewpoints here are about 1,500 feet higher than those at the South Rim and provide a dramatically different perspective of the Canyon. The North Rim area offers lodging, dining, and camping facilities similar to the South Rim's, though on a smaller scale. Unless you ski in (backcountry permit required), the North Rim's high country is open only from mid-May–late October, depending on the arrival of the first big winter storm. Although the rims stand just 10 miles apart, motorists on the South Rim must drive 215 miles and about five hours via Cameron and Jacob Lake to get here.

Adventurous travelers on the North Rim willing to tackle 61 miles of dirt road (each way; impassable when wet) can head west to **Toroweap Overlook,** a 140-mile, 3.5-hour drive from the Bright Angel Point area. This perch sits a dizzying 3,000 feet directly above the Colorado River—one of the Canyon's most spectacular viewpoints. Don't expect any facilities other than the road and outhouses. Bring all supplies, including water. Low elevations of 4,500–5,000 feet allow access most of the year; you can check road conditions with a ranger, tel. 928/638-7888.

South Rim Sights

GRAND CANYON VILLAGE AREA

Parking may be your first thought upon arrival! Maps in the literature given out at the entrance stations show parking areas in Grand Canyon Village. Once you've found a spot, the free Village Shuttle will take you around. Cycling is another option, though it's restricted to roads and bike paths. Walking, especially on the very scenic Rim Trail, is the most enjoyable way of seeing the sights here.

Eventually parking for Grand Canyon Village will be moved south to Tusayan, where buses or a light-rail will convey visitors to Canyon View Information Plaza and beyond.

Canyon View Information Plaza

This new visitor center complex, a short stroll south of Mather Point, opened in late 2000 and has replaced the old visitor center. Because it's designed as part of the public transport system, there's no parking here. You can take the Village Shuttle or walk via the Rim Trail. The Village Shuttle stops on the west side of the Plaza and the Kaibab Trail Shuttle on the east side. Despite the name, there's no view here! You have to walk 300 yards over to Mather Point to see the Canyon.

Large outdoor panels have maps, sightseeing destinations, hiking possibilities, lodging, campgrounds, and other helpful information to get you started on your visit to the park. You can also check listings of ranger-

© BILL WEIR

sunset drama from Mather Point

guided rim walks, Canyon hikes, talks, family activities, photography workshops, campfire programs, and evening presentations. Step inside the Visitor Center for the information desk and some exhibits. Kids 4–14 can sign up to learn skills in the Junior Ranger Program; it's also available at Yavapai Observation Station and Tusayan Museum. The Visitor Center is open daily 8 A.M.–6 P.M. and the outdoor lights stay on until 9 P.M. Call 928/638-7888 to reach the automated switchboard with recordings of scheduled programs and offices or surf over to the website website: www.nps.gov/grca. (People with hearing impairments can call the TDD, tel. 928/638-7804.)

South across the Plaza, you'll find Books & More. This spacious new bookstore of the Grand Canyon Association features a great selection of Canyon-related books (including ones for kids), posters, topo maps, videos, slides, and postcards.

Mather Point

The panorama here is the first view of the Grand Canyon for many visitors. Walk north from the Canyon View Information Plaza or walk east on the Rim Trail from Grand Canyon Village. You may be able to park here, but finding a space takes some luck. Below Mather Point (elev. 7,120 feet) lie Pipe Creek Canyon, the Inner Gorge of the Colorado River, and countless buttes, temples, and points eroded from the rims. Stephen Mather served as the first director of the National Park Service and was in office when the Grand Canyon joined the national park system on February 26, 1919.

Rim Trail

People of all ages enjoy a walk along this easy trail, which offers views from many different vantage points. The four-mile section from Mather Point past the El Tovar Hotel to Maricopa Point is paved and nearly level.

Another paved section, between Mather Point and the first viewpoints on Desert View Drive, should be open in 2002. The Rim Trail continues west 6.7 miles from Maricopa Point as a dirt path to Hermits Rest, at the end of Hermit Road. Shuttle buses stop at both ends of the trail and at many places along the way.

Pick up biology and geology brochures for the trail at the Visitor Center, at Yavapai Observation Station, or outside Verkamp's Curios (near El Tovar Hotel). Start anywhere you like, as there are no keyed trail numbers. Pinyon pine, juniper, cliff rose, and smaller plants grow on exposed areas of the rim; ponderosa pines stick to more protected areas farther back or below the rim.

Yavapai Observation Station

Set on the brink of the Canyon, this overlook makes a great spot to take in the panorama or watch sunrises and sunsets. Panels identify the many buttes, temples, points, and tributary canyons seen through the windows. A few geology exhibits are on display too. It's open daily 8 A.M.–5 P.M., with extended summer hours. Grand Canyon Association sells books, maps, videos, slides, and postcards. Parking is difficult here—the Village Shuttle or a walk along the Rim Trail are the best ways to come.

Hopi House

Designed by Mary Colter to resemble a pueblo, this unusual building opened in 1905. She patterned it after structures in the Hopi village of Old Oraibi with a stone and adobe exterior, thatched ceilings, and corner fireplaces. Hopi not only helped in the construction, but lived inside on the upper floors, worked as craftsmen, displayed their work, and performed nightly dances. Today Hopi House has an outstanding collection of Native American

MARY COLTER, ARCHITECT OF THE SOUTHWEST

In an early 20th-century world dominated by male architects, Mary Colter (1869–1958) succeeded in designing many of the Grand Canyon National Park's most notable structures. After her father died in 1886, her mother gave Colter permission to attend the California School of Design in San Francisco to learn skills to support the remaining members of the family. Upon graduation, Colter moved to St. Paul, Minnesota, and began teaching

Mary Colter shows blueprints to Mrs. Ickes, wife of the Secretary of the Interior, in 1935.

© GRAND CANYON NATIONAL PARK (NEG# 16940)

mechanical drawing. She later applied for work with the Fred Harvey Company and, in 1901, obtained a contract to decorate the Indian Building, a new museum and sales gallery of Native American crafts between the Alvarado Hotel and the railroad depot in Albuquerque. Her association with the Fred Harvey Company eventually spanned more than 40 years.

Colter's keen interest and research in Native American architecture led to a remarkable series of buildings along the Grand Canyon's South Rim, beginning with the Hopi House that opened in 1905. She used Southwestern themes and simple designs with careful attention to detail—interiors had to have just the right colors and furnishings, for example. So much thought went into the design of the buildings that each tells a story about its history or setting. Colter gave the stone Lookout Studio, perched on the Canyon rim, a jagged roof to blend into the scenery; it opened in 1914. In the same year she completed Hermit's Rest at the end of Hermit Rd.; its Great Fireplace and cozy interior seem much like a place that a hermit prospector would inhabit. She sought the "lived-in look" and had workmen smear soot on the new fireplace to enhance the atmosphere. Colter's work also extended to the bottom of the Grand Canyon, where in 1922 she designed the stone lodge and four cabins of Phantom Ranch. In 1932 she finished the Desert View Watchtower using a variety of prehistoric and modern Native American themes; it's the most intriguing of her buildings. After settling on a watchtower patterned after those of the Four Corners region, Colter wrote, "First and most important was to design a building that would. . . create no discordant note against the time eroded walls of this promontory." She not only designed the 1935 Bright Angel Lodge, intended to provide accommodations for tourists with moderate incomes, but she also incorporated into it the 1890s Buckey O'Neill Cabin and Red Horse Station. Without her interest in these historic structures, they would have been torn down. She also designed the unusual geologic fireplace in the lodge's History Room.

La Posada Hotel, which opened in 1930 beside the railroad tracks in downtown Winslow, might be her most exotic commission—a fantasy of arches, halls, and gardens in a Spanish Colonial Revival style. La Posada nearly suffered demolition, the fate of the Alvarado Hotel, but it has been saved and restored; Winslow visitors are welcome to tour the public areas. Train travelers at Union Station in Los Angeles, built in 1939, can admire an interior design that brings a Southwestern style into the geometry of Art Deco. Colter enjoyed her professional life—she never married and was reportedly rarely at home. Only in recent times has the public taken note of Colter's work. Perhaps her position as "house architect" on a relatively small number of major buildings, some in remote areas, led to her relative obscurity. That's changed now, with books, exhibits, and documentaries out on her life. Five Colter structures have become National Historic Landmarks.

© GRAND CANYON NATIONAL PARK [NEG# 8307]

Hopi artist Fred Kabotie worked with Mary Colter on the Desert View Watchtower's interior artwork.

art and crafts for sale on two floors. It's near the Canyon rim just east of El Tovar.

Verkamp's Curios

Just east past Hopi House, this venerable institution is also worth a look for Native American crafts and Canyon souvenirs. John Verkamp found business too slow during his first attempt at a curio shop out of a tent in 1898, but he returned in 1905 and built on the present site. The family continues to run the business.

Lookout Studio

The inspiration and materials of this Mary Colter building came from the Grand Canyon itself. Early visitors, after the 1914 completion, could relax by the fireplace in the lounge, purchase souvenirs and postcards in the art room, or gaze into the Canyon depths with a high-power telescope. It's open today with a gift shop and viewing platform. The studio stands on the Canyon's edge, just west of Bright Angel Lodge.

Kolb Studio

Perched on the rim near Lookout Studio and the Bright Angel Trailhead, this building began in 1904 as a photo studio of the Kolb brothers. Emery Kolb expanded and operated it until his death in 1976 at the age of 95. Canyon visitors could watch movies taken by the Kolbs on an early river-running expedition along with movies and stills of other Canyon subjects. The Grand Canyon Association now has a bookstore inside where you can still see some of the Kolb photography on computer screens. The auditorium where Emery showed his movies now hosts visiting art exhibitions.

GRAND CANYON NAT'L PARK

WEST OF GRAND CANYON VILLAGE

Hermit Road

The Santa Fe Railroad built this eight-mile-long road from Grand Canyon Village to Hermits Rest in 1912. Stops along the way allow visitors to walk to the rim and enjoy the views. Highlights include a great overlook of the Bright Angel Trail from Trailview, the copper and uranium Orphan Mine from Maricopa Point, some of the best views and a large historic marker at Powell Memorial, the Colorado River from Hopi and Mohave Points, the 3,000-foot sheer drop of the Abyss, and, from Pima Point, views of Granite Rapid and foundations of an old hotel below. Your map will help identify Canyon features: Bright Angel Trail switchbacking down to the grove of trees at Indian Garden; Plateau Point at the end of a short trail from Indian Garden; long, straight Bright Angel Canyon on the far side of the river; the many majestic temples rising to the north and east; and the rapids of the Colorado River.

Hermits Rest—with restrooms, gift shop, and drinking water—marks the westernmost viewpoint and end of the drive. Mary Colter designed the imaginative stone building and its Great Fireplace according to what she thought a hermit might like. A free shuttle bus runs the length of the drive except in winter, when you can take your own vehicle. Bicyclists enjoy this drive too, and they aren't affected by the shuttle-season ban on cars. Because Hermit Road is so narrow, cyclists need to pull off and dismount when large vehicles need to pass.

If you've walked to Hermits Rest on the Rim Trail, you'll probably want to rest too. Louis Boucher, the Hermit, came to the Canyon in 1891 and stayed 21 years; he lived at Dripping Springs and constructed the Boucher Trail to his mining claims in Boucher Canyon.

Hermit Trail, built by the Fred Harvey Company after Louis Boucher departed, begins just beyond Hermits Rest at the end of a gravel road. It descends to the Tonto Trail, then continues down to the river at Hermit Rapids. Visitors who took this trail between 1912 and 1930 could stay at a tourist camp partway down on the Tonto Platform; only foundations remain today. A branch in the upper trail goes to Dripping Springs and Boucher Canyon.

EAST OF GRAND CANYON VILLAGE

Desert View Drive

Outstanding overlooks line this 25-mile drive between Grand Canyon Village and Desert View. Each has its own character and is worth a stop, but many people consider the aptly named Grandview Point one of the best. It's 12 miles east of Grand Canyon Village (13 miles before Desert View), then 0.8 mile north. Sweeping panoramas take in much of the Grand Canyon from this commanding site above Horseshoe Mesa. The vastness and intricacies of the Canyon show themselves especially well here.

Other major viewpoints on Desert View Drive include Yaki Point, Moran Point, Lipan Point, and Desert View. At Lipan, by looking both up- and down-canyon, you can see the entire geologic sequence of the Canyon.

Tusayan Ruin

Prehistoric ancestral Puebloans built this village in A.D. 1185–1190, according to tree-ring dating. Perhaps 30 people lived here, contending with poor soil, little rainfall, and scarce drinking water. After staying 35–40 years, they moved on. Archaeologists who excavated the site in 1930 named it Tusayan, a Spanish term for Hopi territory.

A small museum introduces the ancestral Puebloans with artifacts and illustrations of

a painting in the Desert View
Watchtower, 1932

Desert View

This overlook presents a stunning view at the east end of Desert View Drive. Although the surrounding pinyon pines and junipers suggest a lower elevation, this is the highest viewpoint on the South Rim at an elevation of 7,500 feet. Far to the east lies the multi-hued Painted Desert that gave the viewpoint its name. Below, to the north, the Colorado River comes out of Marble Canyon, then curves west through the Grand Canyon.

The strange-looking **Desert View Watchtower**, designed by Mary Colter, incorporates design elements from both prehistoric and modern tribes of the Four Corners region. The Fred Harvey Company built the 70-foot structure in 1932, using stone around a steel frame. The interior contains reproductions of Hopi paintings and petroglyphs; stairs lead to several levels inside and to an outdoor terrace. You enter the watchtower through a room shaped like a Navajo hogan with a traditional log ceiling.

Desert View has a small information center/bookstore, gift shop, snack bar, general store, service station, and campground. There is a $10 fee for the campsites, which have drinking water but no hookups; they're open mid-May to the end of October, weather permitting; no reservations taken.

Vicinity of Desert View

Highway AZ 64 continues east 33 miles from Desert View to Cameron and US 89. On the way you'll pass two impressive overlooks of the **Little Colorado River**—signed Scenic View—on the Navajo Reservation. The sheer 800-foot cliffs of the Little Colorado create a spectacular sight. The first overlook, 16.5 miles from Desert View, requires a half-mile walk out to the best viewpoints. The second overlook, 5.2 miles farther east, offers a large market of Native American jewelry, pottery, and other crafts with just a short walk to the views.

dwellings. An exhibit about archaic cultures has some split-twig figures dating as far back as 4,000 years; other exhibits introduce modern tribes of the region. Outside, a short, self-guided trail leads around the plaza and ruins of living quarters, storage rooms, and two kivas. A leaflet (pick one up at the trailhead) and interpretive signs describe how the ancestral Puebloans farmed and obtained some of their wild foods. You can also take a free guided 45-minute tour, check *The Guide* for times. Related books can be purchased.

The museum is open daily 9 A.M.–5 P.M., except in winter when it may close some days, but the trail stays open then, weather permitting. It's on Desert View Drive, 22 miles east of Grand Canyon Village and three miles west of Desert View, tel. 928/638-2305.

GRAND CANYON NAT'L PARK

SILENCE IN THE CANYON

Wilderness can provide a refuge from the ever busier worlds that we create. Just being out in the canyons turns out to be a delightful experience. Part of this delight seems to come from the space and the silence, which then reflects back on our own minds. "Preserving the power of presence," as Jack Turner terms it in his book, *The Abstract Wild*, is far more complex than just looking after the biodiversity. Rather than believing that presence is something that we can add on to make the wilderness whole, he states that "the loss of aura and presence is the main reason we are losing so much of the natural world." Turner thinks that by viewing wilderness as amusement and resource, we lose sight of the magic and sacred nature of it.

In the Grand Canyon, this value of presence or silence has come under assault from a steady stream of aircraft circling over the heart of the Canyon. No local topic has become as heated or difficult to resolve. Pilots and passengers enjoy flying so much that they refuse to consider a ban on flights, yet proponents of presence will not be satisfied until the skies over the park become silent. Congress first addressed the noise problem in 1987, banning nonemergency flights below the rims and requiring the designation of flight-free zones. The current compromise of restricted flight paths reduces the noise over some parts of the park, but it comes far short of the tranquility that early tourists to the park must have experienced. Only public opinion, expressed to representatives in Congress and to the Grand Canyon National Park administration, will determine how much natural silence the Canyon will offer to future visitors.

Cape Solitude, directly above the confluence of the Little Colorado and Colorado Rivers, lives up to its name and features amazing views of both canyons. The jeep road has been closed to vehicles, but adventurous drivers with 4WD can take back roads on the Navajo Reservation (tribal permit needed) to the park boundary, then walk the last 6.7 miles. When the Little Colorado isn't in flood, you'll see turquoise-blue waters from mineral-rich springs in its canyon. Hikers can reach Blue Springs on a very rough route, estimated at 1.5 miles one way and an elevation change of 2,100 feet; it's on the Navajo Reservation (tribal permit required) and approached on 4WD roads from Desert View via Cedar Mountain or from the Kaibab National Forest farther east. The Little Colorado offers a challenging hiking route between Cameron and the Colorado River; conditions constantly change, and it should be avoided when in flood. Hiking books describe some of these routes. Ask around at Desert View, Tusayan Ruins, and the Backcountry Office to find a ranger knowledgeable in these areas. See **Cameron** (Northeastern Arizona chapter) for details on obtaining Navajo tribal permits to explore this remote country east of the Grand Canyon.

KAIBAB NATIONAL FOREST (TUSAYAN RANGER DISTRICT)

Tusayan Bike Trails

Three interconnected loops for mountain bikers begin from a trailhead on the west side of AZ 64 between Moqui Lodge and Tusayan. Trail 1 is three miles (it takes about half an hour); Trail 2 goes eight miles (just over an hour); and Trail 3 runs nine miles (about an hour and a half).

Grandview Lookout

Some of the prettiest country of the Tusayan Ranger District surrounds the lookout. You can climb the 80-foot steel tower, built by the Civilian Conservation Corps in 1936, for a panorama of the region. The tower is easily reached from the Desert View Drive, two miles east of the Grandview Point turnoff; turn south at the sign for "Arizona Trail" between Mileposts 252 and 253 and proceed 1.3 miles on a dirt road. You can also drive east 15 miles on unpaved Forest Road 302 from the south edge of Tusayan.

Cross-country ski loops begin one-third of a mile north of Grandview Lookout; the Forest Service grooms trails here in the snow season, beginning about late December.

The historic **Hull Cabin** and outbuildings, two miles from the lookout by bumpy dirt road, once belonged to a sheep ranch. You're welcome to visit the grounds. The Kaibab Forest Map (Tusayan District) shows the way in.

Hikers have several options at the trailhead beside Grandview Lookout. **Vishnu Trail** makes a 2.2-mile loop with a spur trail to Grand Canyon viewpoints. The trail heads northeast from the tower, then loops back on the Arizona Trail. Whether you're setting out on a months-long expedition or just a short stroll, the **Arizona Trail** offers some scenic hiking and mountain biking. The first mile southeast from the trailhead has interpretive signs about mistletoe. Altogether, the Arizona Trail runs 24.2 miles one way between the lookout and the south boundary of the Tusayan Ranger District. The Coconino Rim Trail segment follows the top of 500-foot cliffs southeast of Grandview Lookout; it's 12 miles one way to Russell Tank with views of the Painted Desert, moderate grades, and some switchbacks. The 12.2-mile, mostly level Russell Wash segment farther south crosses the transition from ponderosa forest in the north to pinyon pine and juniper in the south and parallels the old Moqui Stage route (1893–1901) from near Russell Tank past the station site, reached by a .25-mile-long trail, to the south forest boundary. Forest roads intersect the Arizona Trail allowing a variety of loops for mountain bikers.

Red Butte Trail

Few hikers know about this mountain south of Tusayan, despite the good trail and fine views. It's a remnant of the red-colored Moenkopi Formation, protected from erosion by a thick lava cap. The hike is 2.4 miles roundtrip and takes about 1.5 hours to the summit (7,326 ft.), an 866-foot elevation gain. You can visit the lookout tower for the best 360-degree panorama. The large meadows just to the north once hosted Grand Canyon's original airport; a bit farther north stands the green tower of a uranium mine, currently inactive due to low ore prices. A long stretch of the

confluence of the Little Colorado and Colorado Rivers from the air

© BILL WEIR

GRAND CANYON NAT'L PARK

North Rim rises farther to the north, Grand-view Lookout can just be seen on the wooded ridge to the northeast, and the San Francisco Peaks and Volcanic Field lie to the south. From Tusayan, head south nine miles on AZ 64 to between Mileposts 226 and 227, then turn east 4.3 miles on Forest Roads 305, 340, and 340A. From the south, you can take AZ 64 to Milepost 224, then turn east 2.7 miles via Forest Roads 320, 340, and 340A to the trailhead. As on all trails in the Southwest, keep an eye out for rattlesnakes.

VALLE

Highways US 180 from Flagstaff and AZ 64 from Williams meet at this road junction 28 miles south of Grand Canyon Village. The tiny community has an excellent aviation museum, a simple theme park based on the cartoon Flintstones, two motels, a campground, convenience stores, gift shops, and a gas station. The desolate high-desert spot isn't a place to linger, except for the museum. The motels are poor value compared with those in Flagstaff or Williams, and the restaurants lack a smoke-free area. The campground at the theme park is exposed to winds, and the café here also fails to provide a non-smoking area.

Planes of Fame Air Museum

Outstanding aircraft of the past, along with some oddities and replicas, reside beside Valle's airport on the south side of town. During the Korean War, General Douglas MacArthur flew aboard the Lockheed Constellation C-121A named "Bataan," which has been beautifully restored and opened for tours. The 1928 Ford Trimotor, said to have been a personal aircraft of Henry Ford, still flies; it's a type of plane used in early tourist flights over the Grand Canyon. You'll see replicas of a few famous WW I aircraft. World War II highlights include a Fuji Ohka 11 piloted suicide rocket, a Messerschmitt Bf 109G Gustav fighter plane, and an early P-51A Mustang. Newer fighters represent the dawn of the jet age. Some homebuilts and other light aircraft, a Link Trainer Model C-3 ("the sweat box"), and a timeline of women in aviation round out the collection. The museum, open daily 9 A.M.–6 P.M. (to 5 P.M. in winter) except Thanksgiving and Christmas, is part of the Planes of Fame Air Museum based in Chino, California; some planes rotate between the two collections. The website www.planesoffame.org has information on both, or call 928/635-1000 for information. Admission is adults $5, children 5–12 $2, and "Bataan" tours cost an extra $3.

Around the last weekend in June, the museum sponsors the **High Country Warbirds Air Display** with flybys of vintage aircraft and ground displays.

Flintstones Bedrock City

Fans of the cartoon series *The Flintstones* may enjoy walking around this life-size town. It has the houses of Fred and Barney and their families, businesses, dinosaur statues (one is a kid's slide), a little ride through a "volcano," and a theater where the cartoons play. The park, tel. 928/635-2600, is open year-round but the volcano ride and theater don't run in winter; admission is $5 for ages two and up. There's also a campground here (see below for details).

South Rim Practicalities

SOUTH RIM ACCOMMODATIONS

The Grand Canyon offers too much to see in one day. In Grand Canyon Village you can stay right on the rim at Bright Angel Lodge, Thunderbird Lodge, Kachina Lodge, or El Tovar Hotel. Other lodges lie back in the woods. The town of Tusayan, just outside the park seven miles south of Grand Canyon Village, provides additional places to stay. One can usually find a room anytime, but reservations from six up to 23 months in advance will give you the best choice. If planning a late arrival, you might consider either a reservation or staying in one of the gateway towns surrounding the park.

Grand Canyon Village

Grand Canyon National Park Lodges operates all the lodges here, as well as Phantom Ranch at the bottom of the Canyon, Moqui Lodge just outside the South Entrance Station, and the lodge and cabins at the North Rim's Bright Angel Point. All the lodges have non-smoking rooms and totally smoke-free public areas. Make reservations at 14001 E. Iliff Ave., Suite 600, Aurora, CO 80014; tel. 303/297-2757 (advance reservations) or 928/638-2631 (same-day reservations), or fax 303/297-3175; www.grand-canyonlodges.com.

One of the grand old hotels of the West, **El Tovar** has offered the Canyon's finest accommodations and food since 1905. This national historic landmark offers rooms—no two alike—with modern conveniences, yet it retains an old-fashioned lodge ambience; guests enjoy a restaurant, lounge, and concierge service. Four suites have Canyon views. Room rates run $118 d for a standard double up to $176 d for a deluxe and $201–286 for a suite.

Kachina and **Thunderbird** Lodges, on the rim between El Tovar and Bright Angel Lodge,

offer modern rooms for $116 d back side or $126 d canyon side.

Historic 1935 **Bright Angel Lodge** sits on the rim a short distance from the Bright Angel trailhead. Hikers and other visitors gather in the lobby, patio, restaurant, and lounge of this popular place. Rates for historic cabins run $76 d, rim cabins $98 d, and rim cabins with fireplace $118 d. Rooms in the lodge cost $48 with sink only, $54 with toilet, $66 d with toilet and shower or tub; other facilities are down the hall. The Buckey O'Neill Suite dates from the early 1890s and is one of the oldest structures in the park; it costs $236 d. The Bright Angel History Room displays memorabilia from early tourist days and a "geological fireplace" in which Canyon rocks have been laid, floor to ceiling, in the proper stratigraphic sequence. The transportation desk in the lobby organizes scheduled bus service, bus and air tours, mule trips, and Phantom Ranch accommodations. The lodge also features two restaurants, an ice cream fountain, lounge, and a gift shop.

Maswik Lodge, two blocks south of Bright Angel Lodge, has a cafeteria and cozy cabins for $64 d (closed in winter) and modern rooms for $76 d in the south section, $119 d in the north section. **Yavapai Lodge,** one mile east of Bright Angel Lodge, then one-third mile south near Market Plaza, offers modern rooms for $89 d in the west section and $103 d in the east section; there's also a cafeteria here; the lodge closes for part of the winter.

Tusayan

Motels, restaurants, a campground, an IMAX Theater, and other tourist services line AZ 64 in this compact town, seven miles south of Grand Canyon Village. They're all well signed. Prices run on the high side for accommoda-

GRAND CANYON NAT'L PARK

POINT-AND-SHOOT POINTERS

Compact cameras can take wonderful pictures—if their pea-sized electronic brains aren't too heavily relied upon! The small size of compacts makes it easy to keep your camera ready for those "magic moments." Here's a checklist of ideas to obtain rewarding images:

• Moving in close to your subject gives striking results! Too often a person steps back and tries to take a photo of his sweetheart AND the Grand Canyon without doing justice to either. A closer snap of the sweetheart with a bit of Canyon background would make a better shot. Simple backgrounds give a sense of place without distracting from the subject.

• To zoom or not to zoom? Wide-angle settings often work best for landscapes and in confined spaces. Normal or telephoto lens settings do well for portraits.

• People busy enjoying themselves make memorable photos.

• The early photographer gets the greatest shots. Morning's warm, soft, misty light creates wonderful effects for both landscapes and portraits. Evening's light is almost as good.

• Foregrounds add depth and interest to scenics. The infinity or spot button on many cameras ensures that the camera focuses on the distant scenery—not a nearby tree.

• To flash or not to flash? Cameras optimistically think their flash will illuminate the entire Grand Canyon for that evening shot! Then it's best to turn off the flash, prop up the camera on something (a tripod if you're lucky enough to have one handy), and use the self-timer or remote to release the shutter without jarring the camera; you can obtain surprisingly good night and interior shots this way. Some cameras have a "night scene" mode that illuminates near objects with flash, then leaves the shutter open to expose the distant background; again, you'll need to prop up the camera. Flash can work well in daytime to "fill in" dark shadows. You can dust off the camera's instruction manual to see what flash modes, flash ranges, and shutter-speed range you have.

• Flash ranges: If you copy the flash-range distances out of the instruction manual for the film speeds you use and write it on a label on the back of the camera, you'll always know when you're "in the light." Typically compact camera flashes work from the minimum focusing distance up to about 16 feet at wide angle, decreasing to about 9 feet at telephoto settings with ISO 100 films; distances double with ISO 400 and double again at ISO 1600.

• Steady cameras get the sharp shots. If you hold the camera securely but not tightly, and let out half of your breath and hold it while clicking the shutter, you'll get the best results. In low light or with telephoto settings, you might consider propping up the camera.

• Prints or slides? The old adage "take print film for prints, slide film for slides" is fine, but if you'd really like both, great prints can be made from slides, though at a higher cost.

• What film speed? ISO 100 gives very sharp, fine-grained pictures if you have steady hands. ISO 200 or 400 makes a good alternative for low light, fast-moving subjects, and telephoto shots.

• 35mm, APS, or digital? Despite its age, 35mm has yet to be surpassed as a format for compact cameras. APS offers quality nearly as good as 35mm, but with a bit more convenience (smaller size and easier film loading), three selectable formats (normal, wide, and panoramic on some models), and minor enhancements (strips store processing and picture information on the more expensive models). APS has a smaller format than 35mm and usually comes only in print film, so slide photographers will want to stick with 35mm. Digital photography has made a big splash with its instant results (you can see the

photo immediately on cameras with preview screens!) and ease of hooking to a computer to do all kinds of "darkroom" modifications; you can then email the photo to friends or see it emerge from an inexpensive color printer. Digital photography can be lots of fun, though you'll have to pay more for cameras and printing supplies than you would for film cameras. Results may not be quite as good as with film, and prints may have a shorter life. Alternatively, you can use a film camera and scan the prints or slides into your computer; some scanners go for less than $100.
• Out in the weather or on a river-rafting trip, you'll find a water-resistant camera handy. The best models for outdoors feature weatherproofing, a glass lens protector (can't jam), and a zoom lens with only a slightly higher cost and weight than unprotected models. Waterproof disposable cameras provide a low-cost alternative.
• A critical look at professional photos in *Arizona Highways* magazine will provide a wealth of ideas—you can see how lighting, camera angle, foreground, background, and placement of subjects lead your eye into and around each photo for a delightful experience.
• Books and websites offer examples and tips. Kodak has many how-to books; its website features picture-taking advice at website: www.kodak.com. Sun Spot Photography offers picture-taking instruction at website: www.sunspotphoto.com. The author of website: www.photo.net provides lots of how-to and equipment advice. Short Courses at website: www.shortcourses.com specializes in digital photography.

tions, though they drop a bit in winter or any time business is slow. You're unlikely to find any rooms under $50.

$50–100: Seven Mile Lodge, tel. 928/638-2291, offers basic rooms at $68 d in summer, less in winter; no reservations taken.

Moqui Lodge, one mile north of Tusayan and just outside the South Entrance Station, tel. 928/638-2424 or 303/297-2757 (central reservations), offers rooms at $94 d from April 15–October 15 (closed in winter). Rooms lack air-conditioning, but nights are always cool. The lodge has a restaurant open daily for a breakfast buffet, a cantina that serves light meals, an information desk where you can arrange tours and horseback riding, a gift shop, and a service station.

$100–150: Red Feather Lodge/Rodeway Inn, tel. 928/638-2414 or 800/538-2345, or 800/228-2000 (Rodeway reservations), has standard rooms at $79–119 d in the older motel-style annex and deluxe rooms at $99–129 d in the new building with lower rates off-season; guests can enjoy an outdoor pool and hot tub, fitness room, and adjacent restaurant.

Grand Canyon Quality Inn & Suites, tel. 928/638-2673 or 800/228-5151, features a restaurant, the Wintergarten Lounge, and an 18-foot hot tub in a huge atrium; there's also an outdoor pool and hot tub and a gift shop. Standard rooms are $118–128 d and suites go for $188 d from April–October 15, less off-season.

Best Western Grand Canyon Squire Inn, tel. 928/638-2681 or 800/622-6966, offers three restaurants, lounge, sports bar, outdoor pool, hot tub, sauna, exercise room, tennis courts, bowling alley, beauty salon, and gift shop. Rooms cost $135 d standard, $150 d deluxe, and the few suites are $175–225 d; www.grandcanyonsquire.com.

Holiday Inn Express, tel. 928/638-3000 or 888/538-5353, or 800/HOLIDAY, includes a continental breakfast with its rooms, which run $139 d in summer. A nearby building offers suites with one bedroom at about $148 d and two bedrooms for about $250.

The Grand Hotel, tel. 928/638-3333 or 888/634-7263, presents a dinner theater with Native American programs and cowboy songs, a restaurant, and an indoor pool and hot tub on the south side of town; rooms go for $139 d ($149 with a balcony) in summer; www.gcanyon.com/grand.htm.

Valle

You'll pass through this little town, 28 miles south of Grand Canyon Village, if coming on the direct routes from Williams or Flagstaff. **Grand Canyon Motel** ($79 d) and the nearby **Grand Canyon Inn** ($49–69 d) are under the same management, tel. 928/635-9203 or 800/635-9203. Both may close mid-winter. The inn has a smoky restaurant, summer pool, and a gift shop.

SOUTH RIM CAMPGROUNDS

Grand Canyon Village

Campgrounds tend to be crowded in the warmer months and it's strongly recommended to have a reservation from mid-March–Oct.; otherwise, try to arrive before noon to look for a site. Rangers enforce the "No Camping Outside Designated Sites" policy with stiff fines. Backpackers inside the Canyon or in backcountry areas atop the rim need a permit from the Backcountry Office. RVs have a dump station near the road to the campgrounds.

Mather Campground, tel. 928/638-7851, in Grand Canyon Village accepts both tenters and RVers; it's open year-round with drinking water but no hookups for $15 per night, $7.50 with a Golden Age or Access pass. Make reservations for family and group sites at tel. 800/365-2267 (365-CAMP) or on the Internet at reservations.nps.gov. Backpackers and bicyclists can camp in a walk-in area for $4 per person, no reservations needed; it has space even when the campground is signed "FULL." Coin-operated showers and laundromat and ice sales are nearby. You can attend free campfire programs during the warmer months.

Trailer Village, just east of Mather Campground, has RV sites for $24 with hookups all year. Reservations are highly recommended from the week before Easter to the end of October; you can make them with Grand Canyon National Park Lodges, 14001 E. Iliff Ave., Suite 600, Aurora, CO 80014, tel. 303/297-2757 (advance reservations) or 928/638-2631 (same-day reservations), fax 303/297-3175; www.grandcanyonlodges.com. Coin-operated showers and laundry lie within walking distance.

Desert View

This campground, near the East Entrance Station (25 miles east of Grand Canyon Village), has sites in a pinyon-juniper forest with drinking water but no hookups. It's open mid-May–October, weather permitting, for $10; no reservations taken.

Tusayan

Grand Canyon Camper Village, tel. 928/638-2887, offers sites for tents ($18) and RVs ($22–26 including hookups) with coin showers and a playground. Tepee tents ($20) are available during the warmer months. Reservations can be made only for the hookup sites, though spaces are usually available. The campground may close in winter.

Ten X Campground in the ponderosa pines of the Kaibab National Forest has drinking water but no hookups or showers; it's open May–Sept. for $10 per vehicle and usually has room. Amphitheater programs take place many nights. From Tusayan, go south two miles (between Mileposts 233 and 234), then turn east a quarter mile. **Charley Tank Group Site** nearby can be reserved; tel. 928/638-2443 (Tusayan Ranger Station).

Dispersed camping in the Kaibab National Forest south of the park is another possibility—just practice no-trace camping, carry your own drinking water and a shovel, and stay at least a quarter mile from the nearest paved road and from any surface water. Check with the ranger station, on the right one mile north of Tusayan, to learn whether campfires are permitted; staff can also suggest areas for dispersed camping. The Kaibab Forest map (Williams and Tusayan Districts) shows the back roads.

Valle

Flintstones Bedrock City campsites in Valle, 28 miles south of Grand Canyon Village on AZ 64, tel. 928/635-2600, cost $12 for tents or RVs ($16 w/hookups). It has coin showers, a store, snack bar (smoky), and theme park. The campground is open year-round.

SOUTH RIM FOOD

Grand Canyon Village Area

El Tovar Hotel, tel. 928/638-2526 ext. 6432, offers elegant continental and American dining daily for breakfast, lunch, and dinner at moderate to expensive prices; you'll need to make reservations for dinner.

Bright Angel Lodge features two moderately priced restaurants, the **Bright Angel Restaurant,** tel. 928/638-2526 ext. 6189, serving breakfast, lunch, and dinner daily, and the **Arizona Room,** tel. 928/638-2526 ext. 6296, offering Southwestern fare nightly for dinner. The Arizona Room closes Jan.–February. Neither restaurant takes reservations but you can often get in for dinner without much waiting by arriving before sunset.

Maswik Lodge, two blocks south of Bright Angel Lodge, and **Yavapai Lodge,** one mile east of Bright Angel Lodge, then one-third

mile south near Market Plaza, both have large cafeterias open daily for breakfast, lunch, and dinner at relatively low prices.

The **Canyon Village Marketplace** in Market Plaza has a supermarket and a deli counter with tables. You can also buy groceries at general stores in Desert View and Tusayan. **Bright Angel Fountain** serves ice cream and other snacks on the Canyon rim behind Bright Angel Lodge; it's closed in the winter.

Tusayan

Moqui Lodge's restaurant, tel. 928/638-2424, prepares a breakfast buffet daily and the cantina serves light meals during the April 15–October 15 season. The spacious atrium and greenery in the **Grand Canyon Quality Inn & Suites'** restaurant, tel. 928/638-2673, provide an enjoyable setting. Diners have a choice of ala carte or buffets daily for breakfast, lunch, and dinner. The large selection of salads and fruit in the buffets will appeal to vegetarians; non-veggies will appreciate steak and seafood on the menu as well as a variety of meat dishes in the buffet. **Canyon Star** at the Grand Hotel, tel. 928/638-3333, features a dinner theater with Native American programs and cowboy songs as well as breakfast, lunch, and dinner daily; buffet options for breakfast, lunch, and dinner run in summer and early autumn. **Café Tusayan,** tel. 928/638-2150, serves American favorites daily for breakfast, lunch, and dinner next to the Red Feather Lodge. The **Grand Canyon Squire Inn's** Coronado Room offers fine dining of steak, barbecued ribs, prime rib, seafood, pasta, and some Mexican items nightly for dinner; the Canyon Room serves ala carte meals (year-round) and buffets (summer only) daily for breakfast and lunch; tel. 928/638-2681. **The Steakhouse,** tel. 928/638-2780, serves up steak, chicken, shrimp, and even a few veggie options; it's open daily for lunch (summer only) and dinner. **We Cook Pizza & Pasta,** tel. 928/638-2278, offers pizza, pasta, calzones, and sandwiches

© GRAND CANYON NATIONAL PARK (NEG# 5423)

Hopi dancer Chester Dennis (right) leads other dancers at the dedication of the Desert View Watchtower, 1933.

daily for lunch and dinner. **Pizza Hut** and **Taco Bell** can be found in the Grand Canyon IMAX Theater complex. **McDonald's** is nearby across the highway.

SOUTH RIM SERVICES

Entertainment

Rangers present **evening programs** and **campfire talks;** see *The Guide* listings for times and places, check the panels outside the Visitor Center, or call 928/638-7888 for the day's topics. Chamber music comes to the Grand Canyon in September during the **Grand Canyon Music Festival,** held at Shrine of the Ages auditorium on the South Rim. The **Grand Canyon IMAX Theatre,** tel. 928/638-2468/2203, in Tusayan projects an impressive movie, *The Grand Canyon—The Hidden Secrets,* on a 70-foot screen with six-track stereo sound. The spectacular photography of the 34-minute presentation portrays prehistoric tribes, explorers, wildlife, river running, and flying. Showings take place every day on the half hour 8:30 A.M.–8:30 P.M. March–October,

then 10:30 A.M.–6:30 P.M. in winter. Admission is $9.50 adults, $6.50 children 3–11. You'll also find fast-food restaurants, gift shops, ATM, and tourist information here.

Shopping

Grand Canyon Association has excellent selections of regional books, children's books, topo maps, posters, and videos in its shops at Canyon View Information Plaza, Kolb Studio, Yavapai Observation Station, Tusayan Ruin, and Desert View; www.grandcanyon.org. **General stores,** at Market Plaza in Grand Canyon Village, at Tusayan, and at Desert View, sell groceries, camping and hiking supplies, clothing, books, maps, souvenirs, and offer one of the best selections of camera film. The Market Plaza store is the largest and has a deli. There's a gift shop almost everywhere you turn in the developed areas of the South Rim! El Tovar, other lodges, most motels, helicopter terminals, and the airport have them. **Hopi House,** the pueblo replica just east of El Tovar, has an impressive array of Native American crafts and art from the Southwest; it's worth a visit to see both the architecture—interior and exterior—and the high-quality merchandise. A bit farther east is **Verkamp's Curio** with Native American crafts and other souvenirs. **Lookout Studio,** on the rim's edge near Bright Angel Lodge, features curios and books in a picturesque stone building. Other places to shop in the park include Hermits Rest and Desert View Watchtower, at opposite ends of the South Rim drives.

Other Services

Backpackers can stow their bags with staff in the Bright Angel Lodge lobby. The **post office,** near the general store in Market Plaza, tel. 928/638-2512, is open Mon.–Fri. 9 A.M.–4 P.M. and Saturday 11 A.M.–3 P.M.; stamp machines in the lobby are available after hours. **Bank One** next door has a 24-hour ATM; it cannot change foreign currency or cash out-of-town checks. The **general store** in Tusayan also includes a **post office** and an ATM, and there's another ATM at the IMAX Theater across the highway. **Western Union,** tel. 928/638-2608, does wire transfers at Canyon Food Mart in Tusayan. **Print film processing** is offered at the general stores and several places in Tusayan. **Grand Canyon Garage,** tel. 928/638-2225 (638-2631 ext. 6502 after hours), fixes ailing cars and provides 24-hour emergency service. **Grand Canyon Clinic,** tel. 928/638-2551, offers medical services, open in summer Mon.–Fri. 8 A.M.–8 P.M. and Sat. noon–6 P.M. (shorter hours in winter); for a dentist, call tel. 928/638-2395. For an ambulance or other emergency, dial 911.

National Park Service staff provide wheelchairs, the *Accessibility Guide,* and other services for visitors with special needs; ask at the entrance stations, visitor centers, or write ahead to the park, Box 129, Grand Canyon, AZ 86023.

The **Pet Kennel,** tel. 928/638-0534, houses the furry companions who won't be welcome in the park lodges or permitted on the inner-canyon trails; reservations are suggested. Leashed pets may walk the rim trails in developed areas and may be able to stay in some of the motels in Tusayan. Service animals may be allowed below the rim—check in first at the Backcountry Information Center. You'll find a coin-operated **laundromat** and **showers**—a welcome sight to any traveler who's been a long time on the road or trail—near Mather Campground.

Theft has become a problem at the Canyon—be sure to keep valuables hidden or carry them with you. Park rangers patrol the park, serving as law enforcement officers and firefighters; see them if you have difficulties.

SOUTH RIM INFORMATION

Visitor Center

Canyon View Information Center, just south of Mather Point, provides on its outdoor panels an overview of things to see and do in the park; step inside the Visitor Center for the information desk; it's open daily 8 A.M.–6 P.M. with extended hours in summer. At the entrance stations, you'll receive a copy of *The Guide* newspaper with the latest visitor information including sightseeing, hiking, programs, places to stay and eat, and other visitor services. You can contact the park at Box 129, Grand Canyon, AZ 86023 or on the Web at www.nps.gov/grca.

The **automated switchboard,** tel. 928/638-7888, has a **weather forecast** and other recordings, and it connects to all park offices if you're patient. The **hearing-impaired** can use the TDD number for park information, tel. 928/638-7804.

Tusayan's tourist information counter offers local and regional information daily 9 A.M.–5 P.M. beside the IMAX Theater's ticket office.

Planes of Fame Air Museum in Valle also has Arizona tourist information.

GRAND CANYON NAT'L PARK

Backcountry Information Center

For trail information and backcountry camping permits, drop by this office in the Maswik Transportation Center, open daily 8 A.M.–noon and 1–5 P.M.; tel. 928/638-7875. Call between 1–5 P.M. to speak with someone in person. Day-hikers don't need a permit.

Kaibab National Forest

Though often ignored in the shadow of Grand Canyon National Park, the Kaibab offers hiking, mountain biking, and both developed and primitive camping. Stop by the **Tusayan Ranger Station** for handouts on hiking and biking trails, scenic drives, and other attractions. The Kaibab National Forest map for the Tusayan District shows the trails and back roads. Staff can also provide directions for hiking the Red Butte Trail, the prominent butte 12 miles south of Tusayan, as well as the Arizona Trail just south of the park. In winter, cross-country skiers can glide along loops near the Grandview Lookout. The station, open Mon.–Fri. 8 A.M.–4:30 P.M., is in the Tusayan Administrative Site, across and 0.2 mile south of Moqui Lodge just outside the South Entrance Station. Contact the Tusayan District, tel. 928/638-2443, at Box 3088, Grand Canyon, AZ 86023; www.fs.fed.us/r3/kai.

Internet Sites

A "virtual tour" can give you ideas of things to do on your visit. The National Park Service site contains news, visiting tips, hiking information, and river running opportunities at www.nps.gov/grca. The "Unofficial Grand Canyon National Park Home Page" is also a good source at www.kaibab.org. Canyon Web-Works, a commercial site, offers a good introduction to the park and links to surrounding towns at www.thecanyon.com.

Grand Canyon Community Library

This small collection resides in an old schoolhouse tucked behind the garage and general office for the lodges in Grand Canyon Village. It's open daily 1–6 P.M. with general and Southwestern reading, periodicals, and Internet computers; tel. 928/638-2718.

SOUTH RIM TOURS

Most of the lodges in the park, along with Moqui Lodge just outside, and the airport have a transportation desk where you can arrange tours.

Mule Rides

Sure-footed mules have carried prospectors and tourists in and out of the Canyon for more than a century. These large animals, a crossbreed of female horses and male donkeys, depart daily year-round on day and overnight trips. Although easier than hiking, a mule ride should still be considered strenuous—you need to be able to sit in the saddle for long hours and control your mount. These trips are definitely not for those afraid of heights or large animals.

Day trips proceed down the Bright Angel Trail to Indian Garden and out to Plateau Point, a spectacular overlook directly above the river; the 12-mile, seven-hour roundtrip costs $118 per person. On the overnight trip you follow the Bright Angel Trail all the way to the river, cross a suspension bridge to Phantom Ranch, spend the night in a cabin, then come out the next day via the South Kaibab Trail. This costs $334 for one person, $598 for two, and $275 for each additional person; meals are included. Three-day, two-night trips offered mid-November–March 31 cost $457 for one, $773 for two, and $338 for each additional person. Mules will also carry hikers' overnight gear to Phantom Ranch, $52 each way (30-pound limit). All these rates include tax.

Enforced requirements for riders include good health, weight under 200 pounds (91 kg), fluency in English, height at least four feet seven inches (138 cm), and ability to the first train to carry passengers to the Grand Canyon, 1901

mount and dismount without assistance. No pregnant women are allowed. A broad-rimmed hat, tied under the chin, long pants, a long-sleeved shirt, and sturdy shoes (no open-toed footwear) are necessary. Don't bring bags, purses, canteen, or backpacks, but you can carry a camera or binoculars. A bota (water carrier), which ties on the saddle horn, is supplied.

Reservations should be made 9–12 months in advance for summer and holidays. Also be sure to claim your reservation at least one hour before departure. Without a reservation, there's a chance of getting on via the waiting list, especially off-season; register in person between 6 and 10 A.M. the day before you want to go.

For information and reservations less than two days in advance, see the Bright Angel transportation desk, tel. 928/638-3283. To make reservations more than two days in advance, contact Grand Canyon National Park Lodges at 14001 E. Iliff Ave., Suite 600, Aurora, CO 80014, tel. 303/297-2757; www.grandcanyonlodges.com.

Trail Rides

Apache Stables, tel. 928/638-2891 (stables) or 638-2424 (Moqui Lodge), offers mule and horse rides through the Kaibab National Forest for one hour ($30.50), two hours ($55.50), and all the way to the South Rim and back in four hours ($95.50) from the stables near Moqui Lodge, one mile north of Tusayan. Campfire trips ($40.50) ride out and take a wagon back, or you can take the wagon both ways ($12.50); bring your own food. Riding season runs spring to autumn depending on the weather. Reservations are recommended two weeks ahead in summer or two days the rest of the year—though last-minute openings are possible; www.apachestables.com.

Bus Tours

Fred Harvey Transportation Co., tel. 928/638-3283, will show you the sights of the South Rim and narrate the Canyon's history, geology, wildlife, and architecture. Hermits Rest Tour visits viewpoints on Hermit Road (two hours, $15.25). Desert View Tour travels along Desert View Drive (just under four hours, $27.25). Begin or end the day with sunrise or sunset tours (hour and a half, $11.75 each, May–Oct. only). Children under 16 go free. You can purchase the Desert View Tour and any other excursion at $32.50 and take the tours on separate days if you wish.

Railroad Express drives you to Williams early in the morning to catch the train ride back to Grand Canyon Village, $40 adult, $20 children 16 and under. A river raft excursion runs the smooth-flowing Colorado River in Glen Canyon from the dam to Lees Ferry; at stops on the drive to the dam you'll see highlights along Desert View Drive and the Navajo Indian Reservation (12 hours, $101 adult, $53 age 12 and under, April–early November). Tours in the park leave daily (twice a day in summer for the Hermits Rest and Desert View tours). Lodge transportation desks have tickets. Reservations recommended; contact Box 699, Grand Canyon, AZ 86023; www.grandcanyonlodges.com.

Jeep Tours

Grand Canyon Jeep Tours & Safaris, tel. 928/638-5337 or 800/320-5337, in Tusayan visits backcountry historic and scenic spots in the Kaibab National Forest and the Grand Canyon. The two-hour Canyon Pines Tour departs mid-day for $48 adult ($35 age 12 and under). The three-hour Grand Sunset Tour goes late in the afternoon—a good time to spot wildlife—and includes a stop to watch the sunset for $53 ($40 age 12 and under).

The Indian Cave Paintings Tour visits a site with petroglyphs and pictographs in the Kaibab National Forest at $35 adult ($25 age 12 and younger). Tours run March–Oct.; www.grandcanyonjeeptours.com.

Grand Canyon Field Institute

Small groups explore the Grand Canyon with day hikes, backpacking, river-running trips, van tours, and classroom instruction. You can pick up a schedule at the Grand Canyon Association bookstores in the park or write the institute at Box 399, Grand Canyon, AZ 86023, tel. 928/638-2485; www.grandcanyon.org/fieldinstitute.

Air Tours

Flights over the Canyon provide breathtaking views and a look at some of the park's more remote areas. About 40 scenic flight companies operate helicopters or fixed-wing aircraft here, mostly out of Las Vegas. The 50,000-plus flights a year sometimes detract from the wilderness experience of backcountry users—Tusayan's airport is the third busiest in the state. However, restrictions on flight routes and elevations help minimize the noise.

Scenic flights depart all year from Tusayan Airport. Helicopters fly near rim-level and offer the novelty of their takeoffs and landings, but they cost more. Fixed wing aircraft fly about 1,000 feet higher and provide more air time for your dollar; they also offer better children's discounts. Most fixed-wing aircraft leave from the main terminal, while Grand Canyon Airlines and the helicopter companies fly from separate terminals nearby.

Grand Canyon Airlines, tel. 928/638-2407 or 800/528-2413, started flying here in 1927 with Ford Trimotors. Today the company uses high-wing, twin-engine planes on a 45–55-minute loop over the South Rim, Little Colorado River, and back over the North Rim

SHUTTLING OUT TO THE SOUTH RIM

The park already provides public transit to ease vehicle congestion in the popular Grand Canyon Village area. In the future, the inadequate spaces here will be replaced by new parking areas in Tusayan, just outside the park. Visitors will be able to park and quickly check out a menu of sightseeing options before hopping on a bus or light rail shuttle to the Canyon View Information Plaza near Mather Point, already open with its new visitor center and bookstore. Lodge and campground guests will be able to drive into Grand Canyon Village on a new road, but once in the park, everyone will walk, cycle, or use shuttles.

Cyclists, walkers, and eventually equestrians will have a new Greenway trail network totaling about 73 miles on both rims. The first sections—connecting Canyon View Information Plaza with Grand Canyon Village and Tusayan—should open in summer 2002. Eventually the Greenway system will go all the way to

Desert View and have a spur trail to Yaki Point. The Desert View Drive will continue to be open to motorists for at least the near future, though private vehicles may not be able to go all the way out to some overlooks. (South Kaibab Trailhead and Yaki Point are already on a shuttle-only route.)

The **Heritage Education Campus,** planned for central Grand Canyon Village, will have exhibits on natural and cultural aspects of the park, current issues, and Native American cultures, but it will be several years before this facility is open.

People unable to take shuttle buses may request an **accessibility permit** that allows a private vehicle to travel on the shuttle-only routes. Accessibility passes are available at park entrances, the visitor center at Canyon View Information Plaza, and Yavapai Observation Station. Accessible shuttle buses can be arranged by calling at least two days ahead at 928/638-0591.

GRAND CANYON NAT'L PARK

($75 adult, $45 children under 12). Planes leave from just north of the main terminal; www.grandcanyonairlines.com.

Air Grand Canyon, tel. 928/638-2686 or 800/247-4726, flies high-wing Cessnas on: a 30–40-minute flight over the eastern Canyon ($79 adult, $57 children 12 and under); a 50–60-minute loop over the eastern Canyon and North Rim ($95 adult, $52 children 12 and under); a 90–100-minute grand tour of the Grand and Marble Canyons to Lake Powell ($186 adult, $100 children 12 and under), a three-hour trip to Monument Valley and Lake Powell ($260 adult, $240 children 12 and under; add $35 for a ground tour), and an all-day excursion with a flight to Page, smooth-water river trip to Lees Ferry, then by road back to the Grand Canyon ($260 adult, $240 children 12 and under). A full-day com-

bination flying and rafting tour to the lower Grand Canyon can be arranged with two days notice ($635 per person); www.airgrandcanyon.com.

AirStar Airlines, tel. 928/638-2139 or 800/962-3869, takes off in high-wing Cessnas on a 50-minute tour to the eastern Grand Canyon and over the North Rim ($81 adult, $61 children under 15); www.airstar.com.

Papillon Grand Canyon Helicopters, tel. 928/638-2419 or 800/528-2418, flies across the Canyon to the North Rim (25–30 minutes, $104 adult, $85 children 2–11) and over the eastern Grand Canyon and North Rim (45–50 minutes, $164 adult, $132 children 2–11). You can also arrange to land at Supai village in Havasu Canyon and visit the waterfalls on day and overnight excursions. Helicopters fly from a site across the street and north of the main terminal; there's a gift shop and photo lab here; www.papillon.com.

AirStar Helicopters, tel. 928/638-2622 or 800/962-3869, will take you across the Canyon to the North Rim and back (25–30 minutes, $99), around the eastern Grand Canyon (40–45 minutes, $145), and over both the eastern and North Rim areas (50–55 minutes; $165) from the hill just east of the main terminal; www.airstar.com.

Kenai Helicopters, tel. 928/638-2764 or 800/541-4537, heads across the Canyon to the North Rim (25–30 minutes, $105 adult, $99 children 2–12) and over the eastern Grand Canyon and North Rim (40–45 minutes, $164 adult, $154 children) from the hill just east of the main terminal; www.flykenai.com.

SOUTH RIM TRANSPORTATION

Shuttle Services

The park offers free shuttle services to reduce traffic congestion. You can get the schedules in *The Guide* newspaper, free at entrance stations and information desks. Hermit Road and the Yaki Point/S. Kaibab Trailhead road are closed to private vehicles when the shuttles are running, but people with accessibility needs can obtain a permit at the Visitor Center to drive their own vehicles.

Village Shuttle connects Canyon View Information Plaza, Yavapai Observation Station, campgrounds, lodges, shops, and offices of Grand Canyon Village; buses operate daily year-round about every 10–15 minutes from early morning to late at night. The route takes about 50 minutes roundtrip.

Hermits Rest Shuttle leaves from the West Rim Interchange near Bright Angel Lodge and goes to Hermits Rest with stops at overlooks along the way; it operates daily every 10–30 minutes from an hour before sunrise to an hour after sunset. The trip out and back takes 90 minutes if you don't get off. Shuttles may

not run in winter, in which case you can take your own vehicle.

The Kaibab Trail Shuttle connects Canyon View Information Plaza with the South Kaibab Trailhead and Yaki Point from one hour before sunrise to one hour after sunset about every 30 minutes.

Eco Shuttle, tel. 928/638-0821, serves Bright Angel Lodge and other places in Grand Canyon Village from Tusayan and the airport April–Oct. for a small charge; charter tours can be arranged too; you can also check with the lodge transportation desks.

Trans-Canyon Shuttle, tel. 928/638-2820, offers daily roundtrip van service to the North Rim from May–Oct., $60 one way, $100 roundtrip; or contact any lodge transportation desk. Call ahead for details.

Auto Rentals and Taxi

Enterprise Rent-a-Car, tel. 928/638-2871 or 800/736-8222, is at the Tusayan airport. For a taxi, call **Fred Harvey Transportation Dispatch** at 928/638-2822.

Bus

Nava-Hopi, tel. 928/774-5003 (Flagstaff) or 800/892-8687, runs buses between Bright Angel Lodge and Flagstaff, $14 each way. See lodge transportation desks for schedules, but no reservations are needed; www.navahopitours.com.

Train

Passenger trains rolled into the railroad station at the Grand Canyon from 1901–1968. Twenty-one years later, steam locomotives of the **Grand Canyon Railway** began a new service pulling vintage railway cars from downtown Williams to the historic 1909 log depot in Grand Canyon Village.

Trains run daily except December 24th and 25th out of Williams. Steam engines lead the way in summer, then diesels are used the rest of the year. See the Williams section for the many options and entertainment provided; tel. 800/THE-TRAIN; www.thetrain.com. Transportation Services desks in the lodges have a tour that combines a bus to Williams with the train back to the Grand Canyon.

Air

The airport just southwest of Tusayan has both north and south entrances from AZ 64. The main terminal offers scheduled flights, fixed-wing scenic tours, a Harveycar Excursions desk (ground tours), and a gift shop.

Scenic Airlines flies large F-27 and some smaller aircraft from Las Vegas at least twice a day year-round. Fares run $139 one way, $227 roundtrip; tour packages are offered out of Las Vegas; tel. 928/638-2617 (Grand Canyon), 702/638-3300 (Las Vegas), or 800/634-6801; www.scenic.com.

Air Vegas Airlines offers both scheduled and tour flights four or five times daily all year in small twin-engine turbo prop planes. Tickets are $139 one way, $278 roundtrip, or you can sign up for one of the many tours out of Las Vegas; tel. 928/638-9351 (Grand Canyon), 702/736-3599 (Las Vegas), or 800/255-7474; www.airvegas.com.

North Rim Sights

The North Rim offers an experience very different from that of the South Rim. Elevations 1,000–1,500 feet higher result in lower temperatures and nearly 60 percent more precipitation. Rain and snowmelt have cut deeply into the North Rim so that it is now about twice as far back from the Colorado River as the South Rim. Dramatic vistas from the north inspired early explorers to choose names like Point Sublime, Cape Royal, Angels Window, and Point Imperial.

Even away from the viewpoints, the North Rim displays great beauty. Spruce, fir, pine, and aspen forests thrive in the cool air. Wildflowers bloom in blazes of color in the meadows and along the roadsides.

You'll find visitor facilities and major trailheads near Bright Angel Point, a 45-mile drive south on AZ 67 from Jacob Lake in the far north of Arizona. The road to Bright Angel Point opens in mid-May, then closes after the first big winter storm, anytime from early October to the end of November.

In winter, a deep blanket of snow covers the Kaibab Plateau's rolling meadow and forest country. The snow cover typically reaches a depth of 4–10 feet, and during the winter of 1994–95 it was more than 19 feet deep. Cross-country skiers and snowshoers find the conditions ideal. The park itself has no facilities open on the North Rim in winter; you can camp here, however, with a permit from the Backcountry Information Center.

BRIGHT ANGEL POINT AND VICINITY

Bright Angel Point

You'll get a North Rim edition of *The Guide* at the entrance station on the drive in. Park at the end of the highway, near Grand Canyon Lodge, and follow the paved foot trail to the tip of Bright Angel Point, an easy half-mile roundtrip walk. Shells and other fossils can be spotted in the outcrop of Kaibab limestone on your right, just after a stone bridge. Roaring Springs Canyon on the left and The Transept on the right join the long Bright Angel Canyon below. John Wesley Powell's 1869 expedition camped at the mouth of this canyon and gave the name Bright Angel Creek to its crystal-clear waters. Listen for Roaring Springs far below on the left and you'll see where the springs shoot out of the cliff. A pumping station at the base sup-

GRAND CANYON NAT'L PARK

plies drinking water to both North and South rims. Roaring Springs makes a good day-hike or mule-ride destination via the North Kaibab Trail. (See the "Corridor Trails of the Inner Canyon" section later in the book.) The volcanic summits on the horizon to the south are, from left to right, O'Leary, San Francisco Peaks, Kendrick, and Sitgreaves. Red Butte, on the right and closer, preserves a remnant of Moenkopi Formation under a lava cap.

Transept Trail

This easy level trail winds along The Transept's rim between Grand Canyon Lodge and the campground, 1.5 miles one way. You can enter the mouth of this canyon, which usually has only a small flow, from the North Kaibab Trail; it's best attempted on an overnight trip, when you can stay at nearby Cottonwood Campground.

Cape Royal Scenic Drive

The paved Cape Royal Road, which begins three miles north of the lodge, leads to some of the North Rim's most spectacular viewpoints. Follow it 5.3 miles, then turn left 2.7 miles for **Point Imperial** (elev. 8,803 feet), which offers picnic tables and the highest vantage point from either rim. Views encompass impressive geology in the park's eastern section. You'll see Nankoweap Creek below, Vermilion Cliffs on the horizon to the north, rounded Navajo Mountain on the horizon in Utah to the northeast, the Painted Desert far to the east, and the Little Colorado River Canyon to the southeast.

Hikers can descend to Nankoweap Creek and the Colorado River on the difficult Nankoweap Trail. (See the "Inner Canyon Hiking" section later in the book.) You can hike to Saddle Mountain Trailhead on a four-mile trail through the forest from Point Imperial; it begins on the far side of the road loop from the overlook. You can also drive there on Forest Service roads from De Motte Park.

Transept, Bright Angel, and Grand Canyon from near Bright Angel Point

© BILL WEIR

Cape Royal Road continues beyond the Point Imperial turnoff past **Vista Encantadora** (with picnic tables), **Roosevelt Point, Walhalla Overlook,** and other viewpoints to a parking area and a few picnic tables at the end of the road, just before Cape Royal. Total driving distance from Grand Canyon Lodge is 23 miles one way. A paved level trail continues south 0.3 mile from the parking lot to Cape Royal. Trailside signs identify plants growing on this high, arid ridge. On the way you'll see **Angels Window,** a massive natural arch, which you can walk out on via a short side trail. **Cape Royal** (elev. 7,865 feet) features a fantastic panorama; it's the southernmost viewpoint of the North Rim in this part of the Grand Canyon. Signs point out Freya Castle to the southeast, Vishnu Temple and the distant San Francisco Peaks to the south, and a branch of Clear Creek Canyon and flat-topped Wotans Throne to the southwest.

Cliff Spring Trail

Hikers enjoy pretty scenery on this trail, which takes you into a forested ravine, past a small prehistoric ruin, and under an overhang to the spring in half a mile one way. The canyon walls open up impressively as you near the spring. It's possible to continue on a rougher trail another half mile for more canyon views. Cliff Spring Trail begins from Angels Window Overlook, a small pullout on a curve of Cape Royal Road, 1.1 miles past Walhalla Overlook and 0.6 mile before road's end.

Cape Final

An easy two-mile (each way) hike brings you east of Cape Royal Road to a unique perspective from the Kaibab Plateau above Unkar Creek Canyon. The trailhead at a small unpaved parking area on the east side of the road can be difficult to spot—it may or may not be signed. Drive 5.5 miles past Roosevelt Point to the parking spot, which is one mile before Walhalla Overlook and 2.7 miles

before road's end at Cape Royal. Other scenic vistas on the North Rim can be reached on back-road hikes on the Walhalla Plateau; consult a ranger for suggestions.

Walhalla Ruins

Ancestral Puebloans, known by archaeologists as Kayenta Anasazi, farmed more than 300 sites on the plateau, most of them near the rim where warm air currents extended the growing season. The villagers probably occupied the pueblo at Walhalla (elev. 8,000 feet) in summer and wintered at Unkar Delta (visible from Walhalla Overlook); they departed from the Grand Canyon about A.D. 1150. A 100-yard walk across the road from Walhalla Overlook leads to this site.

Widforss Trail

Gently rolling terrain, fine Canyon views, and a variety of forest types attract hikers to the Widforss Trail. From the edge of a meadow, the trail climbs a bit, skirts the head of The Transept, then leads through ponderosa pines to an overlook near Widforss Point. The trail and point honor Swedish artist Gunnar Widforss, who painted the national parks of the West between 1921 and 1934.

Haunted Canyon lies below at trail's end, flanked by The Colonnade on the right and Manu Temple, Buddha Temple, and Schellbach Butte on the left; beyond lie countless more temples, towers, canyons, and the cliffs of the South Rim.

Widforss Trail is 10 miles roundtrip and takes about six hours to hike. Many people enjoy going just part way. You'll often see mule deer along the trail. From Grand Canyon Lodge, go 2.7 miles north on the highway, then turn left and go one mile on a dirt road; the turnoff is 0.3 mile south of the Cape Royal Road junction.

Ken Patrick Trail

This trail, 10 miles one way, offers forest

GRAND CANYON NAT'L PARK

scenery and views across the headwaters of Nankoweap Creek. From Point Imperial, the Ken Patrick winds about three miles along the rim to Cape Royal Road, then continues seven miles through forest to the North Kaibab trailhead, with an elevation drop of 560 feet. Allow six hours for the entire hike, one way.

You can start either from trailheads near the south end of the Point Imperial parking area, on Cape Royal Road one mile east of the Point Imperial junction, or from the upper end of the North Kaibab trailhead parking area, two miles north of Grand Canyon Lodge.

Ken Patrick worked as a ranger on the North Rim for several seasons in the early 1970s. He was shot and killed by escaped convicts while on duty at California's Point Reyes National Seashore in 1973.

Uncle Jim Trail

The first mile follows the Ken Patrick Trail—from the North Kaibab trailhead—then turns southeast to make a loop around Uncle Jim Point. Allow three hours for the five-mile roundtrip. Views from the point include Roaring Springs Canyon and North Kaibab Trail. James "Uncle Jim" Owens served as the Grand Canyon Game Reserve's first warden from 1906 until establishment of the national park.

North Rim Practicalities

The road from Jacob Lake to the North Rim may be open earlier in the spring and later in the fall than the Grand Canyon Lodge, restaurants, gas station, and campground. A sign at Jacob Lake near the turnoff for the North Rim lists the services available. If you're looking for a room in summer, be sure to make reservations as far in advance as possible, as every lodge on the Kaibab Plateau will be full! Alternatives are to stay to the west in Fredonia or Kanab, or to the east in the lodges along US 89A or in Page. In autumn, you have a chance of getting in on short notice. During winter and spring, when the North Rim is closed, Jacob Lake Inn stays open and should have plenty of rooms.

BRIGHT ANGEL POINT

Accommodations and Campgrounds

Grand Canyon Lodge, overlooking The Transept near Bright Angel Point, offers the only accommodations within the park on the North Rim. Lodging comes in five types: Rim Cabins with a view from the porch, $109 d; Western Cabins, $99 d; two-bedroom Pioneer Cabins, $94 for one–four persons; Frontier Cabins, $80 d; and modern motel rooms, $87 d. The season runs mid-May–mid-October, when reservations and a deposit are highly recommended. Call 303/297-2757 for advance reservations, 928/638-2611 for same-day reservations, or fax 303/297-3175; the lodges can also be reached at 14001 E. Iliff Ave., Suite 600, Aurora, CO 80014; www.grandcanyonnorthrim.com.

North Rim Campground, 1.5 miles north and west of Grand Canyon Lodge, provides drinking water but no hookups. It's open mid-May–mid- or late October at $15 per night, $7.50 with Golden Age or Access passes; reservations are required. Four rim sites have views—and winds—at a higher cost. Backpackers and bicyclists can camp at a walk-in area for $4 per person; a "FULL" sign at the campground means that all drive-in spaces are taken but spaces will be available for walk-ins. Coin-operated showers, a laundromat, store, and ice are available nearby. Reservations for family and group sites can be made one day–three months in advance at tel. 800/365-2267 (365-CAMP); reservations.nps.gov.

Food and Services

Grand Canyon Lodge, tel. 928/638-2611, serves moderately priced breakfasts, lunches, and dinners in a huge rustic dining room with Canyon views; open daily mid-May–mid-October. You'll need reservations for dinner. A cafeteria style **snack bar,** also part of the lodge, offers faster service and lower prices but no atmosphere; it's open for breakfast, lunch, and dinner. The **Saloon** in the lodge serves gourmet coffees as well as more potent beverages.

You'll also find a **post office** and **gift shop** in Grand Canyon Lodge. A **service station** is near the campground, along with a small **general store/snack bar** offering camping supplies, groceries, and cooked food.

Information

The **North Rim Visitor Center,** tel. 928/638-7864, near the lodge has an information desk, book sales, and a few exhibits; it's open daily 8 A.M.–6 P.M.; signs list times of nature walks, talks, and children's programs. Kids 4–14 can take part in Junior Ranger activities.

Obtain overnight camping permits and trail information from the **Backcountry Information Center** (Box 129, Grand Canyon, AZ 86023) on the South Rim or at the ranger station on the North Rim. The North Rim ranger station, tel. 928/638-7868, is open daily 8 A.M.–noon and 1–5 P.M. from May 15–October 15, weather permitting. The turnoff from the highway is a quarter mile north of the campground turnoff; walk around to the window on the side of the building. The park's automated switchboard, tel. 928/638-7888, has recorded **weather forecasts** and other information and will connect you to any office. Or visit the website www.nps.gov/grca.

Mule Rides, Tours, and Transportation

Mule rides take you along the rim and into the Canyon. One-hour rim rides cost $20 (minimum age seven), half-day trips down the North Kaibab Trail to the tunnel are $45 (minimum age eight), and full-day rides to Roaring Springs are $95 including lunch (minimum age 12). Requirements for riders are similar to those for South Rim trips, including proper riding attire (long pants and wide-brimmed hat), good health, weight under 200 pounds/91 kilograms for the full-day (220 pounds/100 kilograms for the shorter rides), and fluency in English. Reservations with the mule rides desk in the Grand Canyon Lodge lobby are a good idea; call 928/638-9875 at the lodge or 435/679-8665 (residence).

A **Hiker Shuttle** goes to the North Kaibab trailhead early in the morning from Grand Canyon Lodge; make advance reservations at the lodge's front desk. **Trans-Canyon Shuttle,** tel. 928/638-2820, offers daily roundtrip van service between the South and North Rims from May–Oct., $60 one way, $100 roundtrip.

NORTH OF THE PARK

Accommodations, Campgrounds, and Services

Kaibab Lodge, tel. 938/638-2389 in season, then 928/526-0924 or 800/525-0924 the rest of the year, lies 18.5 miles north of Bright Angel Point and 26 miles south of Jacob Lake at the edge of a large meadow just west of AZ 67. Guests stay in cabins ($80 d–$130 for four people) and dine at the restaurant (breakfast and dinner daily) during the mid-May–late Oct. season; www.canyoneers.com. Across the highway, **North Rim Country Store** sells groceries, camping and auto supplies, and gas and diesel.

De Motte Park Campground, just south of Kaibab Lodge, is open early June–late September with drinking water and interpretive programs but no showers or hookups; $12 per night. Try to arrive before noon for the best chance of getting a space—no reservations are taken.

Jacob Lake Inn, 45 miles north of the North Rim at the junction of AZ 67 and US 89A, tel. 928/643-7232, stays open all year with basic motel rooms ($90–92 d;$98–105 four persons), cabins (April–November only, $72–118), restaurant (American food daily for breakfast, lunch, and dinner), grocery store, Native American crafts shop, and service station; www.jacoblake.com.

Jacob Lake Campground, tel. 928/643-7770, has sites in the ponderosa pines with drinking water but no hookups or showers from mid-May–mid-Oct. for $12 per night; there's usually room. Campers can enjoy summer interpretive programs and nearby hiking trails. Head west 0.1 mile on US 89 A from AZ 67, then turn right at the sign. Only groups can reserve sites with Recreation Resource Management at tel. 928/204-1698; www.camprrm.com.

Kaibab Camper Village, tel. 928/643-7804 or 800/525-0924 (reservations), overlooks tiny Jacob Lake just 0.3 mile south on AZ 67 from US 89A, then west 0.7 mile; it's open May 15–October 15 with coin showers. Tent spaces and dry RV sites run $12 and sites with hookups cost $22. Tent sites are usually available, though RVers should make reservations or arrive by noon.

Allen's Outfitters, tel. 435/644-8150 or 435/689-1979, offers trail rides of one and two hours in the forest, half- and full-day trips to overlooks, and pack trips from about mid-May–early September at their stables 0.3 mile south on AZ 67 from US 89A and year-round in Kanab.

Information

Staff at the U.S. Forest Service's **Kaibab Plateau Visitor Center,** tel. 928/643-7298, in Jacob Lake provide information on the many viewpoints, trails, campgrounds, and historic sites in the Kaibab National Forest along the North Rim; they also issue backcountry permits for most areas of Grand Canyon National Park.

Cream-colored blossoms of the cliffrose *(Cowania stansburiana)*, an evergreen member of the rose family, festoon canyon rims in early summer and then transform into long, white, plumed seeds.

Exhibits include a 3-D model of the Grand Canyon and wildlife displays. You can purchase books and maps. It's open daily 8 A.M.–5 P.M. from about mid-May–mid-Oct. and possibly later in the year with a shorter schedule; www.fs.fed.us/r3/kai.

THE WESTERN KAIBAB PLATEAU

Kanab Creek Wilderness

Kanab Creek has the largest canyon system in the Grand Canyon's North Rim, with headwaters 100 miles north on the Paunsaugunt Plateau in Utah. The wilderness area protects

© BILL WEIR

77,100 acres along the Kanab and its tributaries. Springs in Kanab Canyon nourish large cottonwood trees and lush growths of desert willow, tamarisk, maidenhair fern, and grass. From Hack Canyon, a popular entry point on the west, hikers can descend 21 miles down Kanab Creek to the Colorado River; allow three days each way. You'll need a Grand Canyon backcountry permit to camp below the junction with Jumpup Canyon. Hack Canyon and a bit of the wilderness lie on BLM land; the office in Kanab, Utah, has information on trailhead access and hiking. The trailhead is also worthwhile as a scenic drive if you don't mind the bumpy road; see the Hack Canyon entry in the Arizona Strip section. Other trailheads lie on the Kaibab National Forest; contact the Fredonia or Kaibab Plateau Visitor Center offices for road and trail information. The easy to moderate, 17-mile **Ranger Trail** wraps around the base of Jumpup Point in the heart of the wilderness. You can reach it on the west side via the easy, 21.5-mile **Snake Gulch-Kanab Creek Trail #59,** as well as from Kanab or Hack Canyons. On the east side, Jumpup Cabin Trailhead and the difficult, six-mile **Jumpup-Nail Trail #8** provide access.

Jumpup Point

An amazing canyon panorama greets the rare visitor who ventures out along the rough road on this long point in the western Kaibab Plateau. Five miles before the end of the point, the vast Jumpup Canyon first appears on the left, along with its tributaries Sowats Canyon and Indian Hollow. Much of this canyon country belongs to the Kanab Creek Wilderness, which almost completely surrounds Jumpup Point. Although there's no trail access to the canyons from here, Ranger Trail can be seen far below, where it's joined by Jumpup-Nail Trail, which descends from Sowats Point across to the east. You might spot a bighorn sheep on one of their precarious

ledges. At road's end, a short walk reveals more views. Lower Kanab Canyon and the Grand Canyon seem almost lost in the vastness. Kanab Canyon and the broad Hack Canyon lie to the west. Mt. Trumbull stands as the highest of the volcanoes across Kanab Canyon. The summit of Mt. Logan, identified by its cliff profile, is just to the left and farther back. Vermilion Cliffs and other high points of Utah lie to the northwest and north.

Sparse pinyon pine, juniper, sage, and cactus of the high desert cover the point at an elevation of 5,650 feet. The Kaibab National Forest map (North Kaibab District) shows the ways in. From Jacob Lake, go south 0.3 mile on AZ 67, turn west on Forest Road 461, and take Forest Roads 462, 22, 423, 235, 423, then 201 to its end. Forest Road 22 provides access from either the east edge of Fredonia (US 89A between Mileposts 607 and 608) or DeMotte Park (0.8 mile south of the North Rim Store on AZ 67), then you'll follow Forest Roads 423, 235, 423, and 201. A high-clearance vehicle will be needed for the rocky sections of the last 10 miles of road. Mountain bikers enjoy this ride too.

Sowats Point

This viewpoint of Jumpup Canyon lies east across from Jumpup Point at an elevation of 6,200 feet. **Jumpup-Nail Trail #8** descends into the depths here, six miles and a drop of 2,000 feet—steep in places—to Ranger Trail #41 in Kanab Creek Wilderness. You can start on the same roads as those to Jumpup Point, but take Forest Roads 425 and 233 off Forest Road 22. High-clearance vehicles will be needed for the last several miles.

Indian Hollow and Thunder River Trailhead

A tiny campground with an outhouse and tables is 0.4 mile before the end of Forest Road 232 at an elevation of 6,300 feet. Ponderosa pine start to thin out closer to the rim, where pinyon pine, juniper, and Gambel oak predominate. At the rim, a short walk from road's end, you'll have a view of the Deer Creek drainage of the Grand Canyon. Great Thumb Mesa lies directly across to the south. The full length of the Powell Plateau presents itself to the southeast. Down canyon, Mt. Sinyala stands near the mouth of Havasu Canyon.

Thunder River Trail drops steeply from the rim for the first few hundred yards, then contours west half a mile to a break in the cliffs, a good day-hike destination. (See the "Inner Canyon Hiking" section for a description of the hike to Thunder River and Deer Creek Falls.) Forest Road 22 provides access either from the east edge of Fredonia (US 89A between Mileposts 607 and 608) or from DeMotte Park (0.8 mile south of the North Rim Store on AZ 67), then you'll follow Forest Roads 425 and 232 to the end of 232. Cautiously driven cars might be able to make it; check with Kaibab National Forest staff.

Crazy Jug Point

This point features great views and good access roads at an elevation of 7,500 feet. Pinyon pine, cliff rose, and some ponderosa grow here. A walk of a few hundred feet from the parking area leads to the overlook. The Colorado River comes out from behind the Powell Plateau, wraps around Great Thumb Mesa, then winds far downstream. Dark, forested volcanoes of Mt. Trumbull and the rest of the Uinkaret Mountains rise to the west. Directly below are Crazy Jug Canyon, Tapeats Amphitheater, and other parts of the Tapeats Creek drainage. The lineup of Fence, Locust, North Timp, Timp, and Fire Points marks the Kaibab Plateau to the southeast; all of these points can be reached by road for a variety of perspectives of this part of the Grand Canyon. Directions for Crazy Jug Point are the same as those for Indian Hollow except that you continue south on Forest Roads 425 and 292B, following signs. Cars can do this trip in dry weather.

Monument Point and Bill Hall Trailhead

Bill Hall Trail climbs west up along the rim nearly a mile before plunging steeply to the Thunder River Trail. The ridge just above the trail has a sweeping panorama up Tapeats Canyon and down the Grand Canyon. Near the trailhead area (elev. 7,050 feet), you'll see effects of the Bridger Burn of 1996. This fire affected 54,000 acres—a large portion of the western Kaibab Plateau—but pinyon pine, juniper, and lots of cliff rose and wildflowers grow here. Follow directions for Crazy Jug Point until the junction half a mile before the point, then keep straight 1.7 miles on Forest Road 292A; it's okay for cars in dry weather.

Timp, North Timp, and Parissawampitts Point

Walk about one-third mile out on Timp Point from the parking area for the best panoramas and to see Thunder River emerge from the north wall of Tapeats Canyon and drop in two large cascades amidst lush cottonwoods. You can also spot the trail that climbs from Thunder River to the top of cliffs and over into Surprise Valley. Binoculars give the best view. Nearby North Timp and Parissawampitts Points also provide good perspectives.

Rainbow Rim Trail #10 follows the convoluted rim between Timp and Parissawampitts for 18 miles one way. Mountain bikers can make many pleasant loops on this trail and on forest roads in the area. Forest Road 250 connects roads to these points, though you'll need a high-clearance vehicle or mountain bike for it. Cars can reach Timp Point (elev. 7,600 feet) in good weather by turning off AZ 67 at DeMotte Park (0.8 mile south of the North Rim Store on AZ 67), then following Forest Roads 22, 270, 222, 206, and 271. Forest Road 271A branches to North Timp Point from 271. Parissawampitts Point may also be okay for cars; take Forest Roads 22, 270, 222, 206, then 214 to its end.

Fire Point

The panorama here takes in Tapeats Amphitheater, Steamboat Mountain, and Powell Plateau (you can spot the trail to its top); Great Thumb Mesa lies across the river. Walk 100 feet out on the rocks for an even better look. A fine stand of ponderosa pine grows on the point. Carefully driven cars can negotiate the roads in good weather.

Turn west two miles on Forest Road 22 from AZ 67 in De Motte Park (0.8 mile south of the North Rim Country Store), head south two miles on Forest Road 270, then turn west 13 miles on Forest Road 223 to its end. The last mile is within Grand Canyon National Park and will probably be closed to vehicles.

Point Sublime

This well-named overlook and picnic area, southeast of Fire Point and west of Bright Angel Point, lies at the end of a 17-mile dirt road negotiable by high-clearance vehicles, mountain bicycles, on horseback, or on foot. Point Sublime extends far into the Grand Canyon for awesome views. You can scan a great length of both North and South Rims and spot a section of Colorado River. The South Rim can be traced from below Bass Canyon upcanyon nearly to Desert View. Binoculars help you to see parts of the Tonto, Hermit, and South Kaibab Trails along with Grand Canyon Village and Hermits Rest. On the North Rim, the Powell Plateau lies to the northwest, Confucius and Mencius Temples to the southeast, and Tiyo Point and Cape Royal to the east, truly sublime. Closer in, cliffs drop into the Tuna Creek drainage. Point Sublime makes a great place to camp, but you'll need a backcountry permit to do so.

The route is bumpy and not always passable; check at the North Rim Backcountry Office or the North Rim Visitor Center. You can enter from the Kaibab National Forest by turning west two miles on Forest Road 22 from the AZ 67 turnoff in De Motte Park (0.8 mile south of the North Rim Country Store), heading south two miles on Forest Road 270, turning west six miles on Forest Road 223, then south 1.5 miles on Forest Roads 268 and 268B to the park boundary, where the road becomes rougher and less well signed on the last 15 miles to Point Sublime. Keep left at the junction 0.2 mile inside the park (the right fork goes to Swamp Point), then keep right past the junctions for Kanabownits Lookout and the road to AZ 67. The Kaibab National Forest map (North Kaibab District) is essential for navigating these back roads. A second way in begins near Bright Angel Point—go north 2.7 miles on AZ 67 from Grand Canyon Lodge, then turn left on the unpaved Point Sublime Road (high-clearance vehicle needed) past the Widforss and Tiyo Point trailheads to Point Sublime.

Tiyo Point has been closed to vehicles, but you can hike in or go by horseback. Turn south 6.3 miles from Point Sublime Road at a large meadow, 4.2 miles in from AZ 67.

THE EASTERN KAIBAB PLATEAU

Saddle Mountain Wilderness

This 40,610-acre wilderness includes part of the densely forested Kaibab Plateau, along with sheer cliffs and narrow canyons. Mountain lions, bears, and mule deer roam the area. North Canyon Wash is noted for its pure strain of native Apache trout. Saddle Mountain (elev. 8,424 feet) stands northeast of the Bright Angel Point area on the Grand Canyon's North Rim. (You can see Saddle Mountain from Point Imperial.) Nankoweap, South Canyon, and North Canyon trails cross the wilderness from the Kaibab Plateau to House Rock Valley.

East Rim Viewpoint

Expansive vistas across the Marble Canyon

area greet visitors at this overlook on the east edge of the Kaibab Plateau. The site (elev. 8,800 feet) lies on Kaibab National Forest land several miles north of Grand Canyon National Park. Cars and small RVs can easily travel the gravel roads in good weather. East Rim Viewpoint features great sunrises and sunsets; colors reflect off the distant Vermilion Cliffs and Painted Desert. The Forest Service offers some outhouses but no other facilities. Camping may be restricted at the viewpoint, but good places for primitive camping lie in the conifer and aspen forests nearby; no camping permit or fee is required. From AZ 67 in De Motte Park (0.8 mile south of the North Rim Country Store), turn east about four miles on Forest Road 611. Another fine panorama lies farther north at the end of Forest Road 611, 6.9 miles from AZ 67 (keep right at the fork 6.5 miles in; this last 0.4 mile is too rough for cars); walk a few hundred feet beyond road's end for the views. Still farther north, **Dog Point** also features a fine view; head east 1.2 miles on Forest Road

611 from AZ 67, then turn left (north) 7.2 miles on Forest Road 610 to its end; keep right at the fork 6.4 miles in.

Hikers can follow some of the Kaibab Plateau/Arizona Trail #101 along the rim or descend into North Canyon in the Saddle Mountain Wilderness from East Rim Overlook. East Rim Trail #7 descends from a trailhead 300 feet north of the overlook, and North Canyon Trail #4 descends from the rim two miles south. Together, these three trails make a loop of about six miles into the valley below. North Canyon Trail #4 continues down North Canyon to House Rock Valley, a total of seven miles one way.

Marble Viewpoint

This overlook, southeast of East Rim Viewpoint, provides another perspective. From AZ 67 in De Motte Park (0.8 mile south of the North Rim Country Store), turn east 1.3 miles on Forest Road 611, right 6.7 miles on 610, then left 4.6 miles on 219 to its end.

© BILL WEIR

the view east from Forest Road 610 at Saddle Mountain Trailhead

Saddle Mountain Trailhead

The drive out Forest Road 610 is worthwhile for the spectacular views of Marble Canyon, Nankoweap, and House Rock Valley areas. From the trailhead (elev. 8,800 feet), Nankoweap Trail #57 drops several hundred feet to the best viewpoints; this trail continues to the Nankoweap Trailhead (three miles) and on to Road 8910/445G (5–6 miles) in House Rock Valley. From the AZ 67 turnoff in De Motte Park, 0.8 mile south of the North Rim Country Store, head east 1.3 miles on 611, then turn right 12 miles on 610 to the trailhead. Cautiously driven cars should be able to do this in dry weather. A trail to Point Imperial begins on the right 0.2 mile before Saddle Mountain Trailhead; it follows a former fire road about four miles through the forest. The national park border is just south of 611, so do not camp here without a backcountry permit. The Kaibab National Forest has many spots suitable for dispersed camping.

Although not shown on the Kaibab Forest map, the road continues 1.4 miles past Saddle Mountain Trailhead to another great viewpoint of Marble Canyon, House Rock Valley, and far beyond. Use a high-clearance vehicle or hike in.

House Rock Valley

Rolling hills of grasslands and pinyon-juniper woodlands of this valley separate cliffs of the Kaibab Plateau above and Marble Canyon below. Viewpoints provide intimate and detailed views of Marble Canyon. The turnoff for House Rock Buffalo Ranch Road (Road 8910/445) from AZ 89A is between Mileposts 559 and 560, 20 miles east of Jacob Lake and 21.5 miles west of Marble Canyon Lodge. About 90 **buffalo** roam freely across 67,000 acres of the valley; you're most likely to see them in summer, least likely during hunting season in autumn.

For **Buck Farm Overlook,** head south 23.5 miles from US 89A to a fork; take the left fork

east two miles, then turn left three miles on Forest Road 445H to its end.

Triple Alcoves Overlook features a different panorama; go 2.5 miles south on Forest Road 445 from the 445–445H junction, then hike east a half mile on an old jeep road to the overlook. Signs mark the trailhead. House Rock Buffalo Ranch Road provides nearly year-round access to these and other viewpoints as well as to Saddle Mountain Wilderness.

The very scenic Forest Roads 213 and 220 connect the Kaibab Plateau with House Rock Valley. You'll need a high-clearance vehicle for the steep and winding sections. Turnoff from AZ 67 is between Mileposts 601 and 602, about three miles north of the North Rim Country Store. Forest Road 213 crosses the Arizona Trail 2.6 miles in. Seven miles in from AZ 67, Forest Road 213 begins the descent on short switchbacks. It skirts the north edge of Saddle Mountain Wilderness before ending after 8.6 miles at the East Side Game Road (Forest Road 220). Turn right 8.2 miles to continue down to House Rock Valley, following Tater Canyon part of the way to a T-junction with Road 8910/445, 17 miles south of US 89A. Turn left here for US 89A or turn right for Buffalo Ranch, Saddle Mountain trailheads, and Marble Canyon overlooks.

TOROWEAP

This remote area of the North Rim lies between Kanab Canyon to the east and the Pine Mountains (Uinkaret Mountains) to the west. An overlook (elev. 4,552 feet) provides awesome Canyon views from sheer cliffs nearly 3,000 feet high above the river. Toroweap, also known as Tuweep, lies 140 road miles west of the developed North Rim area of Bright Angel Point. The views, many hiking possibilities, and solitude reward visitors who make it here. No park entry or campground fee was charged here at press time, though user fees may be

GRAND CANYON NAT'L PARK

forthcoming. Obtain hiking information, backcountry permits, and emergency help at the Tuweep Ranger Station, open all year though the ranger does take a few days off now and then. There's an emergency phone here and possibly emergency water. If you'll need a backcountry permit, it's safer to obtain it beforehand, though you could try for a last-minute permit here or at Pipe Spring National Monument.

Pinyon pine, juniper, cactus, and small flowering plants cover the plateau. Watch for rattlesnakes. Hikers can enjoy many easy rambles near the rim, a difficult descent to the river near Lava Falls, a scramble up Vulcan's Throne, or multi-day trips on the Tuckup Trail.

© BILL WEIR

view up the Colorado River from Toroweap Overlook

Toroweap Overlook

The views begin at road's end, where sheer cliffs drop to the Colorado River. **Mount Sinyala,** a butte 25 miles east of the overlook, marks the mouth of Havasu Canyon. Most of the Havasupai who live on the reservation dwell in Supai village, nine miles up Havasu Canyon. The **Hualapai Indian Reservation** lies directly across the Colorado River from the overlook. **Vulcan's Anvil,** also known as Vulcan's Forge or Thor's Hammer, rises in the middle of the river directly below. This 50-foot-high lava neck is all that remains of an extinct lava vent.

Lava Falls, visible 1.5 miles downstream, roars with a vengeance. You can see it from a point just one-eighth mile to the right from the overlook. Debris from Prospect Canyon on the South Rim forms the rapids, perhaps the roughest water in the Grand Canyon. Water flowing between 8,000–20,000 cubic feet per second drops abruptly, then explodes into foam and spray. River-runners commonly rate these rapids a 10-plus on a scale of 1–10. Lava Falls Route is a steep and very strenuous hike that leads down to the rapids from a nearby trailhead; see "Inner Canyon Hiking" below.

Saddle Horse Canyon Trail

The trailhead for this easy hike lies beside the main road 5.7 miles south of the ranger station. The path heads east to a Colorado River overlook, then north with views of wonderfully weathered rock near Saddle Horse Canyon; it's about 1.6 miles roundtrip.

Esplanade Loop Trail

This 2.9-mile hiking trail begins at the campground, 5.4 miles south of the ranger station.

Vulcan's Throne

Vulcan's Throne, the 600-foot-high rounded cinder cone west of the overlook, is one of the youngest volcanoes in the area. The hike to the top (no trail) is about 1.5 miles roundtrip with a 500-foot elevation gain; it's most easily reached by road via normally dry Toroweap Lake. Between 30,000 and 1.2 million years ago, eruptions of red-hot lava built about 60 volcanic cones here, even forming dams across the Colorado River. One of the dams towered nearly 2,000 feet, but the river washed it away long ago.

More adventurous hikes in the area include the Lava Falls Route and Tuckup Trail (see "Inner Canyon Hiking").

Toroweap Campground

The small campground has a great setting backed by low cliffs and overlooking small canyons; it's 5.4 miles past the ranger station and 0.9 mile before the overlook at the end of the road. The overlook itself is planned to become a day-use area. There's no water, no camping charge, no reservations accepted, and no permit needed for the established sites; an eight-person, two-vehicle limit per site applies. If all campsites are full, you must obtain the backcountry permit for other areas in the park or simply drive north and find an undeveloped spot on BLM land. Bring lots of water, extra food, and camping gear.

Getting There

Three roads lead in to the area. The most popular one begins at AZ 389, nine miles west of Fredonia; turn south 40 miles on Road 109 at the sign for "Toroweap 61," continue straight seven miles on Road 5, and straight 14 miles on Road 115. These dirt roads are usually in good condition when dry but have washboard sections. Watch for livestock and take it slow through washes and cattleguards. The last few miles are slow and rocky, but careful drivers should make it through fine. The Tuweep Ranger Station is on the left 6.3 miles before the overlook. Beyond the ranger station, Toroweap Point (summit elev. 6,393 feet) towers on the left;

TUWEEP AREA CLIMATE

ANNUAL AVERAGE
71.5°F/21.9°C
44.3°F/6.8°C

ANNUAL
12.1"/307.3mm

——— MAXIMUM TEMPERATURE
——— MINIMUM TEMPERATURE

GRAND CANYON NAT'L PARK

dumpy Vulcan's Throne (summit elev. 5,102 feet) sits on the right.

You can also drive to Toroweap on a 90-mile dirt road from St. George (Roads 1069 and 5 for 76 miles, then right 14 miles on Road 115) or a 58-mile road from Colorado City (Road 5 for 44 miles, then continue straight 14 miles on Road 115). Avoid driving these roads after heavy rain or snow, especially the route from Colorado City. Snows usually block the road from St. George between October and May. Water, food, and gas are not available in this country. Bring a map—the BLM's Arizona Strip one is best—as signs may be missing at some junctions.

Inner Canyon Hiking

The wonders of the Canyon reveal themselves best to those who enter its depths. Just remember that the Inner Canyon is a wilderness area, subject to temperature extremes, flash floods, rockslides, and other natural hazards. You can have a successful trip in the Canyon only by taking enough food, water, and other supplies.

Always carry—and drink—water. All too often people will walk merrily down a trail without a canteen, and then suffer terribly on the climb out. Only the Bright Angel and North Kaibab trails have sources of treated water. In summer, carry one quart or liter of water for each hour of hiking; half a quart per hour should be enough in the cooler months. Electrolyte-replacement drinks may be helpful too.

Canyon trails offer little shade—you'll probably need a hat, sunglasses, and sunscreen. Footgear should have good traction for the steep trails; lightweight boots work well. During winter and early spring, instep crampons—metal plates with small spikes—greatly improve footing on icy trails at the higher elevations. Rain gear will keep you dry during rainstorms; ponchos, on the other hand, provide poor protection against wind-driven rain. Be careful when rock-scrambling—soft and fractured rocks dominate in the Canyon. Don't swim in the Colorado River—its cold waters and swift currents are simply too dangerous.

Zones

Backcountry areas of the Grand Canyon have been divided into zones to give hikers an idea of what conditions to expect.

Corridor Zone trails receive regular maintenance and have signs, emergency phones, toilets, and easy trailhead access. They're the best choice for first-time visitors because some-

one will likely be around in case of difficulty. Drinking water is available at some places along the way, but ask before relying on them. You should still carry water because water sources may be hours apart. Camping is permitted only in established campgrounds.

Threshold Zone areas receive less maintenance and have fewer signs; you'll need to know where water sources are and purify before drinking. The more heavily used areas have designated camping sites. Most trailheads are reached by dirt roads.

Primitive Zone hiking requires route finding and Canyon experience because you'll see only the occasional sign. The long distances between water make this zone best in autumn through spring. Trails and routes receive no maintenance—you could encounter difficult or hazardous conditions. Some trailheads require a 4WD vehicle.

Wild Zone routes should be tackled only by highly experienced Canyon hikers who can find their way on indistinct or non-existent routes. Water may be unavailable or scarce, so this zone is best suited for the cooler months.

Information and Permits

Rangers are the best source of up-to-the-minute information for trails and permit procedures. On the South Rim, the **Backcountry Information Center** at Maswik Transportation Center is open daily 8 A.M.–noon and 1–5 P.M. all year. Staff answer the **Backcountry Information Line,** tel. 928/638-7875, Mon.–Fri. 1–5 P.M. The Backcountry Information Center at the North Rim Ranger Station is open daily 8 A.M.–noon and 1–5 P.M. from May 15–October 15, weather permitting. Bookstores in the park sell hiking guides and topographical maps. Also see the booklist at the back of this book for suggested titles.

ARIZONA TRAIL: THE GRAND CANYON SECTION

This part of the Arizona Trail presents one of the biggest challenges for trail users. Besides the deep descent into the chasm and long climb out the other side, hikers must plan ahead to obtain the required backcountry permit or to make a reservation at Phantom Ranch. The rim-to-rim distance is just too great to hike and enjoy in one day. If you don't get a permit or reservation ahead of time, you can show up at the Backcountry Office for a camping permit or at the Bright Angel Lodge Transportation Desk for a Phantom Ranch bed and hope that space is available. Obtaining a last-minute permit or reservation may delay transcanyon hikers for several days.

Bicyclists face a long detour. Not even the most experienced mountain biker will be permitted to ride down any of the trails into the Canyon because of dangers to the cyclist and other trail users. Also, the Park Service won't allow cyclists to carry their bikes across the Canyon on pack frames, because a wide load could knock hikers off the trail. So cyclists will have to follow the same route as cars—adding more than 200 miles to the route. Cyclists planning to camp on the Navajo Nation should obtain permission from the local landowner first.

The Arizona Trail reaches Grandview Lookout Tower from the south. (This area has some good day hiking, too; see "Kaibab National Forest.") The Arizona Trail turns west to Tusayan, then north to Grand Canyon Village to join the 9.3-mile Bright Angel Trail. One could also hike the short distance from Grandview Lookout to Grandview Trailhead, then take the Grandview, Tonto, and either South Kaibab or Bright Angel Trails down to the Colorado River. From the Colorado, North Kaibab Trail climbs 14 miles to the top of the North Rim. From here one can continue north 9.9 miles on the Ken Patrick Trail to Point Imperial. A former road continues north four miles from the Point Imperial Road, opposite the viewpoint, and parallels the rim to the Kaibab National Forest and the Saddle Mountain Trailhead near the end of FR 610.

From the Saddle Mountain Trailhead, one can hike west 7.5 miles along the park boundary on FR 610 to the trailhead for Kaibab Plateau/Arizona Trail 101, which goes north seven miles to East Rim View and on to AZ 89A. If you drive to the south end of Trail 101, take the AZ 67 turnoff in De Motte Park, 0.8 mile south of the North Rim Country Store, and head east 1.3 miles on 611, then turn right 4.8 miles on 610 to the trailhead, marked by log fences and an outhouse. Arizona Trail ends on the Utah border at Stateline Trailhead, which has a tiny campground; you can get here by turning 19 miles north on unpaved House Rock Valley Road from US 89A (between Mileposts 565 and 566) or south 11 miles on House Rock Valley Road from US 89 in Utah (between Mileposts 25 and 26). The North Kaibab Ranger District office, tel. 928/643-7395, has handouts and advice for this part of the Arizona Trail at 430 S. Main St. in Fredonia, open Mon.–Fri. 7 A.M.–5 P.M., or write Box 248, Fredonia, AZ 86022; website: www.fs.fed.us/r3/kai. You can also stop by the Kaibab Visitor Center at Jacob Lake, tel. 928/643-7298, open daily 8 A.M.–5 P.M. from about mid-May–mid-Oct. and possibly later in the year with a shorter schedule.

You'll need a permit for all overnight camping trips in the backcountry, but not for day hikes or stays at Phantom Ranch. Permits can be requested in person or by mail through the Backcountry Information Center, Grand Canyon National Park, P.O. Box 129, Grand Canyon, AZ 86023 or by fax at 928/638-2125. Ask for the *Backcountry Trip Planner*, which includes regulations, a map, and a permit request form, or obtain the information over the Internet at website: www.nps.gov/grca. Permits will be sent through the mail.

Each permit costs a nonrefundable $10 plus $5 per person per night. If you plan on doing a lot of trips, the 12-month Frequent Hiker membership of $25 will let you purchase permits for just the $5 per person per night fee. The Park Service limits the number of campers in each section of the Canyon to provide visitors with a quality wilderness experience and to protect the land from overuse. Try to submit your choices early, especially for holidays and the popular months of March–May. Requests are not accepted more than four months in advance, starting with the first day of the month of that four-month period. Small groups (fewer than six people) have a greater chance of getting a permit, because the backcountry has only a few spots for larger ones; 11 is the maximum group size.

Permits can sometimes be obtained from rangers on duty at Tuweep, Meadview, and Lees Ferry Ranger Stations. However, these rangers are often hard to find because patrol duties have priority. Two other options in the Arizona Strip area are Pipe Spring National Monument and Kaibab Plateau Visitor Center, which can issue last-minute permits for some areas if space is available. Do not depend on obtaining a permit on a walk-in basis.

If you arrive without a permit, show up at the Backcountry Information Center by 8 A.M. to find out what's available or to get on a waiting list. If you're flexible and have extra days, there's a good chance of getting into the Canyon.

Other Areas

Not all of the Grand Canyon lies within the park. The Havasupai Indian Reservation contains Havasu Canyon, famous for its waterfalls, travertine pools, and blue-green waters. The Hualapai have the only road access to the bottom of the Grand Canyon via Diamond Creek and some spectacular rim viewpoints. The Arizona Strip has trailheads and amazing views from the North Rim; these places—some very remote—lie on lands of the Kaibab National Forest, Bureau of Land Management, and Lake Mead National Recreation Area.

CORRIDOR TRAILS OF THE INNER CANYON

Park Service rangers usually recommend that first-time visitors try one of the trails in the Corridor Zone to get the feel of Canyon hiking. These trails are wide and well signed. Rangers and other hikers will be close by in case of problems.

Camping along Corridor trails is restricted to established sites at Indian Garden, Bright Angel, and Cottonwood. Mice and other small varmints at these campgrounds have voracious appetites for campers' food—keep yours in the steel boxes provided or risk losing it.

Bright Angel Trail

Havasupai used this route from the South Rim to reach their fields and the spring at Indian Garden. Prospectors widened the trail in 1890, later extending it to the Colorado River. Now it's the best-graded and most popular trail into the Canyon.

The trailhead lies just west of Bright Angel Lodge in Grand Canyon Village. Resthouses one and a half miles and three miles below the rim contain emergency telephones and usually offer water from May 1–September 30. Pipeline breaks commonly occur, so it's best to check that water is available by asking at the Visitor Center or Backcountry Information

Center. One-way distances from the top are 4.6 miles to Indian Garden (campground, water, and ranger station), 7.7 miles to the Colorado River, and 9.3 miles to Bright Angel Creek (campground, water, ranger station, and Phantom Ranch). Allow 4–5 hours for the descent to the river and 8–10 hours coming out (elevation change 4,500 feet).

Plateau Point makes a good all-day hike during the cooler months. Perched 1,300 feet directly above the swirling Colorado River, you'll enjoy a 360-degree panorama of the Canyon. To reach Plateau Point, take the Bright Angel Trail to Indian Garden, then follow the signs. This strenuous day hike is 12.2 miles roundtrip from the rim with elevation change of 3,080 feet.

River Trail

This short, 1.7-mile trail parallels the river in the twisted rocks of the Inner Gorge, connecting the bottoms of the Bright Angel and South Kaibab trails. There's little elevation change. Two suspension bridges cross the river to Bright Angel Creek.

South Kaibab Trail

Hikers enjoy sweeping views up and down the Canyon on this trail. From the trailhead near Yaki Point, 4.5 miles east of Grand Canyon Village, the South Kaibab drops steeply, following Cedar Ridge toward the river and Bright Angel Creek (6.4 miles one way). There's an emergency telephone at the Tipoff, 4.4 miles below the rim, where the trail begins to descend into the Inner Gorge.

Lack of shade and water and the steep grade make this trail especially difficult in summer. Allow 3–5 hours for the descent and 6–8 hours coming out (elevation change 4,800 feet). Cedar Ridge, partway down, is a good day hike destination—three miles roundtrip and an elevation change of 1,160 feet. Strong hikers enjoy continuing down to the nearly level Tonto Trail (4.4 miles from the rim), turning left 4.1 miles on the Tonto to Indian Garden, then heading 4.6 miles up the Bright Angel Trail. The park's shuttles connect the trailheads for this 13.1-mile hike. Only very strong hikers can make it all the way from rim to river and back in one day. During summer, however, this is grueling and dangerous for *anyone* and isn't recommended.

North Kaibab Trail

Few other Canyon trails compare in the number of interesting side trips and variety of scenery. Hikers on this trail start in the cool forests of the North Rim, descend through the woods into Roaring Springs Canyon, then follow rushing Bright Angel Creek all the way to the Colorado River. Look for the trailhead at the lower end of the parking lot, two miles north of Grand Canyon Lodge. Snows close the road from some time in October or November until mid-May, but you can reach the lower end of the North Kaibab at Bright Angel Campground year-round on trails from the South Rim. A long section of trail between the rim and Roaring Springs has been cut into sheer cliffs; waterfalls cascade over the rock face in spring and after rains. A picnic area near Roaring Springs makes a good destination for strong day hikers; it's 9.4 miles roundtrip from the North Rim and has an elevation change of 3,160 feet. Water is available from May–September.

Cottonwood Campground, 6.8 miles below the rim, is a good stopping point for the night or a base for day trips—it has a ranger station and, from May–September, water; winter campers must obtain and purify water from the creek. Ribbon Falls pours into a miniature paradise of travertine and lush greenery, nestled in a side canyon 1.5 miles from Cottonwood Campground. The Transept, a canyon just upstream and across the creek, offers good exploring too.

From Cottonwood Campground, the North Kaibab Trail continues downstream

GRAND CANYON NAT'L PARK

FUN ON THE TRAIL CHECKLIST

- In summer to avoid the heat, it's well worthwhile to hit the trail at first light, before 7 A.M. at the latest—or start after 4 P.M.; a lightweight flashlight provides the option of hiking after dark.
- Water and sun protection will come in handy even on short hikes, as the grand scenery will try to draw you in farther than you'd planned!
- Keep your body humming with frequent water and food (carbohydrate) breaks. All water and no food can lead to water intoxication—a dangerous condition caused by low electrolytes. Salty snacks are beneficial.
- Rangers recommend one gallon of water for an eight-hour hike in hot weather.
- Drinking water *before* you get thirsty will prevent the 10–20 percent loss of efficiency caused by even slight dehydration.
- If it's hot, try soaking your clothing in water for refreshing coolness.
- An easy pace allows the body to function more efficiently and feel better.
- Kicking back and putting your legs up for a 5–7-minute break once or twice an hour will refresh your leg muscles.
- It's best to ignore that temptation to try a rim-to-river-to-rim hike unless you're sure you can do it AND the weather is cool.
- The Canyon Rule is to allow one-third of the time and energy on the descent and the rest for the climb back up.
- Wind and rain can cause hypothermia even in summer, so raingear can save the day year-round.
- Traveling light increases the fun; food and water should be the heaviest items. You might be able to replace a heavy tent with a tarp and ground sheet, a heavy sleeping bag with a lightweight blanket, and the Walkman with sounds of the Canyon.
- Rangers will be happy to advise you on your trip plans and possible difficulties that may lie ahead.

along Bright Angel Creek, entering the dark contorted schists and other rocks of the ancient Vishnu Group. Near the bottom you'll walk through Phantom Ranch, then Bright Angel Campground. Most people can descend the 14.2-mile North Kaibab in 8–9 hours of steady hiking (elevation change 5,700 feet). Climbing out requires 10–12 hours and is best attempted over two days. Anglers are often successful in pulling rainbow trout from Bright Angel Creek, especially in winter.

Phantom Ranch

Rustic buildings along Bright Angel Creek at the bottom of the Canyon offer dormitory beds ($22), cabins ($64 d, $11 each extra person), meals (breakfast $12, box lunch $8, stew dinner $18, steak dinner $28), drinks, snacks, and souvenirs. You must make reservations for meals and accommodations with transportation desks in the lodges or contact Grand Canyon National Park Lodges, 14001 E. Iliff Ave., Suite 600, Aurora, CO 80014, tel. 303/297-2757 in advance or 928/638-3283 if four days or less in advance, website: www.grandcanyonlodges.com. Reservations can be difficult to get; make them up to 23 months in advance. If you'd rather have your gear carried by someone else, mules are available for $53 in or out with a weight limit of 30 pounds. Mules will carry you, too (see **Mule Rides** in "South Rim Tours").

THRESHOLD, PRIMITIVE, AND WILD ZONES OF THE INNER CANYON (SOUTH RIM)

Trails and routes in these zones lead to some beautiful corners of the park, offering solitude and new Canyon perspectives. Hikers here must be self-reliant—know where water sources are, how to use map and compass, and how to handle emergencies. Most trails follow prehistoric Indian routes or game trails that miners improved in the late 1800s. Conditions vary widely; some trails are in excellent condition, while others are dangerous or require careful map reading. Hermit and Grandview get some maintenance, and other trails may receive attention if they become impassable. Hermit Trail, Hermit and Granite Rapids, Horseshoe Mesa, and parts of the Tonto Trail have designated camping areas, which you're required to use.

The Canyon offers thousands of possible routes for the experienced hiker. Harvey Butchart, master of Canyon off-trail hiking, describes many routes in his books (see the Booklist at the back of the book). Staff at the Backcountry Information Center will suggest interesting routes as well, and they'll give you an idea of current conditions. You'll no doubt come up with route ideas of your own while hiking through the Canyon and studying maps.

© GRAND CANYON NATIONAL PARK (NEG#833)

GRAND CANYON NAT'L PARK

prospector and tourist guide William Bass, dog Shep, and burro Joe, circa 1899

Just keep in mind that much of the Canyon's exposed rock is soft or fractured—a handhold or foothold can easily break off. The Colorado River presents a major barrier, as the water is too cold, wide, and full of treacherous currents to swim.

The following South Rim trails and routes are listed from west to east.

Tonto Trail

Canyon views change continually along this 92-mile trail as it contours along the Tonto Platform, winding in and out of countless canyons and sometimes revealing spectacular panoramas from the edge of the Inner Gorge. The Tonto connects most of the trails below the South Rim between the mouth of Red Canyon at Hance Rapids and Garnet Canyon far downstream. Average elevation on the gently rolling trail is 3,000 feet. You might lose the trail occasionally, but with attention to rock cairns and the map, you'll soon find it again. The sun bears down relentlessly in summer, when it's best to hike elsewhere.

South Bass Trail

William Bass learned about this route from the Havasupai in the 1880s, then used it to start a small tourist operation. Bass also built a trail up to the North Rim, crossing the river by boat and later by a cage suspended from a cable. No crossing exists today.

The South Bass Trail is generally in good condition and easy to follow. It drops to the Esplanade, a broad terrace, then down to the river. You'll need a high-clearance vehicle to reach the trailhead, four miles north of Pasture Wash Ranger Station; ask at the Backcountry Information Center for directions.. Hiking the nine-mile trail to the river takes about five hours down and nine hours up, with an elevation change of 4,400 feet. No reliable water is available before the river. You may be asked to purchase a tribal permit to cross a small corner of the Havasupai reservation.

Dripping Springs

Boucher Trail

Louis Boucher, the Hermit, came to the Canyon in 1891 and mined copper along the creek that bears his name until 1912. Steep terrain and rockslides can make the trail difficult—it's best for experienced hikers with light packs.

Take Hermit and Dripping Springs trails to Boucher Trail, which contours along the base of the Hermit Shale, high above the west side of Hermit Canyon with excellent views. You'll reach Tonto Trail just before Boucher Creek. The route down the creek to Boucher Rapids on the Colorado River is an easy 1.5 miles. From the Hermit trailhead at the end of Hermit Rd., it's 11 miles to Boucher Creek; allow 7–8 hours down and 9–10 hours coming up, with an elevation change of 3,800 feet. The Boucher,

Tonto, and Hermit Trails make a fine three- or four-day loop hike. Boucher and Hermit Creeks usually have water year-round.

Hermit Trail

Although named for Boucher, the trail was actually built for tourists by the Santa Fe Railroad in 1912. Visitors took this route to Hermit Camp, which operated until 1930. Most of Hermit Trail is in good condition; the few places covered by rockslides can be easily crossed. The trail begins just beyond Hermits Rest, at the end of Hermit Road. Water is available at Santa Maria Spring (two miles one way) and Hermit Creek (seven miles one way). Hermit Rapids on the Colorado River is an easy 1.5-mile walk down the bed of Hermit Creek; a sign on the Tonto Trail points the way down to Hermit Creek. The elevation change from rim to river is 4,300 feet, so allow 5–6 hours going down and 8–10 hours climbing out.

Hermit Trail also connects with Waldron, Dripping Springs, and Tonto Trails. Day-hikers can head to Dripping Springs, a six-mile roundtrip hike requiring 4–6 hours with an elevation change of 800 feet. Descend the Hermit Trail 1.5 miles, then turn left 1.5 miles on Dripping Springs Trail. Carry water for the entire trip, as the springs offer only a tiny flow. The 22.5-mile Hermit Loop hike, which follows the Hermit, Tonto, and Bright Angel Trails, is quite popular. You can find water on this loop year-round at Monument Creek and Indian Garden. Hikers can easily walk down the bed of Monument Creek to Granite Rapids, 1.5 miles one way.

Grandview Trail

Day-hikers frequently use this steep but scenic trail to Horseshoe Mesa. The trailhead lies at Grandview Point on Desert View Drive. Miners improved an old Indian route in 1892 so they could bring out high-grade copper ore from Horseshoe Mesa. Mining ceased in 1907, but mine shafts, machinery, and ruins of buildings remain. Trail is a bit steep and rugged, may not be best in summer.

Cave of the Domes, a limestone cavern on the west side of the mesa, has some good passages; take the trail fork that goes west of the butte atop the mesa. Three trails descend Horseshoe Mesa to the Tonto Trail. Bring water, as the springs are either unreliable or difficult to reach. Allow two hours down and four up for the six-mile roundtrip hike to Horseshoe Mesa, with an elevation change of 2,600 feet.

New Hance Trail

John Hance, one of the first prospectors to take up the tourist business, built this trail down Red Canyon in 1895. The unsigned trailhead lies about one mile southwest of the Moran Point turnoff on Desert View Drive; obtain directions from a ranger. Suited for more experienced hikers, the trail—with poor footing in places—descends steeply to the river at Hance Rapids. Most of the trail is easy to follow, especially when you're descending. No reliable water is available before the river. The eight-mile trail takes about six hours to descend and 8–10 hours to ascend, with an elevation change of 4,400 feet.

Capt. John Hance (1835–1919) was one of the first to promote tourism on the South Rim. He spent the last 40 years of his life entertaining Canyon visitors with wild tales.

GEOLOGIC CROSS SECTION OF THE GRAND CANYON REGION

Triassic
- Chinle Formation
- Cedar Mountain
- Moenkopi Formation

Permian
- Kaibab Limestone
- Toroweap Formation
- Coconino Sandstone
- Hermit Shale

Pennsylvanian
- SUPAI GROUP
  - Esplanade Sandstone
  - Wescogame Formation
  - Manakacha Formation
  - Watahomigi Formation

Mississippian
- Redwall Limestone

Devonian
- Temple Butte Limestone

Cambrian
- Muav Limestone
- Bright Angel Shale
- Tapeats Sandstone

Dox Sandstone
Shinumo Quartzite
Hakatai Shale
Bass Limestone
Vishnu Schist
Zoroaster Granite
Vishnu Schist

The Esplanade

Foraminifera including fusulinids, corals, bryozoans, brachiopods, gastropods, pelecypods, conodonts, fish

Foraminifers, corals, bryozoans, gastropods, pelecypods, cephalopods, blastoids, crinoids, fish

Brachiopods, hyolithids, eocrinoids, trilobites, ostracodes

Tonto Platform
Inner Gorge
Colorado River

FEET
1000
750
500
250
0

GRAND CANYON NAT'L PARK

© EDWIN D. MCKEE, U.S. GEOLOGICAL SURVEY PROFESSIONAL PAPER 1173

Escalante Route

The Tonto Trail's upper end gives out at Hance Rapids, but you can continue upstream to Tanner Rapids and the Tanner Trail. Cairns mark the 15-mile Escalante Route. Expect rough terrain and a difficult time finding the route in some sections. The Colorado River, easily accessible only at the ends of the route, provides the only reliable source of water. The route is somewhat easier to hike in the downstream direction, Tanner to Hance.

Tanner Trail

Seth Tanner improved this Indian trail in the 1880s to reach his copper and silver mines along the Colorado River. Although in good condition and easy to follow, the Tanner Trail is long—10 miles one-way—and dry, and best attempted in the cooler months. Hikers often cache water partway down for the return trip.

The trailhead lies about 100 yards back down the road from Lipan Point, off Desert View Drive. Allow 6–8 hours for the descent and 8–10 hours for the return, with an elevation change of 4,700 feet.

Beamer Trail

This slim path begins at Tanner Canyon Rapids (lower end of Tanner Trail) and follows the river four miles upstream to Palisades Creek, then climbs to a high terrace for the remaining five miles to the Little Colorado River confluence. No camping is allowed within in a half mile of the confluence.

THRESHOLD, PRIMITIVE, AND WILD ZONES OF THE INNER CANYON (NORTH RIM)

Whitmore Wash Trail

Although little known or used, this three-quarter-mile-long trail offers the park's easiest hike from trailhead to river. The trick is in reaching the trailhead! You'll need a high-clearance 4WD vehicle and lots of time. Follow County 5 and other dirt roads on the Arizona Strip from Toroweap, Fredonia, Colorado City, or St. George to the four-way intersection at Mt. Trumbull Schoolhouse, turn south 1.8 miles on BLM Rd. 257, then bear left 21.7 miles on BLM Rd. 1045 its end. The last 7.5 miles are rough, as the road crosses lava flows from Mt. Emma. This lava acts as a ramp for the road to descend deep into the Grand Canyon. The trail appears to drop off the rim where the road ends, but that's not the real trailhead. Instead, climb up above the barbed-wire fence to the trail.

You'll drop about 850 feet as the trail switchbacks, then skirts the base of a massive cliff of columnar basalt before ending on a sandy beach. Remnants of ancient lava dams can be seen on both sides of the river. A small trail near the bottom leads a half mile downstream to Whitmore Rapids and lower Whitmore Canyon, which you can explore for about a half mile upstream.

CANYON ROCKS

With 94 types of rock discovered in the Grand Canyon, how can you remember even the major formations? All you have to do is keep in mind, "Know the canyon history. See rocks made by time very slowly." From top to bottom,

Know	Kaibab Limestone
the	Toroweap Formation
canyon	Coconino Sandstone
history.	Hermit Shale
See	Supai Group
rocks	Redwall Limestone
made	Muav Limestone
by	Bright Angel Shale
time	Tapeats Sandstone
very slowly.	Vishnu Schist

GRAND CANYON NAT'L PARK

Lava Falls Route

The Colorado River explodes in a fury of foam and waves at Lava Falls, reached by this short but steep route from the Toroweap area. Cairns mark the way down a lunarlike landscape of volcanic lava. Barrel cacti thrive on the dark, twisted rock. Although the route is only 1.5 miles one way, it's considered difficult because of steep grades and poor footing. It is not a developed or maintained trail. Summer temperatures get *extremely* hot; elevation at the river is only 1,700 feet. Summer hikers should start at dawn and carry plenty of water.

From Toroweap Overlook, backtrack on the road 2.8 miles and look for a dirt track on the left (3.5 miles south of Tuweep Ranger Station); follow it 2.5 miles across normally dry Toroweap Lake and around the west side of Vulcan's Throne. The route is too rough for cars and impassable for any vehicle when the lake contains water. At road's end, the route descends to a hill of red cinders about two-thirds of the way down; the last part of the descent follows a steep gully. Lava Falls lies 0.3 mile downstream. Camping is allowed along the river with a permit. Allow two hours going down and 3–6 hours coming out, with an elevation change of 2,500 feet.

Tuckup Trail

Experienced Canyon hikers looking for solitude and expansive vistas can try this faint trail. It follows the Esplanade of the North Rim for more than 70 miles between the Toroweap Point area and Hundred and Fifty Mile Canyon. Back roads lead to trailheads near these two areas and to upper Tuckup Canyon, about the halfway point on the trail.

The trailhead lies just east of the Toroweap Overlook road, 4.7 miles south of the ranger station and 1.6 miles north of the overlook. You can wander off on a variety of jaunts in this remote area. Hikers have followed the Tuckup Trail from Toroweap Point to Cottonwood Canyon, descended Cottonwood and Tuckup canyons to the Colorado River (rope needed), hiked the shore downstream to Lava Falls Route, and climbed back up to Toroweap in a week or so of travel. Springs of varying reliability may provide water along the Tuckup Trail. Talk with rangers knowledgeable about the area for trailhead, spring, and hiking conditions.

Thunder River and Bill Hall Trails

Thunder River blasts out of a cave in the Muav Limestone, cascades a half mile, then enters Tapeats Creek. It's not only the world's shortest river but suffers the humiliation of being a tributary to a creek!

Deer Creek Falls, another area attraction, plummets more than 100 feet onto the banks of the Colorado River. Cottonwood trees, willows, and other cool greenery grace the banks of Thunder River and both creeks. Trails are generally good and easy to follow, though spring runoff and rains can make Tapeats Creek too high to cross safely.

Two trails descend from the North Rim: the **Thunder River Trail** from the end of Forest Rd. 232 (just past Indian Hollow Campground) and the **Bill Hall Trail** from the east side of Monument Point at the end of Forest Rd. 292A. The Bill Hall Trail saves five miles of walking but the steep grade can be slippery and hard on the knees.

Reach the trailheads by turning west on Forest Rd. 22 from AZ 67 in De Motte Park, 0.8 mile south of the North Rim Store and 17.5 miles north of Bright Angel Point; consult a Kaibab National Forest map (North Kaibab Ranger District). It's about 35 miles of dirt road and an hour and a half from AZ 67 to either trailhead. Cars can negotiate the roads in good weather, but winter snows bury this high country from about mid-November–mid-May. Thunder River and Bill Hall Trails both drop to the Esplanade, where they meet. The Esplanade could be used for dry camping, and you may wish to cache some water here for the climb back out. Thunder River Trail then switchbacks down to Surprise Valley, a giant piece of the rim that long ago slumped thousands of feet to its present position. The valley turns into an oven in summer and lacks water; it's about eight miles from the Bill Hall Trailhead.

In another two miles, **Thunder River Trail** goes east across Surprise Valley, drops to Thunder River, and follows it to Tapeats Creek. Except at high water, Tapeats Creek can be followed 2.5 miles upstream to its source in a cave. The Colorado River is a 2.5-mile hike downstream from the junction of Thunder River and Tapeats Creek. If the creek runs too deep to cross, you can stay on a west-side trail all the way to the Colorado. Upper Tapeats Campsite is just below the Thunder River-Tapeats Creek confluence; Lower Tapeats Campsite lies downstream on the Colorado River. Good fishing attracts anglers to Tapeats Creek and perhaps has for a long time—prehistoric Cohonina left ruins here. The trek from Bill Hall trailhead at Monument Point to Tapeats Rapids is about 12.5 miles one way, with an elevation change of 5,250 feet. Figure seven hours to reach the upper campsite on Tapeats Creek and nine hours to hike all the way to Tapeats Rapids; return times are nearly double. Thunder River, 9.5 miles from the Bill Hall trailhead, is the first source of water.

Deer Creek Trail, marked by a large cairn in Surprise Valley, splits off to the west and drops about 1.5 miles to Deer Creek (Dutton) Spring, another cave system from which a waterfall gushes. You can hike up to the falls for a closer look or take the path that goes higher and behind the falls. The creekside trail winds down one mile past some remarkable Tapeats narrows, then drops to the base of Deer Creek Falls at the river. Watch out for poison ivy here. Campsites lie along Deer Creek between Deer Creek Springs and the head of the narrows. Distance from the Bill

Hall Trailhead to the Colorado River is about 11 miles one way with a descent of 5,400 feet; Deer Creek Springs, 9.5 miles in, is the first water source. Allow about seven hours to reach Deer Creek and 45 minutes more to descend to the Colorado River, then almost double that to return.

North Bass Trail

This long and faint trail drops from Swamp Point on the North Rim to Muav Saddle, where there's a 1925 Park Service cabin. The trail makes a sharp left toward Muav Springs, drops steeply to White Creek in Muav Canyon, follows a long bypass to a safe descent through the Redwall Limestone, winds down White Creek to Shinumo Creek, continues to Bass Camp, then cuts over a ridge to the left and drops down to a fine beach on the Colorado River. The trail reaches the Colorado about 0.3 mile below where the South Bass Trail comes down on the other side. No crossing exists today, though people occasionally hitch rides to the far shore with river-rafters. A waterfall blocks travel down Shinumo Creek just before the river, which is why the trail climbs over the ridge. The Muav and Shinumo drainages create their own canyon worlds— you're not really exposed to the Grand Canyon until you reach the ridge above the Colorado River near trail's end.

Once at the Colorado River via the main trail, you can loop back to Bass Camp on another trail; it begins at the downstream end of the beach and crosses over to lower Shinumo Creek, which you can then follow upstream back to Bass Camp and the North Bass Trail. Many routes off the North Bass Trail invite exploration, such as the Redwall Narrows of White Creek above the trail junction, Shinumo Creek drainage above White Creek, and Burro Canyon.

Muav Saddle Springs offers water just off the trail. White Creek has intermittent water above and below the Redwall. Shinumo Creek's abundant flow supports some small trout. Shinumo can be difficult to cross in spring and after summer storms; at other times you can hop across on rocks. Allow 3–4 days for the 28-mile roundtrip to the river, with an elevation change of 5,300 feet; the trail is best suited for experienced hikers.

With a high-clearance vehicle you can reach the trailhead at Swamp Point from AZ 67 in DeMotte Park via Forest Roads 22, 270, 223, 268, 268B, and Swamp Point Road. You'll need the current Kaibab Forest map, as old ones may not show these roads correctly. The drive from DeMotte Park to Swamp Point takes nearly two hours due to the roughness of Swamp Point Road.

Powell Plateau Trail

A good trail from Swamp Point connects this isolated "island" that lies within the vast reaches of the Grand Canyon. Once part of the North Rim, the plateau has been completely severed from the rim by erosion, except for the Muav Saddle connection. The trail is about 1.5 miles one way; you drop 800 feet to Muav Saddle on the North Bass Trail, then continue straight across the saddle and up another set of switchbacks to a ponderosa pine forest on the Powell Plateau. Here the trail fades out. Many places on the seven-mile-long plateau offer outstanding views. Travel is cross-country, so you'll need a map and compass; expect to do some bushwhacking.

The easiest viewpoint to reach lies to the northwest; just follow the north edge of the plateau (no trail) to a large rock cairn about one mile from where the trail from Swamp Point tops out on the plateau. You can camp on the Powell Plateau with a backcountry permit; all water must be carried in from the trailhead or Muav Saddle Springs. See **North Bass Trail** for directions to Swamp Point.

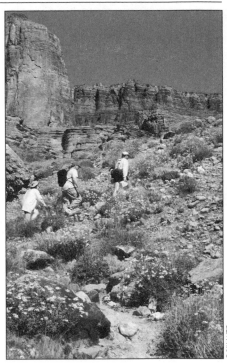

hiking across Nankoweap Delta to Little Nankoweap Canyon

© BILL WEIR

Clear Creek Trail

This trail, in very good condition and easy to follow, is the North Rim's version of the Tonto Trail. It begins 0.3 mile north of Phantom Ranch and climbs 1,500 feet to the Tonto Platform, which it follows—winding in and out of canyons—until dropping at the last possible place into Clear Creek, nine miles from Phantom Ranch. Carry water—there's no source before Clear Creek—and be prepared for very hot weather in summer. The best camping sites lie scattered among the cottonwood trees where the trail meets the creek.

Day-hikers enjoy the first mile or so of Clear Creek Trail for its scenic views of the river and Inner Gorge. Strong hikers can walk all the way to Clear Creek and back in a long day. Better still is a trip of several days.

The route to **Cheyava Falls,** the highest waterfall in the Canyon, takes 6–8 hours roundtrip up the long northeast fork of Clear Creek. Cheyava Falls puts on an impressive show only in spring and after heavy rains. Other arms of the creek offer good hiking as well. The canyon that branches east about a half mile downstream from the end of Clear Creek Trail cuts through a narrow canyon of quartzite. You can also walk along Clear Creek to the Colorado River, a 5–7-hour roundtrip hike through contorted granite and schist, a dark, easily split metamorphic rock with closely spaced bands of mica. The 10-foot-high waterfall a half mile from the river is bypassed by clambering around to the right.

Nankoweap Trail

Thrilling ledges on the Nankoweap Trail discourage hikers afraid of heights. But if you don't mind tiptoeing on the brink of sheer cliffs, this trail will open up a large section of the park for your exploration. The trailhead lies at Saddle Mountain Saddle, 2.4 crow-flying miles northeast of Point Imperial. You can't drive to the trailhead, however; it must be approached on foot, either three miles one way from House Rock Buffalo Ranch Rd. (south from US 89A), or three miles one way from near the end of Forest Rd. 610 (east off AZ 67). Both access roads are dirt, passable by cars, but House Rock Buffalo Ranch Rd. lies at a lower elevation and is less likely to be snowed in.

The Nankoweap Trail drops several hundred feet, then contours along a ledge all the way to Tilted Mesa before descending to Nankoweap Creek. Some care in route finding is needed between Tilted Mesa and the creek. Nankoweap Creek, 10 miles from the trailhead, is the first source of water; you may want to cache water partway down to drink on your return. The remaining four miles to the river is easy. Allow 3–4 days for a roundtrip journey, with an elevation change of 4,800 feet.

GRAND CANYON NAT'L PARK

Running the Colorado River

Running the Colorado River through the Grand Canyon provides the excitement of roaring rapids and the tranquility of gliding in silent passages. It rates as one of the world's greatest adventures! A journey through the Canyon by river with some side hikes might be the single best way to see and appreciate the grandeur and beauty here. Many beautifully sculptured side canyons, some with lush vegetation, can be easily reached only from the river. Just being at the bottom of the Canyon is a delight, whether you're riding atop the waves, strolling between the convoluted walls of an unnamed side canyon, or enjoying life at camp.

Within the Grand Canyon, the Colorado River flows 277 miles, drops 2,200 feet, and thunders through 70 major rapids. Although explorers of the 19th century feared this section of the river, rendering it in dark and gloomy drawings, boating the Canyon has become a safe and enjoyable experience. It opens some of the grandest and most remote corners of the Canyon. River parties stop frequently to explore the twisting side canyons, old mining camps, and prehistoric ruins along the way.

A river trip through the Grand Canyon requires a large commitment in time, whitewater experience, equipment, expense, and permit procedures. About one-third of river runners do it themselves with a noncommercial river trip permit from the park. The easier option, taken by most people, simply involves setting aside the time for the trip and paying a river company to handle the many details.

YOUR OPTIONS

Boats

Both oar-powered and motor-powered craft run the river. Motor-powered rafts can zip through the entire Canyon in six days, or zoom

When Major John Wesley Powell encountered dangerous rapids, he normally took the precaution of portaging his boats around or lowering them on lines through the tumultuous waves, but this narrow section of the Upper Granite Gorge offered no foothold. With only the options of running the rapids or abandoning the river, Powell and his men headed down into the breakers and whirlpools.

© THE EXPLORATION OF THE COLORADO RIVER AND ITS CANYONS

from Lees Ferry to Phantom Ranch in two days. The oar-powered boat trips take half again as much time but provide a quieter and more natural experience. On these smaller boats, passengers have the advantage of being able to talk easily with the crew and one another. Whether in a little or a big rig, you can be assured that the crew will work hard to provide a safe and enjoyable trip.

GRAND CANYON NAT'L PARK

All but two of the tour companies use rafts of various sizes; the exceptions are Grand Canyon Dories and Grand Canyon Expeditions, which employ sturdy, hard-shelled dories with upturned ends. The dories ride high in the water as they dance through the waves. They're small—16–18 feet long—with one person at the oars and just four passengers. Only the most skilled boaters can handle dories because, unlike rafts, they can't bounce off rocks without damage.

Small rafts typically measure 18 feet and carry four or five passengers plus one crew member to do the rowing. Some companies provide a paddle-boat option—not a Mississippi-type paddle wheeler, but a small raft in which everyone has a paddle! The guide sits at the stern to steer and give instructions, but it's up to the passengers to succeed in running each rapid.

The motor-powered rigs can be 30 feet long or more and have pontoon outriggers for extra stability. A small outboard motor near the stern provides steering and speed. Some people dislike the use of motors in a wilderness, but these boats do allow more people to run the Colorado than would be possible if everyone went in non-motorized rigs.

Routes

Most tours put in at Lees Ferry, just upstream from the park, and end downstream at Diamond Creek or Pearce (also spelled Pierce) Ferry on Lake Mead. You can also travel just half the distance by joining or leaving the rafts at Phantom Ranch, which requires a hike or mule trip to get in or out. You can leave or join a tour in the lower section of river via a helicopter ride from or to Hualapai land near Whitmore Wash, at Mile 187 below Lava Falls. If you'd like just a taste of river-running, try a one-day smooth-water trip from Glen Canyon Dam to Lees Ferry, just above Grand Canyon National Park,

with **Wilderness River Adventures,** based in Page. Or you can visit the lowermost part of the Grand Canyon and run a few rapids on a one-day trip with **Hualapai River Runners,** based in Peach Springs.

A typical commercial oar trip takes 12–16 days from Lees Ferry to Diamond Creek, covering 226 miles. The upper half takes five or six days from Lees Ferry to Phantom Ranch, 87.5 miles; the lower half requires eight or nine days from Phantom Ranch to Diamond Creek, 138.5 miles. Continuing to Pearce Ferry on Lake Mead adds just a day or two. Equivalent motorized trips typically run eight days from Lees Ferry to Diamond Creek or Pearce Ferry with three or four days from Lees Ferry to Phantom Ranch and four or five days from Phantom Ranch to Diamond Creek or Pearce Ferry.

Those preferring shorter trips can end a trip or begin a two- or three-day run in the lowermost Grand Canyon at Whitmore Wash. Although a trail from the North Rim ends here, river parties use helicopters between the river (on Hualapai land) and the Bar 10 guest ranch, where small planes shuttle people to Las Vegas or other destinations.

Other combinations are available too. Extra days may be added to some trips for hiking or layovers, especially early or late in the season. Expect to pay about $250 per day; discounts may be available for groups, children under 14, early booking, and off-season journeys.

If you have children in tow, check for minimum age requirements. Sometimes these are left up to the passenger; at other times operators require minimum ages of 8–16 years. Most trips depart from Flagstaff, Page, St. George, or Las Vegas. Meals, camping gear, waterproof bags, and land transportation are usually included in the price. Experienced kayakers can tag along with many tours, paying a lower rate.

GRAND CANYON NAT'L PARK

Seasons

The river-running season normally lasts April–Oct., with only non-motorized craft departing mid-September–mid-December. When you choose to go makes a big difference in the river experience. Most people go during summer because that's when they take their vacations. The Canyon gets very hot then, but a splash of river water will always be cooling. Hiking at this time is limited to shady side canyons with water. Spring—April–early June—offers many advantages. The redbud trees and many plants bloom in beautiful colors, hiking weather will be near perfect, days get long, trip operators often add a couple of extra days for long hikes or layovers, and it's much easier to get a reservation for a trip. The downside is the possibility of cold weather, even sleet, which the author woke up to on one April morning in the upper Canyon! Some boaters think that early June offers the best weather for a boat trip, though hiking can get hot then. Autumn brings shorter days, along with cooler temperatures. The Canyon quiets after mid-September, when all the motorized rigs have left the river. Heavy-duty rain gear with sweaters underneath can keep spring and autumn boaters warm during cool spells.

Rafting the Lower Grand Canyon

This last section, beginning at Diamond Creek, offers beautiful Canyon scenery and some rapids. You can get on a trip here much more easily than in the upper Canyon, either with Hualapai River Runners or on your own. The Park Service gives free permits for up to two private parties (16 people maximum in each) per day. River runners will need to pay for a Hualapai permit to use the Diamond Creek Rd. access or to camp on the south shore. The lower canyon bakes in summer, so spring, autumn, or even winter offer better weather for exploring side canyons.

Boating into the Lower Grand Canyon from Lake Mead

Boats—but not personal watercraft—may go up as far as Separation Canyon (Mile 240 on the river) from Lake Mead National Recreation Area without a permit. Primitive camping is allowed on the Park's shore in this section without permits, though high lake levels can flood all the spots; you'll need a backcountry permit from the Park Service to camp inland. A permit from the Hualapai is required to camp on their lands (the south shore). Boats must have a toilet. South Cove offers the closest paved boat ramp, reached by the paved road via Dolan Springs from US 93. Pearce Ferry nearby is closer with a primitive boat ramp and camping, but the last four miles in are unpaved.

Canoeing the Lower Grand Canyon

Canoes in the Grand Canyon? Yes, indeed, in the last 40 miles within the park. You'll need a powerboat to carry the canoes from Lake Mead to Separation Canyon. Most of the south shore on this trip belongs to the Hualapai, so obtain tribal permits if you plan to camp or hike on their land.

Private River Trips

Step One is to read Grand Canyon National Park's regulations and procedures! Obtain them from the River Trips Office, Box 129, Grand Canyon, AZ 86023, tel. 928/638-7884 or 800/959-9164 (call Mon.–Fri. 8 A.M.–5 P.M. to reach someone in person), or online at website: www.nps.gov/grca. Step Two—getting the permit—will be the hard part. Unfortunately, you'll be at the end of a very long line. So many groups have applied that the waiting list extends for more than 12 years! Cancellations do occur during this lengthy wait, so flexible and lucky groups might get on sooner, even the same year. The River Permits Office has worked out a system for applications that's as fair as possible to everyone during this waiting period. To get on the waiting list, carefully follow the instructions for an initial application ($100 fee at press time) and annual renewals (no charge), all of which you must submit within specified date ranges.

RIVER COMPANIES

The following companies offer a wide variety of trips through the Canyon, ranging from one- or two-day introductions to adventurous 19-day expeditions. Write Grand Canyon National Park for the latest list of companies (Box 129, Grand Canyon, AZ 86023), ask at the visitor center, or check listings on the Internet at website: www.nps.gov/grca. The Internet works best because you get not only a list, but also links to the companies, which have colorful and informative sites. If possible, make reservations (with deposit) six months to a year in advance. It's possible to get on a trip with short notice, especially if there are just a few in your group and you're going early or late in the season. **Rivers and Oceans,** tel. 928/526-4575 or 800/473-4576, specializes in river trips and will supply information about companies, make reservations, and let you know about last-minute openings at 12620 N. Copeland Lane, Flagstaff, AZ 86004; website: www.rivers-oceans.com.

All of the companies put in at Lees Ferry except for Wilderness River Adventure's day trips, which start from Glen Canyon Dam, and Hualapai River Runners trips, which begin at Diamond Creek in the lower Grand Canyon. Prices will be lower if you start or leave from Phantom Ranch or Whitmore Wash.

Arizona Raft Adventures, tel. 928/526-8200 or 800/786-7238, goes to Diamond Creek on 12–15-day oar ($2,550–2,870) and eight- or 10-day motorized trips ($1,840–2,170), most with the option of ending or starting at Phantom Ranch. It offers paddle raft trips too, either in combination with oar-powered rafts

or all by themselves. Contact 4050 E. Huntington Dr., Flagstaff, AZ 86004; website: www.azraft.com.

Arizona River Runners, tel. 602/867-4866 or 800/477-7238, offers a 13-day oar trip to Diamond Creek ($2,520) with an option to end or start at Phantom Ranch and an eight-day motorized run to Pearce Ferry ($1,745) which you can leave or join at Whitmore Wash. Contact Box 47788, Phoenix, AZ 85068-7788; website: www.raftarizona.com.

Canyon Explorations/Expeditions, tel. 928/774-4559 or 800/654-0723, uses oar boats on runs to Diamond Creek of 13–16 days ($2,565–3,165); a paddle raft and inflatable kayaks come along on selected trips too. Some departures have a Phantom Ranch exit/entry option. Contact Box 310, Flagstaff, AZ 86002; website: www.canyonexplorations.com.

Canyoneers, tel. 928/526-0924 or 800/525-0924, runs motorized rafts to Pearce Ferry in seven days for $1,725 ($1,525 in April) with the option of ending/starting at Phantom Ranch. Contact Box 2997, Flagstaff, AZ 86003; website: www.canyoneers.com.

Colorado River & Trail Expeditions, tel. 801/261-1789 or 800/253-7328, goes to Pearce Ferry in 12 days by oar-powered raft ($2,550) and eight or nine days in motorized rafts ($1,850); a paddleboat goes along on the oar trips. You can leave or join at Phantom Ranch on both trips. Contact Box 57575, Salt Lake City, UT 84157-0575; website: www.crateinc.com.

Diamond River Adventures, tel. 928/645-8866 or 800/343-3121, offers 12-day oar trips ($2,397) and eight-day motorized trips ($1,812) to Diamond Creek with options of leaving or joining at Phantom Ranch; an excursion just to Whitmore Wash from Lees Ferry takes 10 days by oar ($2,365) and seven days by motor ($1,725). Contact Box 1316, Page, AZ 86040; website: www.diamondriver.com.

GRAND CANYON NAT'L PARK

Grand Canyon Dories, tel. 209/736-0805 or 800/877-3679, features dories on 16-day trips ($3,953) to Pearce Ferry; 19-day trips also run in spring and autumn ($4,026). You can join or leave the trip at Phantom Ranch or Whitmore Wash. Contact Box 216, Altaville, CA 95221; website: www.oars.com.

Grand Canyon Expeditions, tel. 435/644-2691 or 800/544-2691, runs dories on 14-day trips to Pearce Ferry ($2,705); motorized rafts do this run in eight days ($1,933). All trips go straight through without any passenger exchanges. Contact Box O, Kanab, UT 84741; website: www.gcex.com.

Hatch River Expeditions, tel. 435/789-3813 or 800/433-8966, runs motorized rafts to Whitmore Wash in six and a half days for $1,625 with the option to leave or join at Phantom Ranch. Contact Box 1200, Vernal, UT 84078.

High Desert Adventures, tel. 435/673-1733 or 800/673-1733, offers oar rafts to Pearce Ferry in 14 days ($3,115) with an exchange option at Phantom Ranch, and motorized rafts to Pearce Ferry ($2,135) in eight days without passenger exchanges. Contact Box 40, St. George, UT 84771-0040; website: www.boathda.com.

Hualapai River Runners, tel. 928/769-2219 or 800/255-9550, travels just the lower Grand Canyon on motorized rafts, putting in at Diamond Creek and coming out by helicopter to Grand Canyon West on a one-day run for $250. Overnight trips to Lake Mead can be chartered. Contact Box 246, Peach Springs, AZ 86434; website: www.river-runners.com.

Moki Mac River Expeditions, tel. 801/268-6667 or 800/284-7280, heads down to Pearce Ferry in 14-day oar trips ($2,795), with an option to end or begin from Phantom Ranch, and eight-day motorized rafts ($1,855) without a passenger exchange. Contact Box 71242, Salt Lake City, UT 84171; website: www.mokimac.com.

O.A.R.S., tel. 209/736-4677 or 800/346-6277, offers oar rafts to Diamond Creek in 13 days for $3,368 and 14–17-day runs all the way to Pearce Ferry for $3,579–3956 with options to leave or join at Phantom Ranch (and Whitmore Wash, for the Pearce Ferry trips). Contact Box 67, Angels Camp, CA 95222; website: www.oars.com.

Outdoors Unlimited, tel. 928/526-2852 or 800/637-7238, goes to Pearce Ferry on oar rafts in 13 days ($2,690) with an option to leave or join at Phantom Ranch; a paddle raft comes along too, and some trips are all paddle rafts. Contact 6900 Townsend Winona Rd., Flagstaff, AZ 86004; website: www.outdoorsunlimited.com.

Tour West, tel. 801/225-0755 or 800/453-9107, runs oar rafts to Whitmore Wash in 12 days ($2,363) without any passenger exchanges; paddle rafts can be added on request. Motorized rafts go to Whitmore Wash in six days ($1,695), then another three days to Pearce Ferry ($2,095 from Lees Ferry or $830–885 from Whitmore Wash). Contact Box 333, Orem, UT 84059; website: www.twriver.com.

Western River Expeditions, tel. 801/942-6669 or 800/453-7450, motorized rafts go to Pearce Ferry in eight days ($1,740 April, $1,930 May–Sept.) with a passenger exchange at Whitmore Wash. Contact 7258 Racquet Club Dr., Salt Lake City, UT 84121; website: www.westernriver.com.

Wilderness River Adventures, tel. 928/645-3296 or 800/992-8022, heads for Whitmore Wash on 12-day oar trips at $2,655 with a Phantom Ranch end or start option. Motorized trips take eight days to Whitmore Wash for $2,094 and can be joined or left at Phantom Ranch. The company also offers a day trip from Glen Canyon Dam to Lees Ferry, a scenic ride on smooth water. Contact Box 717, Page, AZ 86040; website: www.riveradventures.com.

DOWN THE COLORADO THROUGH THE GRAND CANYON

This miniguide of river-running highlights contains just a sampling of the sights along the river. Even so, it would be impossible to fit them all into a single trip. Experienced river guides know far more places, including some "secret" ones they may share with you. Weather, schedules, and where other river parties have stopped will affect which places your group will decide to take in. Rapids with ratings of five or more on the 1–10 scale are listed in parentheses. (The 1–10 scale is unique to the Colorado River; other rivers are rated on a 1–6 scale.)

The place descriptions come from the author's experience on two river trips and advice from river guides and National Park Service staff. Geologic information is mostly from the out-of-print book *River Runner's Guide to the Canyons of the Green and Colorado Rivers: With Emphasis on Geologic Features, Vol. III* by George C. Simmons and David L. Gaskill (Northland Publishing, 1969).

Mile 0: Lees Ferry
This historic site on the Colorado River, once the only easily accessible crossing for hundreds of miles upstream or down, now marks the beginning of river voyages into the Grand Canyon. Most boaters have only one thing on their minds here—getting on the river and embarking on their adventure. Yet it's worthwhile to come early or at another time to explore Lonely Dell Ranch, other historic buildings, and remnants of past mining attempts at Lees Ferry. Spencer Trail beckons hikers from the rim of the Canyon and the far more gentle Cathedral Wash route offers a walk to the river below. The Paria Canyon hike, one of the finest in the region, ends here after 4–6 days of twisting through its wonderful sandstone walls from a trailhead

north across the Utah border. Some people come just to relax or fish by the cold, clear, trout-filled river. See the **Lees Ferry** section later in this book for details on the area, including lodging, camping, and restaurant information.

You're now at an elevation of 3,116 feet. A descent of 1,936 vertical feet lies ahead as you plummet deep within the Grand Canyon through more than a dozen geologic formations before meeting the Canyon's last riffles near Separation Canyon, where the Colorado River joins Lake Mead. Note how the types of rock affect the river and thus your ride—wide and smooth through the soft shales, then narrower and bumpier in the sandstone, limestone, granite, and schist—but be ready for surprises where tributaries have dumped huge piles of rocks into the river!

Rock layers visible near Lees Ferry formed during the Triassic and Jurassic Periods, roughly 240–140 million years ago, when the dinosaurs first appeared and walked this land. Rocks of this age actually once lay atop the older layers seen on the much higher rims of the Grand Canyon, but there they've been reduced by erosion to just a few remnants such as Cedar Mountain, visible from Desert View. Dramatic folding and faulting downstream have raised the Colorado Plateau thousands of feet, whose increasingly older rock layers you'll soon plunge into. The sights mentioned below follow the convention of "river right" and "river left" facing downstream.

Mile 0.8: Kaibab Formation
Look on the left for the emergence of the Kaibab Formation, the cream-colored, weather-resistant limestone that caps much of the Grand Canyon rims. Scientists have found fossils of marine invertebrates and some fish. You've now crossed a major geologic time boundary into the Permian Period (290–240 million years ago) of the Paleozoic era.

GRAND CANYON NAT'L PARK

Mile 1: Paria Riffle
The Colorado gets some of its namesake reddish color here if the Paria River (on the right) is flowing. Major John Wesley Powell and his men saw the sheer, polished walls from here down to the Little Colorado confluence and named this section Marble Canyon, although no marble is actually present.

Mile 2: Toroweap Formation
This silty limestone, formed near the ancient sea's edge, was also deposited during the Permian Period. The Toroweap has thinner beds and less chert than the Kaibab.

Mile 4: Coconino Sandstone
Tilted crossbedding, reptile tracks, and even imprints of raindrops indicate windblown deposits—ancient sand dunes built up during the middle of the Permian Period. By comparing the angles of the crossbedding with those of modern sand dunes, geologists have concluded that winds had blown the sand from the north.

Mile 4.5: Navajo Bridge
The bridge, recently built beside the 1929 original, connects the Canyon rims 470 feet above the river. In 1937, river runner Buzz Holmstrum stopped near here to get supplies at what looked on his map like the nearby Marble Canyon store. He did make it up and down the cliff somehow and then went on to make the first intentional solo run through the Grand Canyon.

Mile 7: Hermit Shale
Fossils of ferns, other plants, and even some insects have been collected from this soft reddish shale. The rock formed in a vast river floodplain in the early part of the Permian Period.

Mile 8: Badger Creek Rapid (5–8)
River runners rate this, your first of many exciting rapids, at five–eight, depending on flow.

The outwash from ephemeral streams of Badger Canyon on the right and Jackass Canyon on the left creates the rapid. A rough three-mile trail connects the river to US 89A via Jackass Canyon; Navajo sometimes come down this way to fish. Hikers can scramble up Badger Canyon for about a mile. Badger and nearby Soap Creek got their names when 19th-century Mormon explorer Jacob Hamblin shot a badger, took it back to camp, stewed it overnight, and then found that the alkaline water had turned the fat in his breakfast into soap!

Mile 11.2: Soap Creek Rapid (5–6)
Soap Creek comes in from the right. This rapid marks the beginning of a series of tragic sites for the 1889 Stanton-Brown survey, which came to study a proposed railroad route through the Grand Canyon. Despite having portaged the rapid, Frank M. Brown, the organizer of the Denver, Colorado Canyon, and Pacific Railroad Company, drowned below here. Five days later, two other members drowned before the group abandoned its work and climbed out of the Canyon. The following year, Robert B. Stanton and a team returned equipped with lifejackets and better gear to complete the survey.

The Supai Group exposed here comprises four formations that contain fossils of plants deposited in ancient deltas. Tracks of primitive reptiles have been found in the upper half of the group. First, you'll see reddish-brown sandstone from the early part of the Permian Period (about 280 million years ago) with thinner layers of ripple-marked siltstone and shale. The rock commonly weathers into ledges. Below are rocks of the Pennsylvanian Period (330–290 million years ago)—crossbedded sandstone in the middle part of the group, then thin-bedded sandstone with much interbedded siltstone and mudstone in the lower part.

Mile 12: Salt Water Wash
A rough route on the left climbs about four

miles to US 89A; lots of boulders in the lower half make for slow going.

Mile 16.9: House Rock Rapid (7–9)
Rider Canyon comes in from the right. Robert B. Stanton used this difficult canyon route during his second expedition in 1890 to carry out an injured photographer who had fallen from a 20-foot cliff.

Mile 20.5: North Canyon Rapid (5)
You've now entered the "Roaring 20s"—a lively section of rapids in Marble Canyon. North Canyon, on the right, offers beautiful hiking. It's less than a mile to where cliffs block the way; you may see pools and small waterfalls.

Mile 21.2: 21 Mile Rapid (5)

Mile 23: Redwall Limestone
Perhaps the most distinct layer in the Grand Canyon, the Redwall forms long, unbroken cliffs. Here it makes up much of the impressive walls of Marble Canyon. The Redwall challenges skills of trailbuilders and hikers who attempt rim-to-river routes. The upper Redwall contains many caves; sometimes you'll even see matching caves on both sides of the river. The namesake color comes not from the limestone itself, but from staining by the Hermit Shale above. Fossils of nautiloids (straight and spiraled), corals, brachiopods, crinoids, and sponges show that the limestone was deposited on the floor of a shallow sea in the Mississippian Period (360–330 million years ago).

Mile 23.3: 23 Mile Rapid (4–6)

Mile 24.2: 24 Mile Rapid (6–8)

Mile 24.5: 24½ Mile Rapid (5–6)

Mile 24.9: 25 Mile Rapid (5–7)
It's also known as Hansbrough-Richards Rapid in memory of two members of the trouble-plagued Stanton-Brown railroad survey expedition of 1889. They drowned when their boat capsized just after they lined it through the rapid.

Mile 25.3: Cave Springs Rapid (5–6)

Mile 26.6: Tiger Wash Rapid (4–5)
Tiger Wash is on the left.

Mile 29.2: Silver Grotto and Shinumo Wash
In warm weather, boaters clamber up into the narrow canyon of lower Shinumo Wash on the left and swim through several icy pools to Silver Grotto. You can also see Silver Grotto from above by pulling over on the left at Mile 30.1 and hiking back upstream on the Fence Fault Route. Shinumo Altar rises from the south side of Shinumo Wash; the name comes from the Paiute word for the former inhabitants (ancestral Puebloans).

Mile 30: Redwall Dam Site
This spot is remarkable for what you *don't* see. Recognized as one of a series of potential dam sites by government surveys in the 1920s, it was later proposed by the Bureau of Reclamation as the site for a dam that would have raised the water 222 feet in a lake stretching nearly to Lees Ferry.

Mile 31.6: South Canyon
South Canyon, on the right, provides hikers with a route from the rim.

Mile 31.8: Stanton's Cave
High up (150 feet) and to the right in the Redwall you'll see a large cave entrance. The name honors Robert B. Stanton, chief engineer of the 1889 and 1890 Brown-Stanton railroad expeditions, who used the cave to store gear when the demoralized first expedition walked out South Canyon. Archaeologists value the cave for the split-twig figurines left behind thousands of years ago and for more recent

GRAND CANYON NAT'L PARK

Redwall Cavern

pottery and granaries left by the ancestral Puebloans. The Park Service has closed it to the public.

Mile 31.9: Vasey's Paradise
Springs transform the right shore into a beautiful oasis of flowers, maidenhair fern, mosses, and poison ivy. The Park Service recommends that visitors don't enter the vegetated area because of endangered Kanab ambersnails, found only here and at one spot in southern Utah. George W. Vasey worked as a botanist with Major Powell on an 1868 expedition to what's now the state of Colorado.

Mile 33: Redwall Cavern
Major Powell thought that this giant alcove on the left could serve as a theater seating 50,000 people, but he allowed that "at high water the floor is covered with a raging flood." Today it's a popular stop, though camping isn't permitted.

Mile 34.8: Nautiloid Canyon
On the left, stop to see large fossils embedded in the floor of the canyon. They are chambered shells of an animal related to squid.

Mile 35: Muav Limestone and The Bridge of Sighs
The contact between the Redwall and the underlying Muav (at river level) can be difficult to see; at some places a small slope or a bench marks the line. The Muav was deposited in a sea about 535 million years ago during the Cambrian Period and has very few fossils. The Bridge of Sighs, a natural arch, appears high on the right.

Mile 43: Point Hansbrough and Anasazi Bridge
A log bridge high on the right survives from a prehistoric trail of ancestral Puebloans. The river begins a big loop to the right around the point. The second Stanton expedition found the skeleton of Peter Hansbrough here six months after he had drowned at 25 Mile Rapid.

Mile 43.7: President Harding Rapid
A U.S. Geological Survey expedition, led by Claude Birdseye, came through in 1923 to make the first detailed maps of the Canyon and to survey potential dam sites. The expedition carried the first radio receiver into the Canyon. Having heard earlier on the radio of the president's death, the group stopped here for a day in observance of the president's funeral. Eminence Break Trail on the left beside the rapid climbs out to the rim; you'll enjoy great panoramas on the way up. You can reach the upper trailhead (difficult to find) by road (difficult to navigate); see **Tatahatso Point** in the section, Western Navajo Country.

Mile 46.6: Triple Alcoves
The alcoves appear on the right.

Mile 47: Saddle Canyon
Hike up this canyon on the right one mile, past redbud trees flowering in the spring in shady recesses, to pools and a little waterfall.

Mile 50: Bright Angel Shale
This purple and green shale formed in the sea during the Cambrian Period about 550 million years ago.

Mile 51.9: Little Nankoweap Creek
Like many tributaries, this canyon on the right becomes prettier as you head upstream; cliffs eventually block the way. Redbud trees and pools add to the beauty.

Mile 52.2: Nankoweap Area
Nankoweap Rapid (3) offers a long ride, but hiking in the area draws more attention. The Nankoweap and Little Nankoweap form a large delta with many places to camp and explore. A short, steep hike leads to an impressive row of granaries constructed by ancestral Puebloans. Between 900 and 1150 A.D., they built many structures on the section of river between here and Unkar Delta (Mile 72.5). Hikers could spend days exploring Nankoweap Canyon and its tributaries or even hike out to the North Rim on the Nankoweap Trail. Most river runners prefer shorter explorations in the area. A good loop day trip begins by hiking up the Nankoweap about two miles, turning south up the first major draw and going down the other side to Kwagunt Creek, and then following Kwagunt back to the river, where you can either meet the other boaters in your party or hike up the Colorado back to Nankoweap. Bring plenty of water and a sun hat for this spring or autumn trek.

Mile 56: Kwagunt Rapid (6)
You can explore Kwagunt Creek on the right on foot.

Mile 60: Tapeats Sandstone

The brown, medium—coarse-grained sandstone formed about 570 million years ago during the Cambrian Period.

Mile 61.4: Little Colorado River
This major tributary of the Colorado flows from the left in two colors. During spring snowmelt or summer storms in the mountains of eastern Arizona, the Little Colorado carries a heavy load of brown silt. In dry periods, the only flow comes from mineral-laden Blue Spring, 12.5 miles upstream. Salts and calcium carbonate turn the water a beautiful aquamarine, but it's not recommended for drinking. Endangered fish hang out near the confluence, so no fishing or camping is permitted here.

You can hike up the Little Colorado nearly a mile to see Ben Beamer's stone-slab cabin on the south bank. Beamer came here in 1889 to prospect and do a bit of farming; he likely "borrowed" stones from ruins left by ancestral Puebloans to build his cabin. Beamer's Trail still connects the confluence with Tanner Rapid downstream and the Tanner Trail to the South Rim.

Back on the Colorado River, you'll spot some salt deposits along the left bank in the next three miles. Hopi once made long pilgrimages from their villages to collect this salt. The salt mines remain sacred to the Hopi, so Park Service rangers prohibit others from visiting them. Instead, wait until Mile 119.8, where you can stop and take a close look at a salt deposit.

Mile 63.4: The Great Unconformity
About 250 million years have been lost from the geologic record at this unconformity between the Tapeats Sandstone above and the Unkar Group of the Precambrian Period below. The Unkar contains five formations of about 1,250–825 million years ago. From the oldest (lowermost), they are the Bass Limestone, Hakatai Shale, Shinumo Quartzite,

GRAND CANYON NAT'L PARK

Dox Sandstone, and the Cardenas Lavas. You'll also hear the term "Grand Canyon Supergroup," which includes the Unkar Group and three formations of roughly the same age that occur in the Colorado River's tributaries but not at river level: Nankoweap Formation (Nankoweap and Basalt Canyons); Chuar Group (Nankoweap, Carbon, and Lava Canyons); and Sixtymile Formation (Nankoweap Butte and upper Sixtymile Canyon). Faulting has tilted these formations and caused large offsets between one side of the Canyon and the other.

Mile 64.7: Carbon Creek
For a look at the complex geology in this part of the Canyon, you can hike up Carbon Creek (on the right), cut south over a pass, and then descend Lava Canyon to the river, where you should arrange to be picked up. The pass has especially fine views of the Unkar Group and lava flows. On the way down Lava Canyon, look for a trail to the left that passes a dry fall.

Mile 65.6: Lava Canyon (Chuar) Rapid (3–5)
Lava Canyon is on the right, Palisades Creek on the left. A park naturalist found a moonshine still in Lava Canyon in 1928, but you'd be safer to carry your own liquid refreshment on hikes here.

Mile 68.5: Tanner Canyon
Hikers descend from the South Rim on the Tanner Trail to the beach and the small rapid at the river. The Beamer Trail goes upstream to the Little Colorado. The Escalante Route winds downstream to connect with the Tonto and New Hance (Red Canyon) Trails.

Mile 71: Cardenas Creek
You can scramble south up the ridge for a wonderful panorama of the Canyon and a look at a stone structure left by ancestral Puebloans; it may have been a watchtower. Spanish explorer García López de Cárdenas, ar-

riving on the South Rim in 1540, was the first White man to see the Grand Canyon; his group tried but failed to reach the river.

Mile 72.5: Unkar Rapid (6–7)
Ancestral Puebloans once farmed the Unkar delta on the right. You can stop to look at stone foundations of their village.

Mile 75.5: Nevills Rapid (6)
Norm Nevills led the first commercial river trip through the Grand Canyon in 1938.

Mile 76.8: Hance Rapid (8–10)
Rock gardens in the river present a real challenge, especially to the hard-shelled dories. Red Canyon on the left is the start of the long Tonto Trail that heads downstream and the Hance (Red Canyon) Trail that climbs to the South Rim. John Hance arrived at the Grand Canyon in 1883, built the first lodge on the South Rim two years later, made trails, did some mining, and guided tourists. All the while he entertained his tour guests with amazing yarns, such as the tale about the Canyon filling with clouds, when he just strapped on his snowshoes and walked across. On stretches where trails parallel the river, the difference in time between foot and boat travel is amazing. A lazy day on the river with just an oar-powered boat can cover as much distance as several hard days on the trail.

Mile 77: Upper Granite Gorge
Another Great Unconformity marks the boundary between the Unkar Group and rocks even more ancient, perhaps 1.7 billion years old, formed in the early part of the Precambrian Period. Unimaginable extremes of time, pressure, and heat have folded, twisted, and crystallized these rocks, which probably once lay beneath a mountain range. Despite the gorge's name, you'll find mostly gneiss (a coarse-grained metamorphic rock with bands of visibly different minerals) and schist (a dark, easily split, meta-

morphic rock with closely spaced bands of mica). Pink pegmatite (a coarse-grained igneous rock) was injected into these rocks. You'll see milky quartz too. The Upper Granite Gorge extends about 48 miles downstream. The Canyon's character changes dramatically as the dark walls close in, constrict the river, and speed up the water's flow.

Mile 78.7: Sockdolager Rapid (8–9)
Major Powell's second expedition used a slang word meaning "knockout blow" for this one. Powell's men weren't able to portage their frail craft here, so they ran the rapid with the loud roar of the waves reverberating off the Canyon walls.

Mile 81.5: Grapevine Rapid (8)
Grapevine Creek comes in from the left, Vishnu Creek from the right. Many of the rock "temples" and canyons below the North Rim bear names of Eastern gods and philosophers. The Hindu god Vishnu preserves the world. Geologist Clarence Dutton started the "heroic nomenclature" for Grand Canyon features.

Mile 83.5: 83 Mile Rapid (3–5)

Mile 84: Clear Creek Canyon
You wouldn't think such a small stream and canyon could drain a large area of the North Rim. It's worth making the short hike of about half a mile up to a small waterfall. You could also climb around the waterfall and continue far upstream. Clear Creek Trail connects the creek with the North Kaibab Trail near Phantom Ranch.

Mile 84.6: Zoroaster Rapid (5–8)
Zoroaster Creek on the right descends from the south side of Zoroaster Temple. About 700 b.c., the Persian philosopher Zoroaster founded what became a major religion of that region.

Mile 85: 85 Mile Rapid (2–6)

Mile 87.5: Kaibab Bridge
The South Kaibab Trail from the South Rim crosses the river here on its way to Phantom Ranch after a very scenic descent of 6.8 miles to Bright Angel Camp via Cedar Ridge. The bridge warns you that a touch of civilization lies just ahead. River trips put in at the beach on the right past the bridge to exchange passengers leaving or joining at this point. You can wander over to Phantom Ranch to use a telephone, mail your postcards via mule train, buy snacks or souvenirs at the store, or ogle a flush toilet, which you won't have seen for days.

If you have time for a hike, try part of the North Kaibab or climb the Clear Creek Trail for views. Or leave the crowds and head up Phantom Creek to lush greenery and small waterfalls; walk about one mile up the North Kaibab Trail until you see the creek on the other side of Bright Angel Creek, which you'll have to ford.

Mile 87.8: Bright Angel Rapid and Bright Angel Bridge
Major Powell named the swift and clear-flowing Bright Angel Creek to honor the forces of good, after earlier naming the muddy Dirty Devil River upstream in Utah. Much of the Bright Angel's flow comes from Roaring Springs, which blasts out of caves in the Redwall Limestone below the North Rim. Hikers can reach the North Rim on the 14.2-mile North Kaibab Trail.

Mile 89: Pipe Springs Rapid (4–5)
The Bright Angel Trail turns up Pipe Creek Canyon on its well-graded, 7.8-mile-long ascent to the South Rim.

Mile 90.2: Horn Creek Rapid (8–10)
Horn Creek comes in on the left. Two boulders near midstream give the rapid its name.

Mile 93.5: Granite Rapid (9)

Monument Creek on the left offers an easy walk up to the Tonto Trail.

Mile 95: Hermit Rapid (8–9)
Hermit Creek on the left also provides a scenic walk up the Tonto Trail. Louis Boucher, the Hermit, mined copper and guided tourists in the area during his stay from 1891–1912. He wore a white beard, rode a white mule, and told only "white lies."

Mile 96.8: Boucher Rapid (3–5)
The route along Boucher Creek on the left is an easy walk to the Tonto and Boucher Trails.

Mile 98.2: Crystal Rapid (10)
This fierce rapid has weakened the knees of many a river-runner scouting it from the shore. Places in the Grand Canyon may stay nearly unchanged for more than a century, only to be turned topsy-turvy by a single storm. That happened here in 1966, when a massive flood tore through Crystal Creek (on the right), washing many huge boulders into the Colorado and forcing the river into the left wall. Now boaters must pick out a route that stays clear of the rocks, the wall, and giant, boat-flipping holes. If you're camping near here, Crystal Creek offers a pleasant stroll up its relatively open canyon.

Mile 99.2: Tuna Creek Rapid (6)

Mile 101.3: Sapphire Rapid (7)
One of a series of rapids here called "The Jewels." Sapphire Canyon is on the left.

Mile 102: Turquoise Rapid (3–6)
Turquoise Canyon is on the left.

Mile 103.9: 104 Mile Rapid (5–7)

Mile 104.6: Ruby Rapid (6–7)
Ruby Canyon is on the left.

Mile 106: Serpentine Rapid (6–8)
Serpentine Canyon is on the left. Serpentine (an ornamental stone) and asbestos (sought by Hance, Bass, and other prospectors) occur in the Canyon where molten volcanic rock subjected the Bass Limestone to intense heat.

Mile 107.8: Bass Rapid (3–6)
Bass Canyon on the left and the South Bass Trail, just upstream of the rapid, provide access to the Tonto Trail and South Rim. William Bass arrived in the 1880s, did some prospecting, raised a family, and ran a tourist operation until he left the area in 1923. He built tourist camps and constructed trails to both South and North Rims. Boats, and in 1908 a cableway with a cage big enough for horses, connected his trails. The Park Service cut the cable in 1968, so there's no crossing today. A metal boat, the *Ross Wheeler,* lies on the left bank just above the rapid, where it was abandoned about 1914.

Mile 108.2: Beach and Trailhead for Bass's Camp
From this popular campsite on the right, a trail climbs high over a ridge (blazing with yellow brittlebush in spring), drops to Shinumo Creek, and then winds upstream to Bass's Camp. You'll discover relics of his camp and small farm along the swift, sparkling creek. Cottonwood trees shade the banks. Be sure to carry lots of water and a sun hat for this hike of two miles each way. The North Bass Trail continues another 12 miles upcanyon to the pine-forested North Rim.

Mile 108.7: Shinumo Rapid
Boats can pull in at lower Shinumo Creek on the right so that you can take a short walk to a pool and waterfall. The waterfall blocks hikers from continuing upstream to Bass's Camp.

Mile 112.2: Waltenberg Rapid (6–9)
John Waltenberg worked with William Bass in developing copper and asbestos mines in the area during the early 20th century.

© BILL WEIR

the boat-flipping Crystal Rapid

Mile 112.6: 112¹/2 Mile Rapid (1–6)

Mile 113.1: Rancid Tuna Rapid (6)
One can only assume that this rapid was named by an unlucky early boating expedition that discovered the terrible truth about its food situation here.

Mile 114.4: Garnet Canyon
The Tonto Trail ends its 92-mile meandering at this canyon on the left.

Mile 116.5: Elves Chasm
Royal Arch Creek creates this beauty spot on the left with a waterfall, greenery and flowers, and extensive travertine deposits.

Mile 116.9: Stephen Aisle
This straight section of Canyon runs about two miles. The Upper Granite Gorge ends at a fault where the river cuts into Tapeats Sandstone. From here until the start of the Middle Granite Gorge at Mile 126.6, you'll be seeing stretches of Tapeats Sandstone, Precambrian gneiss, and Bright Angel Shale.

Mile 119.8: Salt Deposits

Look on the right for alcoves filled with salty stalactites, stalagmites, and columns. It's possible to stop here or walk back from the Blacktail Canyon camp 0.3 mile farther.

Mile 120.1: Blacktail Canyon and Conquistador Aisle
Blacktail Canyon on the right offers a short hike into Tapeats Sandstone narrows. Conquistador Aisle, another two-mile straight section of canyon, lies downstream.

Mile 121.7: 122 Mile Rapid (4–6) and Bright Angel Shale

Mile 122.8: Forster Rapid (6)
Forster Canyon is on the left.

Mile 125: Fossil Rapid (6–7)
Fossil Canyon is on the left.

Mile 126.6: Middle Granite Gorge
Schist and quartzite make up most of the low walls of this narrow, 3.9-mile gorge. Sheetlike dikes of igneous pegmatite (coarse-grained rock) and amphibolite (dark rock composed mostly of the mineral hornblende) have cut

into the older rocks. You'll see salt deposits on the left.

Mile 129: Specter Rapid (5–8)
Specter Chasm is on the left.

Mile 130.5: Bedrock Rapid (8) and Unkar Group
Bedrock Canyon and the "Doll's House" are on the right. Middle Granite Gorge ends just below, where the river cuts into the Unkar Group. Bass Limestone, with its igneous intrusions, dominates the next five miles.

Mile 131.7: Deubendorff Rapid (7–9), Galloway Canyon, and Stone Creek
Galloway Canyon, on the right just above the rapid, and Stone Creek, on the right just below, invite exploration. Galloway is dry, but Stone Creek features pools, waterfalls, greenery, flowers, and a magical narrows. Stone Creek makes a great spot for a layover day. The whole walk up offers pretty scenery, so just tramp as far as the spirit moves you. Look for a bypass trail on your right around the first high waterfall about one mile up; another mile of climbing will take you to the short narrows that end in a waterfall.

In 1909, Julius Stone earned the distinction of being the first to boat through the Grand Canyon for the fun of it. A president of a gold-dredging company, he had met pioneering boatman Nathaniel Galloway in Glen Canyon and hired him to supervise construction of four wooden, flat-bottomed boats. Galloway had devised not only superior riverboat designs but also a better way of rowing them in the rapids. He found that it made no sense to row blindly into the dangerous rapids when one could simply turn the boat around, face the rapids, and pull upstream to give more time and control to make a safe descent. The new boats, 16.5 feet long and four feet wide, featured sealed compartments and lightweight construction. Stone and four companions, including Galloway and helper Seymour Deubendorff, pushed off from Green River, Wyoming, and reached Needles, California, just over two months later. Galloway became the first to make two complete transits of the canyons, and his rowing technique endures today. Deubendorff capsized here, much to his embarrassment at the time.

Mile 133.7: Tapeats Rapid (5–8), Tapeats Creek, and Thunder River
Two sets of voluminous springs feed crystal-clear Tapeats Creek, on the right just above the rapid. Thunder Spring rates as one of the Grand Canyon's top hiking destinations—you're not likely to be disappointed! Trails run up both sides of Tapeats Creek from the Colorado. In spring, when the creek can be too high and swift to ford easily, it's best to get off the boats on the downriver side of the creek. In

A hike into the Shinumo Quartz in Stone Canyon narrows leads to this pretty waterfall.

© BILL WEIR

2.5 miles you'll reach Thunder River, which suffers the indignity of both being short and serving as a tributary to a creek.

A trail climbs steeply half a mile to good vantage points of Thunder Spring as it blasts out of a cave system in the Muav Limestone. Large Fremont cottonwood trees provide shade. In spring or autumn, you can continue 1.5 miles up the trail past Thunder Spring and down into the gently sloping Surprise Valley, renowned for its ovenlike heat in summer. A cairn marks the junction of the Thunder River Trail to the North Rim, but continue west 1.5 miles on the Deer Creek Trail, which drops to Deer Creek (Dutton) Spring, another cave system gushing a waterfall. You can hike up to the falls for a closer look or take the path that goes higher and behind the falls. The creekside trail winds down one mile past the remarkably narrow and twisting Tapeats narrows, then drops to the base of Deer Creek Falls at the river. Watch out for poison ivy here. If it's too hot to hike or you can't arrange to be met by boats, Deer Creek makes a great stop on its own.

Mile 134.7: 135 Mile Rapid (5) (Helicopter Eddy)

Mile 135.4: Granite Narrows
The Colorado constricts to just 76 feet in the Granite Narrows, its smallest width in the Grand Canyon.

Mile 136.2: Deer Creek Falls
See the Mile 133.7: Tapeats Creek/Thunder River entry above for hiking details on the Deer Creek Trail (on the right).

Mile 136.6: Unconformable contact (a gap in the geologic record) of Precambrian rocks and overlying Tapeats Sandstone
Tapeats predominates for the next 3.5 miles; you'll also see some Precambrian quartzite and spring-deposited travertine.

Mile 137.7: 137¹/₂ Mile (Doris) Rapid (5–7)
Doris, wife of Norm Nevills, took a swim here after getting washed overboard on one of the early commercial river trips in 1940.

Mile 139: Fishtail Rapid (5–7)
Fishtail Canyon is on the right.

Mile 140.1: Conformable Contact (no gap in the geologic record) between the underlying Tapeats Sandstone and Bright Angel Shale
The river cuts through Bright Angel Shale for the next seven miles.

Mile 143.5: Kanab Rapid and Kanab Canyon
A major canyon system with many tributaries of its own, Kanab Creek on the right extends far north into Utah past the town of Kanab to the Paunsaugunt Plateau, 100 miles from the Grand Canyon. Kanab means "willows" in Paiute. Major Powell ended his second river expedition here in 1872 and walked out Kanab Canyon. Whispering Falls makes a good hiking destination; walk up about four miles from the river and turn right into the first tributary.

Mile 145.6: Olo Canyon
The overhanging cliff to the left with a waterfall doesn't look promising for hikers, but some groups will send a rock climber on a bypass just downriver to put in a cable ladder at the pour-off. Two other steep sections a little farther upstream can be rigged with ropes to aid hikers. The climb is worthwhile to view the water-sculpted canyon full of pools. Upstream, the canyon widens a bit, and vegetation finds soil to take root. Olo is Havasupai for "little horse."

Mile 147.1: Conformable Contact between the Bright Angel Shale and overlying Muav Limestone
The river flows through the Muav for the next 18.6 miles.

GRAND CANYON NAT'L PARK

Mile 147.9: Matkatamiba Canyon
"Matkat" on the left presents a beautiful show of rock sculpture and pools similar to those in Olo Canyon. Agile hikers should be able to make it up Matkat without ropes. As in Olo, you can hike a long way in, limited mainly by the time you have. Matkatamiba is a Native American family name.

Mile 149.7: Upset Rapid (6–9) and 150 Mile Canyon
The 1923 Birdseye (U.S. Geological Survey) River Expedition had made it this far when the head boatman, Emery Kolb, performed the group's first flip. On the right is 150 Mile Canyon.

Mile 156.8: Havasu Canyon
The turquoise-blue waters and Shangri-La reputation of this canyon on the left put it at the top of many river runners' favorite hikes. Trees, grass, and flowers fill the canyon floor. Havasupai live in their secluded Supai village about nine miles upcanyon; *havasu* means "blue water" and *pai* means "people." Everyone wants to visit Havasu Canyon, yet there's no beach to land boats. So boaters have to tie up in the canyon mouth—an amazingly complex network of interconnected ropes at times.

The trail upstream crosses the creek many times, but has little elevation gain to Beaver Falls, four miles away, the most popular destination for river runners. Here you can swim in large pools enclosed by travertine terraces. Fleet-of-foot hikers can continue two more miles to see 196-foot Mooney Falls, the most impressive in Havasu Canyon. No camping is allowed in the lower canyon, so boaters are limited to day trips. For a longer visit, it's best to hike in from the top at another time to visit Supai Village and the other waterfalls; see the **Havasupai Indian Reservation** section later in this book.

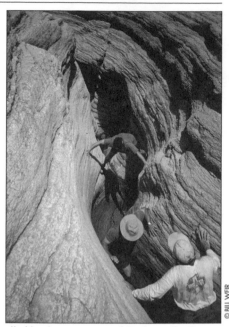

climbing lower narrows of Matkatamiba Canyon

© BILL WEIR

Mile 165.7: Contact of Muav Limestone and the underlying Bright Angel Shale
The river flows through Bright Angel Shale for the next 10.2 miles.

Mile 166.5: National Canyon
The canyon on the left, sometimes with a small stream, is an easy one-mile walk; you'll need a rope to go farther.

Mile 168: Fern Glen Rapid (3) and Fern Glen Canyon
A worthwhile hike of about half a mile through the canyon on the right takes you to seeps that support expanses of maidenhair fern.

Mile 175.9: Contact of Bright Angel Shale and the underlying Tapeats
The river flows through Tapeats for the next 3.2 miles.

ENDANGERED FISH OF THE COLORADO RIVER

Colorado pikeminnow *(Ptychocheilus lucius)*

Native only to the Colorado and its tributaries, this species is the largest minnow in North America. It has been reported as weighing up to 100 pounds and measuring six feet long. Loss of habitat due to dam construction has greatly curtailed its size and range. Fishermen often confuse the smaller more common roundtail chub *(Gila robusta)* with the Colorado pikeminnow; the chub is distinguished by a smaller mouth extending back only to the front of the

Humpback chub *(Gila cypha)*

Scientists first described this fish only in 1946 and now know little about its life. The small fish usually weighs in under two pounds and under 13 inches. Today the humpback chub hangs on the verge of extinction: it has retreated to a few small areas of the Colorado River where the water still runs warm, muddy and swift. The bonytail chub *(Gila robusta elegans)* has a similar size and shape, but without a hump; its numbers are also rapidly declining.

Humpback or Razorback sucker *(Xyrauchen texanus)*

This large sucker grows to weights of 10–16 pounds and lengths of about three feet. Its numbers have been slowly decreasing, especially above the Grand Canyon. They require warm, fast-flowing water to reproduce. Mating is done as a bizarre ritual in the spring. When the female has selected a suitable spawning site, two male fish press against the sides of her body. The female begins to shake her body until the eggs and males' spermatozoa are expelled simultaneously. One female can spawn three times, but she uses a different pair of males each time.

© LOUISE FOOTE

GRAND CANYON NAT'L PARK

Mile 178: Vulcan's Anvil
The Anvil, a remnant of a lava vent, rises in the middle of the river. The Anvil marks the beginning of a long stretch of volcanic features in the Grand Canyon. A series of eruptions took place over the last million years, burying the countryside under lava and cinders and even filling the Grand Canyon with massive

lava dams. Much of the basaltic lava formed columnar jointing. The fractures developed as the basalt cooled; cooler spots commonly formed three radial fracture planes (120 degrees apart) that grew outward and intersected other fracture planes to create the columnar joints—usually hexagons. The faster the basalt cooled, the more fractures occurred, so you'll sometimes see cross-sections of fanlike columns near the surface branching out from larger "trunks" below.

Toroweap Overlook stands high above on the North Rim with some classic Canyon views. Lava Falls Route connects the river and the Toroweap area, though it's probably best to come by road at another time to explore this region; see **Toroweap** earlier in this book.

Mile 179.1: Crossing the Toroweap Fault
The downstream side of the fault has dropped 580 feet, so you go from Tapeats Sandstone to the younger Muav Limestone without seeing the intervening Bright Angel Shale; look for the fault on the left (the right side is covered by lava). From here to the head of the Lower Granite Gorge at Mile 215.1, you'll be in one of these three formations or some Precambrian rocks at river level.

Mile 179.3: Lava Falls Rapid (10)
Boaters may discuss whether Crystal or Lava Falls is the more difficult, but there's no denying that both are BIG and receive lots of respect. After a lengthy scout of the rapid from shore, you're in the boats and into the wild waves for an exhilarating ride.

Mile 183: Plugged Channel
An old river channel on the right is filled with lava.

Mile 187: Whitmore Wash
When lava filled the mouth of Whitmore Wash on the right, the stream cut a new channel farther downriver. You can easily hike about a half mile up this new canyon. Whitmore Trail climbs from river to rim in only three-quarters of a mile—the shortest access trail within Grand Canyon National Park—but you're still a very long and bumpy road from the nearest town. Some river parties do a passenger exchange here, not by trail, but by helicopter using a pad on Hualapai land across the river.

The helicopter flies to the North Rim's Bar 10 guest ranch, where a day of activities is usually included; small planes then take departing guests to Las Vegas or other destinations.

Mile 205.5: 205 Mile (Kolb) Rapid (7–8)
205 Mile Creek is on the left.

Mile 208.5: Granite Park
The large beach on the left makes an attractive campsite. Nearby canyons invite exploration. The river splits around a large, low island just downstream.

Mile 212.2: Little Bastard Rapid (1–7)

Mile 214.3: Shady Ledges (below 214 Mile Creek)
The lower Canyon can get mighty hot even in spring and autumn. These ledges on the right provide a shady lunch spot.

Mile 215.1: Entering Lower Granite Gorge
The Tapeats Sandstone makes an unconformable contact with the underlying Precambrian granite.

Mile 217.4: 217 Mile Rapid (6–7)
217 Mile Canyon is on the left.

Mile 225.6: Diamond Creek Rapid (4) and Diamond Creek
The name comes from the distinctive 3,512-foot peak that you see long before reaching the creek; the summit is only 400 feet higher in elevation than Lees Ferry. This left side of the Colorado River belongs to the Hualapai, who maintain a 21-mile unpaved road from here to Peach Springs on old Route 66. If you were to stay on the Colorado, there's only one day's river running remaining, and then a long stretch of lake to Pearce Ferry, the next road access. Still, this last section offers great beauty, well worth seeing if you can do it. You can also start river trips

here; contact the Hualapai River Runner's office in Peach Springs.

Mile 229: Travertine Rapid (3) and Travertine Canyon
A bit of steep scrambling (a rope is handy) up some travertine on the left will take you into a large cavelike room with a refreshing waterfall.

Mile 230.6: Travertine Falls
A waterfall near the river splashes thousands of sparkling drops off large travertine deposits on the left.

Mile 230.8: 231 Mile Rapid (4–7)

Mile 232.2: 232 Mile Rapid (4–7)

Mile 233.5: 234 Mile Rapid (4–6)

Mile 235.3: Bridge Canyon Rapid (3–6)
Bridge Canyon, with a spring and a natural bridge, is on the left.

Mile 236: Gneiss Canyon Rapid (3–6)
Gneiss Canyon is on the left.

Mile 237.2: 237 Mile Rapid (3–6)

Mile 239.6: Separation Canyon
On August 28, 1869, during Major Powell's first river expedition, the hardships of the unknown, the rapids, and dwindling food supplies brought three of the crew to the breaking point; they decided to hike out here through this canyon on the right. Rapids roared just downstream, and what lay beyond, Powell and the men could only guess. When they separated here, each group assumed the other to be embracing the greater danger. Powell and his remaining party safely negotiated the last rapids and left the Grand Canyon at noon on the following day. The three who climbed out never made it home. Powell later personally investigated and concluded that the men met their deaths at the hands of Shivwits tribesmen.

Today there's not much more than riffles where rapids once terrified Powell's men. You're on Lake Mead now, though the Colorado still provides a current and the Canyon still reveals magnificent views. Most groups start motoring out or arrange to be met by motorboats somewhere below Separation, even if they've been rowing so far.

Mile 259.3: End of the Lower Granite Gorge
Exposures of Tapeats Sandstone and Bright Angel Shale appear at lake level, though they're likely to be covered by silt. In pre-dam days, scattered exposures of Precambrian rocks reportedly extended all the way to the end of the Grand Canyon.

Mile 266.3: Bat Cave and Guano Point
U.S. Guano sank a lot of money into the mining of a deposit of bat guano (dung used as fertilizer) in a cave during the late 1950s. Cables suspended from the towers once carried the guano from Bat Cave high on the north side across the Canyon to Guano Point high on the Hualapai Plateau. The Park Service prohibits entry to the cave because it disturbs the bats. You can visit Guano Point by road or air for spectacular views and a close look at one of the towers; see **Grand Canyon West** in the Hualapai Indian Reservation section.

Mile 277.7: Grand Wash Fault and End of the Grand Canyon
The Canyon abruptly ends at Grand Wash Fault because rock layers on the west side lie several thousand feet lower—the Colorado never had a chance to carve a canyon in them. You're now on the vast expanse of water in Lake Mead National Recreation Area.

Mile 280: Pearce Ferry
Takeout and the road home.

GRAND CANYON NAT'L PARK

Western Grand Canyon and the Arizona Strip

Havasupai and Hualapai Indian Reservations

VISITING HAVASU CANYON

The towering cliffs of Havasu Canyon enclose a land of blue-green waters, breathtaking waterfalls, and lush vegetation. Havasu Creek rushes through the canyon past the village of Supai before beginning its wild cascade down to the Colorado River. The canyon and its creek, about 35 air miles northwest of Grand Canyon Village, belong to the Havasupai (*havasu* means "blue water," and *pai* means "people").

Havasupai lived here long before the first White people arrived. The tribe farmed the fertile canyon floor each summer, then moved to the plateau after harvest to gather abundant wild foods and firewood during winter.

Coyote Buttes North, west of Page

© BILL WEIR

Spanish missionary Francisco Tomás Garcés visited the Havasupai in 1776 and thought them a peaceful and industrious tribe. However, as was often the case, White settlers grabbed tribal lands over the following years. The Havasupai protested, and the tribe's winter homelands were finally returned in 1975. The Havasupai Reservation now spans 188,077 acres and houses 500–600 members, most of whom live in Supai village.

Getting There

The tribe wisely decided against allowing road construction in the canyon, so most residents and tourists enter by mule, horse, or on foot. Helicopters provide another option, though the noisy machines seem out of place here.

The eight-mile trail from Hualapai Hilltop to Supai is the usual way in. From Seligman on I-40, take AZ 66 northwest for 28 miles (to between Mileposts 110 and 111), then turn right and go 63 miles on signed Indian 18, paved all the way to Hualapai Hilltop. If coming from the west, take AZ 66 northeast out of Kingman for 60 miles, then turn left and drive the 63 miles. Fill up with gas before leaving AZ 66, as no water, supplies, or stores are available after the turnoff. The road to Hualapai Hilltop climbs into forests of ponderosa pine that give way to pinyon and juniper, then desert grasslands close to the rim. Parking areas and stables mark road's end. Various dirt-road shortcuts to Hualapai Hilltop suffer from poor signing and rough surfaces.

Hiking In

You *must* obtain reservations to camp or to stay in the lodge. From Hualapai Hilltop (elev. 5,200 feet), the trail descends at a moderate grade into Hualapai Canyon for the first 1.5 miles, then levels off slightly for the remaining 6.5 miles to Supai village (elev. 3,200 feet). About 1.5 miles before the village, the trail joins the sparkling waters of Havasu Canyon. Avoid the heat of the day in summer when temperatures soar past 100°F, and always carry drinking water. All visitors must pay a $20 entrance fee on arrival at Supai. The tribe asks you to leave pets, alcohol, and firearms at home. To preserve the canyon floor, no fires or charcoal are allowed, so campers need to bring stoves if they plan to cook.

Riding In

If you'd rather ride than walk, local families will take you and your gear on horses or mules from the parking lot at Hualapai Hilltop to Supai ($70 one-way or $120 roundtrip) or all the way to the campground ($75 each way), 2.75 miles farther. One animal can carry about four backpacks. Try to get an early start from Hualapai Hilltop, especially in the warmer months; a small surcharge is added for departures after 10 A.M. A sightseeing ride from Supai to the falls and back can be arranged with the lodge. You should make reservations at least six weeks in advance and pay a 50 percent deposit. Campers make arrangements through Havasupai Tourist Enterprise; lodge guests through the lodge. Also call two weeks before arrival to make sure your animal is available. Visitors may bring their own horses if they take along feed and pay a $20 trail fee.

Sights

The famous waterfalls of the canyon begin 1.5 miles downstream from Supai—three cascades plunge over cliffs of Redwall Limestone in a space of just two miles. You'll first come to 75-foot-high **Navajo Falls** which has several widely spaced branches. It's named after a 19th-century Havasupai tribal chief kidnapped by Navajo as an infant and raised as a Navajo. Not until he grew to manhood did he learn of his true origin and return to the Havasupai.

A bit farther, spectacular **Havasu Falls** drops 100 feet into a beautiful turquoise-colored pool rimmed by travertine deposits. Clear, inviting waters make this a perfect spot for swimming or picnicking.

WESTERN GRAND CANYON

Awe-inspiring **Mooney Falls** plummets 196 feet into a colorful pool one mile beyond Havasu Falls. The Havasupai named this most sacred of waterfalls, Mother of the Waters. The present name is that of a prospector who died here in 1880. When assistants lowered Daniel Mooney down the cliffs next to the falls, the rope jammed and Mooney hung helpless as the rope frayed and broke. He fell to his death on the rocks below, and 10 months passed before his companions could build a wooden ladder down the falls to reach and bury the travertine-encrusted body. A rough trail descends beside the falls along the same route hacked through the travertine by miners in those months after Mooney's death. You'll pass through two tunnels and then ease down with the aid of chains and iron stakes. At the bottom—as soon as your knees stop shaking—you can enjoy a picnic or swim in the large pool. Miners extracting silver, lead, zinc, and vanadium drilled the holes that you see high on the canyon walls.

Beaver Falls, two miles downstream from Mooney, makes a good day-hike from the campground or Supai village. You'll pass countless inviting travertine pools and small cascades, of which Beaver Falls is the largest. The trail, rough in places, crosses the creek three times, climbs high up a cliff, then descends and crosses a fourth time below Beaver Falls. The trail continues downstream along Havasu Creek four more miles to the Colorado River. Travel fast and light if going to the river, as camping is prohibited below Mooney Falls. Photographing the falls can be a challenge; the best time to snap them in full sunlight is in May, June, and July.

WESTERN GRAND CANYON AND ARIZONA STRIP HIGHLIGHTS

Havasu Canyon: Waterfalls and travertine pools in this beautiful canyon create a "Shangri-La" setting.

Diamond Creek: You can drive along this creek to the bottom of the Grand Canyon on an unpaved road on the Hualapai Indian Reservation.

Grand Canyon West: Spectacular panoramas take in the lower Grand Canyon from remote viewpoints.

Arizona Strip: Adventurous travelers who love wilderness and solitude seek out the canyons and mountains of this vast area.

Pipe Spring National Monument: You can experience life on a ranch straight out of the Old West.

Paria Canyon and Coyote Buttes: Exquisitely sculptured rock awaits hikers in the Paria Canyon-Vermilion Cliffs Wilderness.

Havasu Campground

Most visitors prefer to camp, listening to the sounds of the canyon and enjoying the brilliant display of stars in the nighttime sky. Havasu Campground begins a quarter mile below Havasu Falls (or 10.75 miles from Hualapai Hilltop) and provides spring water, picnic tables, litter barrels, and pit toilets. It's recommended that campers treat or filter the spring water. Most people don't realize that the campground extends three-quarters of a mile along Havasu Creek to the brink of Mooney Falls. You'll enjoy more solitude if you walk to the far end. Theft is a serious problem in the campground, so don't leave valuables in your tents or lying around.

To camp, you must have reservations and pay $10 per person per night. Camping outside the established campground is prohibited. Call 928/448-2141 or write Havasupai Tourist Enterprise, P.O. Box 160, Supai, AZ 86435. Try to make reservations far ahead, especially for holidays, weekends, and all of April, May,

© BILL WEIR

the steep descent to the base of Mooney Falls

June, and July. The tribe now accepts Visa and Master Card.

Accommodations and Food

The modern **Havasupai Lodge,** tel. 928/448-2111, in Supai village offers rooms with air-conditioning, two double beds, and private bath for $75 s, $80 d. Obtain the required reservations—recommended two–three months in advance; P.O. Box 159, Supai, AZ 86435.

A cafe nearby serves breakfast, lunch, and dinner daily 6 A.M.–7 P.M. (8 A.M.–5 P.M. in winter) Try the Indian taco—red beans, beef, cheese, onion, and lettuce on Indian fry bread. Ice cream prices are high, though not so bad when you consider what it takes to bring the frozen dessert to such a remote area. A store across the street, open daily, sells meat, groceries, and cold drinks.

Services

Send your postcard home via pack train—with a postmark to prove it. The **post office** is open weekdays 9 A.M.–4 P.M. next to the store. A **health clinic** in Supai provides emergency medical care.

VISITING THE HUALAPAI INDIAN RESERVATION

The Hualapai (Pine Tree People) once occupied a large area of northwestern Arizona. In language and culture, they're closely tied to the Havasupai and Yavapai tribes. Though the Hualapai were friendly to early white visitors, land seizures and murders by the newcomers led to warfare. In 1869 the tribe surrendered to the U.S. Army and were held at camp Beale Springs (present-day Kingman) and other locations before being forced south onto the Colorado river Indian Reservation in 1874. Many died there due to the oppressive climate, hard labor, and lack of food. Survivors escaped the following year and fled back to their traditional lands, only to find the best areas had already been taken by white people. In 1883, the government gave the Hualapai a 993,000-acre reservation, now housing about half the tribe's 1,500 members. Much of the lower Grand Canyon's South Rim belongs to the Hualapai. Highlights for visitors include the drive into the grand Canyon at Diamond Creek, Colorado River trips, and spectacular viewpoints froom the rim of the lowermost Grand Canyon. Respect the privacy of the tribal residents and obtain permits for sightseeing or other activities off the main highway.

Peach Springs

This community, 54 miles northeast of Kingman on AZ 66, is the only town on the reservation. Peach Springs offers neither charm nor anything to see, but it does have lodging and offices where you can obtain required permits for back-road drives and outdoor

WESTERN GRAND CANYON

© MOJAVE COUNTY HISTORICAL SOCIETY

Farlee Hotel near Diamond Creek, built in 1884 and in ruins when this photo was taken, circa 1914

WESTERN GRAND CANYON

recreation. **Hualapai Lodge,** tel. 928/769-2230 or 888/255-9550, has comfortable rooms ($75 d, less in winter) and a restaurant that serves breakfast, lunch, and dinner daily. The lodge's front desk sells permits to drive into the Grand Canyon via Diamond Creek Road, detailed below. Grand Canyon West permits, also described below, can be obtained when you arrive there. For other areas, you'll need to contact the tribe's Wildlife office, across the highway from the lodge and several doors to the west; open Mon.–Fri. 8 A.M.–4:30 P.M.; tel. 928/769-2227. **Hualapai Office of Tourism,** tel. 888/255-9550, has a desk open daily 9 AM.–5 P.M. in the lobby of Hualapai Lodge, where you can arrange rafting trips through the lower Grand Canyon and get information about visits to Grand Canyon West; contact P.O. Box 359, Peach Springs, AZ 86434; website: www.hualapaitours.com. After hours, ask at the front desk. A grocery store and post office lie across the highway and a few doors west. Craft vendors may set up in the park across from the lodge.

Grand Canyon Caverns Inn, 13 miles southeast on AZ 66, tel. 928/422-3223, offers

accommodations ($45 s, $50 d, lower rates in winter), an RV park for self-contained vehicles ($6.50), pool, and snack bar.

Frontier Motel, nine miles southwest in Truxton on AZ 66, tel. 928/769-2277, has motel rooms ($35 s, $40 d), an RV park ($20 w/hookups; self-contained only), and a smoky cafe.

Diamond Creek Road

This scenic 21-mile gravel road winds north from Peach Springs to the Colorado River at Diamond Creek, providing the only road access to the river within the Grand Canyon. You'll see fine canyon views, though not as spectacular as those in the developed areas of Grand Canyon National Park. Except for river-runners, who use the road to take out or put in boats, few people visit this spot. Yet the very first organized groups of tourists to the Canyon arrived at Diamond Creek in 1883. A hotel built here and used in 1884–89 was the first in the Grand Canyon.

If the weather has been dry for several days, cars with good ground clearance can traverse the road. Summer rains in July and August may wash out sections and require use of a truck. A camping area near the Colorado River has some picnic tables and an outhouse or two. Hikers can explore Diamond Creek and other canyons. Before turning down Diamond Creek Road, you must stop at the Hualapai Lodge front desk to obtain permits; hikers may also need to visit the Wildlife office for a hiking permit. Staff at either place can advise on road conditions. Sightseeing permits cost $5 per day per person (ages 6 and over). Camping is $10 per day per person and includes the sightseeing fee. Fishing is an extra $8 per day per person. Diamond Creek Road turns off AZ 66 opposite the Hualapai Lodge.

River-Running

Hualapai River Runners, tel. 928/769-2219 or 888/255-9550, will take you on a one-day motorized-raft trip down the lower Grand Canyon from Diamond Creek, lift you out by helicopter to the rim at Grand Canyon West, then return you by road to Peach Springs, $250. Overnight trips to Lake Mead can be chartered. This is the only company to offer a day trip within the Grand Canyon. Rates during the March–Oct. season cover food, waterproof bag for personal gear, and transportation from Peach Springs. Contact the office at Hualapai Lodge or write P.O. Box 246, Peach Springs, AZ 86434; website: www.river-runners.com.

view down Grand Canyon from Guano Point

Grand Canyon West

The Hualapai tribe offers a 4.5-mile tour along the rim of the western Grand Canyon to Guano Point, where visitors enjoy a great panorama of this little-visited part of the Canyon. The Colorado River, placid now that it has met the waters of Lake Mead, lies nearly 4,000 feet directly below. Sheer, terraced cliffs rise even higher on the North Rim than where you're standing. The Canyon remains grand to the end, as you'll see. The Grand Wash Cliffs, which lie just out of sight downstream, mark the west end of both the Grand Canyon and the Colorado Plateau. One of the steel towers and some of its machinery once used in a guano mining operation still stand on the point, and another tower is visible below. When in use, a tram carried guano from a bat cave located across the river. The tour also makes a short stop at an overlook on Eagle Point, an exceptionally long and narrow neck of land extending out into the Canyon.

Cost for the bus tour and a barbecue lunch at Guano Point runs $35 adult, $22 children 3–12; the lunch contains enough vegetables to satisfy most vegetarians too. Tours depart frequently during the day year-round and last about two hours; the first is at 10 A.M. and the last about 3 P.M.; no reservations are needed. Tickets, Quartermaster Point permits, and a gift shop are in the terminal building at the Grand Canyon West airport. It's a good idea to call ahead and allow plenty of time, because this is such a long drive out. Contact the Hualapai Office of Tourism for information (see Peach Springs, above).

While at Grand Canyon West, you can also enjoy a visit on your own to **Quartermaster Point,** another outstanding panorama of the Grand Canyon farther upstream. A quarter-mile trail from road's end leads down to the best views at the top of sheer cliffs. Quartermaster Canyon lies to your right, and Burnt Canyon is across the river. Twin Point stands above Burnt Canyon. Farther

WESTERN GRAND CANYON

THE DESERT TORTOISE

(Gopherus agassizii)

A threatened species, the desert tortoise survives the harsh climate of western Arizona by burrowing underground for about 95 percent of its lifetime. Here it escapes the 140°F surface temperatures in summer and the freezes of winter. It also seeks out catchment basins, where it will lie waiting when the rare rains seem likely. A tortoise's bladder can store a cup of liquid for later use, and they've been known to expel the bladder's contents at intruders. Wastes are excreted in a nearly dry form. Tortoises can withstand dehydration, then increase their weight 43 percent by drinking after a storm. Growth and sexual maturity depend much on availability of food and moisture. Several growth rings may appear each year. The female reaches maturity when about 7–8 inches long (mid-carapace), perhaps at 15 years of age. Mating peaks in late summer/early autumn, though egg laying won't take place until May–June, when tortoises lay two or three batches of 2–9 eggs. Babies emerge 3–4 months later. Oddly, experiments have shown that eggs incubated at 79–87°F turn out to be all males, at 88–91°F all females.

The tortoise's diet includes grasses, herbs, flowers, and new cactus growth. Males may fight each other for territory until one flees or gets flipped onto its back. If the defeated rival cannot right himself, he will die in the sun. Because the tortoise needs sand or gravel to burrow, you're most likely to see them in washes and canyon bottoms. Life span may be 70 years or more. The male has a longer protruding plate (used in jousting matches) under his neck; he may be as much as 14 inches long and weigh up to 20 pounds. The female is a bit smaller. Laws forbid disturbing or collecting a wild tortoise, but habitat loss and "kidnappers" have left their future in doubt. The western box turtle (*Terrapene ornata*), sometimes confused with the desert tortoise, is much smaller at about five inches long and has distinctive light and dark striping on its shell.

BOB RACE

the desert tortoise

upcanyon, Kelly Point extends even farther out from the North Rim. (Both of these points can be visited via back roads; see "The Arizona Strip" section.) You can also picnic at Quartermaster Point; the spot has a few tables and an outhouse. First, obtain a permit from the Grand Canyon West Terminal, $10 per person (free if you also take a tour). The turnoff is 1.1 miles before the Grand Canyon

West Terminal, then 2.3 miles in at the sign to the rim.

Getting to Grand Canyon West is an adventure too. Allow at least two hours for any of the driving routes. Four roads allow loop possibilities, or you can fly from Las Vegas. Buck and Doe Road stays within the reservation all the way. This dirt road is passable by cars when the weather has been dry, but it can be rough—ask about road conditions before you leave. When it's wet, even 4WD vehicles should avoid it. Buck and Doe turns north from AZ 66 between Mileposts 100 and 101, several miles west of Peach Springs; follow it to the end, then turn right 4.3 miles on paved Diamond Bar Road. Antares Road, also dirt but likely to be better graded, turns north off AZ 66 farther west from Peach Springs, between Mileposts 74 and 75; take it 33 miles, turn right 7 miles on Pearce Ferry Road (paved), then go right 21 miles on Diamond Bar Road. The first 14.4 miles on Diamond Bar Road is dirt but very scenic; you pass Joshua trees and enter a canyon through the Grand Wash Cliffs. Another back-road route involves heading north 40 miles on Stockton Hill Road

from Kingman, then right 7.1 miles on Pearce Ferry Road and right 21 miles on Diamond Bar Road. The best road in approaches from the west; take US 93 from Kingman or Las Vegas to paved Pearce Ferry Road, near Milepost 42, follow it 29 miles east, then turn right 21 miles on Diamond Bar Road.

Several fixed wing and helicopter companies offer tours from Las Vegas; check with operators there for the many options. Helicopters also fly from Grand Canyon West into the Canyon and land either near the river or on a bench part way down on Hualapai land. Some flights allow passengers to get out and be picked up later in the day for the flight back to the top.

The Arizona Strip

Lonely and vast, the Arizona Strip lies north and west of the Colorado River. This land of forests, desert grasslands, mountains, and canyons covers 14,000 square miles, yet supports only 3,200 people. The Grand Canyon presents a formidable barrier between these citizens and the rest of the state; all highway traffic has to follow a circuitous route around the mighty chasm. To cover 140 miles as the crow flies, residents of Moccasin in the Arizona Strip must drive 357 miles to the Mohave County seat at Kingman, detouring through Utah and Nevada before reentering Arizona at Hoover Dam.

Historically, the Strip has far more in common with Utah; Mormon pioneers first settled this region. Today, the Strip appeals to those who love wilderness and solitude. In addition to Grand Canyon National Park and Glen Canyon National Recreation Area, nine designated wilderness areas totaling nearly 400,000 acres protect some of the most scenic sections. Much of this land has also been included in the Grand Canyon-Parashant National Monument, which

exceeds one million acres. Travelers can wander along the canyons, back roads, and trails here without meeting another soul. Many viewpoints provide spectacular panoramas of the Grand Canyon, and you'll never have to joust with tour-bus crowds or search for a parking spot. Other attractions include fishing and boating on Lake Powell, historic Lees Ferry (15 river miles below Lake Powell), and Pipe Spring National Monument, an early Mormon ranch.

Several tiny communities in the Arizona Strip offer food and accommodations; more extensive facilities lie just outside in Mesquite across the Nevada border to the west, in St. George and Kanab across the Utah border to the north, and in Page across the Colorado River to the east.

History

Few pioneers took an interest in the prairie here—the ground proved nearly impossible to plow and lacked water for irrigation. Determined Mormons began ranching in the 1860s despite the constant isolation and

WESTERN GRAND CANYON

occasional Navajo raids. They built Winsor Castle, a fortified ranch, in 1870 as a base for a large church-owned cattle herd. Mormons also founded the towns of Fredonia, Short Creek (now Colorado City), and Littlefield.

Some of these settlers had fled Utah to escape federal laws prohibiting polygamy. About 3,000 members of a polygamous, excommunicated Mormon sect still live in Colorado City and neighboring Hildale, Utah. (Note the huge size of "family" houses here!) Federal and state officials raided Colorado City several times, most recently in 1953, when 27 arrests were made—those charged received one year of probation. Since then government policy has been mostly "live and let live."

Information

For hiking and access information for public lands on the Arizona Strip and into Utah, contact the **Interagency Visitor Center,** tel. 435/688-3246, at 345 E. Riverside Dr., St. George, UT 84790; open Mon.–Fri. 7:45 A.M.–5 P.M. (best times for reaching someone with first-hand travel experience) and Saturdays and holidays 9 A.M.–5 P.M.; website: www.az.blm.gov. Take I-15 Bluff Street Exit 6 and turn southeast one-third mile on Riverside Dr.; the office is on your left. This is also the home of the Arizona Strip Interpretive Association (ASIA), which has a good bookshop here.

The BLM's **Kanab Resource Area** office, 318 N. 100 East (Kanab, UT 84741), tel. 435/644-4600, takes care of the Paria Canyon area and Grand Staircase-Escalante National Monument; open Mon.–Fri. 7:45 A.M.–4:30 P.M.; website: www.ut.blm.gov.

The U.S. Forest Service manages Saddle Mountain Wilderness and most of the Kanab Creek Wilderness from the **North Kaibab Ranger District** office, tel. 928/643-7395, at 430 S. Main St. in Fredonia (P.O. Box 248, Fredonia, AZ 86022); open Mon.–Fri. 8 A.M.–5 P.M.; website: www.fs.fed.us/r3/kai.

The BLM's *Arizona Strip District* map shows topography, roads with numbers, and land ownership at a 1:168,960 scale. The St. George Interagency office, Kanab Resource Area office, and most regional bookstores have the map; you can also order it online from the Interagency Internet address. The more detailed USGS 1:100,000 and 1:24,000-scale topo maps will be handy for hikers.

Exploring the Arizona Strip

Paved highways lead to the Virgin River gorge in the northwest corner, Pipe Spring National Monument in the north, the Grand Canyon's North Rim farther east, and Lees Ferry at the east edge. Elsewhere, high-clearance 4WD vehicles are recommended in this remote and rugged land. Cautiously driven 2WD vehicles can negotiate roads to the Trumbull and Toroweap areas in dry weather from St. George, Colorado City, and Fredonia. Parts of these roads are so smooth that one can drive at high speeds, often too fast to spot that washout or rough cattle guard! Drivers of 2WD vehicles need to take extra care not to become stuck on steep, sandy, or washed-out roads.

Mountain bikers can do exciting trips in the mountains and out to Grand Canyon viewpoints. Marked trails for cyclists include the Dutchman Trail, an "easy" nine-mile loop near Little Black Mountain (south of St. George) and the "more difficult" 8.5-mile Sunshine Loop southeast of St. George. The Arizona Trail farther east is another cycling destination.

All visitors must respect the remote location, lack of water, and absence of facilities here. Be sure to carry camping gear, extra food and water, tools, and a first-aid kit in case of breakdown. Distances can be great—make sure you have enough gas. Some roads shown on maps will be very difficult, hazardous, or completely closed; learn of current conditions from the BLM or Forest Service. Major junc-

WESTERN GRAND CANYON

tions have signs and most roads also have a number, which helps with navigation. Some critical intersections lack signs, however, so it's highly recommended to have the BLM's Arizona Strip District map and to make frequent reference to it. Leave an itinerary with a reliable person in case you don't emerge on time. Some people live seasonally on the Arizona Strip, but you cannot count on being able to find anyone in case of trouble. Ranchers run cattle on the strip, so gates should be left as you found them. Drivers need to keep an eye out for endangered desert tortoises that might wander across the road in the Mohave Desert, west of the Grand Wash Cliffs and the Virgin Mountains.

WILDERNESS AND SCENIC AREAS ON THE WESTERN ARIZONA STRIP

Virgin River Canyon Recreation Area

Picnic areas and campsites overlook the Virgin River at this scenic spot just south of I-15 Cedar Pocket Exit 18. It's open year-round with water but no showers or hookups; the gate closes at 9 P.M. Expect hot weather in summer at this 2,260-foot elevation. Campsites cost $8, picnic areas $2; groups can reserve day-use and camping areas with the BLM's Arizona Strip office in St. George, Utah; tel. 435/688-3200. A one-fifth-mile nature trail leads to hilltop views, where interpretive signs explain the unusual geology of the canyon at this transition between the Colorado Plateau and the Basin and Range Province; trailhead parking is on the left where the picnic and campground roads divide. Other trails drop from the picnic and camping areas to the river.

River Running on the Virgin

Experienced whitewater boaters prepared for changing conditions can tackle the Virgin River. A minimum of about 1,000 cubic feet per second (cfs) is needed, which doesn't occur every year; spring, and especially May, offers the best chance of sufficient flow. No permits are needed. The Interagency Visitor Center in St. George can advise on river travel and possibly on local boat rentals and shuttle services. River runners can put in at the Man of War Rd. bridge in Bloomington, just south of St. George. Take-out can be at the last I-15 bridge or farther down on slow water near the Arizona town of Beaver Dam.

Littlefield and Beaver Dam

These two farming communities lie near the Virgin River on opposite sides of I-15 in Arizona's extreme northwest corner. Turn north 0.6 mile from Beaver Dam Exit 8 for **Hamilton Ranch,** a historic hotel on old Highway 91 once used as a movie star retreat; call for rates. The restaurant serves breakfast, lunch, and dinner daily (summer dinners are by reservation); tel. 928/347-5111; website: www.hamiltonranchgolf.com. Golfers have an 18-hole course. A gas station/grocery store is nearby. Mesquite, Nevada, offers motels, restaurants, supermarkets, and glitter just eight miles west on I-15.

Beaver Dam Mountains Wilderness

This 19,600-acre wilderness includes alluvial plains and the rugged mountains of extreme northwestern Arizona and part of adjacent Utah. Desert bighorn sheep, desert tortoises, raptors, the endangered woundfin minnow, Joshua trees, and several rare plant species live here. There are no trails, but hikers enjoy traveling cross-country through the beautiful Joshua tree forest or exploring canyons. Unpaved BLM Rd. 1005, 10 miles long, follows a corridor through the wilderness, providing easy access. The east end begins at I-15 Cedar Pocket Exit 18, opposite the Virgin River Recreation Area, 20 miles southwest of St. George. The west end (unsigned) turns off between Mileposts 14 and

WESTERN GRAND CANYON

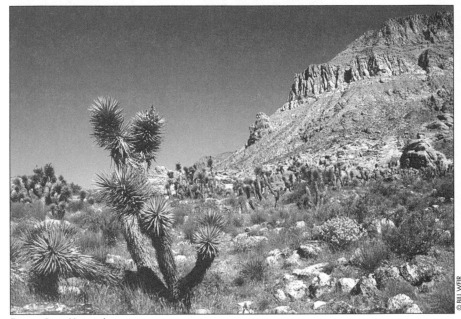

© BILL WEIR

Beaver Dam Mountains

15 of Hwy. 91, 5.5 miles north of I-15 Beaver Dam Exit 8.

Paiute Wilderness

This 84,700-acre wilderness lies south of I-15 and the Virgin River in the northwest corner of Arizona. The jagged Virgin Mountains contain a wide variety of plant and animal life, from desert country at 2,400 feet to pine and fir forests surrounding 8,012-foot Mt. Bangs.

Several hiking trails wind through the rugged terrain. Cougar Spring Trailhead at the wilderness boundary provides the easiest route to the summit. Follow an old road up one mile through the wilderness to a saddle, then turn left one more mile up another old road toward the top. When the road ends, you'll need to bushwhack through some chaparral (look for cairns and wear long pants) and rock scramble the last quarter mile to the top; the

climb takes about four and a half hours roundtrip. Despite the high elevations, only a few pines grow on the upper slopes; you'll see mostly manzanita, jojoba, Gambel oak, and some hedgehog and prickly pear cactus. Surrounding ridges have forests, however.

Other hiking options from Cougar Spring Trailhead area include the ridge north of Mt. Bangs and the Sullivan Trail. The 15-mile Sullivan Trail crosses the wilderness from Cougar Spring Trailhead or Black Rock Rd. to the Virgin River via Atkin Spring and Sullivan Canyon; expect some rough and poorly defined sections. The lower trailhead lies 1.5 miles downstream and across the Virgin River from Virgin River Campground, near I-15, 20 miles southwest of St. George; check the depth of the Virgin River carefully and turn back if it's too high to cross safely.

Hikers have a choice of approaching Cougar Spring Trailhead from the east via Black Rock

Rd. (#1004), a pretty route through ponderosa pines on Black Mountain (good camping and a few picnic tables); from the south via Lime Kiln Canyon (#242) and other roads; or from the west on the very steep Elbow Canyon Rd. (#299; best driven downhill). From Mesquite, Nevada, turn south 0.9 mile on Riverside Rd. (just east of Oasis Casino), then turn left onto Lime Kiln Canyon Rd. #242 (just after crossing the Virgin River bridge). After 0.9 mile you'll see the road to Elbow Canyon on the left, but keep straight 16 miles for Lime Kiln Canyon, cross over a pass and descend past some pretty red sandstone outcrops, then turn left 22 miles on BLM Rd. 1041 to Cougar Spring Trailhead.

From St. George, take the I-15 Bloomington Exit 4, head east 1.8 miles (becomes Brigham Rd.), turn south 3.8 miles on River Rd. to the Arizona border and continue south another 20 miles on Quail Hill Rd. (#1069), turn right 25 miles on Black Rock Rd. (#1004), then right 0.5 mile to the trailhead.

If coming from Toroweap, take County 5 to Mt. Trumbull Schoolhouse, turn north 40 miles on County 5, then left 25 miles on Black Rock Rd. (#1004) and right 0.5 mile to the trailhead. If you're feeling adventurous and have a high-clearance 4WD vehicle, Elbow Canyon Rd. (#299) is an option—head west from the trailhead, climb a bit to a pass, then plummet down the rough road to the desert plains below. Loose rock makes this drive much easier going downhill. Mesquite is about 18 miles from the trailhead. Lots of other very scenic roads head toward the Virgin Mountains too; see the Arizona Strip District Map.

Little Black Mountain Petroglyph Site

Impressive groups of rock art, most believed to have ceremonial or calendar functions, cover boulders at the base of this mesa just south into Arizona from St. George. Archaeologists have discovered more than 500 individual de-

signs. A short trail winds past the petroglyphs, where signs describe some of their features. From St. George, take the I-15 Bloomington Exit 4, head east 1.8 miles (becomes Brigham Rd.), turn south 3.8 miles on River Rd. to the Arizona border and continue south 0.4 mile on unpaved Quail Hill Rd. (#1069), turn east 4.5 miles to a T-junction (there's a gate on the way), then left into the parking area, which has a picnic table and outhouse.

Cottonwood Point Wilderness

The 6,860-acre wilderness contains part of the multicolored 1,000-foot-high Vermilion Cliffs, jagged pinnacles, and wooded canyons. Springs and seeps in the main canyon east of Cottonwood Point support a world of greenery surrounded by desert. The wilderness lies on the Utah border near Colorado City, west of Fredonia. Dirt roads from AZ 389 and Colorado City provide access; check with the BLM for trailhead directions.

Grand Wash Cliffs Wilderness

Grand Wash Cliffs mark the west edge of the Colorado Plateau and the end of the Grand Canyon. The wilderness protects 36,300 acres along a 12-mile section of the cliffs in an extremely remote portion of Arizona. Desert bighorn sheep and raptors live in the high country; desert tortoises forage lower down. **Grand Wash Bench Trail,** a 10-mile gated road, follows a bench between the upper (1,800 feet high) and lower (1,600 feet high) cliffs; trailheads are on the north and south wilderness boundaries. Hikers can also head out cross-country to the cliffs from BLM Rd. 1061 along the west boundary of the wilderness.

An exceptionally scenic 4WD road through Hidden Canyon crosses the Grand Wash Cliffs north of the wilderness. To reach the east end of this drive, follow Parashant Rd. (#103) southwest 16.6 miles from County 5 (turnoff is 11.5 miles north of Mt. Trumbull

WESTERN GRAND CANYON

Schoolhouse and 46 miles south of St. George), then turn right on BLM Rd. 1003 at the sign for Hidden Canyon. Small canyon cliffs appear four miles in, then become higher and higher as the road winds downstream along the canyon floor, repeatedly crisscrossing the normally dry streambed. Juniper and pinyon pine on the Shivwits Plateau in the upper canyon give way to Joshua trees in the desert country below. After about 20 miles, you leave the canyons. BLM Rd. 1061 turns south for the west face of the Grand Wash Cliffs Wilderness and you can continue on BLM Rd. 1003 for Grand Wash Bay of Lake Mead. Other roads turn north to the Virgin Mountains. Numerous sandy washes require a high-clearance 4WD vehicle for Hidden Canyon and for most roads in the Grand Wash Cliffs area.

Mount Dellenbaugh

This small volcano atop the Shivwits Plateau offers a great panorama of the Arizona Strip. Vast forests of juniper and pinyon and ponderosa pine spread across the plateau. A long line of cliffs marks the Grand Canyon to the south. Beyond rise the Hualapai Mountains near Kingman. You can see other mountain ranges in Arizona, Nevada, and Utah as well. Frederick Dellenbaugh served as artist and assistant topographer on Major John Wesley Powell's second river expedition through the Grand Canyon in 1871–72.

From Mt. Trumbull Schoolhouse, go north 11.5 miles on County 5, then turn southwest 42 miles on Parashant Rd. (#103), following signs. Note that this road is *not* the one into Parashant Canyon. From St. George, Utah, it's 46 miles to the junction, then 42 miles to Mt. Dellenbaugh. The last five miles can be negotiated only when dry; high-clearance vehicles are recommended. The trailhead lies just past the BLM's Shivwits Ranger Station; follow an old jeep road, now closed to motor vehicles. The trail is an easy four miles

roundtrip, climbing 900 feet to the 7,072-foot summit.

Twin Point

Beautiful views from this overlook take in the lower Grand Canyon, Surprise Canyon, Burnt Canyon, and Sanup Plateau. Follow Parashant Rd. 103 south 37 miles, keep straight where the road to Mt. Dellenbaugh turns left, and continue south another 14 miles. You'll pass Parashant Field Station on the left two miles beyond the Mt. Dellenbaugh turnoff. Ponderosa pine gives way to juniper and pinyon pine as you near the point. At a fork three miles past the field station, you can detour right one mile to an overlook of upper Burnt Canyon, perhaps named for the colorful yellow and red rock layers. The main road continues south 2.7 miles, then skirts the west rim of Burnt Canyon, offering many fine views. Just before the road ends, it forks left for Twin Point and right for a trailhead to Sanup Plateau. Ranchers run cattle down this trail for winter grazing. Twin Point offers plenty of places to camp, and no permit is needed.

Kelly Point

Located east of Twin Point, this point extends much farther south than any other on the North Rim. Road conditions have so deteriorated that the route is now extremely rough, rocky, and slow—figure 5 mph on the last 20 miles. Getting here can be more an expedition than a casual sightseeing jaunt—Twin Point has similar views without the hardships for you and your vehicle. If you're determined and well prepared, follow Parashant Rd. (#103) past Mt. Dellenbaugh and continue south to road's end.

Whitmore Point

Spectacular views of the Grand Canyon, Parashant Canyon, Mt. Logan, and the Uinkaret Mountains greet those who head out to this 5,500-foot-high perch. Volcanoes and massive lava flows between here and the Toroweap area to the east can be seen clearly. There are plenty of good places to camp, with no permit needed.

From Mt. Trumbull Schoolhouse, head west then south 22.2 miles on BLM Rd. 1063. Some junctions feature signs, but you'll need to refer frequently to a map. At 9.9 miles in, a jeep road to the right heads down Trail Canyon to Parashant Canyon, a good area for adventurous hikers. Continue straight (south) for Whitmore Point. As with most roads on the Arizona Strip, conditions get rougher as you move closer to the Grand Canyon; a high-clearance vehicle is necessary. Whitmore Point and other areas north of the western Grand Canyon are the responsibility of the Lake Mead National Recreation Area; the agency could improve its road maintenance and signing efforts, as you'll see.

Whitmore Wash Road

Lava flows from Mt. Emma in the Uinkaret Mountains enable you to drive a high-clearance, 4WD vehicle deep into the Grand Canyon, though the last part of the drive is very rough. A short trail at road's end leads down to the Colorado River. See **Whitmore Wash Trail** for directions and hiking information.

Bar 10 Ranch, tel. 435/628-4010 or 800/582-4139, lies along this road 80 miles from St. George and about nine miles before the rim. It offers miles of open country, cowboy-style meals, and an informal Western atmosphere. Activities include horseback riding, pack trips, hiking, scenic flights, river trips, ATV tours, and entertainment. Many visitors spend a day here when shuttling in or out from a river trip by helicopter and flying by small plane to Las Vegas or other destinations. You can also drive (high-clearance vehicles recommended) or fly in. Make the required reservations with Bar 10,

which stays open all year, at P.O. Box 910088, St. George, UT 84791-0088; website: www.bar10.com.

Mt. Trumbull School

Homesteaders arrived in this remote valley about 1917 to farm and raise livestock. Population peaked at 200–250 in the 1930s, when a drier climate forced residents to switch their livelihood from crops to cattle and sheep. People gradually drifted away until the last full-time resident departed in 1984. Abandoned houses stand empty, along with some houses that are inhabited seasonally. No trespassing is allowed on private lands, but you can get some good photos from the main roads. Dedicated teachers taught at the remote one-room schoolhouse from 1922 until the bell rang for its last class in 1968. The school recently burned, but volunteers have rebuilt it; photo and document exhibits that show what life was like here. Donations are appreciated.

Mount Trumbull Wilderness

Forests cover the basalt-rock slopes of Mt. Trumbull (8,028 feet), the centerpiece of this 7,900-acre wilderness. Oak, pinyon pine, and juniper woodlands grow on the lower slopes; ponderosa pine, Gambel oak, and some aspen cover the higher and more protected areas. Kaibab squirrels, introduced in the early 1970s, flourish in the forests. You might see or hear a turkey, too. The 5.4-mile roundtrip climb to the summit makes an enjoyable forest ramble with some views through the trees. From the marked trailhead at an elevation of 6,500 feet on the southwest side of Mt. Trumbull, the wide path climbs around to the south side, with some good views across Toroweap Valley, the Grand Canyon, and the San Francisco Peaks. The trail then turns north and becomes faint, but cairns show the way to the summit, marked by a survey tower and some viewpoints. You can reach the trailhead by County

Rd. 5 from Toroweap, Fredonia, Colorado City, or St. George; you'll know that you're close when ponderosa pines appear. The buildings and trailers across the field belong to a BLM site; if staff are in, they may be able to help with local information.

Mormon pioneers built a steam-powered sawmill just west of the trailhead in 1870 to supply timbers for the St. George Temple. A historic marker tells about the sawmill operation and you can explore the site for the scant remnants. Water from Nixon Spring, higher on the slopes, once supplied the sawmill. A faucet near the road between the historic site and trailhead usually has water from the spring—a handy resource for travelers in this arid land. Mount Trumbull and nearby Mount Logan lie northwest of the Toroweap area of the Grand Canyon. John Wesley Powell named both peaks after U.S. senators.

Mount Logan Wilderness

Scenic features of this 14,600-acre volcanic region include Mt. Logan (7,866 feet), other parts of the Uinkaret Mountains, and a large natural amphitheater known as Hell's Hole. Geology, forests, and wildlife resemble those of Mt. Trumbull, a short distance to the northeast. A road climbs the east side of Mt. Logan to within a half mile of the summit; the rest of the way is an easy walk—just continue north along the side of the ridge. On top you can peer into the vast depths of Hell's Hole, a steep canyon of red and white rock. The sweeping panorama takes in much of the Arizona Strip and beyond to mountains in Nevada and Utah. Trees block views to the south.

From County 5, just southeast of the Mt. Trumbull trailhead, turn southwest 4.2 miles on BLM Rd. 1044, then right 2.2 miles on BLM Rd. 1064 until it becomes rough and steep at its end. Many fine spots in the ponderosa pines suitable for camping line the roads in.

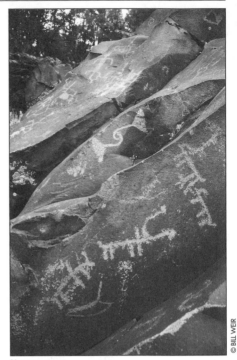

© BILL WEIR

Nampaweap

A rough 4WD road follows a corridor through the wilderness, from which hikers can turn south onto the old Slide Mountain Rd. (closed to vehicles) or enter Hell's Hole from below. You'll need to follow a map closely as none of these destinations will be signed; roads also branch off to other unsigned areas, adding to the navigational challenge. Loose rock and erosion of the corridor road require a high-clearance 4WD; it's slow going, but the road continues all the way down to the Whitmore Wash Rd. (#1045), one mile north of the Bar 10 Ranch.

Nampaweap Rock Art Site

Archaic, ancestral Puebloan, and Paiute tribes have pecked thousands of glyphs into boulders near Mt. Trumbull. Nampaweap means "foot canyon" in Paiute, perhaps referring to it being on a travel corridor dating back to prehistoric times. From the Mt. Trumbull Trailhead, go east 3.5 miles on County Rd. 5 (or west 3.7 miles from the junction with Toroweap Rd.), turn south 1.1 miles on BLM Rd. 1028 toward the private Arkansas Ranch, turn east into the parking area, and then walk three-quarters of a mile to the head of a small canyon. The rock art is on the canyon's north side.

Kanab Point

A great expanse of canyon falls away below your feet from this perch overlooking the confluence of the Kanab and Grand Canyons. Few people know about this lonely spot, yet it's one of the best Grand Canyon viewpoints. The drive out takes some care with navigation as not all the junctions may be signed. You'll need the BLM's Arizona Strip Field Office Visitor Map, a high-clearance vehicle, and dry weather. The turnoff on County 109 is 34 miles north of Toroweap and 34 miles southwest of Fredonia. Head east on BLM Rd. 1058, keep right at a fork 7.5 miles in, turn right on a fork 10.1 miles in (the wider left fork goes to an

uranium mine), turn left at a T-junction 16.4 miles in and continue 0.8 mile to the national park boundary; you'll reach Kanab Point in another 4.0 miles, for a total of 21.2 miles one way from County 109. At the rim, the best panoramas of the Grand Canyon are 0.2 mile to the right and the best ones of Kanab Canyon lie 0.3 mile to the left.

Hack Canyon

This tributary of Kanab Canyon offers both great scenery—you'll feel like you're in the Grand Canyon—and access to the Kanab Creek Wilderness. The road gets rough in the last few miles where 4WD will be handy. The turnoff from County 109 is 4.7 miles north of the Kanab Point junction, or 38 miles north of Toroweap and 30 miles southwest of Fredonia. Head east on BLM Rd. 1123 and you'll see the headwall of Hack Canyon on the left after 1.1 miles. The road drops in and follows the normally dry canyon bottom with ever higher and grander walls on each side. You'll reach the wilderness boundary and road's end at 9.7 miles from County 109. A trail continues into the wilderness toward Kanab Canyon, five miles

© BILL WEIR

view down Hack Canyon in Kanab Creek Wilderness

WESTERN GRAND CANYON

one way, where you could turn downstream another 10.5 miles to the mouth of Jumpup Canyon or 16 miles to the Colorado River; a backcountry permit is needed to camp below Jumpup Canyon. Black Willow Spring, a short distance down the trail on your right in Hack Canyon, is a rare source of water here.

PIPE SPRING NATIONAL MONUMENT

Excellent exhibits in Winsor Castle, an early Mormon ranch southwest of Fredonia, provide a look into frontier life. The abundant spring water here first attracted prehistoric Basket Maker and Pueblo tribes, who settled nearby more than 1,000 years ago, then moved on. Paiute, who believe they're related to these people, arrived more recently and now live on the surrounding Kaibab-Paiute Indian Reservation; in earlier times, they spent summers on the Kaibab Plateau and winters near Pipe Spring.

Mormons found the spring in 1858 and began ranching five years later, despite Navajo raiders who occasionally stole stock and were suspected of having killed two Mormon men who pursued them. Raids ended after 1870 when Mormons and Navajo signed a treaty. Mormon leader Brigham Young then decided to move the church's southern Utah cattle herd to Pipe Spring. A pair of two-story stone houses went up with walls connecting the ends to form a protected courtyard; workers added gun ports just in case, but the settlement was never attacked.

The structure became known as Winsor Castle—the ranch superintendent, Anson P. Winsor, possessed a regal bearing and was thought to be related to the English royal family. Winsor built up a sizable herd of cattle and horses and oversaw farming and the ranch dairy.

A telegraph office—the first in Arizona—opened in 1871, bringing the rest of the world closer. Eventually, so many newlyweds passed

Travelers and ranchers spent many a pleasant evening in the parlor of the Winsor Castle.

© BILL WEIR

through after marriage in the St. George Temple that the route became known as the Honeymoon Trail. In the 1880s, the Mormon Church came under increasing assault from the U.S. government, primarily over the practice of polygamy. Fearing the feds would soon seize church property, the church sold Winsor Castle to a non-Mormon in 1895.

President Harding proclaimed Pipe Spring a national monument in 1923 "as a memorial of Western pioneer life." Today, National Park Service staff keep the frontier spirit alive by maintaining the ranch much as it was in the 1870s. Activities such as gardening, weaving, spinning, quilt-making, cheese-making, and butter-churning still take place, albeit on a smaller scale. You can also see a traditional Paiute shelter (wickiup) and demonstrations of Paiute food and crafts. At times a cowboy or a Paiute speaker tells of life on the Arizona Strip. Short guided tours of Winsor Castle relate how people lived here in the early days, and you can explore the outbuildings and gardens on your own. The half-mile-loop Rim Trail climbs the small ridge behind the ranch to a viewpoint, where signs describe the history and geology of the area. Paiute guides offer a walking tour to a nearby rock art site for a fee; call ahead to the tribal office, tel. 928/643-7245, open weekdays.

Visitor Center

Historic exhibits are open daily 8 A.M.–5 P.M. year-round with extended hours in summer; $3 per person admission (16 and under free); tel. 928/643-7105; website: www.nps.gov/pisp. A short video, photo exhibits, and historic artifacts introduce the monument. Demonstrations, talks, and walks take place mainly in summer. Produce from the garden is often given away. A gift shop has a good selection of regional books, maps, and Southwestern Native American arts and crafts. Hikers may be able to obtain last-minute backcountry permits for the Grand Canyon National Park, a useful service for some North Rim destinations. Pipe Spring National Monument lies north off AZ 389, 14 miles southwest of Fredonia.

The Paiute tribe operates a **campground** one quarter mile northeast of the monument. It has showers and is open all year at a bargain-priced $5 tent or $10 RV with hookups; non-campers can use the showers for $3; tel. 928/643-7245 (tribal office). There's a gas station/convenience store at the highway turnoff. Colorado City and Fredonia also offer gas and grocery stores. The nearest restaurants and motels are in Fredonia, but Kanab has more extensive services, including supermarkets.

KANAB AND VICINITY

Striking scenery surrounds this small Utah town just north across the Arizona border. The Vermilion Cliffs to the west and east glow with a fiery intensity at sunrise and sunset. Streams have cut splendid canyons into surrounding plateaus. The Paiute knew the spot as Kanab, meaning "Place of the Willows," which still grow along Kanab Creek. Mormon pioneers arrived in the mid-1860s and tried to farm along the unpredictable creek. Irrigation difficulties culminated in the massive floods of 1883, which in just two days gouged a section of creekbed 40 feet below its previous level. Ranching proved better suited to this rugged and arid land.

Hollywood discovered the dramatic scenery in the 1920s and has filmed more than 150 movies and TV series here, including *The Greatest Story Ever Told, The Outlaw Josey Wales, Rin Tin Tin, The Lone Ranger, Gunsmoke,* and *F Troop.* Film crews have constructed several Western sets near town, but most lie on private land. You can see some sets right in Kanab at Frontier Movie Town and the reconstructed Pahreah set east of Kanab. Ask at the visitor center for advice on visiting other sets.

Travelers find Kanab (pop. 5,500) a handy stopover on trips to Bryce, Zion, and Grand Canyon National Parks and to Glen Canyon National Recreation Area. A good selection of motels and restaurants lines US 89, which zigzags through town. Short detours on many of the side streets reveal 19th-century houses from Kanab's pioneer days.

Kanab Heritage House

This 1893 Queen Anne-style Victorian house reflects the prosperity of two of Kanab's early Mormon residents. Henry Bowman built it, but he lived here only two years before going on a mission. He sold the property to Thomas Chamberlain, who led a busy life serving as a leader in the Mormons' United Order and car-

WESTERN GRAND CANYON

ing for his six wives and 55 children. (There's a family photo in the sitting room.) A guide will show you around the house and explain its architectural details. Photos, furnishings, and artifacts give an idea of what life was like in early Kanab. The town had no stores when the house was built, so each family grew its own vegetables and fruit. The grape arbor, berry bushes, and trees here represent those grown during pioneer times; fruit is free for the picking to visitors. The house is usually open for tours Mon.–Sat. 10 A.M.–5 P.M. from April–Sept.; tel. 435/644-3506. Admission is $3 adult, $1 age 5–12, or $6 family. You might be able to visit at other times by appointment; check with the Kanab Visitor Center. The house is located one block west of US 89 at the corner of Main and 100 South.

Frontier Movie Town

Movie-set buildings here portray local movie history and a bit of the Old West. You may recognize some of the structures used in *The Outlaw Josey Wales* and other movies and TV shows. Many small exhibits display Western and movie memorabilia. There's a photo studio where you can dress up in Old West costumes.

The buildings and gift shop stay open all year. A steak house serves lunch and dinner daily along with Western entertainment from May–October; reservations are recommended. The only saloon in town is here too. Turn in at 297 W. Center; tel. 435/644-5337 or 800/551-1714.

Squaw Trail

This well-graded trail provides a close look at the geology, plant life, and animals of the Vermilion Cliffs just north of town. Allow about an hour on the moderately difficult trail to reach the first overlook (two miles roundtrip with a 400-foot elevation gain) or one and a half hours to go all the way up (three miles roundtrip with an 800-foot ele-

vation gain). Views to the south take in Kanab, Fredonia, Kanab Canyon, and the vast Kaibab Plateau. At the top, look north to see the White, Gray, and Pink Cliffs of the Grand Staircase. The trail is planned to continue across the mesa to Hog Canyon; ask in town. The Kanab trailhead is at the north end of 100 East just past the city park. Pick up a trail guide at the visitor center. Brochures may also be available at the trailhead or BLM office. Bring water, and try to get a very early start in summer.

Best Friends Animal Sanctuary

Angel Canyon, a beautiful area on Kanab Creek above town, is now home to the largest no-kill animal shelter in the country. The sanctuary is Kanab's top visitors' attraction and one of the more unusual destinations in Utah. Filmmakers shot several Western movies and TV shows, including *Rin Tin Tin* and *The Lone Ranger* here; a barn from a Disney picture is still in use. Best Friends takes in unwanted or abandoned creatures—mostly companion animals—and gives them a home. Cats and dogs comprise the majority of the animal population, which is never less than 1,800 at any given time. Birds, bunnies, and farm denizens make up the balance. About 85 percent get adopted; those that don't get a lifetime of care.

To see the 3,000-acre sanctuary, you'll need to join a guided bus or van tour; call ahead for tour times and reservations. Tours of 45 or 90 minutes depart daily; the longer tours include stops to meet some of the cats and dogs. There's no charge, but donations are welcome. Before or after the tour, you can watch a video about the work done here and visit the gift shop. Many people like the facility so much that they volunteer to care for the animals. The sanctuary and tours operate all year; it's open daily 8:30 A.M.–5 P.M. You can stay here at Angel Canyon Guest Cottages, tel. 435/644-2001, extension 102, but advance reservations are needed. The canyon's scenery and history can be enjoyed on a self-guided hiking trail that begins across the road from the visitor center parking. Head down a dirt road, turn left and descend a trail to a bridge across Kanab Creek, then wind up to a series of prehistoric ruins under a cliff; the walk is about one mile roundtrip and takes 40 minutes. From downtown Kanab, drive five miles north on US 89, then turn right 1.4 miles on paved Kanab Canyon road (between Mileposts 69 and 70); tel. 435/644-2001; website: www.bestfriends.org.

towers of the Vermilion Cliffs

© THE EXPLORATION OF THE COLORADO RIVER AND ITS CANYONS

Moqui Cave

A huge cave in Navajo Sandstone holds a large collection of Native American artifacts—most excavated locally—plus minerals and dinosaur tracks. A diorama re-creates a prehistoric ruin located five miles away in Cottonwood Wash. You'll also see what's claimed to be one of the largest fluorescent mineral displays in the country. The exhibits and a gift shop inside the spacious cave stay pleasantly cool even in the hottest weather. Open Mon.–Sat. from early March–mid-November, with summer hours of 9 A.M.–7 P.M., then shorter hours in spring and autumn; admission costs $4 adults, $3.50 seniors, $2.50 children 13–17, and $2 ages 6–12. The cave is six miles north of Kanab on US 89; tel. 435/644-2987.

Accommodations

Nearly all of the motels and campgrounds lie along US 89, which follows 300 South, 100 East, Center, and 300 West through town. Reservations are a good idea during the busy summer months. The summer rates listed may drop in winter.

Under $50: Canyonlands International Youth Hostel, a half block off US 89 at 143 E. 100 South, tel. 435/644-5554, is a great place to meet other travelers, many from foreign countries. Guests stay in simple dorm-style accommodations with use of the kitchen, laun-

dry, TV room, patio, lawn, locked storage, and a reference library of regional maps and books. Open year-round; check-in is all day; $10 per person (no hostel card needed).

Travelers Motel, 544 E. 300 South, tel. 435/644-2228, has the basics at $35 d.

Kanab Mission Inn Motel, 386 E. 300 South, tel. 435/644-5373, costs $42–47 d.

Sun-N-Sand Motel, 347 S. 100 East, tel. 435/644-5050 or 800/654-1868, features a pool, hot tub, and four kitchenettes; rooms start at $38 s, $40 d.

Aiken's Lodge National 9 Inn, 79 W. Center, tel. 435/644-2625 or 800/524-9999, offers a pool; $43 s, $47 d; it closes Jan.–February.

Treasure Trail Motel, 150 W. Center, tel. 435/644-2687 or 800/603-2687, has a pool, $42–48 s, $42–56 d.

Quail Park Lodge, 125 Hwy. 89 North, tel. 435/644-5094, has a pool; rooms run $38–89 d.

WESTERN GRAND CANYON

$50–100: Holiday Inn Express, one mile east of downtown at 815 E. US 89, tel. 435/644-8888 or 800/HOLIDAY, offers a round on the nine-hole golf course next door, a free breakfast bar, pool, and hot tub; rooms are $99 d.

You can stay where the stars stayed at **Parry Lodge,** 89 E. Center, tel. 435/644-2601 or 800/748-4104. Room doors have names of the movie stars who stayed there and you'll see their photos in the lobby and restaurant. There's also a pool here. Rates run $64–69 s, $69–74 d.

Red Hills Motel (Best Western), 125 W. Center, tel. 435/644-2675 or 800/528-1234, has a pool and costs $89 d.

Super 8, 70 S. 200 West, tel. 435/644-5500 or 800/800-8000, includes a pool, $69 s, $72 d.

Shiloh Inn, 296 W. 100 North, tel. 435/644-2562 or 800/222-2224, features all mini-suites and a pool, $70 d.

Four Seasons Motel, 36 N. 300 West, tel. 435/644-2635, includes a pool; rooms start at $59 s, $69 d.

Campgrounds

Crazy Horse RV Campark, 625 E. 300 South, tel. 435/644-2782, has spacious sites with lots of grass and trees on the east side of town; amenities include a pool, store, game room, and showers; open mid-April–late October. Spaces cost $13.50 tents or RVs without hookups, $15 RVs with hookups.

Hitch'n Post RV Park, 196 E. 300 South, tel. 435/644-2142, has sites with showers open all year; rates are $14 tents, $16 RV with hookups.

Kanab RV Corral, 483 S. 100 East, tel. 435/644-5330, has sites with hot showers, pool, and laundromat open all year on the south side of town; RVs with hookups cost $20; no tents.

Food

Parry's Lodge, 89 E. Center, tel. 435/644-2601, features steak, prime rib, seafood, and chicken and dumplings; open daily for breakfast and dinner.

Houston's Trail's End Restaurant, 32 E. Center, tel. 435/644-2488, rustles up steak, prime rib, chicken, seafood, and pasta with a western atmosphere, open daily for breakfast, lunch, and dinner.

Wildflower Café & Natural Foods, 18 E. Center, tel. 435/644-3200, has a vegetarian deli and baked goods along with a grocery store of organic and natural foods.

Rocking V Café, 97 W. Center, tel. 435/644-8001, offers a diverse menu including Southwestern and Italian favorites, open daily in summer for breakfast, lunch, and dinner; closed Jan.–February.

Chef's Palace Restaurant, 176 W. Center, tel. 435/644-5052, is open daily for breakfast, lunch, and dinner. Dinner fare includes steak, prime rib, and seafood.

Rainbow Cafe, 198 S. 100 East, tel. 435/644-8295, serves up American food daily for breakfast, lunch, and dinner with indoor and patio seating.

For Mexican food, including steak and seafood, try **Fernando's Hideaway** in the west end of town at 332 W. 300 North, tel. 435/644-3222, open daily for lunch and dinner, and **Nedra's Too,** 310 S. 100 East in Heritage Center, tel. 435/644-2030, open daily for breakfast, lunch, and dinner.

The **Wok Inn,** 86 S. 200 West, tel. 435/644-5400, serves Hunan and Szechuan cuisine. It's open Mon.–Fri. for lunch and nightly for dinner; closed in winter.

R&R Pizza Express, 365 S. 100 East, tel. 435/644-2500, and **Pizza Hut,** 421 S. 100 East, tel. 435/644-2513, cook pizza daily for lunch and dinner.

Entertainment and Events

In July and August, free musical concerts or

other entertainment take place Wednesday evenings at the gazebo in the center of town. **Kanab Theatre** has movies at 29 W. Center, tel. 435/644-2334.

Sleek dogs come to Kanab in May for the **Greyhound Gathering** with a parade, race, and howl-in. Humans get their turn in the **Kanab 10K** run in May on the day before Mother's Day. **Southern Utah Bluegrass Festival** plays lively tunes in mid-July. **Western Legends Round Up** honors the Old West with a parade, rodeo, music, cowboy poetry, art, demonstrations, and other festivities in September; website: www.westernlegendsroundup.com.

Services and Shopping

The **city park** provides picnic tables, playground, tennis courts, and a baseball field at the north end of 100 West; the trailhead for Squaw Trail also starts here (see "Squaw Trail," above). An outdoor **swimming pool,** 44 N. 100 West (behind the State Bank), tel. 435/644-5870, opens in summer. **Coral Cliffs Golf Course,** tel. 435/644-5005, has nine holes and a driving range on the east edge of town. **Allen's Outfitters,** 584 E. 300 South, tel. 435/644-8150 or 435/689-1370, offers trail rides year-round.

The **post office,** tel. 435/644-2760, is at 34 S. Main. **Kane County Hospital,** 355 N. Main, tel. 435/644-5811, provides emergency care. The **public library,** 374 N. Main, tel. 435/644-2394, offers reading and Internet access; closed Sunday.

Nature's Showcase, 288 W. Center across from Four Seasons Motel, specializes in "Kanab Wonderstone" slabs; this natural sandstone found nearby has curious patterns (possibly caused by deposits from mineral springs) that resemble scenic landscapes. Prices range from a few dollars for a pocket-sized piece to $1,000 for a five-foot by two-and-a-half-foot specimen. Several other shops sell Native American crafts and assorted .
Denny's Wigwam, 78 E. Center, tel.

435/644-2452, is a landmark Old West trading post with lots of quality Western jewelry, cowboy hats and boots, and souvenirs.

Alderman & Son Photo, 19 W. Center, tel. 435/644-5981, supplies film and camera needs (including repairs) beyond what you would expect in a town this size. The shop almost qualifies as an antique camera museum. It closes in winter but there are other photo shops nearby on Center.

Information

Staff at the **Kanab Visitor Center,** 78 S. 100 East (Kanab, UT 84741), tel. 435/644-5033 or 800/733-5263, offer literature and advice for services in Kanab and travel in Kane County. The center, conveniently located in the center of town, also has movie exhibits, local art, video programs, and regional books. In summer (May–Oct.), the visitor center is open Mon.–Fri. 8 A.M.–8 P.M., Sat. 9 A.M.–5 P.M., and Sun. 9 A.M.–1 P.M.; hours the rest of the year run Mon.–Fri. 9 A.M.–6 P.M., Sat. 9 A.M.–4 P.M., and closed Sunday; website: www.kaneutah.com.

Visit the BLM's **Kanab Resource Area** office, 318 N. 100 East (Kanab, UT 84741), tel. 435/644-4600, to learn about hiking and back roads in the Kanab area, including the Grand Staircase-Escalante National Monument and the Paria Canyon area; it's open Mon.–Fri. 7:45 A.M.–4:30 P.M.; website: www.ut.blm.gov.

Tours

Lake Mead Air, tel. 435/644-2299, will take you over the Grand Canyon on a 40–45-minute flight for $89 per person or a 60–90-minute flight for $119 per person. Flights require a two-person minimum and leave from the airport three miles south of town, toward Fredonia.

Backcountry driving tours feature the beautiful yet seldom seen areas near Kanab; ask at the visitor center.

CORAL PINK SAND DUNES STATE PARK

Churning air currents funneled by surrounding mountains have deposited huge sand dunes in this valley west of Kanab. The ever-changing dunes reach heights of several hundred feet and cover about 2,000 of the park's 3,700 acres. Moviemakers have used the location for filming. Tiny particles of quartz make up the sand—the "coral pink" refers only to the color. Average summer temperatures at the 6,000-foot elevation range from about 55°F at night–95°F during the day; winter days have highs of about 55°F to lows below freezing at night. Most wildlife is difficult to spot, though you may see tracks in the sand and hear coyotes at night. Wildflowers put on a fine show in June and July. Different areas in the park have been set aside for hiking, off-road vehicles, and a campground. If you see what looks like a family reunion, it might be just a man and his wives from the nearby polygamist settlements of Colorado City or Hildale!

From Kanab, the shortest drive is to go north eight miles on US 89 (to between Mileposts 72 and 73), turn left 9.3 miles on the paved Hancock Road to its end, then turn left (south) one mile on a paved road into the park. From the north, you can follow US 89 3.5 miles south of Mount Carmel Junction, then turn right (south) 11 miles on a paved road. The back road from Cane Beds in Arizona has about 16 miles of gravel and dirt with some sandy spots; ask a park ranger for current conditions. Entrance fees are $4 per vehicle for day use or $12 per vehicle for camping. Contact the park at P.O. Box 95, Kanab, UT 84741, tel. 435/648-2800 or 800/322-3770 (reservations).

Day-Use Area

On the left just past the contact station, a short boardwalk leads into a protected section of the dunes; signs explain the geology and illustrate some animals and plants that live in this semiarid desert. Photographers and families can explore on foot and use the sheltered picnic tables.

Riding the Dunes

Drivers of off-road vehicles can head for the sands from a trailhead between the day-use area and the campground. The thrills of traveling across the Sahara-like landscape attract motorcyclists, ATVers, and dune-buggy enthusiasts. Paddle-type tires work best on the soft sand. Park regulations ask drivers to attach an eight-foot whip with a flag to their vehicles, observe quiet hours from 10 P.M.–9 A.M., and avoid riding across vegetation. All vehicles owned by Utah residents must be registered for off- or on-highway use. It's a good idea to ride where other drivers can see you. Rangers have a complete list of regulations.

Campground

The pleasant campground sits in a pinyon pine, juniper, and oak woodland. Facilities include restrooms with showers, paved pull-through sites, and a dump station. Park staff may sell ice, firewood, and off-road vehicle whips. It's open all year; reservations are recommended for the busy Memorial Day to Labor Day season.

Other Areas

The canyon country surrounding the park has good opportunities for hiking and off-road vehicle travel; the BLM office in Kanab can supply maps and information. The BLM maintains **Ponderosa Grove Campground** on the north edge of the dunes; no water but a $5 fee; it's on the paved Hancock Road that turns off one mile north of the park or eight miles north of Kanab from US 89 (between Mileposts 72 and 73). The campground is two miles in from the road to the park and 7.3 miles in from US 89. Drivers with 4WD vehicles can turn south on Sand Springs Road

(1.5 miles east of Ponderosa Grove Campground) and go one mile to Sand Springs and another four miles to South Fork Indian Canyon Pictograph Site in a pretty canyon. Visitors may not enter the Kaibab-Paiute Indian Reservation, which is south across the Arizona state line, from this side.

FREDONIA TO MARBLE CANYON ON US 89A

Fredonia

Though just a tiny town, Fredonia (pop. 1,220) is the largest community on the Arizona Strip. Mormon polygamists, seeking refuge from federal agents, settled here in 1885. They first called the place Hardscrabble but later chose the name Fredonia, perhaps a contraction of the words "freedom" and "doña" (Spanish for wife).

The town's modest places to stay, listed north to south, lie along Main St. (US 89A). **Grand Canyon Motel,** 175 S. Main St., tel. 928/643-7646, offers a choice of motel rooms at $32.50–38 d and hotel rooms at $27.50–32.50 with no extra charge for tax or kitchenettes. **Ship Rock Motel,** 337 S. Main St., tel. 928/643-7355, is $30–37 d; it closes in winter. **Blue Sage Motel and RV,** across the highway at 330 S. Main St., tel. 928/643-7125, runs $35–45 d, $15 RV with hookups; the motel closes in winter. **Crazy Jug Motel,** 465 S. Main St., tel. 928/643-7752; costs $35–45 d. The town of Kanab, seven miles north, offers a much larger selection of accommodations (including a hostel), restaurants, shopping, and recreation.

For Mexican and American food, dine at **Nedra's Cafe,** 165 N. Main St., tel. 928/643-7591, open daily for breakfast, lunch, and dinner in summer, then closed Mon. the rest of the year. **Crazy Jug Restaurant,** next to the motel at 465 S. Main St., tel. 928/643-7712, has American food daily for breakfast, lunch and dinner. A couple of convenience stores offer groceries in town.

the heart of Marble Canyon

The **post office** is downtown at 85 N. Main Street. A **city park** offers picnic tables and playground on 2nd East; turn east three blocks on Brown or Hortt from Main Street. The **public library,** 130 N. Main St., tel. 928/643-7137, has reading and Internet computers downtown; closed Sunday.

Fredonia is building a **welcome center** at the north end of town to offer information about local services and area attractions; tel. 928/643-7241 (town office).

Folks at the **North Kaibab Ranger District** office, 430 S. Main St. (P.O. Box 248, Fredonia, AZ 86022), tel. 928/643-7395, will tell you about hiking, Grand Canyon viewpoints, and the back roads of the national forest north of the Grand Canyon. The Kaibab National Forest map (North Kaibab Ranger District) sold here is a must for exploring the

WESTERN GRAND CANYON

Kaibab Plateau. Hours run Mon.–Fri. 8 A.M.–5 P.M. and you can pick up information at other times inside the vestibule; website: www.fs.fed.us/r3/kai.

Jacob Lake

High in the pine forests at an elevation of 7,925 feet, this tiny village is on US 89A at the AZ 67 turnoff for the Grand Canyon North Rim. The nearby lake honors Mormon missionary and explorer Jacob Hamblin. A **1910 forest cabin** that overlooks the lake has been restored and opened to visitors; from US 89A, head south 0.3 mile on AZ 67, turn right 0.6 mile, then go south 0.2 mile on Forest Road 282; check hours at the Kaibab Plateau Visitor Center. **Jacob Lake Lookout** offers views of plateaus and mountains in Utah to the north; it's one mile south on AZ 67, between Mileposts 580 and 581, from US 89A. **Dry Park Lookout** features great views from a 125-foot tower southwest of Jacob Lake. These and other lookouts, all shown on the Kaibab National Forest map, welcome visitors when they're staffed.

Jacob Lake Inn, tel. 928/643-7232, stays open all year with basic motel rooms ($90–92 d; $98–105 four persons), cabins (April–November only, $72–118), restaurant (American food daily for breakfast, lunch, and dinner), grocery store, Native American crafts shop, and service station; website: www.jacoblake.com.

Jacob Lake Campground, tel. 928/643-7770, offers sites in the ponderosa pines with drinking water but no hookups or showers from mid-May–mid-Oct. at $12 per night; there's usually room. Campers can enjoy summer interpretive programs and nearby hiking trails. Groups (only) can reserve sites with Recreation Resource Management at tel. 928/204-1698. It's on the north side of US 89A just west of the AZ 67 turnoff.

Jacob Lake Picnic Area is on the left 0.1 mile south on AZ 67.

Kaibab Camper Village overlooks the lake just 0.3 mile south on AZ 67 from US 89A, then west 0.7 mile; it's open May 15–October 15 with coin showers and a modem jack. Tent spaces and dry RV sites run $12 and sites with hookups cost $22; tel. 928/643-7804 or 800/525-0924 (reservations). Tent sites are usually available, though RVers should make reservations or arrive by noon.

Allen's Outfitters offers trail rides of one and two hours in the forest, half- and full-day trips to overlooks, and pack trips from about mid-May–early September at its stables 0.3 mile south on AZ 67 and year-round in Kanab; tel. 435/644-8150 or 435/689-1370.

Staff at the Forest Service's **Kaibab Plateau Visitor Center,** tel. 928/643-7298, in Jacob Lake provide information on the many viewpoints, trails, campgrounds, and historic sites in the Kaibab National Forest along the North Rim; they also issue backcountry permits for most areas of Grand Canyon National Park. Exhibits include a 3-D model of the Grand Canyon and wildlife displays. You can purchase books and maps. It's open daily 8 A.M.–5 P.M. from about mid-May–mid-Oct. and possibly later in the year with a shorter schedule; website: www.fs.fed.us/r3/kai.

Vermilion Cliffs

These sheer cliffs, a striking red, appear to burst into flames at sunrise and sunset. The cliffs dominate the northern horizon for many miles; a hilltop pullout 11 miles east of Jacob Lake on US 89A offers the best view. John Wesley Powell described them as "a long bank of purple cliffs plowed from the horizon high into the heavens."

San Bartolome Historic Site

Markers tell the story of the Dominguez-Escalante Expedition, which camped near here in 1776. Returning from a failed attempt to reach Monterey, California, the group struggled to find a route through the forbidding terrain to

Santa Fe. The site is signed on the north side of US 89A between Mileposts 557 and 558, about midway between Marble Canyon and Jacob Lake.

Cliff Dweller's Lodge

About 1890, White traders built an unusual trading post underneath a giant boulder. You can still see the old buildings beside the modern establishment. The lodge, tel. 928/355-2228 or 800/433-2543, offers rooms ($60 d and $72 d, less in winter), restaurant (American food for breakfast, lunch, and dinner), small store, and a gas station. It's on US 89A, nine miles west of Marble Canyon and 32 miles east of Jacob Lake.

Lee's Ferry Anglers Guides & Fly Shop, tel. 928/355-2261 or 800/962-9755, has guides and supplies for fishermen; website: www.leesferry.com.

Lees Ferry Lodge (Vermilion Cliffs)

The lodge, tel. 928/355-2231, has motel rooms ($45 s, $50 d) and a smoky restaurant (American food for breakfast, lunch, and dinner daily). It's on US 89A, three miles west of Marble Canyon and 38 miles east of Jacob Lake; website: www.leesferrylodge.com.

Badger Canyon-Marble Canyon Overlook

A dirt road leads to the edge of precipitous cliffs where these two canyons meet. The cold waters of the Colorado glide below. You may see river runners bouncing through Badger Creek Rapid or camped on the shore. Jackass Canyon meets Marble Canyon on the opposite side. There's no sign for the turnoff on US 89A, but it's on the left just 0.1 mile southwest (toward Jacob Lake) from Lees Ferry Lodge. Go through a gate and continue two miles to road's end. On the way you'll have views of Badger Canyon. Endangered cacti live here, so keep to the existing road and pullouts when driving or camping.

Marble Canyon Lodge

Major John Wesley Powell named the nearby section of Colorado River canyon for its smooth, marblelike appearance. The lodge, tel. 928/355-2225 or 800/726-1789, is on US 89A at the turnoff for Lees Ferry. You can stay in motel rooms ($54 s, $64–70 d), a cottage ($86 with four beds), and two-bedroom apartments ($134). Other amenities are a smoky restaurant (American food for breakfast, lunch, and dinner daily), store (Native American crafts, regional books, and supplies for camping, river-running, and fishing), post office, laundromat, coin showers, gas station, convenience store, and paved airstrip.

Marble Canyon Outfitters, tel. 928/355-2245 or 800/533-7339, offers guided trips and a shop for fishermen; website: www.leesferryflyfishing.com.

LEES FERRY

The Colorado River cuts one gorge after another as it crosses the high plateaus of southern Utah and northern Arizona. Settlers and travelers found the river a dangerous and difficult barrier until well into the 20th century. A break in the cliffs above Marble Canyon provided one of the few places where a road could be built to the water's edge. Until 1929, when Navajo Bridge finally spanned the canyon, vehicles and passengers had to cross by ferry. Zane Grey expressed his thoughts about this crossing—Lees Ferry—in *The Last of the Plainsmen* (1908):

I saw the constricted rapids, where the Colorado took its plunge into the box-like head of the Grand Canyon of Arizona; and the deep, reverberating boom of the river, at flood height, was a fearful thing to hear. I could not repress a shudder at the thought of crossing above that rapid.

The Dominguez-Escalante Expedition tried to cross at what's now known as Lees Ferry in 1776, but without success. The river proved too cold and wide to swim safely, and winds frustrated attempts to raft across. The Spaniards traveled 40 miles upriver into present-day Utah before finding a safe ford.

About 100 years later, Mormon leaders determined the Lees Ferry crossing to be the most convenient route for expanding Mormon settlements from Utah into Arizona. Jacob Hamblin led a failed rafting attempt in 1860, but he returned four years later and made it safely across.

Although Hamblin first recognized the value of this crossing, it now bears the name of John D. Lee, a colorful character who gained notoriety in the 1857 Mountain Meadows Massacre. One account of this unfortunate chain of events relates that Paiute, allied to the Mormons, attacked an unfriendly wagon train; Lee and fellow Mormons then joined in the fighting until all but the small children, too young to tell the story, lay dead.

When a federal investigation some years later uncovered Mormon complicity in the slaughter, the Mormon Church leaders, seeking to move Lee out of sight, asked him to start a regular ferry service on the Colorado River. This he did in 1872. One of Lee's wives remarked on seeing the isolated spot, "Oh, what a lonely dell," and thus Lonely Dell became the name of their ranch. Lee managed to succeed with the ferry service despite boat accidents and sometimes hostile Navajo, but eventually his past caught up with him. In 1877, authorities took Lee back to Mountain Meadows, where a firing squad and casket awaited.

Miners and farmers came to try their luck along the Colorado River and its tributaries. Charles Spencer, manager of the American Placer Company, brought in sluicing machinery, an amalgamator, and drilling equipment. In 1910 his company tried using mule trains to pack coal from Warm Creek Canyon, 15 miles upstream. When the mules

proved inadequate, company financiers shipped a 92-foot-long steamboat in sections from San Francisco. The boat, the *Charles H. Spencer,* performed poorly, burning almost its entire load of coal in just one roundtrip, and was used only five times. The boiler, decking, and hull can still be seen at low water on the shore upstream from Lees Ferry Fort (see below). Although Spencer's efforts to extract fine gold particles proved futile, he persisted in his prospecting here as late as 1965 and made an unsuccessful attempt to develop a rhenium mine.

The ferry service continued after Lee's departure, though fatal accidents occurred from

NAVAJO BRIDGE: THE OLD AND THE NEW

A new, wider bridge for traffic has replaced the old Navajo Bridge across Marble Canyon. The old bridge, admired for its design and beauty, has been preserved as a pedestrian path just upstream from the new one. Now you can enjoy a walk 470 feet above the water on the old bridge's 834-foot length. (Do not throw anything off the bridge, as even a small object can pick up lethal velocity from such a height and hurt boaters below.) A 1930s stone shelter built by the Civilian Conservation Corps and a new visitor center stand just west of the bridges. Indoor and outdoor exhibits illustrate the history and construction details of both structures. You'll find local travel information for the Grand Canyon and Glen Canyon National Recreation Area and a large selection of books, maps, videos, music (Native American and Southwest), and posters in the Navajo Bridge Interpretive Center; it's open daily 8 A.M.–5 P.M. from mid-April–mid-November. Navajo sell crafts on the old bridge's east end. Both ends of the old bridge have parking.

time to time. The last run took place in June 1928, while the bridge was going up six miles downstream. The ferry operator lost control in strong currents and the boat capsized; all three people aboard and a Model-T were lost. Fifty-five years of ferryboating had come to an end. Navajo Bridge opened in January 1929, an event hailed by the Flagstaff *Coconino Sun* as the "Biggest News in Southwest History."

Today, the Lees Ferry area and the canyon upstream belong to the Glen Canyon National Recreation Area. Grand Canyon National Park begins just downstream. Rangers of the National Park Service administer both areas.

Lonely Dell Ranch and Lees Ferry

You can tour old buildings, mining machinery, the ferry site, and trails in these two historic districts. A self-guided tour booklet, available on site as well as at the Carl Hayden Visitor Center at Glen Canyon Dam, identifies historic features and traces their backgrounds. A log cabin thought to have been built by Lee, root cellar, blacksmith shop, ranch house, orchards, and cemetery survive at Lonely Dell Ranch, a short distance up the Paria River. Historic buildings on the Colorado River include Lees Ferry Fort (built in 1874 to protect settlers from possible Indian attack, but used as a trading post and residence), a small stone post office (in use 1913–23), and structures occupied by the American Placer Company and the U.S. Geological Survey. A trail along the Colorado leads about one mile upstream to the main ferry site, now marked by ruins of ferrymen's stone houses. On the way you'll pass the partially submerged wreck of Spencer's steamboat.

A paved road to Lees Ferry turns north from US 89A just west of Navajo Bridge. Follow the road in 5.1 miles and turn left 0.2 mile for Lonely Dell Ranch Historic District or continue 0.7 mile on the main road to its end for Lees Ferry Historic District. The **ranger station** offers boating, fishing, and

hiking information and sells some books and maps but is open irregular hours; it's on the left 0.4 mile after the campground turnoff; tel. 928/355-2234.

Entry fees for Glen Canyon National Recreation Area, which can be paid at a self-service station half a mile in from US 89A, cost $10 per vehicle or $3 per cyclist or hiker for seven days; admission is free if you have Golden Eagle, Golden Age, or Golden Access card.

Spencer Trail

Energetic hikers climb this unmaintained trail for fine views of Marble Canyon from the rim 1,500 feet above the river. The ingeniously planned route switchbacks up sheer ledges above Lees Ferry. It's a moderately difficult hike to the top, three miles roundtrip; you should carry water. From Lees Ferry parking lot at the end of the road, follow the path through the historic district to the sign, then take the trail leading to the cliffs.

Cathedral Wash Route

This 2.5-mile roundtrip hike follows a narrow canyon to Cathedral Rapid and back. Park at the second pullout, overlooking the wash, on the road to Lees Ferry, 1.4 miles in from US 89A and three miles before the campground.

Boating and Fishing

Rainbow trout flourish in the cold, clear waters released from Lake Powell through Glen Canyon Dam. Special fishing regulations apply here and are posted. Anglers should be able to identify and must return to the river any of the endangered native fish—the Colorado pikeminnow, bonytail chub, humpback chub, and razorback sucker. There's a fish-cleaning station and parking area on the left just before the launch areas. At road's end, you'll reach a paved upriver launch site used by boaters headed toward Glen Canyon Dam; Grand Canyon river-running groups use the unpaved downriver launch area. Powerboats can travel 14.5 miles up Glen Canyon almost to the dam. The Park Service recommends a boat with a minimum 10-hp motor to negotiate the swift currents. Boating below Lees Ferry is prohibited without a permit from Grand Canyon National Park.

Campground

The $10 sites at Lees Ferry Campground have drinking water but no hookups or showers; there's usually space available. Campers can use showers and laundry facilities beside Marble Canyon Lodge. From US 89A, take Lees Ferry Road in 4.4 miles and turn left at the sign. A dump station is on the right on the main road, 0.4 mile past the campground turnoff. The National Park Service allows boat camping on the Colorado River above Lees Ferry only at the plentiful developed campsites. These sites lack piped water but are free. Remember to purify river water before drinking and pack out what you pack in.

PARIA CANYON—VERMILION CLIFFS WILDERNESS

The wild and twisting canyons of the Paria River and its tributaries offer a memorable adventure for experienced hikers. Silt-laden waters have sculpted the colorful canyon walls, revealing 200 million years of geologic history. You enter the 2,000-foot-deep gorge of the Paria in southern Utah, then hike 38 miles downstream to Lees Ferry in Arizona, where the Paria empties into the Colorado River. Besides the canyons, this 110,000-acre wilderness area protects colorful cliffs, giant natural amphitheaters, sandstone arches, and parts of the Paria Plateau. On top of the plateau, wonderful swirling patterns in sandstone hills, known as the "Coyote Buttes," enthrall visitors. The 1,000-foot-high, rosy-hued Vermilion Cliffs meet the mouth of Paria Canyon at Lees Ferry.

The river's name, sometimes spelled Pahreah, is Paiute for "muddy water."

History

Ancient petroglyphs and campsites indicate that ancestral Puebloan people traveled the Paria more than 700 years ago. They hunted mule deer and bighorn sheep while using the broad lower end of the canyon to grow corn, beans, and squash.

The Dominguez-Escalante Expedition, the first White people to see the Paria, stopped at its mouth in 1776. After John Lee began his Colorado River ferry service in 1872, he and others farmed the lower Paria Canyon. Though outlaws used it and prospectors came in search of gold, uranium, and other minerals, much of the Paria Canyon remained little visited.

In the late 1960s, the Bureau of Land Man-

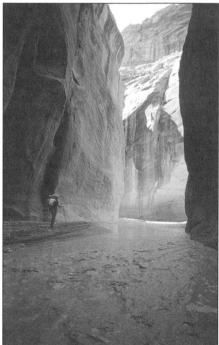

the Narrows of Paria Canyon

agement (BLM) organized a small expedition whose research led to protection of the canyon as a primitive area. The Arizona Wilderness Act in 1984 designated Paria Canyon a wilderness, together with parts of the Paria Plateau and Vermilion Cliffs. In 2000, the Arizona portion of the wilderness and surrounding lands became the 294,000-acre Vermilion Cliffs National Monument.

Hiking

You can hike Paria Canyon in four days, though it's better to have five or six because there are many river crossings, and you'll want to take side trips up some of the tributary canyons. The hike is considered moderately difficult. Hikers should have enough backpacking experience to be self-sufficient, as help may lie days away. Flash floods can race through the canyon, especially from July–September. Rangers will advise if they think danger exists, but they no longer close the canyon when storms threaten. The upper end contains narrow passages, particularly between Miles 4.2 and 9.0. Rangers suggest all hikers obtain up-to-date weather information. For safety in case of flood, one should register at White House, Buckskin, Wire Pass, or Lees Ferry Trailheads when entering or exiting the canyons.

All visitors need to take special care to minimize impact on this beautiful canyon. Check the BLM "Visitor Use Regulations" before you go. Rules include no campfires in the Paria and its tributaries, a pack-in/pack-out policy (including toilet paper!), and a latrine location at least 100 feet away from river and campsites. Hiking parties may not exceed 10 people.

The best times to travel along the Paria are mid-March–June and late September–November. May, especially Memorial Day weekend, is the most popular time. Winter hikers often complain of painfully cold feet. Wear shoes suitable for frequent wading; light fabric and leather boots or jungle boots work better than heavy leather hiking boots.

You can draw good drinking water from springs along the way—see the BLM's book noted below. It's best not to use river water because of possible chemical pollution from farms and ranches upstream. Normally the river flows only ankle deep, but can rise to waist-deep levels in the spring or after rainy spells. During thunderstorms, the river can roar up to 20 feet deep in the Paria Narrows, so heed weather warnings. Floods usually subside within 12 hours. Quicksand, most prevalent after flooding, is more a nuisance than a danger—rarely more than knee deep. Many hikers carry a walking stick for probing the opaque waters before crossing. Conditions can change dramatically after a flood, especially in the narrow sections of Paria, Buckskin, and Wire Pass canyons, so it's best to get the latest advice from BLM staff.

Permits and Information

Backpackers need to apply in advance for a permit that costs $5/person or dog per day. Day-hikers simply pay $5/person or dog at any of the trailheads for a pass that's good for all three canyons—Paria, Buckskin, and Wire Pass. Backpacking permits, Coyote Buttes permits, weather forecasts, and up-to-date information are available from BLM staff at the Paria Information Station, which is in Utah, 30 miles northwest of Page on US 89 near Milepost 21, on the south side of the highway just east of the Paria River. The station is open daily 8:30 A.M.–4:15 P.M. (Daylight Savings Time!) about mid-March–mid-Nov. and intermittently the rest of the year. Hikers can get drinking water at a faucet in front and see the current weather forecast. You can check Paria and Coyote Buttes dates by phone and obtain permits by mail by writing **Arizona Strip Interpretive Association,** 345 E. Riverside Dr., St. George, UT 84790; tel. 435/688-3246. Information and permits are also available from the Kanab Area Office, 318 N. 100 East, Kanab, Utah 84741, tel. 435/644-4600, open Mon.–Fri. 7:45 A.M.–4:30 P.M. year-round. An interactive Website shows available dates and gives reservation procedures at paria.az.blm.gov. The BLM's *Hiker's Guide to Paria Canyon* book ($8) has detailed maps and information.

Trailheads and Shuttle Services

Most hikers start from White House Trailhead, which lies two miles south of Paria Information Station on a dirt road near an old homestead site called White House Ruins, of which only rubble remains. You may camp here (pit toilets and picnic tables) for a $5 fee (up to five persons). The exit trailhead is at Lonely Dell Ranch near Lees Ferry, 44 miles southwest of Page via US 89 and 89A; vehicles can be left at the 14-day parking area.

The hike requires a 150-mile roundtrip car shuttle. You can make arrangements for someone else to do it for you, using either your car, or theirs. Staff at the Arizona Strip Interpretive Association, Paria Information Center, or BLM Kanab Resource District can supply you with a list of shuttle services.

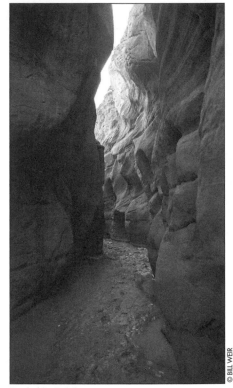

Buckskin Gulch

Wrather Canyon Arch

One of Arizona's largest natural arches lies about one mile up this side canyon off Paria Canyon. The massive structure has a 200-foot span. Veer right (southwest) at Mile 20.6 on the Paria hike. The mouth of Wrather Canyon, which is easily missed, and other points along the Paria are unsigned; you need to follow your map. No camping is allowed in this canyon.

Buckskin Gulch

This amazing Paria tributary—said to be the world's longest slot canyon—features convoluted walls hundreds of feet high, yet narrows to as little as four feet in width. In some places

the walls block out so much light that you'll think you're walking in a cave. Be *very* careful to avoid times of flash floods. Hiking can be strenuous, with rough terrain, deep pools of water, and log and rock jams that sometimes require the use of ropes.

You can descend into Buckskin from two trailheads, Buckskin and Wire Pass, both approached by a dirt road passable for cars in dry weather. The hike from Buckskin trailhead to the Paria River is 16.3 miles one-way and takes 6–8 or more hours. From Wire Pass Trailhead it's 1.7 miles to Buckskin Gulch, then 11.8 miles to the Paria. You can climb out to a safe camping place on a hazardous route—extremely hazardous if you're not an experienced climber—about halfway down Buckskin Gulch; this way out should not be counted on as an escape route. Carry enough water to last until you reach the mouth of Buckskin Gulch.

Wire Pass and upper Buckskin Canyons make a great day-hike loop—you can follow Buckskin 4.5 miles from its trailhead to the confluence of Wire Pass Canyon, then turn 1.7 miles up Wire Pass; you could then walk, do a car shuttle, or hitch the four miles by road back to Buckskin Trailhead. Only the last mile of Buckskin enters narrows on this loop, but all of this country has pretty scenery. Wire Pass Canyon, which is even narrower in spots than Buckskin, may have some ledges. Look for petroglyphs on the right at the lower end of Wire Pass. Try to allow time for exploration into the narrows below the confluence.

To reach these trailheads, go 4.9 miles west on US 89 from Paria Information Station to the unsigned House Rock Road (Road 700) between Mileposts 25 and 26, then turn south 4.5 miles to Buckskin or another 4 miles for Wire Pass. The Arizona border is just 1.2 miles farther, where you'll find the north end of the Arizona Trail at Stateline Trailhead; a tiny campground (no water) is here too. House Rock Road, signed in Arizona as Road 1065, continues 20 miles south to US 89A between Mileposts 565 and 566, near where the highway begins its climb to the Kaibab Plateau. California condor information panels 2.9 miles before US 89A tell of the birds' release site atop the Vermilion Cliffs nearby; an observer may be stationed here who will answer questions and let you take a look through a telescope.

Coyote Buttes

The secret is out on this colorful swirling sandstone atop the Paria Plateau! You've probably seen photos of these wonderful features, but not directions on how to reach them. The buttes lie mostly in Arizona south of Wire

the Wave at Coyote Buttes North

© BILL WEIR

Pass Canyon and have been divided into Coyote North and Coyote South. The famous "Wave" is in the north, so this region is the most popular. Once you get the required permit, BLM staff will give you a map and directions to the Wave, but you're then on your own, as the wilderness lacks signs. Even if you get permits by mail, it's worth dropping by the Paria Information Station for directions. The Wave is about six miles roundtrip and takes half a day, though there's more to see in the area. Photographers will find a wide-angle lens handy to take in the sweep of the curved rock. Both north and south areas have countless beauty spots to discover, so it's worth making a full day of it and carrying food and lots of water.

The BLM issues the required permits for Coyote Buttes, which are day-use only; there's a $5/person fee, and permit procedures are the same as for the Paria River. Permits sell out far ahead in spring and autumn—the best times to visit—and on weekends. If you don't have a permit but your schedule is flexible, try for a walk-in permit—check the procedure with BLM staff or on the website.

WESTERN GRAND CANYON

Only a small number of people may visit each area per day because the Navajo Sandstone rock here is so fragile. It can break if climbed on—causing damage to both the scenery and hikers' bones—so it's important to stay on existing hiking routes and wear soft-soled footwear. Hikers need to carry water and keep an eye out for rattlesnakes. Lightning storms occur most often in late summer but can appear at any time of year.

Trailhead access is off House Rock Road. You can reach Coyote North from Wire Pass Trailhead or the more difficult Notch Access, about two miles south of Wire Pass Trailhead. Coyote South requires 4WD for Paw Hole Access, 2.6 miles in, and Cottonwood Cove Access farther back; deep sand

may make these areas impassable during summer. You could walk in to Paw Hole but it would be a tough slog. BLM staff can advise on road conditions.

The Toadstools

An easy hike of about a mile roundtrip leads to these fanciful rock formations. From the Paria Information Station, drive east 1.5 miles on US 89 and look for the unsigned parking on the north side where power lines turn away from the highway between Mileposts 19 and 20. Go through the pedestrian gate and follow footprints up the valley to red and white balanced rocks; more can be seen if you continue around to the left. No permits or fees are needed.

Page

WESTERN GRAND CANYON

Until 1957, only sand and desert vegetation lay atop Manson Mesa in far northern Arizona, where Page now sits. In that year the U.S. Bureau of Reclamation decided to build a giant reservoir in Glen Canyon on the Colorado River. Glen Canyon Dam became one of the largest construction projects ever undertaken: the 710-foot-high structure created a lake covering 250 square miles with a shoreline of nearly 2,000 miles.

The town of Page, named by the Bureau of Reclamation for one of its commissioners, was born when workers set up prefabricated metal buildings for barracks, dining hall, and offices. Trailers rolled in, one serving as a bank, another as a school. Newly planted grass and trees brought a touch of green to the desert. The remote spot (elev. 4,300 ft.) gradually turned into a modern town with schools, businesses, and churches. Though small (pop. 9,500), it's the largest community close to Lake Powell and offers travelers a variety of places to stay and eat.

With the Arizona Strip to the west, Glen Canyon National Recreation Area to the north, and the Navajo Reservation to the east and south, Page makes a useful base for visiting all of these areas. The town overlooks Lake Powell and Glen Canyon Dam. Wahweap Resort and Marina's extensive services lie just six miles away.

SIGHTS AND HIKES

Powell Museum

This collection honors scientist and explorer John Wesley Powell. In 1869 Powell led the first expedition down the Green and Colorado River canyons, then ran the rivers a second time in 1871–72. It was he who named the most splendid section the Grand Canyon.

Old drawings and photographs illustrate Powell's life and voyages. Fossil and mineral displays interpret the thick geologic sections revealed by the canyons of the Colorado River system. Other exhibits contain pottery, baskets, weapons, and tools of Southwestern

PAGE

CARL HAYDEN VISITOR CENTER
GLEN CANYON DAM
To Wahweap and Kanab
89
Colorado River
TRAILHEAD FOR RIMVIEW AND NATURE TRAILS
20TH AVE
GRANDVIEW
RIMVIEW DR.
12TH AVE.
COURTYARD BY MARRIOTT
MCDONALD'S
AIRPORT
BEST DAM VIEW
CLUBHOUSE DR.
TERMINAL
N. 10TH AVE.
S. 10TH AVE.
DENNY'S
CLUBHOUSE
AERO AVE.
N. VISTA
SCENIC VIEW RD
LAKE
N. LAKE POWELL BLVD. /89L
89
POWELL
DR.
THUNDERBIRD AVE.
COLORADO ST.
SAGE AVE.
7TH ST.
TOWER BUTTE
9TH AVE.
8TH AVE.
GLEN CANYON GOLF AND COUNTRY CLUB
NATIONAL
NAVAJO
6TH AVE
SEE "DOWNTOWN PAGE" MAP
1ST AVE.
DATE
ELM
5TH AVE.
DR.
SUNRISE AVE.
GOLF
3RD AVE.
S.
NAVAJO
PAGE HIGH SCHOOL
CHURCH ROW
ASPEN ST.
N.
COURSE
S. LAKE POWELL BLVD./89L
TENNIS COURTS
PAGE PUBLIC LIBRARY
COPPERMINE RD.
GATEWAY PLAZA (WAL-MART, BASHAS', AND MANDARIN GOURMET RESTAURANT)
MOTEL 6
COMFORT INN
COCONINO COMMUNITY COLLEGE
MOON
To Flagstaff
89
HAUL RD.
PAGE-LAKE POWELL CAMPGROUND
NAVAJO VILLAGE
PALOMINO RD.
APPALOOSA RD.
MORGAN RD.
ELK RD.
CLYDESDALE RD.
BIG LAKE TRADING POST
PINTO RD.
98
To Antelope Canyon and Kayenta
98
FRONTAGE RD.
INDUSTRIAL RD.
MIKE'S WAY
To Leche-e

0   0.5 mi
0   0.5 km

© AVALON TRAVEL PUBLISHING, INC.

WESTERN GRAND CANYON

tribes, as well as memorabilia of early river runners, Page's early days, and Glen Canyon Dam. You can ask to see related videos and purchase regional books as well. Staff offer travel info and can book Lake Powell boat tours, all-day and half-day float trips, Antelope Canyon tours, and scenic flights.

In summer (June–Aug.), the museum is open Mon.–Fri. 8:30 A.M.–5:30 P.M.; spring and autumn hours are Mon.–Fri. 9 A.M.–5 P.M.; it's closed mid-December–mid-February. Admission is $1 adult, $.50 children

kindergarten–8th grade. The museum is in downtown Page at the corner of 6 N. Lake Powell Blvd. and N. Navajo Dr., tel. 928/645-9496 or 888/597-6873, website: www.powellmuseum.org.

Navajo Village

Navajo offer cultural programs about their beliefs and traditional skills from April–October at this living museum on the edge of town. **An Evening with the Navajo** begins with demonstrations of cooking, weaving, and sil-

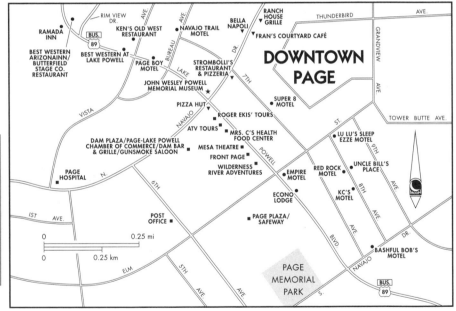

WESTERN GRAND CANYON

© AVALON TRAVEL PUBLISHING, INC.

versmithing. Your hosts will also explain features of the sweat lodge and the two types of hogans here. You'll enjoy a dinner of traditional foods, watch song and dance performances, and listen to campfire stories. The four-hour evening presentations cost $50 adults and $35 children 6–13 plus tax. You can also sign up for a shorter evening program or take a guided tour of the exhibits during the day. Call 928/660-0304 for information or check the website at website: www.navajovillage.net. Page/Lake Powell Chamber of Commerce and Powell Museum also sell tickets.

The Best Dam View

An excellent panorama of Glen Canyon Dam and the Colorado River can be enjoyed just west of town. It's reached via Scenic View Road behind Denny's Restaurant off US 89; turn west at the junction of US 89 and N. Lake Powell Blvd. or west beside the Glen Canyon N.R.A. headquarters building and turn at the sign for "scenic overlook." A short trail leads down to the best viewpoint.

Rimview Trail

An eight-mile trail for walkers, joggers, and cyclists encircles Page with many views of the surrounding desert and Lake Powell. The unpaved route generally follows the edge of the mesa and has some sandy and rocky sections that will challenge novice bike riders. If you find yourself more than 30 vertical feet below the mesa rim, you're off the trail. You can pick up a map from the chamber office. A popular starting point is at the short nature trail loop near Lake View School at N. Navajo Dr. and 20th Ave. in the northern part of town.

Antelope Canyon

You'll see photos around town of the beautifully convoluted red rock in this canyon, so narrow in places that you have to squeeze through. Sunshine reflects off the smooth

arch in Lower Antelope Canyon

© BILL WEIR

Horseshoe Bend

Navajo Sandstone to create extraordinary light and colors that entrance visitors. Light beams reach the floor of upper Antelope only at midday from May–August. Photographers, not wishing to spoil the effect of light and shadow in the dark interior with a flash, bring a tripod to help capture the infinite shapes and patterns.

Antelope Canyon has a wider upper section known as "Corkscrew" that's exceptionally user-friendly—it's an easy walk on the sandy floor all the way through. The narrower lower section has ladders and a bit of scrambling. The shallow wash in between that you see from the highway gives no hint of the marvels up or downstream. Both sections can easily be reached from Page by driving south on Coppermine Road or east on AZ 98 to the junction at Big Lake Trading Post, then continuing east one mile on AZ 98 toward the power plant. Turn right into the parking area for the upper canyon, or stay on AZ 98 just 0.15 mile farther and then turn left half a mile on paved Antelope Point Road for the lower

canyon. You'll pay $5 for a tribal entry permit—good for both sections—plus shuttle or entry fees. Sightseers can tour either section easily in an hour; photographers will probably wish to spend more time. The upper section has a $12.50 shuttle charge for the 3.5-mile drive to the trailhead and a one-hour visit; no walk-ins or private drive-ins are permitted. The shuttle cost increases to $17.50 for a two-hour visit, $22.50 for 3–4 hours, and $32.50 for all day. The lower canyon can be visited on self-guided walks of $12.50 plus the $5 entry fee. Children pay less. You can also take a guided excursion from Page that costs little more and may be more convenient.

The upper canyon ticket booth is usually open daily 8 A.M.–5 P.M. from April–October; you can also obtain Rainbow Bridge hiking permits here. The lower canyon closes by 4 P.M. For information and off-season access, call the Antelope Canyon Navajo Tribal Park at 928/698-2808; the office is 4 miles south of Page in Leche-e. From early April–late October, the canyon hours run on the Navajo

PAGE AREA CLIMATE

F° J F M A M J J A S O N D C°

ANNUAL
AVERAGE
69.8°F/69.8°C
46.5°F/8.1°C

ANNUAL
6.39"/14.2mm

——— MAXIMUM TEMPERATURE
——— MINIMUM TEMPERATURE

Reservation's daylight saving time (when it's 4 P.M. in Page, it's 5 P.M. at Antelope). Late starts also run the risk of canyon access closing early if business is slow. In winter (Nov.–March) you may need to telephone ahead to arrange a visit. Check the weather forecast before heading out, as slot canyons are deadly during a flash flood.

Horseshoe Bend View

The Colorado River makes a sharp bend below this spectacular viewpoint. Look for the parking area just west of US 89, 0.2 mile south of Milepost 545; it's 2.5 miles south of Page's Gateway Plaza. A three-quarter-mile trail (one way) leads from the parking over a sandy ridge

to the overlook. Photographers will find a wide-angle lens handy to take in the whole scene. Mornings have good light for pictures; afternoons can be dramatic if the sky is filled with clouds.

PRACTICALITIES

Accommodations

Nearly all Page motels lie on or near Lake Powell Blvd./Hwy 89L, a 3.25-mile loop that branches off the main highway. Page is a busy place in summer, however, and a call ahead is a good idea if you don't want to chase around town looking for vacancies. Expect to pay top dollar for views of the lake. The summer rates listed here drop in winter (Nov.–March).

The Eighth Ave. places lie in Page's "historic district," a quiet residential area two blocks off Lake Powell Boulevard. These apartments date back to 1958–59 when they housed supervisors and foremen for the dam; today some have been fixed up as pensions and motels.

Under $50

Lu Lu's Sleep EZZe Motel, 105 Eighth Ave., tel. 928/608-0273 or 800/553-6211, features some of the most luxurious rooms on this street, $43–59 d.

Red Rock Motel, 114 Eighth Ave., tel. 928/645-0062, has private baths and some kitchens plus two-bedroom suites at $39 s, $49 d and up; website: www.redrockmotel.com.

Uncle Bill's Place, 117 Eighth Ave., tel. 928/645-1224, provides a quiet garden in back and a choice of rooms with shared bath and kitchen ($30 s, $36–39 d) and private suites ($59–69 d and up); website: www.canyon-country.com/unclebill.

KC's Motel, 126 Eighth Ave., tel. 928/645-2947, offers rooms with shared bath at $36 d, private bath for $39 d, and two-bedroom units with private bath at $59–79 d.

Bashful Bob's Motel around the corner at 750 S. Navajo Dr., tel. 928/645-3919, offers mostly two-bedroom apartments, all with kitchens, $39–45 d; website: www.page.az.net/bashfulbobsmotel.

Navajo Trail Motel has rooms at two downtown locations and on the southern outskirts; contact the office for all three places at 800 Bureau downtown, where rooms are $35 s, $39 d; tel. 928/645-9508. The nearby motel at 630 Vista, behind Glen Canyon Steak House, costs $39 s, $44 d; the third unit is at 524 Haul Road, where rooms go for $35 s, $39 d.

$50–100

Courtyard by Marriott, 600 Clubhouse Dr., tel. 928/645-5000 or 800/321-2211, offers views, a restaurant, a pool, hot tub, exercise room, and adjacent 18-hole golf course, $94–109 d.

Best Western ArizonaInn, 716 Rim View Dr. and N. Lake Powell Blvd., tel. 928/645-2466 or 800/826-2718, provides fine views, swimming pool, adjacent restaurant, and continental breakfast, $89 d.

Best Western at Lake Powell, 208 N. Lake Powell Blvd., tel. 928/645-5988 or 800/528-1234, has mountain views, a pool, hot tub, and exercise room, $79–99 d.

Page Boy Motel, 150 N. Lake Powell Blvd., tel. 928/645-2416, offers a swimming pool, $45–49 d.

Empire Motel, 107 S. Lake Powell Blvd., tel. 928/645-2406 or 800/551-9005, features a swimming pool, $49 s, $54 d.

Econo Lodge, 121 S. Lake Powell Blvd., tel. 928/645-2488 or 800/553-2666, has a pool, $60 d.

Super 8 Motel, is at 75 S. Seventh Ave., tel. 928/645-2858 or 800/800-8000, $60 d.

Holiday Inn Express, 751 S. Navajo Dr., tel. 928/645-9000 or 800/HOLIDAY, offers two-bedded rooms, pool, hot tub, and continental breakfast, $79 d.

South from downtown, you'll find the **Motel 6,** 637 S. Lake Powell Blvd., tel. 928/645-5888 or 800/4MOTEL6, with a pool, $64–72 s, $70–78 d.

Next door, **Comfort Inn,** 649 S. Lake Powell Blvd., tel. 928/645-5858 or 800/228-5150, offers a pool, $70 s, $75 d.

Lake Powell Days Inn & Suites, 961 Hwy. 89, tel. 928/645-2800 or 877/525-3769, lies on the south edge of town beside US 89 with a pool and hot tub, $69–94 d.

Canyon Colors Bed & Breakfast, tel. 928/645-5979 or 800/536-2530, has a pool, patio, and fireplaces, $70–90 d; website: www.canyon-country.com/colors.

Sunrise View Bed & Breakfast, tel. 928/608-4763, offers a shaded backyard and views of lake and mountains, $85–95 d; website: www.canyon-country.com/sunrise.

$100–150

Quality Inn, 287 N. Lake Powell Blvd., tel. 928/645-8851 or 800/808-6682, features a swimming pool, restaurant, and great views over Lake Powell, $104–114 d.

Campgrounds

Page-Lake Powell Campground, tel. 928/645-3374, offers sites for tents ($17) and RVs ($20–26 w/hookups) with an indoor pool and hot tub, store, laundry, and showers; non-guests may use the showers or dump station for a small fee; the campground is 0.7 mile southeast of downtown on Coppermine Road. Other campgrounds, an RV park, and motels are in the Wahweap area (see "Wahweap" under "Glen Canyon National Recreation Area").

Food and Entertainment

Ken's Old West, 718 Vista Ave., tel. 928/645-5160, serves up Western dinners and music nightly; the menu includes steaks, prime rib, chicken, and seafood; closed Sun.–Mon. in winter. **Dam Bar & Grille,** 644 N. Navajo

Dr. in the Dam Plaza, tel. 928/645-2161, fixes steak, barbecue, seafood, pasta, and sandwiches daily for dinner; it also has a sports bar. The adjacent **Gunsmoke Saloon** features country bands and a variety of other music Wed.–Saturday. **Ranch House Grille,** 819 N. Navajo Dr., tel. 928/645-1420, is a handy place for breakfast and does lunch too; it's open daily. **Family Tree Restaurant,** in the Quality Inn at 287 N. Lake Powell Blvd., tel. 928/645-8851, offers a varied menu daily for breakfast and dinner; in summer, you can choose a breakfast buffet and a Friday seafood buffet dinner. **Butterfield Stage Co. Restaurant,** 704 Rim View Dr. next to Best Western ArizonaInn, tel. 928/645-2467, serves American food daily for breakfast, lunch, and dinner; dinner choices include steak, prime rib, and seafood. **Pepper's Restaurant** at the Courtyard by Marriott on 600 Clubhouse Dr., tel. 928/645-1247, offers American and continental cuisine with a Southwestern touch and is open daily for breakfast (also a buffet), lunch (buffet summer weekdays), and dinner. **Denny's,** 669 Scenic View Dr. (turn west at the US 89-N. Lake Powell Blvd. junction), tel. 928/645-3999, is open 24 hours and serves popular American fare for breakfast, lunch, and dinner.

Bella Napoli, 810 N. Navajo Dr., tel. 928/645-2706, offers fine Italian cuisine daily for dinner in summer and Mon.–Sat. for dinner the rest of the year; closed late Dec.–mid-February. **Strombolli's Restaurant & Pizzeria,** 711 N. Navajo Dr., tel. 928/645-2605, provides diners have a choice of indoor seating or the outdoor deck—a popular gathering spot for boaters in the summer; it's open daily for lunch and dinner except closed Dec.–March. **Pizza Hut,** 6 S. Lake Powell Blvd. in Dam Square, tel. 928/645-2455, serves pizza, spaghetti, and other Italian fare daily for lunch and dinner.

For Chinese cuisine, try **Mandarin Gourmet Restaurant** in Gateway Plaza, tel. 928/645-5516, open daily for lunch and dinner.

You can buy **groceries** at Safeway (Page Plaza at corner of S. Lake Powell Blvd. and Elm St.), Bashas' (Gateway Plaza), or at Mrs. C's Health Food Center (34 S. Lake Powell Blvd.). Catch movies at **Mesa Theatre,** 42 S. Lake Powell Blvd., tel. 928/645-9565.

Events

In March, fishermen test their skills in the Bullfrog Open bass tournament. On July 4th, there's a parade followed by fireworks that light the sky over Glen Canyon Dam. Mr. Burfel's Softball Tournament plays in September. Lake Powell Stampede, over Labor Day weekend in September, presents a rodeo, parade, arts and crafts, and entertainment. In October, Air Affaire takes off over Page with airplane acrobatics and parachutists. Bullfrog's Festival of Lights Parade takes place on the Saturday after Thanksgiving. In December, the Here Comes Santa Parade marks the holiday season in Page. Wahweap Festival of Lights Parade on Lake Powell glides by on the first Saturday.

For more information on any Lake Powell event, ask at the marina where it's held. To learn about other events, contact Page/Lake Powell Chamber of Commerce, tel. 928/645-2741.

Shopping, Services, and Recreation

Blair's Dinnebito Trading Post, 626 N. Navajo Dr., tel. 928/645-3008 or 800/644-3008, has the feel of an old-style trading post; if you're interested in its history, staff will show you old Native American works and mementos of the family's trading business in the exhibit rooms upstairs; website: www.blairstradingpost.com.

The **post office** is at 44 Sixth Ave.; tel. 928/645-2571. **Page Hospital,** tel. 928/645-2424, stands at the corner of 501 N. Navajo Dr. and Vista Avenue. In **emergencies**—police, fire, medical—dial 911.

City of Page Memorial Park, off S. Navajo Dr., offers tables, playground, and greenery in the middle of town.

Play **tennis** at the courts on S. Lake Powell Blvd. (Church Row). **Lake Powell National Golf Course,** tel. 928/645-2023, offers an 18-hole championship golf course that wraps around the west side of the mesa; turn in on Clubhouse Dr. adjacent to the Courtyard by Marriott. **Glen Canyon Golf and Country Club,** tel. 928/645-2715, has a 9-hole golf course west across US 89 from the 18-hole course. Both stay open all year. **Twin Finn Diving Center,** 811 Vista Ave., tel. 928/645-3114, offers a variety of diving and snorkeling activities, classes, and rentals; you can also rent both touring and sit-on-top kayaks; website: www.twinfinn.com.

Information

The **Page/Lake Powell Chamber of Commerce,** 644 N. Navajo Dr. in the Dam Plaza (Box 727, Page, AZ 86040), tel. 928/645-2741 or 888/261-7243, offers information about area sights and services and books lake and river tours, Antelope Canyon tours, and scenic flights; open Mon.–Sat. 8 A.M.–8 P.M. and Sun. 9 A.M.–6 P.M. from May 16–October 16, then Mon.–Fri. 9 A.M.–5 P.M. the rest of the year; website: www.pagelakepowellchamber.org.

The semi-circular **Page Public Library,** 479 S. Lake Powell Blvd., tel. 928/645-4270, rises impressively from the mesa rim with fine views; it has an Arizona/Native American collection and Internet computers; hours run Mon.–Thurs. 10 A.M.–8 P.M. and Fri.–Sat. 10 A.M.–5 P.M. **Front Page,** tel. 928/645-5333, has regional titles, general reading, and office supplies at 48 S. Lake Powell Boulevard.

Tours

You can obtain information and make reservations for many area tours through the Page/Lake Powell Chamber of Commerce or Powell Museum. Staff can tell you of additional tour operators, not listed here, that offer kayaking, cycling, or hiking trips.

Overland Canyon Tours, 18 N. Lake Powell Blvd., tel. 928/608-4072, heads to upper Antelope Canyon; a six-hour photographic tour visits "Canyon X," a relatively unknown and uncrowded slot canyon. **Roger Ekis' Antelope Canyon Tours,** 22 S. Lake Powell Blvd., tel. 928/645-9102 or 435/675-9109, goes to both upper and lower Antelope Canyon except in winter; website: www.antelopecanyon.com. **Grand Circle Adventures,** 48 S. Lake Powell Blvd. in Front Page, tel. 928/645-5594 or 800/835-8859, will take you to upper Antelope year-round. **Lake Powell Jeep Tours,** 104 S. Lake Powell Blvd., tel. 928/645-5501 or 866/645-5501, offers regular and photographers' tours to upper Antelope year-round; website: www.jeeptour.com.

ATV Tours, 26 S. Lake Powell Blvd., tel. 928/645-9557 or 800/962-9706, takes visitors on guided ATV tours year-round in the Page and Kaibab Plateau areas; beginners receive instruction; website: www.atvtours.net.

Wilderness River Adventures, 50 S. Lake Powell Blvd., tel. 928/645-3279 or 800/528-6154, offers raft trips down the Colorado River from just below Glen Canyon Dam to Lees Ferry, traveling over 15 miles of smooth-flowing water through the beautiful canyon of Navajo Sandstone. You'll stop to inspect some fine petroglyphs, and you're likely to see condors, blue herons, ducks, and other birds. Half-day trips leave once or twice daily March–Oct., weather permitting; the cost is $55 adults, $47 children 12 and under. All-day trips have more time on the water and include a lunch buffet; they run May 15–Sept. 15 and cost $77 adults, $69 children 12 and under.

Classic Helicopter Tours, tel. 928/645-5356, takes to the air with a variety of tours: 10 minutes for Tower Butte ($39), 15 minutes for Tower Butte & Antelope Creek ($59), about 30 minutes for Rainbow Bridge ($95), and 50–55 rafting the Colorado River through Glen Canyon

minutes to Rainbow Bridge and Escalante ($160); there's a four-person minimum; website: www.helicoptours.com. **Boat tours** to Rainbow Bridge and other destinations leave from nearby Wahweap Marina; see below.

Transport
Great Lakes Aviation operates daily scheduled flights south to Phoenix and northeast to Moab and denver; make reservations with United Airlines, 800/241-6522, or visit www.greatlakesav.com.

Wahweap Lodge operates **Page Shuttle,** tel. 928/645-2433, frequently to Page and the airport. Most area motels also provide transportation for guests to and from the airport. **R&S Pickup & Delivery,** tel. 928/645-0069, runs a shuttle van to area cities. **Avis,** tel. 928/645-2024 or 800/331-1212, rents cars at the airport.

Glen Canyon National Recreation Area

This vast recreation area covers 1.25 million acres, most of which spreads northeast into Utah. Lake Powell is the centerpiece, surrounded by beautiful canyon country. Just a handful of roads approach the lake, so you'll need to go by boat or on foot to truly explore this unique land of water and rock. The recreation area also includes a beautiful remnant of Glen Canyon in a 15-mile section of the Colorado River from Glen Canyon Dam to Lees Ferry. As big as the lake is, it comprises only 13 percent of the vast Glen Canyon National Recreation Area—there's much more to discover!

Rainbow Bridge National Monument— 50 miles uplake from the dam—holds the world's largest natural bridge; it's easily reached on boat tours from Wahweap or Bullfrog or by your own boat. You can also hike in on a spectacular trail; see below. The Carl Hayden Visitor Center has information on Rainbow Bridge.

WESTERN GRAND CANYON

Entry Fees

Visits to most areas now cost $10 per vehicle or $3 per cyclist or hiker for seven days—free if you have a Golden Eagle, Golden Age, or Golden Access card; an annual pass to the recreation area is $20. Motorized boats are an extra $10, then $4 for each additional one; an annual boat pass runs $20. Admission to the Carl Hayden Visitor Center is still free.

Climate

Summer, when temperatures rise into the 90s and 100s, is the busiest season for swimming, boating, and water-skiing. Visits during the rest of the year can be enjoyable, too, though more conducive to sightseeing, fishing, and hiking. Spring and autumn are the best times to enjoy the backcountry. Winter temperatures drop to highs in the 40s and 50s, with freezing nights and the possibility of snow. Lake surface temperatures range from a comfortable 80°F in August to a chilly 45°F in January. Chinook winds can blow day and night from February–May. Thunderstorms in late summer bring strong, gusting winds with widely scattered rain showers. Annual precipitation averages about seven inches.

Geology, Flora, and Fauna

Deposits of ancient deserts, oceans, and rivers formed the colorful rock layers that you see rising above the lake's surface. Uplift of the Colorado Plateau, beginning about 60 million years ago, started a cycle of erosion that has carved canyons and created delicately balanced rocks and graceful natural arches and bridges.

The desert comes right to the edge of the water, because fluctuating lake levels prevent plant growth along the shore. Common plants of this high-desert country include prickly pear and hedgehog cacti, rabbitbrush, sand sagebrush, blackbrush, cliffrose, mariposa and sego lilies, globemallow, Indian paintbrush, evening primrose, penstemon, and Indian rice grass. Pinyon pine and juniper trees grow on the high plateaus. Springs and permanent streams support sandbar willow, tamarisk, cattail, willow, and cottonwood. Look for hanging gardens of maidenhair fern, columbine, and other water-loving plants in small alcoves high on the sandstone walls.

Most animals are secretive and nocturnal; you're most likely to see them in early morning or in the evening. Local mammals include desert bighorn sheep, pronghorns, mule deer, mountain lions, coyotes, red and gray foxes, ringtail cats, spotted and striped skunks, bobcats, badgers, river otters, beavers, prairie dogs, Ord kangaroo rats, black-tailed jackrabbits, several species of squirrels and chipmunks, and many species of mice and bats. Types of lizards you might spot sunning on a rock include collared, side-blotched, desert horned, and chuckwalla. Snake species include the common kingsnake, gopher snake, striped whipsnake, western rattlesnake, and western diamondback rattlesnake.

Birds stopping by on their migratory routes include American avocet, Canada goose, and teal. Others, such as blue heron, snowy egret, and bald eagle, come for the winter. Birds in residence all year are American merganser, mallard, canyon wren, pinyon jay, common raven, red-tailed and Swainson's hawks, great horned and long-eared owls, peregrine and prairie falcons, and the golden eagle. The giant California condors, recently released in the area, have been spotted in Glen Canyon downstream of the dam.

Recreation at Lake Powell

Boating: If you don't have your own craft, Wahweap and other marinas will rent you a boat for fishing, water-skiing, or houseboating. Boat tours visit Rainbow Bridge and other destinations from Wahweap, Bullfrog, and Halls Crossing Marinas. Sailboats find the steadiest breezes in Wahweap, Padre, Halls, and Bullfrog Bays, where spring winds average 15–20 knots. Kayaks and canoes can be used in the more protected areas. All boaters need to be alert for approaching storms that can bring wind gusts up to 60 mph. Waves on open expanses of the lake are sometimes steeper than ocean waves and can exceed six feet from trough to crest. Marinas and bookstores sell Lake Powell navigation maps.

Fishing: You'll need an Arizona fishing license for the southern five miles of Lake Powell and a Utah license for the rest. Get licenses and information from marinas on the water or from sporting goods stores in Page. Anglers can catch bass (largemouth, smallmouth, and striped), walleye, channel catfish, black crappie, carp, and bluegill. Wahweap has a swimming beach (no lifeguards), and boaters can find their own remote spots.

Hiking: Hikers can choose between easy day trips or long wilderness backpack treks. The canyons of the Escalante in Utah rate among America's premier hiking areas. Other good areas within or adjacent to Glen Canyon N.R.A. include Rainbow Bridge National Monument, Paria Canyon, Dark Canyon, and Grand Gulch. You'll find descriptions of these last two places as well as Escalante in *Moon Handbooks: Utah*. National Park Service staff at the Carl Hayden Visitor Center and the Bullfrog Visitor Center can suggest trips and supply trail descriptions. Several guidebooks to Lake Powell offer detailed hiking, camping, and boating information. Most of the canyon country near Lake Powell remains wild and little explored—hiking possibilities are limitless. Be sure to carry plenty of water.

Mountain Biking: Cyclists can head out on many back roads. The visitor center has a list of possibilities.

Scuba: Divers can visit the canyon cliffs and rock sculptures beneath the surface. Visibility runs 30–40 feet in late Aug.–Nov., the best season, and there's less boat traffic then. In other seasons, visibility can drop to 10–20 feet.

Packing It Out

Much of the revenue from the fees has gone toward improving water quality and cleaning up the shore. Visitors can help by packing out all trash. Also, anyone camping within one-quarter mile of the lake must have a container (not plastic bags) for solid human wastes unless a toilet is available on the beach or on your own boat. Eight "restrooms/pump-outs/dump stations," shown on maps, are located along the lake between Warm Creek Bay (13 miles from the dam) and Forgotten Canyon (106 miles from the dam).

LAKE POWELL

Of all the artificial lakes in the United States, only Lake Mead, farther downstream, has a greater water-storage capacity. Lake Powell boasts a shoreline of 1,960 miles and holds enough water to cover the state of Pennsylvania a foot deep. Bays and coves offer nearly limitless opportunities for exploration by boaters. Only the southern part extends into Arizona—Glen Canyon Dam, Wahweap Resort and Marina, Antelope and Navajo Canyons, and the lower parts of Labyrinth, Face, and West Canyons. Lake Powell's surface elevation fluctuates an average of 20–30 feet through the year (fluctuation has reached 59 feet), peaking in July; it reaches 3,700 feet when full. The Carl Hayden Visitor Center, perched beside the dam, offers tours of the dam, related exhibits, and an information desk for the Glen Canyon National Recreation Area.

GLEN CANYON DAM

Construction workers labored from 1956–64 to build this giant concrete structure. It stands 710 feet high above bedrock, the top measuring 1,560 feet across. Thickness ranges from 300 feet at the base to just 25 feet at the top. As part of the Upper Colorado River Storage Pro-

© BILL WEIR

Glen Canyon Dam from the Colorado River

WESTERN GRAND CANYON

ject, the dam provides water storage (its main purpose), hydroelectricity, flood control, and recreation on Lake Powell. Eight giant turbine generators churn out a total of 1,150,000 kilowatts at 13,800 volts. Vertigo victims shouldn't look down when driving across Glen Canyon Bridge, just downstream of the dam. The cold green waters of the Colorado River emerge 700 feet below.

Conservationists deplore the loss of remote and beautiful Glen Canyon, buried today beneath Lake Powell, and call for the removal of the dam. That's very unlikely in the near future, so for now, only words, pictures, and memories remind us of Glen Canyon's lost wonders.

Carl Hayden Visitor Center and Dam Tours

Photos, paintings, and video programs in the visitor center present various features of the Glen Canyon National Recreation Area, in-

cluding Lake Powell and the construction of the dam. A giant relief map helps you visualize the rugged terrain surrounding the lake; look closely and you'll spot Rainbow Bridge. Guided one-hour tours visit the top of the dam, tunnels, the generating room, and the transformer platform; they depart daily every 30 or 60 minutes with the first tour at 8:30 A.M. and the last at 3:30 P.M. (4:30 P.M. Memorial Day–Labor Day). No purses or bags may be taken on the tours nor are there storage lockers. Senator Carl Hayden, a major backer of water development in the West, served as an Arizona member of Congress from 1912–69, a record 57 consecutive years.

Staff operate an information desk where you can find out about boating, fishing, camping, and hiking in the immense Glen Canyon National Recreation Area, or you can write P.O. Box 1507, Page, AZ 86040, tel. 928/608-6404; website: www.nps.gov/glca. The Glen Canyon Natural History Association sells a variety of books on the recreation area and its environs. A gift shop in the visitor center building sells souvenirs, snacks, and postcards; website: www.pagelakepowell.com.

The Carl Hayden Visitor Center is open daily 8 A.M.–7 P.M. in summer and 8 A.M.–5 P.M. the rest of the year. Tours, exhibits, and movies are free. In summer, you can attend an evening program most nights at nearby Wahweap Campground amphitheater.

MARINAS

The **National Park Service** provides public boat ramps and ranger offices at most of the marinas. Rangers know current boating and back-road conditions, primitive camping areas, and good places to explore. **Lake Powell Resorts & Marinas** operates marina services, boat rentals, boat tours, accommodations, RV parks, and restaurants; for information and reservations (strongly recommended in summer) write P.O. Box 56909, Phoenix, AZ 85079, call 800/528-6154 or 602/278-8888 in greater Phoenix, or fax 602/331-5258; website: www.visitlakepowell.com. To make reservations seven days or fewer in advance, contact each marina or resort directly. All the marinas stay open year-round; you can avoid crowds and peak prices by arriving in autumn, winter, or spring. Private or chartered aircraft can fly to Page Airport, Bullfrog's small airstrip, and Halls Crossing's large airstrip.

Wahweap

The name means Bitter Water in the Ute language. Wahweap Lodge and Marina, Lake Powell's largest, offers complete boaters' services and rentals, deluxe accommodations, an RV park, and fine dining. Wahweap lies seven miles northwest of Page; turn right on Lake Shore Dr. about 0.7 mile past the visitor center. Fee stations on the way in collect the entry charge for Glen Canyon National Recreation Area.

Wahweap Lodge offers swimming pools and several types of rooms—many with lake views—at $155 d ($165 d lake view) April–Oct. and $109 d ($116 d lake view) in winter. The lodge's fine-dining restaurant, the Rainbow Room, features a panoramic view for its daily breakfast, lunch, and dinner; in summer there's live entertainment and dancing. The nearby Navajo Room serves buffets for breakfast and lunch in summer. A cafe serves pizza, subs, and salads daily in summer. Just off the lobby lie a boat tour desk and a large gift shop (books, Native American crafts, and souvenirs). Contact Lake Powell Resorts & Marinas for reservations at P.O. Box 56909, Phoenix, AZ 85079, tel. 800/528-6154 or 602/278-8888 in greater Phoenix, fax 602/331-5258; website: www.visitlakepowell.com. You can also reach Wahweap Lodge & Marina at P.O. Box 1597, Page, AZ 86040, tel. 928/645-2433.

Lake Powell Motel is on US 89 opposite the Wahweap North Entrance, four miles northwest of Glen Canyon Dam; rooms cost $89 d; closed in winter; call 928/645-2477 or contact Lake Powell Resorts & Marinas for reservations

An **RV park** with coin showers and laundry costs $23 with hookups ($16 in winter). **Wahweap Campground** is operated first-come, first-served by the concessionaire; the $15 sites have drinking water but no showers or hookups. Evening **interpretive programs** take place here most days in the summer. Campers may use the pay showers and laundry at the RV park. Turnoffs for the RV park, campground, a free picnic area, and a fish-cleaning station lie between Wahweap Lodge and Stateline, 1.3 miles northwest of the lodge. Beyond the Stateline area, you'll come to the picturesque **Coves Day-Use Area,** set on low white bluffs overlooking the lake and a few beaches. You'll find public boat ramps just past the lodge and at Stateline. You can obtain maps and brochures from the **Wahweap**

WESTERN GRAND CANYON

Ranger Station (usually unstaffed) near the picnic area and at Carl Hayden Visitor Center.

Primitive camping—outhouses but no drinking water—costs $6 per vehicle at **Lone Rock** in Utah, six miles northwest of Wahweap off US 89. Boaters may also camp along the lakeshore, but not within one mile of developed areas.

The marina offers seven **lake tours,** ranging from an hour-long paddle-wheel cruise around Wahweap Bay ($11 adults, $8 children 2–12) to an all-day trip to Rainbow Bridge, 50 miles away ($88 adults, $58 children 2–12). Half-day trips to Rainbow Bridge cost $63 adults, $43 children 2–12. The other tours are a 90-minute Antelope Canyon cruise, two-and-a-half-hour Canyon Explorer/Navajo Tapestry tour, two-hour sunset cruise, and three-hour dinner cruise. **Boat rentals** at Stateline include kayak, fishing, runabout, patio, and a variety of houseboats. You can rent fishing gear and water skis, too.

Dangling Rope

This floating marina lies 42 miles uplake from Glen Canyon Dam. The only access is by boat. Services include a ranger station, store, minor boat repairs, gas dock, and sanitary pump-out station. A dangling rope left behind in a nearby canyon, perhaps by uranium prospectors, prompted the name. The Rainbow Bridge dock lies 10 miles farther uplake in Bridge Canyon, a tributary of Forbidding Canyon.

San Juan

You can hand-launch boats at **Clay Hills Crossing** at the upper end of the San Juan Arm. An unpaved road that requires a high-clearance vehicle branches 11 miles southwest from UT 276 to the lake; don't attempt the road after rains. River-runners on the San Juan often take out here, but no facilities are provided. Boat access to the lake is sometimes blocked at low water by a bar of sediment dropped by the San Juan

River as it enters Lake Powell. At high water the bar is covered.

Halls Crossing/Bullfrog Ferry

The *John Atlantic Burr* ferry can accommodate vehicles of all sizes as well as passengers for the short 20-minute crossing between these marinas. Halls Crossing and Bullfrog Marinas lie on opposite sides of Lake Powell about 95 lake miles from Glen Canyon Dam, roughly midway up the length of the lake. Highway UT 276 connects both marinas with UT 95. The ferry's daily schedule has six roundtrips from May 15–September 30 and four roundtrips the rest of the year, no reservations needed. You can pick up a schedule at either marina. Service is suspended for a brief time each winter for maintenance; signs at the UT 276 turnoffs warn you when the ferry is closed.

Halls Crossing

In 1880, Charles Hall built the ferry used by the Hole-in-the-Rock pioneers who crossed the Colorado River to settle in southeastern Utah. The approach roads were so bad, however, that in 1881 Hall moved the ferry 35 miles upstream to present-day Halls Crossing. Business remained slow, and Hall quit running the ferry in 1884.

Arriving at Halls Crossing by road, you first pass a small store offering **three-bedroom units** ($180 up to six persons April–late Sept., $125 off season), an **RV park** ($23 with hookups in summer, $16 off season), and gas pumps. The store may close in winter, but services are still available—ask at the trailer office next door. Coin-operated showers and laundry at the RV park are also open to the public. The separate campground just beyond and to the left offers sites with good views of the lake, drinking water, and restrooms for $12. A half mile farther down the main road are the boat ramp and **Halls Crossing Marina.** The marina features a larger store with groceries and fishing and boating supplies, tours to Rainbow Bridge, a boat rental office, a gas dock, slips, and storage. The ranger station is nearby, though rangers are usually out on patrol; look for ranger vehicles in the area if the office is closed.

Contact Lake Powell Resorts & Marinas for accommodations, boat rental, and tour reservations at P.O. Box 56909, Phoenix, AZ 85079, tel. 800/528-6154 or 602/278-8888 in greater Phoenix, fax 602/331-5258; website: www.visitlakepowell.com. You can also reach the marina at P.O. Box 5101, Lake Powell, UT 84533, tel. 435/684-7000.

Stabilized ancestral Puebloan ruins at **Defiance House** in Forgotten Canyon make a good boating destination 12 miles uplake; a sign marks the beginning of the trail to the ruins.

Bullfrog

Before the days of Lake Powell, Bullfrog Rapids offered boaters a fast and bumpy ride. Today, Bullfrog Marina rivals Wahweap in its extensive visitor facilities. When arriving, you'll come first to the **visitor center** on the right, open daily 8 A.M.–5 P.M. April–Oct.; tel. 435/684-7400. The **clinic** is here too; it's open mid-May–mid-October 9:30 A.M.–6 P.M.; tel. 435/684-2288. Next you'll see a large **campground** on the left; the $13 charge includes drinking water and restrooms. Continue on the main road to a junction, where a service station offers repairs and supplies. Continue straight at the junction for a picnic area and the boat ramp, or turn right at the service station for Defiance House Lodge and Restaurant, Trailer Village, Bullfrog Painted Hills RV Park, and Bullfrog Marina.

Defiance House Lodge offers luxury accommodations for $110 d ($120 d with a lake view) April–Sept. and $77 d ($84 d with a lake view) in winter and the **Anasazi Restaurant** (open daily for breakfast, lunch, and dinner). The front desk at the lodge also offers boat tours and handles **three-bedroom**

units and an **RV park,** both nearby with the same rates as at Halls Crossing. Showers, laundry, a convenience store, and post office are at **Trailer Village.** The RV park also has showers. Ask rangers for directions to primitive camping areas at Upper Bullfrog and Stanton Creek near Bullfrog Bay; these cost $6 per vehicle.

All-day **Rainbow Bridge tours** usually leave daily from April 15–October 31 and stop on request to pick up passengers at Halls Crossing Marina; call for dates in winter. The cost is $88 adults, $58 children 2–12. **Canyon Explorer/Navajo Tapestry tours** spend two and a half hours in nearby canyons during the same season from both marinas at $32 adults, $24 children 2–12. **Escalante Canyon excursions** visit this canyon on half-day trips from both marinas for $63 adults, $43 children 2–12. **Bullfrog Resort & Marina** offers boat rentals, gas dock, slips, storage, and a store. Contact Lake Powell Resorts & Marinas for accommodations, boat rental, and tour reservations at P.O. Box 56909, Phoenix, AZ 85079; tel. 800/528-6154 or 602/278-8888 in greater Phoenix, fax 602/331-5258; website: www.visitlakepowell.com. Contact Bullfrog Resort & Marina at P.O. Box 4055-Bullfrog, Lake Powell, UT 84533, tel. 435/684-3000.

Hite

In 1883, Cass Hite came to Glen Canyon in search of gold. He found a few nuggets at a place later named Hite City, setting off a small gold rush. Hite and some of his relatives operated a small store and post office, the only services available for many miles.

Travelers wishing to cross the Colorado River here faced the difficult task of swimming their animals across. Arthur Chaffin put through the first road and opened a ferry service in 1946. The Chaffin Ferry served uranium prospectors and adventurous motorists until the lake backed up to the spot in

WESTERN GRAND CANYON

1964. A steel bridge now spans the Colorado River far upstream; Cass Hite's store and the ferry site lie underwater about five miles downlake from Hite Marina.

The uppermost marina on Lake Powell, Hite lies 141 lake miles from Glen Canyon Dam. From here boats can continue uplake to the mouth of Dark Canyon in Cataract Canyon at low water or into Canyonlands National Park at high water. Hite tends to be quieter than the other marinas and is favored by anglers. The turnoff for the marina from UT 95 lies between Hanksville and Blanding. On the way in, you'll find a small **store** with gas pumps, **three-bedroom units** (same rates as at Halls Crossing), and a primitive **campground** (no drinking water, $6). Primitive camping is also available nearby off UT 95 at Dirty Devil, Farley Canyon, White Canyon, Blue Notch, and other locations for $6. **Hite Marina,** at the end of the access road, features boat rentals (fishing, ski, and houseboat), slips, storage, gas dock,

and a small store. Hikers can make arrangements with the marina for drop-offs and pick-ups at Dark Canyon. A **ranger station,** tel. 435/684-2457, is occasionally open.

Contact Lake Powell Resorts & Marinas for accommodations and boat rentals at P.O. Box 56909, Phoenix, AZ 85079; tel. 800/528-6154 or 602/278-8888 in greater Phoenix, fax 602/331-5258; website: www.visitlake-powell.com. Reach Hite Marina at P.O. Box 501-Hite, Lake Powell, UT 84533, tel. 435/684-2278.

RAINBOW BRIDGE NATIONAL MONUMENT

Rainbow Bridge forms a graceful span 290 feet high and 275 feet wide; the Capitol building in Washington, D.C., would fit neatly underneath. The easiest way to Rainbow Bridge is by boat tour on Lake Powell from Wahweap, Bullfrog, or Halls Crossing Marinas.

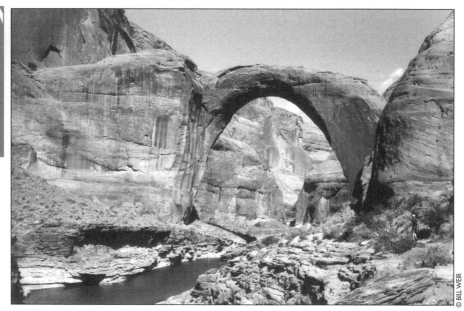

Rainbow Bridge

© BILL WEIR

The more adventurous can hike to the bridge from the Cha Canyon Trailhead (just north across the Arizona-Utah border on the east side of Navajo Mountain) or from the Rainbow Lodge ruins (just south of the Arizona-Utah border on the west side of Navajo Mountain). Rugged trails from each point wind through highly scenic canyons, meet in Bridge Canyon, then continue two miles to the bridge. The hike on either trail, or a loop with both (a car shuttle is needed), is 26–28 miles roundtrip. Hikers must be experienced and self-sufficient, as these trails cross a wilderness. Because the trails are unmaintained and poorly marked, hikers should consult a Navajo Mountain (Utah) 15-minute topo map or the newer 7.5-minute Navajo Begay and Chaiyahi Flat maps.

No camping is allowed at Rainbow Bridge and no supplies are available. You may camp a half mile east of the bridge at Echo camp. The Dangling Rope Marina and National Park Service ranger station are 10 miles away, by water only. The best times to go are April–early June, September, and October. Winter cold and snow discourage visitors, and summer is hot and can bring hazardous flash floods. The National Park Service offers "Hiking to Rainbow Bridge" trail notes; write Glen Canyon N.R.A., P.O. Box 1507, Page, AZ 86040, tel. 928/608-6404; website: www.nps.gov/rabr.

The National Park Service cannot issue hiking permits to Rainbow Bridge. Obtain the required tribal hiking permit ($5 for one person, $10 group of 2–10, $20 group of 11 or more) and camping permit ($2 per person per night) from the Cameron Visitor Center/Ranger Station at P.O. Box 459, Cameron, AZ 86020, tel. 928/679-2303, fax 928/679-2330; or from the Navajo Parks and Recreation Department, P.O. Box 9000, Window Rock, AZ 86515, tel. 928/871-6647 or 871-6635. Both offices are open Mon.–Fri. about 8 A.M.–5 P.M.; the Cameron office may extend its hours to daily 7 A.M.–6 P.M. from Memorial Day–Labor Day weekends. Allow six weeks for permit processing. In the Page area, permits are available at the upper Antelope Canyon ticket booth (usually open daily 8 A.M.–5 P.M. from April–October) and the Antelope Canyon Navajo Tribal Park office, tel. 928/698-2808, four miles south of Page in Leche-e.

The only road access to the Navajo Mountain area is Indian Route 16 from AZ 98, between Page and Kayenta. To reach the east trailhead, drive north 32 miles on Indian Route 16 past Inscription House Trading Post to a road fork, and then turn right six miles to Navajo Mountain Trading Post. Continue on the main road 6.5 miles (go straight at the four-way junction) to an earthen dam. Drive straight across the dam, take the left fork after a half-mile, and then go 1.6 miles to Cha Canyon Trailhead at the end of the road.

You can reach the west trailhead by driving north 32 miles on Indian Rt. 16 to the road fork, then turning left about six miles to the Rainbow Lodge ruins. Always lock vehicles and remove valuables at trailheads. Because Navajo Mountain is sacred to the Navajo, you probably won't get permission to climb it; check with the Navajo Parks Department in Window Rock.

Northeastern Arizona

Introduction

Ancient cultural traditions of Native Americans—ways of life that have survived to the present—make this region a special place. The hardworking Hopi have lived here longest. Ruins, occupied by their ancestors as long ago as 1,500 years, lie scattered over much of northeastern Arizona and adjacent states. The once warlike and greatly feared Navajo came relatively late, perhaps 500–700 years ago. Today, Hopi and Navajo welcome

visitors who respect tribal customs and laws. Here you'll have an opportunity to glimpse a unique way of life in a land of rare beauty.

THE LAND

Multihued desert hills, broad mesas, soaring buttes, vast treeless plains, and massive mountains give an impression of boundless space. The Colorado Plateau, which averages 4,500–7,000 feet in elevation, covers all of northeastern Arizona. Several

Canyon del Muerto and Chuska Mountains

© BILL WEIR

NORTHEASTERN ARIZONA HIGHLIGHTS

Navajo and Hopi lands: Visitors can experience the cultures of these two dynamic, yet very different, Native American peoples.

Navajo National Monument: Two large prehistoric cliff dwellings stand amazingly well preserved, and you can hike to them.

Monument Valley: Towering buttes and pinnacles create an enchanting landscape.

Canyon de Chelly National Monument: Exceptionally beautiful canyons preserve both prehistoric cliff dwellings and traditional Navajo life.

Hopi Country: Centuries-old villages seem to grow out of the mesa tops, where you may be fortunate enough to watch dancers perform religious ceremonies.

pine-forested ranges rise above the desert near Arizona's borders with Utah and New Mexico. Navajo Mountain, just across the border in Utah, is the highest peak in the area at 10,388 feet. Nearby you'll find Rainbow Bridge, the world's highest natural stone span over water. You can reach the bridge by boat on Lake Powell or by a spectacular 26–28-mile roundtrip hike. The beautiful canyons in Navajo and Canyon de Chelly National Monuments also offer excellent scenery and hiking.

Climate

Expect warm to hot summers and moderate to cold winters. Spring and autumn are the ideal times to visit, especially for hiking, though winds in March and April can kick up dust and sand. Afternoon thunderstorms frequently build up from early July–early September. Showers usually pass quickly, but flash floods pose a danger in low-lying areas.

HISTORY

Indian Reservations

In 1878 the federal government began ceding to the Navajo land that has since grown into a giant reservation spreading from northeastern Arizona into adjacent New Mexico and Utah. The Navajo Nation, with more than 200,000 members, ranks as the largest Native American tribe in the country. In 1882 the federal government also recognized the Hopi's age-old land rights and began setting aside land for them. Approximately 10,000 Hopi live today on a reservation completely surrounded by Navajo land. Government officials have redrawn the reservation boundaries of the Navajo and Hopi many times, never to the satisfaction of all parties. In 1978, congressional and court decisions settled a major land dispute between the two tribes in favor of the Hopi. The victorious Hopi regained part of the territory previously designated for joint use but largely settled by Navajo. To the Hopi this was long-overdue justice, while the Navajo called it The Second Long Walk. The Navajo and Hopi Indian Relocation Commissioners faced the daunting task of resettling hundreds of families in their respective reservations.

NATIVE AMERICAN CULTURES

White people have always had difficulty understanding Arizona's tribes, perhaps because these Native American cultures emphasize very different spiritual values. The Hopi and Navajo exist in accord with nature, not against it, adapting to the climate, plants, and animals of the land. Yet when visiting Native American villages, outsiders often see only the material side of the culture—the houses, livestock, dress, pottery, and other crafts. The visitor has to look deeper to gain even a small insight into Native American ways.

N.E. ARIZONA

Hopi and Navajo differ greatly in their lifestyles. The Hopi usually live in compact villages, even if this means a long commute to fields or jobs. The Navajo spread their houses and hogans across the countryside, often far from the nearest neighbor.

Ceremonies

Religion forms a vital part of both Hopi and Navajo cultures. The Hopi have an elaborate, almost year-round schedule of dances in their village plazas and kivas (ceremonial rooms). Some, such as those in the kivas, are closed to outsiders, but others may be open to the public. Nearly all Hopi dances serve as prayers for rain and fertile crops. The elaborate and brilliant masks, the ankle bells, the drums and chanting—all invite the attention of the supernatural spirits (kachinas) who bring rain. Men perform these dances and while they're dancing they *are* kachinas. At the end of the line of dancers, you might see boys who are learning the ritual; dance steps must be performed precisely. When watching, remember that this is a religious service. Dress respectfully, keep clear of the performers, be quiet, and don't ask questions. Hopi ceremonies generally take place on the weekends; call or ask at the Hopi Cultural Center or the Hopi Tribe Cultural Preservation Office.

Most Navajo ceremonies deal with healing. If someone is sick, the family calls in a healer who uses sand paintings, chants, and dancing to effect a cure. These events, often held late at night, aren't publicized. If you're driving at night and see large bonfires outside a house, it's likely there's a healing ceremony going on, but don't go over unless invited.

Visiting the Hopi and Navajo

Learning about Native American cultures can reward visitors with new insights. It's easy to visit Navajo and Hopi lands; the tribes ask guests to follow only a few simple rules.

Hordes of eager photographers besieged Hopi villages from the late 1800s to the early 1900s, when the Hopi cried "No more!" And that's the way it is now—photography, recording, and sketching by visitors are *strictly* forbidden in all Hopi villages. Even the sight of a camera will upset some tribal members. The Navajo are more easygoing about photos, but you should always ask first; expect to pay a posing fee unless attending a public performance.

Reservation land, though held in trust by the government, is private property; obtain permission before leaving the roadways or designated recreational areas. Don't remove anything—a few feathers tied to a bush may make a tempting souvenir, but they're of great religious importance to the person who put them there. Normal good manners, respect, and observance of posted regulations will make your visit pleasurable for both you and your hosts.

You might enjoy tuning in local radio stations to hear favorite tunes and languages of the tribes. Hopi Radio KUYI at 88.1 FM has a large following for its traditional and contemporary Native American and other styles of music.

NORTHEASTERN ARIZONA PRACTICALITIES

Accommodations and Food

Because of the distances involved, visitors usually need to stay overnight on or near the reservations. Most towns have a motel or two that can quickly fill up in the summer tourist season, when reservations come in very handy. Motel prices run on the high side because there's so little competition. Accommodations in towns just outside the reservations—Flagstaff, Winslow, Holbrook, Page, Gallup—are another possibility and generally a much better value. Campgrounds are likely to have space and you'll save a lot of money; only a few have hookups.

Navajo and Hopi enjoy American, Mexican, and Chinese dishes as well as the ever-present fast foods. Try the Navajo taco, a giant tortilla smothered with lettuce, ground beef, beans, tomatoes, chilies, and cheese. The Hopi Cultural Center restaurant on Second Mesa has many local specialties, but chances are the Hopi family at the next table will be munching on hamburgers and fries. No alcohol is sold or permitted on the Navajo and Hopi reservations; you won't find much nightlife, either.

Information

Not always easy to get! Motels and trading posts can be helpful; tribal police know regulations and road conditions. Try the museums run by the Hopi on Second Mesa and by the Navajo at Window Rock and Tsaile. Local newspapers report on politics, sports, and social events, but not religious ceremonies.

The **Hopi Tribe Cultural Preservation Office,** tel. 928/734-2244, provides information for visitors to the Hopi Indian Reservation at its office in Kykotsmovi, one mile south of AZ 264 in the Tribal Headquarters building; contact the office at P.O. Box 123, Kykotsmovi, AZ 86039. The **Hopi Cultural Center,** tel. 928/734-2401, on Second Mesa has a museum, motel, campground, and restaurant; write to P.O. Box 67, Second Mesa, AZ 86043; website: www.hopionline.com. People at either place can tell you about upcoming dances open to the public. The Hopi generally don't allow outsiders to hike, fish, or hunt.

The **Navajo Nation Tourism Department** office, tel. 928/871-7371 or 871-7941, provides literature and information for visitors to the Navajo Indian Reservation. The information desk in the Navajo Museum, Library & Visitor's Center is open Mon. 8 A.M.–5 P.M., Tues.–Fri. 8 A.M.–8 P.M., and Sat. 9 A.M.–5 P.M. in Window Rock on AZ 264; write to P.O. Box 663, Window Rock, AZ 86515; website: www.navajo.org.

© THE EXPLORATION OF THE COLORADO RIVER AND ITS CANYONS

Hopi method of dressing the hair, late 1800s

For hiking and camping information and permits on Navajo lands, contact the **Navajo Parks & Recreation Department,** tel. 928/871-6647 or 871-6635, near the museum and zoo in Window Rock, open Mon.–Fri. 8 A.M.–5 P.M.; P.O. Box 9000, Window Rock, AZ 86515; website: www.navajonationparks.org. Or, in the western Navajo Nation, which contains most of the open backcountry areas, contact the Cameron Visitor Center at the US 89-AZ 64 junction in Cameron, tel. 928/679-2303; it's open Mon.–Fri. 8 A.M.–5 P.M. and may be extended to daily 8 A.M.–6 P.M. from Memorial Day–Labor Day weekends; write P.O. Box 459, Cameron, AZ 86020. Backcountry permits cost only $5 per person per entry and $5 per person per night for camping; allow two weeks for processing.

Fishing and hunting on the Navajo Reservation require tribal permits from **Navajo Fish and Wildlife,** tel. 928/871-6451 or 871-6452, is open Mon.–Fri. 8 A.M.–5 P.M.; P.O. Box 1480, Window Rock, AZ 86515; website: www.navajofishandwildlife.org. Of the 12 lakes stocked with fish on the reservation, the most popular are the trout lakes Wheatfields and Tsaile in eastern Arizona and Whiskey nearby in New Mexico. Arizona Game and Fish has no jurisdiction; you need only tribal permits.

What Time Is It?

This must be the question most frequently asked by reservation visitors! While the Navajo Nation and most of the United States go on Daylight Saving Time from early April–late October, the rest of Arizona stays on Mountain Standard Time. Keep in mind the time difference on Navajo land during Daylight Saving Time or you'll always be one hour late; an easy way to remember is that the reservation follows the same time as its New Mexico and Utah sections. The Hopi, who rarely agree with the Navajo on anything, choose to stay on Mountain Standard Time.

Getting Around

Your own transportation is by far the most convenient, but tours of Navajo country do leave from major centers. **Navajo Transit System,** offers bus service across the Navajo and Hopi reservations Mon.–Fri. and to Gallup on Saturday; no buses run on Sunday and holidays; tel. 928/729-4002. One route connects Fort Defiance and Window Rock in the east with Tuba City in the west, once daily in each direction. Buses also head north from Window Rock and Fort Defiance to Kayenta via Chinle. Other routes connect Fort Defiance and Window Rock with the New Mexico towns of Gallup, Crownpoint, Shiprock, and Farmington.

N.E. ARIZONA

SHOPPING FOR NATIVE AMERICAN ARTS AND CRAFTS

The strength of the Navajo and Hopi cultures appears in their excellent arts and crafts. Trading posts and Native American crafts shops on and off the reservations offer large selections. You'll also have the opportunity to buy directly from the maker. Navajo sell from roadside stands, most numerous on the highways to Grand Canyon National Park. Hopi usually sell directly from their village homes. To learn about Native American art, drop in at the Heard Museum in Phoenix or the Museum of Northern Arizona in Flagstaff. Books—available in trading posts, bookstores, and libraries—describe crafts and what to look for when buying; see the Booklist for more information.

The best work commands high prices but can be a fine memento of a visit to Native American lands. Tribespeople know what their crafts are worth, so bargaining is not normally done. Competition, especially among Navajo at their roadside stands, can make for some very low prices, however. Discounts often mark the end of the tourist season in September and October.

The Navajo have long earned fame for silver jewelry and woven rugs; you'll also see their stonework, pottery, basketry, and sand paintings. Craftsmen learned to work silver from Mexicans in the 19th century, then gradually developed distinctive Navajo styles, such as the squash-blossom necklace with its horseshoe-shaped pendant. Silversmiths also turn out bracelets, rings, concha belts, buckles, and bolo ties. The Navajo are especially fond of turquoise, which appears in much of their work. Navajo once wove fine blankets using sheep obtained from the Spanish and weaving skills learned from pueblo Indians, but factory-made blankets in the late 19th century nearly ended the market for hand-woven ones. At the suggestion of

Navajo jewelry at roadside stall

trader Lorenzo Hubbell, weavers switched to a heavier cloth for use as rugs, which became extremely popular. Rugs have evolved into more than a dozen regional styles and may be made from hand-spun and dyed yarn or less expensive commercial yarn. Navajo once used sandpaintings only in ceremonies but now also produce the distinctive designs and colors for the tourist trade.

The Hopi carve exotic kachina dolls from cottonwood and create jewelry, pottery, and basketry. The kachina dolls originally followed simple designs and served to educate children about Hopi religion. With the rise of interest from outsiders, the Hopi began to carve more elaborate and realistic figures from the diverse Hopi pantheon. The dolls include clowns (painted with black and white stripes and often holding watermelon slices), animal-like forms, solemn masked figures, and fearsome ogres. Much thought and symbolism go into a Hopi carving, so even though its price is high, the doll will be good value. (Some Navajo have cashed in on the kachina-doll trade, but the Hopi may tell you that the Navajo don't really know about the kachina religion; Navajo dolls tend to have more fur, fiercer features, and lower prices.) Hopi silversmiths most often fashion inlay work using traditional symbols. The inlay is made from two sheets of silver, one with a design cut out, sandwiched together. This style, now a Hopi trademark, is seen in earrings, bracelets, rings, bolo ties, and belt buckles. The Hopi also turn out beautiful pottery and baskets, as they have for many centuries.

Artists of both tribes create attractive paintings, prints, and sculpture with Native American motifs.

Western Navajo Country

CAMERON

Cameron Trading Post, built in 1916 overlooking the Little Colorado River, commemorates Ralph Cameron, Arizona's last territorial delegate before statehood. The trading post's strategic location near the Grand Canyon makes it a popular stopping point. Facilities include a motel ($89–159 d, less in winter), RV park across the highway ($15 with hookups, no tents, no showers), restaurant, grocery store, Native American crafts shop, post office, and service station. The excellent restaurant, featuring American with some Mexican and Navajo food, is open daily for breakfast, lunch, and dinner—try the Navajo taco in meat or vegetarian versions. The separate gallery in a stone building in front contains museum-quality Native American crafts and art for sale, well worth a look by aficionados. The trading post is on the west side of US 89, one mile north of the junction with AZ 64 and 54 miles north of Flagstaff; tel. 928/679-2231 or 800/338-7385; website: www.camerontradingpost.com.

Drop in at the **visitor center/ranger station,** at the US 89-AZ 64 junction, for information about the Navajo Reservation; you can buy tribal hiking and camping permits here, too. The center is open Mon.–Fri. 8 A.M.–5 P.M. (may be extended to 7 A.M.–6 P.M. from Memorial Day–Labor Day weekends); write to P.O. Box 459, Cameron, AZ 86020, tel. 928/679-2303, fax 928/679-2330. **Navajo Arts & Craft Enterprise** next door offers a good selection of Native American crafts. An **RV park** across US 89 is open all year with sites for tents ($8.50) and RVs ($14.50 with hookups) as well as showers ($2) and laundry; check in at the Chevron station; tel. 928/679-2532. Nearby, the **Trading Post** sells Native American crafts, and **Simpson's Market** has groceries.

Vicinity of Cameron
You'll see the colorful hills of the **Painted Desert** from roads to the north and east. To

N.E. ARIZONA

the west, the high, sheer walls of the **Little Colorado River Canyon** make an impressive sight, even with the Grand Canyon so near. Viewpoints are 9 and 14 miles west on AZ 64, about halfway to Desert View in Grand Canyon National Park. You'll also have a chance to shop for Navajo jewelry at the many roadside stands in the Cameron area on US 89 and AZ 64.

Gray Mountain Trading Post, 10 miles south of Cameron on US 89, has the **Anasazi Inn** and a gas station/convenience store on the east side of the highway and a restaurant (lacks a smoke-free area) and an Native American crafts shop on the west side. The inn has a pool; rates run $70–90 d; tel. 928/679-2214.

Backcountry Areas

Experienced hikers can explore remote and beautiful areas in the western Navajo lands. The visitor center/ranger station in Cameron sells the required permits and has some information; hiking guidebooks have more detailed descriptions. Navajo permits can also be obtained from staff at the Navajo Parks and Recreation in Window Rock. If you'll be camping in Grand Canyon National Park, permits will also be needed from the Backcountry Office there. Navigating the unsigned jeep roads to many of the trailheads may require as much map reading skill as does hiking the routes. When it's not in flood, you can follow the Little Colorado River all the way from Cameron down to the Colorado River in the Grand Canyon, though deep pools, quicksand, and flash floods can make the way difficult. The Little Colorado Canyon can also be entered via the Blue Springs Trail, Hopi Trail Crossing, and Hopi Salt Trail, all very challenging and only for knowledgeable canyon hikers. Marble Canyon has difficult rim-to-river routes at Eminence Break, Shinumo Wash, Salt Water Wash, and Jackass Canyon. Rainbow Bridge rates as one of the best hiking destinations

on the Colorado Plateau; see "Rainbow Bridge National Monument."

Tatahatso Point

Spectacular views of Marble Canyon greet adventurous drivers who negotiate the confusing network of roads out to the rim. The name comes from the Navajo *dida'a hotsa'a,* meaning "the edge or top of it is big." The rare visitor experiences the precipitous edge, the vastness, and the solitude here. From Cedar Ridge on US 89, the route is about 20 miles to the Point Hansbrough overlook or 25 miles all the way to the end of the road on Tatahatso Point. High-clearance vehicles must be used, and you'll need 4WD if you drive all the way to the end of the point. The trip should be done only in dry weather with good visibility (to see the landmarks); topo maps will be useful. Bring water, food, and camping gear in case of a breakdown, and leave your plans with a reliable person. Although you can drive out in an hour or so, staying overnight will allow you to see the changing colors and patterns in Marble Canyon and on the plateaus all around. *Arizona Highways* did an illustrated article on Tatahatso Point in the July 1998 issue, though the directions seem suspect: "HOW far is it to the stock pond, Sam?"

First obtain a Navajo permit, most easily done at the visitor center/ranger station in Cameron, then you can drive to Cedar Ridge on US 89, 40 miles north of Cameron, and turn west on an unpaved road marked by a cairn 0.2 mile north of Milepost 505. This is Indian Route 6110, a wide and bumpy gravel road. Soon the dark, forested Kaibab Plateau comes into view ahead to the west, then Shinumo Altar to the northwest. It's a good idea to look back occasionally for landmarks to help with navigation on the return drive. The route generally heads west, passing several miles to the south of Shinumo Altar, then at a point southwest of Shinumo, curves northwest toward Tatahatso Point. Don't panic

© BILL WEIR

Point Hansbrough encircled by the Colorado River—view from Tatahatso point

if you lose the way, as there's more than one way across the plateau—rather, be amazed if you don't make a wrong turn! The author counted one (1) sign on the entire drive! Just try not to disturb anyone at the widely scattered ranches out here.

Keep right on 6110 where the road forks after 6.8 miles. After another 0.6 mile, take the left fork (a small earthen dam is on the left here). After 0.8 mile take the right fork, then a left fork after 0.3 mile; there's a little outcrop of white rocks to the south. Take a right fork after 1.6 miles, then a left fork after 0.2 mile, then right at the next two forks just 0.1 mile apart; Shinumo Altar is almost due north and the San Francisco Peaks rise to the south. The route continues west or slightly northwest 2.7 miles past several crossroads, then takes a right fork 0.3 mile down to a watering hole for local livestock. In another 0.3 mile take the right fork, then keep straight on the left fork 0.7 mile farther. After 1.3 miles,

take the right fork, then keep straight on the left fork 0.2 mile farther. In half a mile the road veers to the northwest; there's an earthen ridge to the left in another 0.6 mile. Keep straight on the left fork 0.4 mile past the ridge. Marble Canyon reveals itself to the left after 0.7 mile; the road curves north in another 0.8 mile, then comes to a fork 0.3 mile farther. Turn left here and at the next fork, and you'll have arrived at a cairn marking the end of the road just 0.2 mile farther! The Colorado River makes a sharp 180-degree bend around Point Hansbrough below your feet. President Harding Rapid lies directly below, though only the lower part can be seen. The little side canyon here and cliffs off to your right mark the Eminence Break Fault. Experienced canyon hikers can descend a rough trail from here to President Harding Rapid.

This is the best viewpoint, but you can drive or hike out onto Tatahatso Point for additional views. A rough, steep section of

N.E. ARIZONA

© BILL WEIR

petroglyphs at Inscription Point, north of Wupatki National Monument

rocky road at the fault requires 4WD—don't descend it unless you're sure that you can make it back up! Although just a short walk below the viewpoint, this rough spot is reached by retracing 0.2 mile back to the main road and continuing around and down to the left in 1.7 miles. Once past the rocks, it's an easy three-mile drive across the point, covered in sage, cholla, and Mormon tea, to an old tramway site at road's end. There's a good view downstream to Buck Farm Canyon. One could hike cross-country about 1.5 miles to the southwest corner of Point Tatahatso or drive half a mile north along the rim to the northwest corner of the point and a view upriver.

TUBA CITY

This administrative and trade center for the western Navajo has nothing to do with tubas and is hardly a city. The town (pop. 7,612, elev. 4,936 feet) commemorates Chief Tuba of the Hopi tribe. The business district isn't much to look at, but the area north of Tuba Trading Post has some fine stone buildings in an oasis of green lawns and shade trees. The springs nearby attracted Mormons who founded a settlement in 1877. They could not gain clear title to the land, however, and the U.S. Indian Agency took it over in 1903. Besides the U.S. government offices, the town has a hospital, schools, and a bank.

Sights Nearby

Dinosaur tracks left by several different species lie preserved in sandstone, 5.5 miles west of Tuba City off US 160, about midway between the Tuba City junction and US 89. The turnoff is on the north side of the highway between Mileposts 316 and 317, marked by signs for dinosaur tracks and Moenave. Navajo sell jewelry from stalls here. A guide will probably offer his services, but you can find the several pathway sites on your own—look for the stone-lined paths to them.

Elephant's Feet, a pair of distinctive sandstone pillars, stands near Red Lake, 23 miles northeast of Tuba City on US 160 near Milepost 345.

White Mesa Natural Bridge can be viewed from a distance on a seriously corrugated back road north of Red Lake. Turn north off US 160 between Mileposts 349 and 350 through an oval tunnel under the railroad tracks, continue north 3.7 miles on Indian Route 16, then turn left and go about 5.5 miles on Indian Route 6270; you'll see the huge arch off to the left. There's no access to it because of surrounding private ranches. The AAA *Indian Country* map shows the roads but not the arch.

Accommodations and Camping

Under $50: Greyhills Inn provides one of the few inexpensive places to stay on the Navajo Nation; students of Greyhills High School operate the motel and youth hostel as part of a training program. Rates are $48 s plus $5 for each additional person; people with hostel cards can stay in shared rooms for $16. The bath is down the hall. Guests have use of a kitchen and TV lounge. It's open 24 hours. You can make reservations by phone or mail with the Hotel Management Program, Greyhills High School, P.O. Box 160, Tuba City, AZ 86045, tel. 928/283-4450 or 283-6271, ext. 141/142. From the junction of US 160 and AZ 264, go east a half mile on US 160 to just past the pedestrian overpass, turn left 0.2 mile, turn right, then make the first left into the parking lot.

$50–100: Quality Inn, tel. 928/283-4545 or 800/644-8383, sits in the center of town behind Tuba Trading Post, one mile north of the highway junction; $81 s, $86 d (less in winter). The **RV park** here has some trees, showers, and laundry for $20 RV w/hookups and $12 for tents. **Diné Inn Motel,** tel. 928/283-6107, offers basic rooms—all nonsmoking—on US 160 east of the AZ 264 junction; $65 s, $70 d.

Food

Hogan Restaurant, tel. 928/283-5260, is next to the Quality Inn and serves Mexican-American food daily for breakfast, lunch, and dinner and has a fruit and salad bar. A half block farther east, **Kate's Cafe,** tel. 928/283-6773, serves American and pasta dishes daily for breakfast, lunch, and dinner. Fast food places line the road into town.

The Truck Stop Cafe, at the US 160-AZ 264 junction, tel. 928/283-4975, has American food daily for breakfast, lunch, and dinner. **Szechuan Restaurant** prepares Chinese cuisine in the shopping center. It's open daily for lunch and dinner, and there's often a lunch buffet on weekdays; tel. 928/283-5807. **Pizza Edge** fixes pizza, calzone, subs, sandwiches, and ice cream at the shopping center; it's open Mon.–Sat. for lunch and dinner; tel. 928/283-5938.

Services

Toh Nanees Dizi Shopping Center, a half mile east on US 160, offers two restaurants, a Bashas' supermarket and deli, a movie theater, and other shops.

The unusually shaped **Tuba Trading Post** next door to in the center of town sells Native American crafts. It dates to 1870 and had the two-story octagon added in 1920. **Van Trading Co.,** 1.5 miles west of town on US 160, sells Native American crafts, groceries, and most everything else.

N.E. ARIZONA

Northern Navajo Country

NAVAJO NATIONAL MONUMENT

Navajo National Monument preserves three spectacular prehistoric cliff dwellings, last occupied about 700 years ago. The ancestral Puebloan people who once lived here probably have descendants in present-day Hopi villages. Of the three sites, Betatakin is the most accessible; you can see it from a viewpoint near the visitor center. Rangers lead groups into Betatakin during summer.

Keet Seel, a 16-mile roundtrip hike to the northeast, is the largest cliff dwelling in Arizona. Inscription House, to the west, is the smallest of the three ruins and is closed to the public. The ruins should not be confused with Inscription House Trading Post, which lies some distance away.

You can reach the monument's headquarters and visitor center by following US 160 northeast 52 miles from Tuba City—or southwest 22 miles from Kayenta—then turning north nine miles on AZ 564 at Black Mesa Junction. Tsegi Overlook, on the right just after you enter the Monument, has a fine panorama of canyons.

Visitor Center

The ancestral Puebloan people left many questions behind when they abandoned this area. You can learn what is known about these people and ponder the mysteries at the visitor center. Exhibits of prehistoric pottery and other artifacts attempt to piece together what life was like for them. An excellent 25-minute movie on the ancestral Puebloan people is shown on request. A bulletin board lists campfire programs and ranger-led walks. Navajo often demonstrate their art and crafts in or near the visitor center. You can peek into an old-style Navajo forked-stick hogan and see a

sweathouse and wagon behind the center. Rangers answer questions and sell books and maps. A gift shop offers Navajo crafts and Hopi, Navajo, and Zuni jewelry. There's a **picnic area** across the parking area.

The visitor center is open daily 8 A.M.–5 P.M. except Thanksgiving, Christmas, and New Year's Day. Contact monument staff at HC 71, Box 3, Tonalea, AZ 86044-9704, tel. 928/672-2700; website: www.nps.gov/nava.

Sandal Trail

This easy paved trail begins behind the visitor center and winds through a pinyon-juniper woodland to Betatakin Point Overlook, which has a good view of Betatakin across the canyon. The trail is one mile roundtrip and drops 160 feet to the viewpoint. Signs along the way identify native plants and describe how Native Americans used them.

Aspen Trail branches off to the left 400 feet down Sandal Trail, then drops 300 feet with some steps into the head of Betatakin Canyon, 0.8 mile roundtrip. The trail offers pretty scenery along the way and a view of the quaking aspen, Douglas fir, water birch, and redosier redwood trees on the canyon floor below; there's no ruin view or access from this trail.

Visiting Betatakin

The Betatakin—Navajo for Ledge House—lies tucked in a natural alcove that measures 452 feet high, 370 feet across, and 135 feet deep. It contains 135 rooms and one kiva. Inhabitants built and abandoned the entire village within two generations, between A.D. 1260 and 1300.

You may hike here only with park rangers, who lead one four-hour tour a day from Memorial Day to Labor Day weekends. Groups are limited to 25 people, first-come, first served, so be early. Starting at the trailhead (one mile

© BILL WEIR

Betatakin Cliff Dwelling

from the visitor center), the five-mile roundtrip trail is primitive and drops 700 feet, which you have to climb on the way back, and winds around to a viewpoint of the cliff dwelling. At press time, you couldn't enter the ruins due to rockfall danger. Thin air—the trailhead elevation is 7,300 feet—can make the hike very tiring. People with heart, respiratory, or mobility problems shouldn't attempt it.

Visiting Keet Seel

This isolated cliff dwelling is one of the best preserved in the Southwest. Keet Seel—Navajo for Broken Pottery—has 160 rooms and four kivas. The ruins look as though they were abandoned just a few years back, not seven long centuries ago. The site, 8.5 miles by trail from the visitor center, is open from Memorial Day–Labor Day weekends. A permit is required, and there's a limit of 20 people per day. Visitors should make reservations two months ahead with Navajo National Monument, HC 71, Box 3, Tonalea, AZ 86044-9704, tel. 928/672-2700. To pick up your permit, you must attend a scheduled trail orientation in the morning or the afternoon

before (remember it's Daylight Saving Time).

The trail descends from Tsegi Point to the canyon bottom, travels downstream a short distance, then heads upstream into Keet Seel Canyon. You may have to do some wading. Carry water, as livestock pollute the streams. Visitors may not enter the site without a ranger, stationed nearby. Backpackers can stay in a primitive campground (free, one-night limit) near Keet Seel. Strong hikers can do the roundtrip in a day, though spending a night here makes for an easier, more relaxing visit.

Services

A free **campground** in a pinyon-juniper woodland lies near the visitor center; you can stay year-round but water is on only from about mid-May–mid-October. Campfire programs run many nights in summer. There's nearly always room; no reservations taken. Expect cold and likelihood of snow from November–mid-March. **Anasazi Inn** ($79–99 d, less in winter) and its café (open daily for breakfast, lunch, and dinner) lie 18 miles away on the road to Kayenta; tel. 928/697-3793. Kayenta, 11 miles farther, offers three motels, a basic RV park, and several restaurants.

Black Mesa Shopping Center, nine miles south of the visitor center at the junction of AZ 564 and US 160, has the closest grocery store and service station. The road south from here goes to the coal mines of the Peabody Coal Company, a major place of employment for the Navajo.

Shonto

This Navajo settlement sits in a small canyon southwest of Navajo National Monument. A trading post offers groceries and Navajo crafts. The shaded park in front is a good spot for a picnic. A chapter house and Bureau of Indian Affairs (BIA) boarding school lie nearby. Shonto is 10 miles from the visitor center on a sandy road not recommended for cars (except during the school year, when it's kept graded), or 33 miles via US 160 on paved roads.

KAYENTA

The "Gateway to Monument Valley" has a population of 5,200 in a bleak, windswept valley (elev. 5,660 feet). Its name is loosely derived from the Navajo word *Teehindeeh,* meaning "boghole," as there were once shallow lakes here. Kayenta makes a handy stop for travelers, with three good motels, a basic RV park, several restaurants, and shopping.

Accommodations and Camping

$50–100: Hampton Inn, tel. 928/697-3170 or 800/426-7866, offers spacious rooms at $91–99 s, $98–106 d in summer along with a restaurant, gift shop, and outdoor pool on US 160 west of the Kayenta turnoff. **Best Western Wetherill Inn,** tel. 928/697-3231 or 800/528-1234, lies in the center of town on US 163, one mile north of US 160. Its name honors John Wetherill, an early trader and rancher in the region who discovered Betatakin, Mesa Verde, and other major ancestral Puebloan sites. Rooms cost $98 d in summer, less off-season. Guests can enjoy an indoor pool and a gift shop. **Roland's Navajoland Tours,** tel. 928/697-3524 or 800/368-2785, offers bed and breakfast rooms on US 163, half a mile north of the US 160 junction, for $50–75 d, less in winter; you can also arrange Monument Valley tours here.

$100–150: Holiday Inn, on US 160 at the turnoff for Kayenta, tel. 928/697-3221 or 800/HOLIDAY, offers rooms for $129 d in summer, as well as a restaurant, gift shop, tours, and an outdoor pool;.

The **Coin-Op Laundry** in town offers basic RV spaces for $10.25 with hookups; tent campers are welcome too, though campgrounds at Monument Valley or Navajo National Monument are far more scenic. Showers are also available to noncampers for $2.75; tel. 928/697-3738.

Food

Hampton Inn's **Reuben Heflin Restaurant,** tel. 928/697-3170, serves American and Navajo food daily for lunch and dinner. Holiday Inn's **Wagon Wheel Restaurant** serves up good Navajo tacos and American fare daily for breakfast, lunch, and dinner; there's also a breakfast buffet in season and a salad bar. **Amigo Cafe** prepares Mexican and American food Mon.–Sat. for breakfast, lunch, and dinner. You'll find it 0.2 mile in on US 163 between the Kayenta turnoff and town; tel. 928/697-8448. **Golden Sands Cafe** near the Wetherill Inn offers American food daily for breakfast, lunch, and dinner; tel. 928/697-3684.

For pizza, calzones, and subs, try **Pizza Edge,** open Mon.–Sat. for lunch and dinner in the Teehindeeh Shopping Center; tel. 928/697-8427. Also near the shopping center, **Blue Coffee Pot Cafe,** tel. 928/697-3396, prepares Mexican and American food Mon.–Fri. for breakfast, lunch, and dinner.

McDonalds and **Burger King** also lie near the shopping center; Burger King has exhibits on WW II Navajo Code Talkers. Buy groceries at Bashas' supermarket and deli in the shopping center or at the Kayenta Trading Post behind the Wetherill Inn.

Shopping and Services

Kayenta Visitor Center, tel. 928/697-3572, in front of the shopping center, offers Navajo arts and crafts for sale as well as providing some local information. **Navajo Cultural Center** to the west has traditional forked-stick and octagonal hogans, a sweathouse, and shade house; a weaver demonstrates her craft here during the warmer months. **Navajo Nation Arts & Crafts Showroom,** just east of the highway junction past Thriftway gas station, has a good selection. The motels have Native American arts and crafts, too.

Tours in 4WD vehicles to Monument Valley and the surrounding country can be arranged at the motels and the Kayenta Visitor Center or you can wait until you arrive at Monument Valley, where Navajos offer a variety of driving, horseback riding, and hiking tours.

MONUMENT VALLEY

Towering buttes, jagged pinnacles, and rippled sand dunes make this an otherworldly landscape. Changing colors and shifting shadows add to the feeling of enchantment. Most of the natural monuments are remnants of sandstone eroded by wind and water. Agathla Peak and some lesser summits, roots of ancient volcanoes, rise in the southern part of the valley; their dark rock contrasts with the pale yellow sandstone of the other formations. The desert valley lies at an elevation of 5,564 feet; annual rainfall averages about 8.5 inches.

In 1863–64, when Kit Carson was ravaging Canyon de Chelly and rounding up Navajo, Chief Hoskinini led his people to the safety and freedom of Monument Valley. Merrick Butte and Mitchell Mesa commemorate two miners who discovered rich silver deposits on their first trip to the valley in 1880. On their second trip both were killed, reportedly by Paiutes. Hollywood movies made the splendor of Monument Valley known to the outside world. *Stagecoach,* filmed here by John Ford in 1938, began a long series of movies, television shows, and commercials shot in the valley that continues to this day; warriors from John Wayne to Susan Sarandon have ridden across these sands.

The Navajo have preserved the valley as a tribal park with a visitor center, scenic drive, and campground. The **visitor center,** tel. 435/727-3287 or 727-3353, has an information desk, a few exhibits, and booths where

N.E. ARIZONA

© BILL WEIR

Yei Bi Chei and Totem Pole in Monument Valley

you can sign up for tours; it's open 7 A.M.–7 P.M. in summer and 8 A.M.–5 P.M. the rest of the year; closed Thanksgiving Day afternoon and Christmas; website: www.navajonation-parks.org. Entry to the drive closes half an hour before the visitor center and you must be out before dark. Navajos sell crafts and food from little shops near the highway turnoff. Visitors pay a $3 per person fee (free ages seven and under) collected on the entrance road. From Kayenta, head 24 miles north on US 163 and turn right 3.5 miles.

Monument Valley Drive

A 17-mile, self-guided scenic drive begins at the visitor center and loops through the heart of the valley. Overlooks along the way provide sweeping vistas. The dirt road is normally okay if you drive cautiously, but don't attempt it with RVs over 27 feet or extremely low-clearance vehicles. Avoid stopping and becoming stuck in the loose sand that sometimes blows across the road. Allow one and a half hours for the drive. No hiking or driving is permitted off the signed route. Only the visitor center and campground have water, so you'll probably like to bring some along.

Valley Tours

Navajo guides in the visitor center offer guided tours year-round. The shortest trips last an hour and a half and cover places on the self-guided route. Longer trips of two and a half or three and a half hours visit hogans, cliff dwellings, and petroglyphs in areas beyond the self-guided drive. Horseback rides from stables near the visitor center range from one and a half hours to all day; overnight trips can be arranged too. If you'd like to hike in Monument Valley, you must hire a guide at the visitor center; hiking tours can last from a few hours to a day or more.

Reservations aren't required on the tours. If you'd like to do overnight trips, it's best to call ahead and bring your own food and camping gear. **Totem Pole Tours,** tel. 435/727-3313 or 800/345-8687, offers driving trips, photography tours, trail rides, and hiking including cookouts and overnights. **Homeland Tours,** tel. 435/727-3245 or 800/388-5613, can take you on a variety of backroad drives, trail rides, or hikes. **Roland's Navajoland Tours,** tel. 928/697-3524 or 800/368-2785, offers a variety of backcountry drives, photography tours, hiking trips, and a (in Kayenta). **Sacred Monument Tours,** tel. 435/727-3218, leads jeep, horseback, hiking, and photography tours; website: www.monumentvalley.net. **Monument Valley Horseback Trailrides,** tel. 435/683-2327, will take you out for an hour or more—up to five days.

Accommodations and Food

Sites at **Mitten View Campground** near the visitor center have great views though tent campers must often contend with pesky winds in this exposed location. The cost is $10, with coin-operated showers from early April–mid-October. No hookups are available, but there's a fill and dump station. Off-season the rate drops to $5 and you can use restrooms next to the visitor center. Goulding's Lodge offers the nearest motel, store, and telephone. You'll also find motels at Kayenta in Arizona and at Mexican Hat and Bluff in Utah.

Country of Many Hogan Bed & Breakfast, tel. 928/283-4125, near Monument Valley offers accommodations in hogans with traditional food at $145 d in summer (less in winter) with a continental breakfast. Dinner, camping, sweat lodge, horseback rides, hiking tours, and driving trips can be arranged at extra cost; email: zenbah@hotmail.com; navajoland.com/cmh.

Goulding's Lodge and Trading Post

In 1924, Harry Goulding and his wife, Mike, opened a trading post at this scenic spot, just north of the Arizona-Utah border and 1.5

miles west of the US 163 Monument Valley turnoff. **Goulding's Museum,** in the old trading post building, displays prehistoric and modern Native American artifacts, movie photos, period rooms, and Goulding family memorabilia. It's open daily (on request in winter) and donations are appreciated. Nearby, a shack built for John Wayne in *She Wore a Yellow Ribbon* has exhibits from the movie.

Motel rooms go for $155 d June 1–Oct. 15, dropping to $62 d midwinter; a stiff 17 percent tax is added. Guests enjoy views and an indoor pool. The **Stagecoach Restaurant's** menu offers such American favorites as steak, chicken, pork, fish, sandwiches, and a salad bar. Local specialties include Navajo tacos, both beef and vegetarian, and there are a few pasta and stir-fry items. The Stagecoach is open daily for breakfast, lunch, and dinner.

The large gift shop sells high-quality Native American crafts plus souvenirs and books. A multimedia show, *Earth Spirit,* portrays the region. The nearby gas station has a fast-food counter and there's a convenience store across the road. An airstrip also lies nearby. Monument Valley tours operate year-round at $25.50 for two and a half hours, $30.50 for three and a half hours, and $60.50 full day with lunch; children under 8 pay less. For ac-

commodation and tour information, write P.O. Box 360001, Monument Valley, UT 84536; tel. 435/727-3231 or 800/874-0902; website: www.gouldings.com.

Goulding's Monument Valley Campground, tel. 435/727-3235 or 800/874-0902, offers a spectacular canyon setting one mile west of the lodge turnoff. Tent ($15) and RV ($24 with full hookups) campers have an indoor pool, showers, laundry, and convenience store/gift shop. It's open March 15–Oct. 31. The Seventh-Day Adventist Church founded the nearby hospital and mission.

FOUR CORNERS MONUMENT

An inlaid concrete slab marks the place where Utah, Colorado, New Mexico, and Arizona meet. This is the only spot in the United States where you can put your finger on four states at once. It's said that more than 2,000 people a day stop at the marker in the summer. Average stay? Seven to 10 minutes. On the other hand, five national parks and 18 national monuments lie within a 150-mile radius of this point. Navajo, and occasionally Ute and Pueblo, set up dozens of craft and refreshment booths here in summer. Navajo Parks and Recreation collects a small fee during the tourist season.

Eastern Navajo Country

© BILL WEIR

Navajo paintings in Canyon del Muerto

CANYON DE CHELLY NATIONAL MONUMENT

You'll find prehistoric cliff dwellings and traditional Navajo life preserved in spectacular canyons here. The main canyons are 26-mile-long Canyon de Chelly (pronounced d'SHAY) and adjoining 35-mile-long Canyon del Muerto. Sheer sandstone walls rise up to 1,000 feet, giving the canyons a fortress-like appearance. Rim elevations range from 5,500 feet at the visitor center to 7,000 feet at the end of the scenic drives. Allow at least a full day to see some of the monument's 83,840 acres. April–October is the best time to visit. Winter brings cold weather and a chance of snow. Afternoon thunderstorms arrive almost daily in late summer, bringing thousands of waterfalls that cascade over the rims, stopping when the skies clear.

The small, spread-out town of Chinle, just west of Canyon de Chelly National Monument, takes its name from a Navajo word meaning "Water Outlet"—the Rio de Chelly emerges from its canyon here. Chinle offers motels, several restaurants, a supermarket, shops, post office, laundromat, and service stations.

The First Peoples

Nomadic tribes roamed these canyons more than 2,000 years ago, collecting wild foods and hunting game. Little remains of these early visitors, who must have found welcome shelter from the elements in the natural rock overhangs of the canyons. The ancestral Puebloan people (Anasazi in the Navajo language) made their first appearance about A.D. 1, living in alcoves during the winter and brush shelters in summer. By A.D. 500 they had begun cultivating permanent fields of corn, squash, and beans and fashioning pottery. Villagers lived at that time in year-round pithouses, partly underground structures roofed with sticks and mud.

Around A.D. 700 the population began to move into cliff houses of stone masonry constructed above ground. These pueblos (Spanish for "villages") also contained underground ceremonial rooms, known as kivas, used for social and religious purposes. Most of the cliff houses now visible in Canyon de Chelly date from A.D. 1100–1300, when an estimated 1,000 people occupied the many small villages. At the end of this period the ancestral Puebloan people migrated from these canyons and from other large population centers. Archaeologists speculate that possible causes include floods, drought, overpopulation, and soil erosion.

It's likely that some ancestral Puebloan people moved to the Hopi mesas, as Hopi religion, traditions, and farming practices have many similarities with the Canyon de Chelly cliff dwellers. During the next 400 years, Hopi farmers sometimes used the canyons during the growing season, but they returned to the mesas after each harvest.

The Navajo Arrive

First entering Canyon de Chelly about A.D. 1700, the Navajo found it an ideal base for raiding nearby Native American and Spanish settlements. In 1805 the Spanish launched a punitive expedition; soldiers reported killing 115 Navajo, including 90 warriors. The Navajo identified the dead as mostly women, children, and old men. The site of the killing became known as Massacre Cave. During the Mexican era, raids took place in both directions; the Navajo sought food and livestock, while Mexicans kidnapped women and children to serve as slaves.

Contact with Americans also went badly—settlers encroached on Navajo land and soldiers proved deceitful. Conflict came to an end in the winter of 1863–64, when Colonel Kit Carson led detachments of the U.S. Cavalry into the canyons. The army destroyed the tribe's livestock, fruit trees, and food stores and captured or killed nearly every Navajo it could find. The starving survivors had no choice but to surrender and be herded onto a desolate reservation in eastern New Mexico. In 1868, after four miserable years there, they were permitted to return to their beloved canyons.

Today, Navajo continue farming and grazing sheep on the canyon floors. You can see their distinctive round hogans next to the fields. More than 50 families live in the canyons, but most find it convenient to spend winters on the canyon rims, returning to their fields after the spring floods have subsided.

Visitor Center

Exhibits reveal Native American history from the Archaic period (before A.D. 1) to the present, with many fine artifacts. A 22-minute video, *Canyon Voices,* provides additional insights into the peoples who have lived here, as do regional books for sale here. You can step into a Navajo hogan next to the visitor

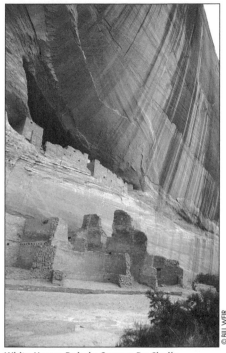

© BILL WEIR

White House Ruin in Canyon De Chelly

center. A bulletin board lists scheduled talks, campfire programs, and hikes. Rangers are happy to answer your questions. The visitor center is open daily 8 A.M.–6 P.M. from about May 1–September 30, and daily 8 A.M.–5 P.M. the rest of the year; contact P.O. Box 588, Chinle, AZ 86503, tel.928/674-5500,www.nps.gov/cach.

Sights

Canyons de Chelly and del Muerto each feature a paved scenic rim drive with viewpoints along the edges, or you can travel inside the canyons by 4WD vehicle, horseback, or foot. With the exception of the White House Ruin Trail, an authorized Navajo guide or monument ranger must accompany visitors entering the canyons. This rule is strictly enforced to protect the ruins and the privacy of families living in the canyons. All land belongs to the Navajo people; the National Park Service administers policies only within monument boundaries.

Vehicle break-ins have become a major problem at overlooks, especially at White House where visitors head down the trail. Sneaky thieves search out cash, cameras, camcorders, computers, and other valuables, which you'll want to keep stored out of sight.

Hiking

White House Ruin Trail is the only hike possible without a guide. If you have a guide, you can hike almost anywhere. Navajos will usually be waiting near the visitor center to accompany you on canyon trips; they can suggest routes depending on your interests and time available. Rangers at the visitor center can help make arrangements and issue the necessary permit. Comfortable walking shoes, water, insect repellent, and a hat will come in handy. Expect to do some wading. In fact, under the hot summer sun with red rocks all around, you may insist on it—the cool water and shade of the trees are irresistible. Autumn can bring especially good hiking weather, with comfortable temperatures and the sight of cottonwoods turning to gold.

Guides charge $15 per hour for up to 15 people. Overnight trips are possible with additional charges for the guide and landowner.

Guides sometimes lead scheduled half-day hikes in the lower canyon from late May to the end of September. Meet the guides at the visitor center, and check departure time the day before—hikes leave promptly. Also, it's a good idea to make reservations the day before, as group size is limited.

Canyon Driving Tours

Tours leave Thunderbird Lodge daily at 9 A.M. and 2 P.M. during the busy season and visit both canyons. In winter, you should call ahead to make sure trips are scheduled; there's

a minimum of six passengers. The trips, very popular with visitors, run half day ($39 adults, $30 children 12 and under) and full day ($63.50 per person—all ages—including lunch). You'll enjoy unobstructed views from the back of an open truck that stops frequently for photography and to view ruins. Half-day trips typically head up Canyon del Muerto to Antelope House Ruin and up Canyon de Chelly to White House Ruin. Full-day excursions can go much farther up each canyon—as far as Mummy Cave in Canyon del Muerto and Spider Rock in Canyon de Chelly.

De Chelly Tours offers private jeep and hiking trips, from three hours to all day or overnight starting at $125 per vehicle for three hours; tel. 928/674-3772.

You can also take your own 4WD vehicles into the canyons with a guide and permit arranged at the visitor center; cost is $15 per hour with a three-hour minimum for up to five vehicles.

Horseback Riding

Justin's Horse Rentals, tel. 928/674-5678, is near the Thunderbird Lodge/Cottonwood Campground turnoff. Rides, available all year, cost $10 per hour for each rider and $15 per hour for the guide (one per group). You can arrange trips of two hours to several days; contact P.O. Box 881, Chinle, AZ 86503.

Tohtsonii Ranch, tel. 928/755-6209, offers four-hour guided horse rides down the Bat Trail in the Spider Rock area and all-day trips that continue to the mouth of the canyon at $10 per hour per person plus $15 per hour for the guide; overnight trips can be arranged too. The ranch is 1.6 miles down a dirt road off the South Rim Drive of Canyon de Chelly (keep straight where the drive turns left for Spider Rock Overlook); contact P.O. Box 434, Chinle, AZ 86503.

You can also ride your own horse by arranging board and feed at one of the stables near the park and by hiring an authorized Navajo guide, preferably from one of the horse concessions.

Accommodations and Camping

Under $50: Many Farms Inn, 17 miles north of Chinle on the way to Monument Valley and Four Corners, tel. 928/781-6362, offers rooms with two beds at $30 (1–4 people, shared baths) in a school training program. Guests can use the coffee room, TV lounge, and laundry. From the junction of US 191 and Indian Route 59, go north 0.7 mile on US 191, turn left 0.7 mile at the Many Farms High School sign, then right 0.3 mile.

$100–150: Thunderbird Lodge, tel. 928/674-5841/5842 or 800/679-2473, has an attractive setting amidst lawns and shade trees a half mile south of the visitor center. The cafeteria, large gift shop, and tours here are a big hit with many visitors. The lodge began as a trading post for the Navajo in 1902, then expanded to accommodate tourists as they began arriving in sizable numbers. Rates from April 1–November 15 start at $97 s, $101 d, less in winter; website: www.tbirdlodge.com. **Holiday Inn,** tel. 928/674-5000 or 800/465-4329 (HOLIDAY), is at the Chinle entrance to the monument; guest enjoy a restaurant, gift shop, and outdoor pool; rates are $99–109 d in season. **Best Western Canyon de Chelly Inn,** tel. 928/674-5875 or 800/327-0354, lies 2.5 miles west of the visitor center and comes with a restaurant, indoor pool, and gift shop; rates run $109 d from May 2–October 31, less off season.

Cottonwood Campground, between the visitor center and Thunderbird Lodge, offers pleasant sites with many large cottonwood trees. It's free and open all year, with water available only from April–October; no showers or hookups are available, though there is a dump station. Rangers present campfire pro-

grams from late May to the end of September. Reservations are accepted only for group sites, though there's usually room at the individual spaces. Cottonwood trees also shade a **picnic area** near the campground; water is available except in winter.

You can escape the crowds at **Spider Rock Campground,** a primitive, privately owned place in a pinyon-juniper woodland; it's eight miles from the visitor center and half a mile before the Spider Rock turnoff on the South Rim Drive; there's a fee with extra charges for water, solar showers, and local tours.

Food

Thunderbird Lodge features a good cafeteria open daily 6:30 A.M.–9 P.M. (8 P.M. in winter). **Holiday Inn's** dining room features the most extensive menu and attractive decor in the area; for dinner you can choose from steaks, ribs, lamb, trout, shrimp, Southwestern, and pasta dishes. In high season, there's a breakfast buffet and a salad bar; the restaurant is open daily for breakfast, lunch, and dinner. **Canyon de Chelly Inn's** Junction Restaurant has American and some Navajo dishes daily for breakfast, lunch, and dinner.

Pizza Edge serves up pizza, calzones, and sandwiches Mon.–Sat. for lunch and dinner in the **Tseyi Shopping Center,** on US 191 just north of the junction with Indian Route 7. **Bashas'** supermarket and deli, **Taco Bell,** and **Burger King,** are in the shopping center too; **A&W** is across the highway. **Church's Chicken** is several blocks east of the junction on Route 7.

Shopping and Services

Navajo Nation Arts & Crafts Showroom sits opposite the Canyon de Chelly turnoff from US 191. The three lodges also display Native American work in their gift shops. The **post office** is in Tseyi Shopping Center.

SOUTH RIM DRIVE OF CANYON DE CHELLY

All pullouts and turns are on the left. Distances include mileage between turnoffs and overlooks. Allow at least two hours for the drive. Parked vehicles should be locked and valuables removed. Binoculars come in handy at the viewpoints.

Mile 0: Visitor Center. The nearby canyon walls stand only about 30 feet high where the Rio de Chelly enters Chinle Wash.

Mile 2.0: Tunnel Canyon Overlook. The canyon is about 275 feet deep here. Guides sometimes lead short hikes down the trail in this side canyon. Don't go hiking without a ranger or Navajo guide.

Mile 2.3: Tsegi Overlook. You'll see a Navajo hogan and farm below. Tsegi is the Navajo word for "rock canyon," which the Spanish pronounced "de chegui." American usage changed it to "de chelly" (d'SHAY).

Mile 3.7: Junction Overlook. Here Canyon del Muerto, across the valley, joins Canyon de Chelly. Canyon depth is about 400 feet. Look for two cliff dwellings of ancestral Puebloan people. First Ruin is located in the cliff at the far side of the canyon. The pueblo has 10 rooms and two kivas, and dates from the late 11th–late 13th centuries. Junction Ruin lies straight across, where the two canyons join. It has 15 rooms and one kiva. These dwellings, like most others in the monument, face south to catch the sun's warmth in winter.

Mile 5.9: White House Overlook. Canyon walls rise about 550 feet at this point. White House Ruin, on the far side, is one of the largest in the monument. The name comes from the original white plaster on the walls in the upper section. Parts of 60 rooms and four kivas remain in the upper and lower sections; there may have been 80 rooms before floodwaters carried away some of the lower ruin. As many as 12 ancestral Puebloan families may have lived in this village about a.d. 1060-1275.

From the overlook, **White House Ruin Trail** begins about 500 feet to the right. Many trails connect the rim with the canyon bottom, but few are as easy as this one. The Navajo often used it to move sheep. Allow two hours for the 2.5-mile roundtrip; bring water but no pets. This is the only hike in the canyon permitted without a guide, but you must stay on the trail. You can buy a pamphlet describing the trail at the visitor center.

Mile 12.0: Sliding House Overlook. These ruins, perched on a narrow ledge across the canyon, are well named. The people who constructed the village on this sloping ledge tried to brace rooms with retaining walls. Natural depressions at the overlook collect water and are still sometimes used by the Navajo.

Mile 19.6: Face Rock Overlook. Small cliff dwellings sit high on the rock face opposite the viewpoint. Though the rooms look impossible to reach, the ancestral Puebloan people cleverly chipped handholds and toeholds into the rock.

Mile 20.6: Spider Rock Overlook. The South Rim Drive ends where rock walls plummet 1,000 feet from the rim to the canyon floor. Spider Rock, the highest of the twin spires, rises 800 feet from the bottom of Canyon de Chelly. Spider Woman, a Navajo deity, makes her home here. A darker side of her character, according to one legend, is her taste for naughty children. When Speaking Rock, the lower pinnacle, reports misbehaving children to Spider Woman, she catches and eats them. Look for the sun-bleached bones on top of her spire.

You can see tiny cliff dwellings in the canyon walls if you look hard enough. Monument Canyon comes in around to the right. Black Rock Butte (7,618 feet high), on the horizon, is either the weathered heart of an extinct volcano or a volcanic intrusion.

© BILL WEIR

Antelope House ruin

NORTH RIM DRIVE OF CANYON DEL MUERTO

All turnoffs are on the right. Distances include mileage between turnoffs and overlooks. Allow at least two hours for the drive. Parked vehicles should be locked and valuables removed. Binoculars come in handy at the viewpoints.

Mile 0: Visitor Center. Cross the nearby Rio de Chelly bridge and continue northeast on Indian Route 64.

Mile 5.9: Ledge Ruin Overlook. The ruin, set in an opening 100 feet above the canyon floor, dates from a.d. 1050–1275 and has 29 rooms, including two kivas in a two-story structure. Walk south a short way to another overlook and a view downcanyon; a solitary kiva is visible high in the cliff face. A hand-

and toehold trail connects it with other rooms in a separate alcove to the west.

Mile 10.0: Antelope House Overlook. Keep right at the fork on the a quarter-mile walk to the viewpoint. Antelope House Ruin had 91 rooms and a four-story building. The village layout is clear—from the overlook you gaze almost straight down on it. The round outlines are kivas. The square rooms were for living or storage. Floods have damaged some of the rooms, perhaps while the ancestral Puebloan people still lived there. The site was abandoned about 1260. Its name comes from paintings of antelope, some believed to be the work of a Navajo artist in the 1830s.

The Tomb of the Weaver sits across from Antelope House in a small alcove 50 feet above the canyon floor. Here, in the 1920s, archaeologists found the elaborate burial site of an old man. The well-preserved body had been wrapped in a blanket made from what appeared to be golden eagle feathers. A cotton blanket was enclosed; these were covered with cotton yarn topped with a spindle whorl.

Look for Navajo Fortress, the sandstone butte across the canyon, from a viewpoint a short walk east from Antelope House Overlook. When danger threatened, the Navajo climbed up the east side using log poles as ladders. They pulled in the uppermost logs and pelted attackers with a hail of rocks. Navajo used this natural fortress from the time of the Spanish until the Kit Carson campaign.

Mile 18.7: Mummy Cave Overlook. Archaeologists in the late 1800s named this large cliff dwelling for two mummies found in the talus slope below. Canyon del Muerto (Spanish for Canyon of the Dead) reportedly also took its name from this find. Mummy Cave Ruin sits within two separate overhangs several hundred feet above the canyon floor. The largest section is on the east (to the left), with 50 rooms and three kivas; the west cave contains 20 rooms. Between these sections is a ledge with seven rooms, including a three-

N.E. ARIZONA

story tower of unknown purpose. The tower dates from about a.d. 1284 and is thought to have been built by ancestral Puebloan people from Mesa Verde in Colorado.

Mile 20.6: Massacre Cave Overlook. The North Rim Drive ends here. In 1805, Antonio de Narbona led an expedition of Spanish soldiers and allied Native Americans to these canyons. A group of fleeing Navajo managed to scale the nearly 1,000 feet to this overhang. Narbona's troops, however, ascended the rim overlooking the cave and fired down. Narbona's account listed 115 Navajo killed and 33 taken captive.

From Yucca Cave Overlook nearby, you can see a cave with at least four rooms and a kiva. A small cave to the left was used for food storage; a hand- and toehold trail connected the two alcoves.

EAST OF CANYON DE CHELLY NATIONAL MONUMENT

Diné College (Tsaile Campus)

Recognizing the need for college education, the Navajo in 1957 established a scholarship fund, financed by royalties from oil. Students had to leave the reservation to receive a college education, but the cultural gap between the Navajo and the outside world proved too great, and many students dropped out. So in 1969, the tribe created Navajo Community College, later renamed Diné College. ("Diné" is the name Navajo prefer when speaking of themselves.) Students used temporary facilities at Many Farms, Arizona, until 1973, when campuses opened at Tsaile and in Shiprock, New Mexico. Students can choose from many Navajo and Native American studies courses—crafts, language, politics, music, dance, herbology, and holistic healing. The colleges offer vocational training and adult education too. The website crystal.ncc.cc.nm.us lists programs, visitor information, museum exhibits, and college-published books.

The unusual campus layout resulted from Navajo elders and healers working together with conventional architects. Because important Navajo activities take place within a circle, the campus grounds and many of the buildings took on that shape. If you know your way around a hogan, you'll find it easy getting around campus: the library is tucked in where the medicine bundle is kept during a ceremony, the cooking area (dining hall) lies in the center, sleeping (dormitories) is centered in the west, the teaching area (classrooms) occupies the south, and the recreation area (student union and gym) is in the north. The central campus entrance, marked by the glass-walled Ned A. Hatathli Center, faces east to the rising sun.

The **Hatathli Museum** claims to be the "first *true* Native American museum." Managed entirely by tribespeople, the collection occupies the third and fourth floors of the hogan-shaped Hatathli Center. Exhibits display art and interpret the cultures of prehistoric peoples as well as Navajo and other modern tribes. The museum and adjacent sales gallery are open Mon.–Fri. 8:30 A.M.–4:30 P.M.; tel. 928/724-6654. A donation is requested. Ned Hatathli was the first Navajo manager of the tribal Arts and Crafts guild and a Tribal Council member.

Diné College Press publishes and sells books on the Navajo and related topics on the first floor of the Hatathli Center. Visitors are welcome in the college cafeteria (on the right) and library (on the left) as you walk west behind the Hatathli Center. The Tsaile campus lies 23 miles east of the Canyon de Chelly Visitor Center and 54 miles north of Window Rock.

Wheatfields Lake

This large mountain lake lies surrounded by a ponderosa forest at an elevation of 7,300 feet, 10 miles south of Tsaile and 44 miles north of Window Rock on Indian Route 12. Visitors enjoy camping and trout fishing at this pretty spot. The rugged Chuska Mountains rise to the east. Campground charges run $2 per person for ages 13 and over; bring water. You'll need Navajo fishing and boat permits, as on all tribal waters. In winter, snow and ice often make driving here unsafe.

Navajo, New Mexico

Trees from the extensive woodlands that surround the town of Navajo supply the town's large sawmill. A supermarket sells groceries and tribal fishing permits. Nearby **Red Lake,** named for the color of its aquatic vegetation, has fishing. Navajo is 17 miles north of Window Rock on Route 12, on the way to Wheatfields Lake, Tsaile, and Canyon de Chelly. **Assayi Lake,** 11 miles northeast in New Mexico at Bowl Canyon Recreation Area, has trout fishing and camping, $10 day use or $15 overnight; it's not suitable for RVs. Whiskey Lake is farther east, also on dirt roads, and offers trout fishing.

WINDOW ROCK

In the early 1930s, "The Rock With a Hole in It" so impressed Commissioner of Indian Affairs John Collier that he chose the site for a Navajo administration center. An octagonal Navajo Council House, representing a great ceremonial hogan, went up, and Window Rock became the capital of the Navajo Nation. Tribal Council delegates meet here to decide on reservation policies and regulations.

Window Rock is a small (area pop. about 8,000) but growing town at an elevation of 6,750 feet. Besides the Council Chambers and offices, the town contains a museum, small zoo, two parks, a motel, and a shopping center. Window Rock's downtown is the shopping center at the junction of AZ 264 and Indian Route 12.

Window Rock hosts the Navajo Nation Fair, said to be the world's largest Native American fair, on the first weekend after Labor Day in September. The five-day festival offers a mixture of traditional and modern attractions,

including singing and dancing, a parade, agricultural shows, food, crafts, concerts, rodeo, and the crowning of Miss Navajo. Write for a free brochure from the Navajo Nation Fair office, P.O. Box 2370, Window Rock, AZ 86515, tel. 928/871-6478 or 871-6702; website: www.navajonationparks.org.

Navajo Museum, Library, and Visitor Center

The entrance of this impressive building opens to the east, like the traditional log hogan in front. Massive wood pillars soar to the central skylight high above. Museum galleries, tel. 928/871-7941, present excellent historical and art exhibits from the permanent collection and visiting shows. The library, across the lobby, has many books on Native American subjects, as well as general reading; tel. 928/871-6376 or 871-6526. A

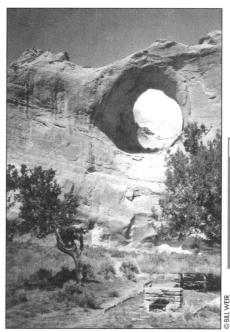

Window Rock

N.E. ARIZONA

gift shop off the lobby offers Native American arts and crafts.

Staff at the information desk in the lobby answer questions and provide Navajo and Arizona travel literature; tel. 928/871-7941 or 871-7371 (tourism office); www.navajo.org. The desk, museum, library, and gift shop all stay open Mon. 8 A.M.–5 P.M., Tues.–Fri. 8 A.M.–8 P.M., and Sat. 9 A.M.–5 P.M. There's also an indoor theater and large outdoor amphitheater. It's on the north side of AZ 264 in Tse Bonito Tribal Park, a half mile east of Window Rock Shopping Center. The park beside the museum and library building offers some shaded picnic tables. A spring, now dry, gave the place its Navajo name, meaning Water Between the Rocks. The Navajo camped here in 1864 on the Long Walk to eastern New Mexico.

Navajo Nation Zoological and Botanical Park

Set beneath towering sandstone pinnacles known as The Haystacks, the zoo offers a close look at animals of the Southwest. Once past the rattlesnakes and other small creatures of the orientation building near the entrance, you'll wander by golden eagles, hawks, elk, coyotes, black bears, mountain lions, wolves, bobcats, and other life. Domestic breeds include the Navajo churro sheep, which has a double fleece and often four horns. Prairie dogs, free of restricting cages, run almost everywhere. Visit daily 8 A.M.–5 P.M.; free admission; tel. 928/871-6573. You'll find it just northeast of the museum and library building.

Window Rock Tribal Park

This beautiful spot shaded by juniper trees lies at the foot of Window Rock. The "window" is a great hole, averaging 47 feet across, in a sandstone ridge. Loose stones just below the hole mark the site of a prehistoric pueblo. You're not allowed to climb up to the hole,

though a trail around to the left passes through wonderfully sculptured hills. The park has picnic tables, water, and restrooms for day-use only. The Navajo Nation Veterans Memorial here honors warriors from all eras of war and peace. Head north about a half mile on Indian Route 12 from AZ 264, turn right at the sign and head a half mile in, passing the Council Chambers on your left just before the park.

Navajo Nation Council Chambers

The Council meets at least four times a year within the circular walls here. At other times twelve standing committees of the Council carry out legislative work. Colorful murals depict Navajo history. If not in use, you can visit the chambers Mon.–Fri. 8 A.M.–5 P.M. For more information, call the Speaker's Office at 928/871-7160.

Accommodations and Camping

$50–100: Navajo Nation Inn, tel. 928/871-4108 or 800/662-6189, features Navajo-style rooms at $62–67 d and has a restaurant; it's on AZ 264, just east of the shopping center. **Days Inn,** tel. 928/871-5690 or 800/325-2525, offers an indoor pool and spa 3.4 miles west in St. Michaels at 392 W. Hwy. 264; rates are $65 s, $75 d.

Window Rock lacks campgrounds; Wheatfields Lake, 44 miles north, and Assayi in New Mexico (17 miles north to Navajo, then 11 miles northeast) are the closest options.

Food

The **Navajo Nation Inn** dining room serves a varied menu of American, Navajo, and Mexican food daily for breakfast, lunch, and dinner, but closes 6 P.M. on weekends. **Hong Kong Restaurant,** tel. 928/871-5622, has Chinese favorites Mon.–Fri. for lunch and dinner in the Window Rock Shopping Center. The shopping center also has **Taco Bell Express, Pizza Hut Express,** and a supermarket.

Bashas' supermarket and deli lies just west on AZ 264; **McDonald's** and **Church's Chicken** are also nearby. A quartet of fast-food places, **Party Time Pizza, Kentucky Fried Chicken, Blakes Lotaburger,** and **Subway** are in New Mexico one mile to the east.

Shopping and Services

Navajo Arts & Crafts Enterprise, tel. 928/871-4095, sells Navajo paintings, rugs, jewelry, jewelry-making supplies, and crafts by other Southwest tribes near the junction of AZ 264 and Indian Route 12. The **post office** is on a hill behind the Navajo Nation Inn.

Information

The **Navajo Nation Tourism Department,** tel. 928/871-7941 or 871-7371, has literature and information for visitors in the lobby of the Navajo Museum, Library & Visitor's Center; it's open Mon. 8 A.M.–5 P.M., Tues.–Fri. 8 A.M.–8 P.M., and Sat. 9 A.M.–5 P.M.; www.navajo.org.

For hiking and camping information and permits on Navajo lands, contact the **Navajo Parks and Recreation Department,** next door to the Zoological and Botanical Park, open Mon.–Fri. 8 A.M.–5 P.M.; P.O. Box 9000, Window Rock, AZ 86515, tel. 928/871-6647 or 871-6635; website: www.navajonationparks.org. Fishing and hunting on the Navajo Nation require tribal permits from **Navajo Fish and Wildlife,** located behind the Motor Pool; open Mon.–Fri. 8 A.M.–5 P.M.; P.O. Box 1480, Window Rock, AZ 86515, tel. 928/871-6451 or 871-6452; website: www.navajofishandwildlife.org. Arizona Game and Fish has no jurisdiction over the reservation—you need only tribal permits.

Transportation

Navajo Transit System connects Window Rock with many communities on the Navajo and Hopi Reservations; tel. 928/729-4002.

VICINITY OF WINDOW ROCK

Fort Defiance

Permanent springs in a nearby canyon attracted the Navajo, who named the area Tsehotsoi, "Meadow between the Rocks." Colonel Edwin Vose Sumner had another name in mind in September 1851, when, in defiance of the Navajo, he established a fort on an overlooking hillside. Though the Navajo nearly overran Fort Defiance in 1860, the army successfully repelled a series of attacks before abandoning it during the Civil War. In 1863–64, Colonel Kit Carson headquartered at the fort while rounding up and moving the Navajo. After the Navajo returned, destitute, in 1868, the first Navajo Agency offices issued them sheep and supplies here. The first school on the reservation opened in 1869, and the first regular medical service arrived in 1880. The old fort is gone now, but the town remains an administrative center with a hospital, schools, and Bureau of Indian Affairs offices.

St. Michael Mission

In 1898, Franciscan friars established a mission to serve the Navajo. St. Michael School, opened by the Sisters of the Blessed Sacrament in 1902, lies a short distance away. The mission's large stone church dates from 1937, when it replaced an earlier adobe structure; it's usually open during the day. The chapel behind the parking area has a circular shape, earthen floor, and a 16-foot woodcarving. The German artist who did the carving called it "The Redemption of Humanity" or "American Pieta"; it shows a dead Native American being lowered from a teepee tarp to a woman in mourning with two attendants, like the body of Jesus being lowered from the cross.

The original mission building has been restored as a **historical museum** with a chapel, missionary room, displays of Native American culture, and information on the life of the early missionaries. A gift shop sells regional books, cards, and posters; admission is free. It's open daily 9 A.M.–5 P.M. from Memorial Day–Labor Day; groups can visit at other times by appointment; tel. 928/871-4171. St. Michael Mission is 2.9 miles west of Window Rock Shopping Center on AZ 264, then 0.2 mile south at the sign.

GANADO

The Spanish called this place Pueblo Colorado ("Colored House") after a nearby ruin left by ancestral Puebloan people. The name later changed to Ganado to honor one of the great Navajo chiefs, Ganado Mucho, or Big Water Clansman, a signer of the treaty of June 1868 that returned the Navajo lands. A Presbyterian mission founded here in 1901 provided the Navajo with a school and hospital. The school grew into the two-year College of Ganado, whose buildings are now used as a hospital. Hubbell Trading Post, Arizona's most famous, comes straight of the Old West. Ganado is on AZ 264, 30 miles west of Window Rock, 44 miles east of Keams Canyon, and 36 miles south of Chinle.

There are no accommodations in the area, but you can find bargain-priced cafeteria meals at the **Sage Cafe** on the old college campus. It's open Mon.–Fri. for breakfast, lunch, and dinner. Turn north into the hospital and follow the signs to a two-story building at the north end of an open park; a playground and some picnic tables lie next to the cafe. A small **museum** off the Sage's food line displays many old photos of the Navajo and has historic exhibits of the school and hospital; ask one of the cafe attendants to open it. **Ramon's Restaurant** nearby has American and Mexican food; turn north one block on the street opposite the junction of AZ 264 and US 191. The Conoco station at the highway junction has a little café open Mon.–Fri. for breakfast and lunch; a grocery store nearby is open daily.

HUBBELL TRADING POST NATIONAL HISTORIC SITE

John Lorenzo Hubbell began trading in 1876, a difficult time for the Navajo, who were still recovering from their traumatic internment

Navajo Fire Dance, late 1800s

at Fort Sumner. Born in New Mexico, Hubbell had already learned some Navajo culture and language by the time he set up shop. Money rarely exchanged hands during transactions; Navajo brought in blankets or jewelry and received credit. They would then select desired items, such as coffee, flour, sugar, cloth, and harnesses. If they had unspent credit left after buying the desired items, Navajo generally preferred silver or turquoise to money. Those bringing wool or sheep to the trading post usually received cash, however.

Hubbell distinguished himself by his honesty and appreciation of the Navajo. His insistence on excellence in weaving and silverwork led to better prices for Navajo craftspeople. The trading post helped bridge the Anglo and Navajo cultures, as Navajo often called on Hubbell to explain government programs and to write letters to officials explaining their concerns.

Visitor Center, Hubbell's House, and Trading Post

Weavers (usually women) often demonstrate their skills in the visitor center, which also has an excellent bookstore with many titles about Native American history, art, and culture. Guides offer free scheduled tours of Hubbell's house and you can take a self-guided tour of the grounds and barn. The house contains superb rugs, paintings, baskets, and other crafts collected by Hubbell before his death in 1930 and by the Hubbell family thereafter.

The trading post still operates much as it always has, offering high-quality crafts or most anything else. Canned and yard goods jam the shelves, glass cases display pocket knives and other small items, horse collars and harnesses still hang from the ceiling, and Navajo still drop in with items for trade. Check out the Native American baskets and other old artifacts on the ceilings and walls of the jewelry and rug rooms. A tree-shaded picnic area sits next to the visitor center. The National Historic Site, tel. 928/755-3475, is open daily 8 A.M.–6 P.M. from June–September, daily 8 A.M.–5 P.M. the rest of the year, and closed Thanksgiving, Christmas, and New Year's Day; website: www.nps.gov/hutr. Major art auctions of works by Navajo and Hopi artists take place in April and August. It's on the south side of AZ 264, one mile west of Ganado.

N.E. ARIZONA

© BILL WEIR

kachina dolls in Hubbell Trading Post

Hopi Country

For centuries the Hopi people have made their homes in villages atop three narrow mesas, fingerlike extensions running south from Black Mesa. Early European visitors dubbed these extensions First Mesa, Second Mesa, and Third Mesa. Arizona 264 skirts First Mesa and crosses over Second and Third Mesas on the way to Tuba City from Window Rock.

The mesas have provided the Hopi with water from reliable springs and protection from enemies, as the 600-foot cliffs discourage assailants. Hardworking farmers, the Hopi are usually peaceable and independent. They keep in close touch with nature and have developed a rich ceremonial life, seeking to maintain balance and harmony with their surroundings and one another. Villages remain largely autonomous even today. The Hopi Tribal Council serves mainly as a liaison between villages and agencies of the federal and state governments.

Visiting Hopi Villages

The Hopi tend to be very private people, though they do welcome visitors to their lands. Policies may vary from village to village and are often posted. All villages *strictly* prohibit such disturbing activities as photography, sketching, and recording. To give residents their privacy, try to visit only between 8 A.M. and 5 P.M. and keep to the main streets and plazas. Walpi asks that visitors enter only with an authorized Hopi guide.

The best time to visit a village is during a ceremony open to the public. Some ceremonies have been placed off limits because of visitors' lack of respect. Please remember that these are important religious rituals and you are

petroglyphs at Hopi Clan Rocks, northwest of Moenave

© BILL WEIR

N.E. ARIZONA

HOPI RESERVATION

N.E. ARIZONA

HOPI KACHINAS AND CALENDAR

Kachinas appear to the Hopi from the winter solstice on December 21 until mid-July. They dance and sing in unison, symbolizing the harmony of good thought and deed, harmony required for rain to fall and for a balanced life. The rest of the year the kachinas remain in their home in the San Francisco Peaks.

A kachina can take three forms: a powerful unseen spirit, a dancer filled with the spirit, or a wooden figure representing the spirit. Kachina dancers are always male, even when the spirit is female. The men may present gifts of kachina figures to women and children during the dances. Each village sponsors its own ceremonies.

HOPI CALENDAR

Wuwuchim and Soyala (November–December)

These months symbolize the time of creation of the world. The villages tend to be quiet, as Hopi spend time in silence, prayer, and meditation.

Wuwuchim, a tribal initiation ceremony, marks the start of the ceremonial calendar year. Young men are initiated into adulthood, joining one of four ceremonial societies. The society a man joins depends on his sponsor. Upon acceptance, the initiate receives instruction in Hopi creation beliefs. He's presented with a new name, and his childhood name is never used again.

Only the Shungopavi village performs the entire Wuwuchim ceremony, and not every year. Other villages engage in parts of the Wuwuchim.

The Soyala Kachina appears from the west in the winter solstice ceremony, marking the beginning of the kachina season. As the days get longer, the Hopi begin planning the upcoming planting season; fertility is a major concern in the ceremony.

Buffalo Dances (January)

Men, women, and children perform these social dances in the plazas. They deal with fertility, especially the need for winter moisture in the form of snow.

Powamuya, the Bean Dance (February)

Bean sprouts are grown in a kiva as part of a 16-day ceremony. On the final day, kachina

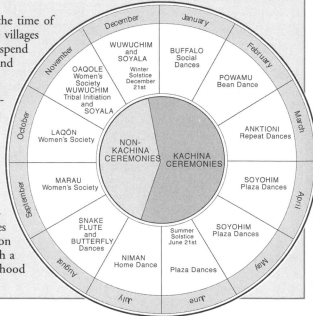

dancers form a long parade through the village. Children of about 10 years are initiated into kachina societies during the Powamuya. Ogre kachinas appear on First and Second mesas.

Kiva Dances (March)

A second set of nighttime kiva dances consists of Anktioni or "repeat dances."

Plaza Dances (April, May, and June)

The kachina dancers perform in all-day ceremonies lasting from sunrise to sunset, with breaks between dances. The group, and the people watching, concentrate in a community prayer calling on the spirits to bring rain for the growing crops.

Niman, the "Home Dance" (July)

At the summer solstice on June 21, the plaza dances end and preparations begin for the Going Home Ceremony. In a 16-day rite, the last of the season, kachina dancers present the first green corn ears, then dance for rain to hasten growth of the remaining crops. Their spiritual work done, the kachinas return to their mountain home.

Snake, Flute, and Butterfly Dances (August)

The Snake and Flute ceremonies, held in alternate years, represent the clan groups who perform them in the interests of a good harvest and prosperity. The Snake Dance, usually closed to non-Hopi, takes place in even-numbered years at Shungopavi and Hotevilla and in odd-numbered years at Mishongnovi. The snakes, often poisonous rattlers, act as messengers to the spirits.

The Flute Ceremony takes place in odd-numbered years at Shungopavi and Walpi.

The Butterfly Dance, a social dance performed mainly by children, takes place in all villages. It also celebrates the harvest.

Women's Society Dances (September, October, and early November)

Held in the plazas, these ceremonies celebrate the harvest with wishes for health and prosperity. Chaos reigns during the Basket Dances; female dancers throw out baskets and other valuables to the audience, who engage in a mad free-for-all to grab the prizes. They mark the end of the ceremonial year.

---

a guest. Check with the village having a dance to make sure that visitors are welcome. If so, residents will expect visitors and you'll be allowed to experience Hopi culture. Dances take place in plazas many weekends. For information, try calling the Second Mesa Cultural Center, tel. 928/734-2401, or the Hopi Tribe's Cultural Preservation Office, tel. 928/734-2244; website: www.hopionline.com. The village names given below have their old spellings, seen on most maps and signs, along with Hopi spellings in parentheses.

KEAMS CANYON

This, the easternmost community on the Hopi Reservation, is not a Hopi village, but an administrative town with various U.S. government agencies. The settlement lies at the mouth of a scenic wooded canyon named after Thomas Keam, who built a trading post here in 1875. From the town, the canyon winds northeast for about eight miles; the first three-mile stretch has a road. Kit Carson engraved his name on Inscription Rock, on the left about two miles in from AZ 264. You'll pass a picturesque Catholic church, then some pleasant picnic spots on the way in.

Practicalities

The motel and campground once here have closed. **Keams Canyon Shopping Center,** on AZ 264 just west of the Keams Canyon turnoff, features McGee's Indian Art Gallery, a grocery store, an ice cream parlor, and a café serving American, Mexican, and Native American food. The café, tel. 928/738-2296, is open Mon.–Fri. for breakfast, lunch, and dinner, and Sat. for breakfast and lunch. A service station is next door. The gallery, tel. 928/738-2295, has a fine selection of Native American arts and crafts and an informative website, website: www.hopi-art.com. Turn north into Keams Canyon for the **post office** (to the right).

Awatovi

Beginning as a small village in the 12th century, Awatovi (ah-WAHT-o-vee) had become an important Hopi town by 1540, when Spanish explorers from Coronado's expedition arrived.

Franciscan friars in 1629 built a large church and friary using Hopi labor. Their mission lasted 51 years until 1680, when, fearing that their culture would be destroyed by Christianity, Hopi villagers joined their New Mexico Pueblo neighbors in successfully overthrowing Spanish rule, wrecking the Awatovi church and killing most of the priests.

Spaniards re-established the mission in 1700, but other Hopi villages became so angered by this continued alien influence that they banded together and promptly destroyed Awatovi. Of the 800 inhabitants, almost all the men were massacred and the women and children removed to other Hopi villages. Spanish troops retaliated a year later with little effect. Further missionary efforts among the Hopi proved futile. Only ghosts live at Awatovi today—it was

never resettled. The ruin sprawls across 23 acres on the southwest tip of Antelope Mesa, with piles of rubble as high as 30 feet. The site is currently closed to the public.

FIRST MESA

Polacca

With an increasing population, some Hopi have built houses in settlements below the mesas, as at Polacca (po-LAH-kah). Still, if you ask residents of Polacca where they're from, they'll likely name one of the three villages on the mesa above. Polacca stretches for about a mile along the highway, but offers little of interest. Thrilling views, however, lie atop First Mesa, reached by a paved road that climbs steeply for 1.3 miles to Sichomovi on the crest. If you have a trailer or large vehicle, you must park it in Polacca or at parking areas 0.6 mile or one mile up. A shuttle may be started in the future, in which case all visitors will park below.

Hano (Hanoki)

The first village you reach looks Hopi but is really a settlement of the Tewa, a Pueblo tribe from the Rio Grande region to the east. Fleeing from the Spanish after an unsuccessful revolt in 1696, a number of Tewa sought refuge with the Hopi. Hopi leaders agreed, on the condition that the Tewa act as guardians of the access path to the mesa. Despite living close to the Hopi for so long, the Tewa have retained their own language and ceremonies. Hano's fascinating history is detailed in *A Tewa Indian Community in Arizona* by Edward P. Dozier (see the Resources).

Sichomovi (Sitsomovi)

To the visitor, Hano and the Hopi village of Sichomovi (see-CHO-mo-vee) appear as one, but residents know exactly where the line is. Sichomovi is considered a branch of Walpi, the village at the tip of the mesa.

Walpi, a village of Tusayan, late 1800s

Walpi (Waalpi)

One of the most inspiring places in Arizona, Walpi (WAHL-pee) stands surrounded by sky and distant horizons. Ancient houses of yellow stone appear to grow from the mesa itself. Coming from Sichomovi, you'll watch the mesa narrow to just 15 feet before widening again at Walpi.

Visitors may enter this traditional village only with an authorized Hopi guide; Walpi is small and its occupants sensitive. Walking tours of about 60 minutes leave daily from Ponsi Hall in Sichomovi 9 A.M.–5 P.M. in summer and 9:30 A.M.–4 P.M. the rest of the year. The tour cost is $8 adults and $5 youth 6–17; tel. 928/737-2262 (Ponsi Hall) or 737-2670 (Community Development office). Tours may not run on weekends, so it's best to call ahead before making a special trip out.

Unlike most other Hopi villages, Walpi lacks electricity and running water. Residents have to walk back toward Sichomovi to get water or to wash. Look for bowl-shaped depressions once used to collect rainwater. Precipitous foot trails and ruins of old defenses and buildings cling to the mesa slopes far below. Inhabited since the 13th century, Walpi is well known for its ceremonial dances and crafts, although most First Mesa dances were

closed to the public at press time. Kachina dolls carved by the men and pottery created by the women are sold in the village; signs indicate which houses sell crafts. With sweeping panoramas at every turn and a determined hold on traditions, Walpi is probably the most rewarding of all the Hopi villages.

SECOND MESA

Second Mesa (Junction)

Highways AZ 264 and AZ 87 meet at the foot of Second Mesa, seven miles west of Polacca and 60 miles north of Winslow. **LKD's Diner,** tel. 928/737-2717, serves Hopi tacos and tostadas, Mexican food, and burgers Mon.–Sat. for lunch and dinner. **Hopi Fine Arts-Alph Secakuku** gallery sells arts and crafts. You'll also find a grocery store and a post office here. **Honani Crafts Gallery** and a service station lie a half mile west at the turnoff for Shipaulovi and Mishongnovi villages.

Shipaulovi (Supawlavi) and Mishongnovi (Musangnuvi)

These villages are close neighbors on an eastern projection of Second Mesa. Dances often take place; ask at the Cultural Center for dates. You reach Shipaulovi (shih-PAW-lo-vee) and Mishongnovi (mih-SHONG-no-vee) by a short paved road that climbs steeply from AZ 264, a half mile west of the intersection with AZ 87, or by a mesa-top road (also paved, but not to be confused with the Pinon-Hard Rock Road) 0.3 mile east of the Cultural Center. Mishongnovi is the easternmost village, at the end of the mesa.

Shungopavi (Songoopavi)

Shungopavi (shong-O-po-vee or shih-MO-pah-vee) is the largest (pop. 742) of the three Second Mesa villages. Dances performed include the Butterfly Dance (a social dance) and the Snake Dance (late August in even-numbered years), though most have been closed to the public. **Dawa's Art and Crafts** on the road into the village sells locally made work. More galleries lie between the village turnoff and the Cultural Center. Shungopavi is 0.8 mile south off AZ 264, midway between the junction with AZ 87 and the Cultural Center.

HOPI CULTURAL CENTER

Proclaiming itself "At the Center of the Universe," this excellent pueblo-style museum/motel/restaurant/gift shop complex is popular with both visitors and local Hopi. The Hopi Cultural Center is situated on the west side of Second Mesa just before the road plunges down on the way to Third Mesa. For a shortcut to Chinle and Canyon de Chelly, turn north off AZ 264 beside the Cultural Center to Pinon Trading Post, proceed 26 miles (mostly rough and only partly paved), then east 42 miles on paved roads.

The museum displays good exhibits of Hopi culture and crafts with many historic photos. It's open all year Mon.–Fri. 8 A.M.–5 P.M.; from late March–late Oct. it's also open Sat.–Sun. 9 A.M.–3 P.M. There's a small gift shop just inside the entrance. Admission runs $3 adults, $1 children 13 and under; tel. 928/734-6650; website: www.hopionline.com. (To learn more of Hopi mythology and customs, dig into off-reservation sources such as the NAU Special Collections or Museum of Northern Arizona libraries, both in Flagstaff.)

The modern motel's nonsmoking rooms run $90 s, ($95 s Fri.–Sat.) and $5 each additional person; rates drop $30 in winter. Reservations are recommended; contact P.O. Box 67, Second Mesa, AZ 86043, tel. 928/734-2401. You'll find a free camping and picnic area next door, between the Cultural Center and the Hopi Arts & Crafts shop. No water or hookups are offered, but you can use the restrooms in the Cultural Center.

The restaurant serves good American and Hopi dishes. This is your big chance to try *paatupsuki* (pinto bean and hominy soup), or maybe some *noqkwivi* (traditional stew of Hopi corn and lamb), or a breakfast of blue pancakes made of Hopi corn. Not to be outdone by Navajo neighbors, the restaurant serves a Hopi taco (with beef) and a Hopi tostada (vegetarian). It's open daily for breakfast, lunch, and dinner.

Hopi Arts & Crafts (Silvercrafts Cooperative Guild), a short walk across the camping area, houses a big selection of traditional works; tel. 928/734-2463; closed Sunday. A small exhibit has examples of early Hopi silver jewelry.

You may also see artwork for sale in a gallery at the Hopi Cultural Center and displayed by vendors on tables outside. Iskasopu Gallery (on the left one mile to the east), Hopi Silver Arts and Crafts (the right 1.1 miles east), and Tsakurshovi (on the left 1.5 miles east) all offer good selections. Joseph and Janice Day at Tsakurshovi are a treasure trove of information about visiting and shopping in the Hopi lands.

Guides offer backcountry trips to petroglyph sites; ask at the motel desk.

THIRD MESA

Kykotsmovi (Kiqötsmovi)

The name means Mound of Ruined Houses. Hopi from Old Oraibi (o-RYE-bee) founded this settlement near a spring at the base of Third Mesa. Peach trees add greenery to the town. Kykotsmovi (kee-KEUTS-mo-vee), also known as New Oraibi, has offices of the Hopi Tribal Council.

The **Hopi Tribe Cultural Preservation Office,** tel. 928/734-2244, provides information for visitors to the Hopi Indian Reservation at its office in Kykotsmovi, one mile south of AZ 264 in the Tribal Headquarters building; contact the office at P.O. Box 123, Kykotsmovi, AZ 86039. The **Kykotsmovi**

Village Store in town sells groceries and fixes pizza, subs, and snacks in the back. **Sockyma's** is a good source of souvenirs.

You can stop for a picnic at Oraibi Wash, 0.8 mile east of the Kykotsmovi turnoff, or the Pumpkin Seed Hill overlook 1.2 miles west on the climb to Old Oraibi. Indian Route 2, leading south to Leupp (pronounced loop), is paved and is the shortest way to Flagstaff.

Old Oraibi (Orayvi)

This dusty pueblo perched on the edge of Third Mesa dates from A.D. 1150 and is probably the oldest continuously inhabited community in the United States.

The 20th century was difficult for this ancient village. In 1900 it ranked as one of the largest Hopi settlements, with a population of more than 800, but dissension caused many to leave. The first major dispute occurred in 1906 between two chiefs, You-ke-oma and Tawa-quap-tewa. Instead of letting fly with bullets and arrows, the leaders staged a "push-of-war" contest. A line was cut into the mesa and the two groups stood on either side. They pushed against each other as hard as they could until one group crossed the line and won. You-ke-oma, the loser, left with his faction to establish Hotevilla four miles away. This event was recorded a quarter mile north of Oraibi with the line and inscription: "Well, it have to be done this way now, that when you pass this LINE it will be DONE, Sept. 8, 1906." A bear paw cut in the rock is the symbol of Tawa-quap-tewa and his Bear Clan, while a skull represents You-ke-oma and his Skeleton Clan. Other residents split off to join New Oraibi at the foot of the mesa.

A ruin near Old Oraibi on the south end of the mesa is all that remains of a church built in 1901 by the Mennonite minister, H.R. Voth. Most villagers disliked having it so close to their homes and were no doubt relieved when lightning destroyed the church in 1942. It's closed to the public but you can see the ruin from the village.

Old Oraibi lies two miles west of Kykotsmovi. Avoid driving through the village and stirring up dust; park outside—or next to Hamana So-o's Arts & Crafts shop—and walk. Hopi arts and crafts are available at the **Calnimptewa Gallery** east of the turnoff for Old Oraibi, **Monongya Gallery** west of the Old Oraibi turnoff, and **Hamana So-o's Arts & Crafts** in the village.

Hotevilla (Hot'vela)

Hotevilla (HOAT-vih-lah) is known for its dances, basketry, and other crafts.

Founded in 1906 after the split from Old Oraibi, Hotevilla got off to a shaky start. Federal officials demanded that the group move back to Old Oraibi so their children could attend school there. Twenty-five men agreed to return with their families, despite continued bad feelings; about 53 others refused to leave Hotevilla. The recalcitrant men were jailed for 90 days while their children were forcibly removed to a Keams Canyon boarding school. That winter the women and infants fended for themselves, with little food and inadequate shelter. In the following year the men returned, building better houses and planting crops. Ex-

Old Oraibi with a kiva entrance in the foreground, late 1800s

N.E. ARIZONA

asperated authorities continued to haul You-ke-oma off to jail for his lack of cooperation and refusal to send village children to school. In 1912, government officials invited the chief to Washington for a meeting with President Taft, but the meeting didn't soften You-ke-oma's stance.

The turnoff for Hotevilla is 3.7 miles northwest of Old Oraibi and 46 miles southeast of Tuba City.

Bacavi (Paaqavi)

The You-ke-oma loyalists who returned to Old Oraibi under federal pressure continued to clash with the people of Tawa-quap-tewa. At one point, when two of the returning women died in quick succession, cries of witchcraft went up. Finally, in November 1909, tensions became unbearable. Members of the unwelcome group packed their bags once more and settled at a new site called Bacavi (BAH-kah-vee) Spring. The name means "jointed reed," after a plant found at the spring. Bacavi lies on the opposite side of the highway from Hotevilla.

Coal Mine Canyon

This scenic little canyon is 31 miles northwest of Bacavi (15 miles southeast of Tuba City) on AZ 264. Look for a windmill and the Coal Mine Mesa Rodeo Ground on the north side of the highway (no signs) between Mileposts 337 and 338, and turn in across the cattle guard. Hopi have long obtained coal from the seam just below the rim. Hoodoos rise out among the white and red cliffs below the overlook.

Moenkopi (Munqapi)

This Hopi village lies two miles southeast of Tuba City. Chief Tuba of Oraibi, 48 miles southeast, founded Moenkopi ("The Place of Running Water") in the 1870s. Mormons constructed a woolen mill in 1879 with plans to use local labor, but the Hopi disliked working with machinery and the project failed. Moenkopi has two sections—only the upper village participates in the Hopi Tribal Council; the more conservative lower village does not. Water from springs irrigates fields, an advantage not enjoyed by other Hopi villages.

Flagstaff and Vicinity

The high country surrounding Flagstaff offers dramatic and remarkably diverse landscapes. Cool forests, which cover much of the region, provide a delightful respite from the desert. Highways wind through many scenic and historic areas, yet backcountry travelers can explore on trails or forest roads all day without ever crossing a paved road. Anglers enjoy the many lakes on the Colorado Plateau and the streams below it. In winter, skiers zip down the runs on the San Francisco Peaks near Flagstaff and the shorter runs on Bill Williams Mountain near Williams. Cross-country skiers can strike out on their own or glide along groomed trails near the San Francisco Peaks, at Mormon Lake, or near Williams.

THE LAND

Flagstaff (elev. 7,000 feet) lies atop the Colorado Plateau, a giant uplifted landmass extending into Utah, Colorado, and New Mexico. As the land rose, vigorous rivers cut deeply through the rock layers, revealing beautiful forms and colors in countless canyons. Sheer cliffs of the Mogollon Rim mark the south edge of the Colorado Plateau.

© BILL WEIR

Wupatki Pueblo

FLAGSTAFF AND
VICINITY

To Grand Canyon
National Park

↑ To Page

64

N a v a j o

Hopi

Indian

Reservation

89

6730

Little

P a i n t e d

I n d i a n

305

545

LOMAKI
PUEBLO ★

Wupatki National
Monument

6730

2

CITADEL ★
PUEBLO

Colorado

DONEY
PICNIC ★
AREA

★
WUPATKI
PUEBLO

WUKOKI
PUEBLO

89

Doney
Mtn.
(5,589 ft.)

D e s e r t

Kachina
Peaks
Wilderness

779

Strawberry
Crater

SUNSET CRATER-
WUPATKI LOOP RD.

River

6732

6812

24

O'Leary Peak
(8,916 ft.) ▲

546

Wilderness

San Francisco Peaks

BONITO

545

418

San Francisco
Humphreys Peak
(12,633 ft.) ▲

▲
Sunset
Crater
(8,029 ft.)

Sunset Crater
Volcano National
Monument

2

▲
ARIZONA
SNOWBOWL

420

LITTLE ELDEN SPRINGS HORSE CAMP

15

15

516

89

Leupp

556

180

510

Flagstaff

Winona

R e s e r v a t i o n

ROUTE
66

★
THE
ARBORETUM

Walnut Canyon
National
Monument

ORT ▲
HILL

✕ FLAGSTAFF
PULLIAM AIRPORT

SEE
"FLAGSTAFF"
MAP

89A

40

To Winslow

17

Lower Lake
Mary

3

Coconino

Upper Lake
Mary

▲
Meteor
Crater
(5,050 ft.)

National

Forest

Oak Creek Canyon

Munds Park

90

Mormon
Lake

0   10 mi

0   10 km

Oak
Creek

Mormon
Lake

17

iona
Mountain
Wilderness
Munds

3

↓ To Phoenix

While rivers cut down, volcanoes shot up. For the last million years, large and small volcanoes sprouted in the San Francisco Volcanic Field around Flagstaff. The most striking include the San Francisco Peaks, of which Humphrey's Peak at 12,633 feet is Arizona's tallest mountain. Sunset Crater, the state's most beautiful volcano, is the youngster of the bunch, last erupting about 800 years ago—just yesterday, geologically speaking.

Climate

Expect a cool, invigorating mountain climate in most of the Flagstaff area. Spring, summer, and autumn bring pleasant weather to this high country, where temperatures generally peak in the 70s and 80s F. From early July into September, thunderstorm clouds billow into the air, letting loose scattered downpours.

Snow and sun battle it out in winter, when temperatures vary greatly—from the bitter cold of storms to the warmth of bright Arizona sunshine. In Flagstaff, average winter lows reach the teens, warming to highs in the lower 40s. The winter visitor should be prepared for anything from sub-zero weather to warm, spring-like temperatures. Skiers enjoy the snow, though not many people brave the higher elevations for camping or backpacking. Annual precipitation, arriving mostly in summer and winter, varies between 10 and 30 inches, depending on elevation and rain shadows.

Flora and Fauna

The great range in elevation, together with a varied topography, provide many different habitats. Tiny alpine plants hug the ground against strong winds and extreme cold on the highest slopes of the San Francisco Peaks, where no trees can survive. At lower elevations, dense groves of aspen, fir, and pine thrive on the mountainsides and in protected canyons. Squirrels busy themselves storing away food for the long winters here, while larger animals just visit for the summer.

Vast forests of ponderosa pine and Gambel oak cover much of the Colorado Plateau. Elk, mule deer, a few black bears, coyotes, and smaller animals make these forests their home. Some of the many birds you'll likely see include the ubiquitous common raven, noisy Steller's jay, and feisty hummingbird. Drier parts of the Flagstaff area support woodlands of juniper, pinyon pine, oak, and Arizona cypress. Herds of pronghorn, a graceful, antelope-like creature, roam the arid grasslands north of the San Francisco Volcanic Field.

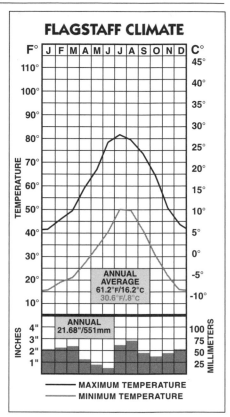

FLAGSTAFF CLIMATE

ANNUAL AVERAGE 61.2°F/16.2°C 30.6°F/.8°C

ANNUAL 21.68"/551mm

——— MAXIMUM TEMPERATURE
——— MINIMUM TEMPERATURE

FLAGSTAFF AREA HIGHLIGHTS

Flagstaff: This lively university town offers history, science, entertainment, and many travelers' facilities.
San Francisco Volcanic Field: Arizona's highest summit and hundreds of other volcanoes rise in scenic splendor.
Walnut Canyon National Monument: Prehistoric cliff dwellings lie tucked in alcoves of this pretty canyon.
Sunset Crater Volcano National Monument: A beautifully formed and colored volcano stands amidst a lunarlike area of lava flows and cinder craters.
Wupatki National Monument: Large, well-constructed pueblos offer a look into the world of the prehistoric people who once lived here.

HISTORY

Native Americans

Archaeologists have dated prehistoric sites along the Little Colorado River as far back as 15,000 B.C., when now-extinct species of bison, camel, antelope, and horse roamed the land. Although some tribes engaged in agriculture between 2,000 and 500 B.C., they maintained a seasonal migration pattern of hunting and gathering. These nomadic groups planted corn, squash, and beans in the spring, continued their travels, then returned to harvest the fields in autumn.

From about A.D. 200–500, as the tribes devoted more time to farming, they built clusters of pithouses near their fields. Regional ancestral Puebloan cultures then began to form, classified by scientists as the Anasazi of the Colorado Plateau, the Mogollon of the eastern Arizona uplands, and the Hohokam of the desert to the south. A fourth culture, the Sinagua, evolved near present-day Flagstaff between A.D. 900 and 1000 as a blend of the three other groups. The Sinagua (Spanish name "without water") could live here despite the area's dry volcanic soil.

As these societies developed further, the people started to build pueblos above ground. Villages, usually situated on hilltops or in cliff overhangs, went up in widely scattered locations over north-central Arizona. By about A.D. 1100 the population reached its peak. Most inhabitants then migrated, abandoning villages and even whole areas. Archaeologists attempt to explain these departures with theories of drought, soil erosion, disease, and raids by the newly arrived Apache. By the 1500s, when Spanish explorers arrived in northern Arizona, the Pueblo tribes had retreated to northeastern Arizona and adjacent New Mexico. Thousands of empty villages remain in the Flagstaff area, some protected in the four national monuments of Wupatki, Walnut Canyon, Tuzigoot, and Montezuma Castle-Montezuma Well. You might also discover ruins while hiking in the backcountry.

Americans Settle In

Beginning in the 1820s, mountain men such as Antoine Leroux became expert trappers and guides in this little-known region between Santa Fe and California. They and other early travelers sent out glowing reports of the climate, water, and scenery of the region, but hostile Apache, Navajo, Yavapai, and Paiute discouraged settlement. As a result, development in the Flagstaff area started later than in southern and central Arizona. Captain Lorenzo Sitgreaves brought a surveying expedition across northern Arizona in 1851, prompting Lieutenant Edward Beale and others to build rough wagon roads, but hostile tribes and poor farming land continued to discourage settlers.

Thomas Forsythe McMillan, who arrived from California with a herd of sheep in 1876, became Flagstaff's first permanent settler. Other ranchers soon moved into the area,

THE MARVELLOUS COUNTRY

In the early 1870s, former Tucson judge Samuel Cozzens traveled east to stir up prospective settlers with a large, well-illustrated book titled *The Marvellous Country; or, Three Years in Arizona and New Mexico, the Apache's Home.* The subtitle expanded upon this theme: *Comprising a Description of this Wonderful Country, Its Immense Mineral Wealth, Its Magnificent Mountain Scenery, the Ruins of Ancient Towns and Cities Found Therein, With a Complete History of the Apache Tribe, and a Description of the Author's Guide Cochise, the Great Apache War Chief, the Whole Interspersed with Strange Events and Adventures.* Cozzens's book sold well in New England and he gave many talks to eager audiences. With each retelling, his descriptions of Arizona's climate, forests, water, and mineral wealth grew and improved. By 1875, the Arizona Colonization Company, with Cozzens as president, was established in Boston. In February 1876, a group of about 50 men, each with 300 pounds of tools and clothing, set off for Arizona under the auspices of the company. In May a second group embarked for the "marvellous country."

After 90 days of arduous travel, the first group arrived at their destination on the Little Colorado River only to find the land already claimed by Mormons. The group continued west to the San Francisco Peaks and started to build a settlement, dubbed Agassiz. But finding no land suitable for farming or mining, they gave up and left for Prescott and California even before the second group arrived. The second group gave up, too, but not before stripping a pine tree and flying a flag from it to celebrate July 4th.

COURTESY OF AISLINN RACE

a coach starting for the Grand Canyon in the late 1880s

bringing the total population to 67 in 1880. The coming of the railroad in 1882, thriving lumber mills, and success in sheep and cattle ranching opened up the region and led to the growth of railroad towns such as Flagstaff and Williams.

TRANSPORTATION

You really need your own vehicle to visit the national monuments and most of the scenic and recreation areas. Tours make brief stops at highlights of the region but tend to be rushed; see "Tours" in the Flagstaff section. Greyhound provides frequent bus service across northern Arizona via Flagstaff and between Flagstaff and Phoenix. Nava-Hopi buses connect Flagstaff with the Grand Canyon to the north and Phoenix to the south. Amtrak runs daily trains across northern Arizona in each direction between Los Angeles and Albuquerque and beyond. A regional airline serves Flagstaff.

Flagstaff

Surrounded by pine forest in the center of northern Arizona, Flagstaff (pop. 63,000) has long served as an important stop for ranchers, Native Americans, and travelers. The older, downtown part of Flagstaff still offers a bit of that frontier feeling, expressed by its many historic buildings. Other parts of this small city may seem like endless lines of motels, restaurants, bars, and service stations, but even here one can find reminders of old Route 66 that once linked Flagstaff with the rest of America.

Downtown is an enjoyable place to stroll, to admire the architecture, and perhaps to sample some of the unique restaurants and shops. Many of the old structures have plaques describing their history. To visit the distant past, when the land rose up, volcanoes erupted, and the early tribes arrived, drop by the Museum of Northern Arizona. To learn about the pioneers of 100 years ago, head over to the Pioneer Historical Museum and the Riordan Mansion State Historic Park. To see the current art scene, swing by the Art Barn and University Art Galleries. For a trip out of this world, visit Lowell Observatory, where astronomers discovered Pluto, or the U.S. Geological Survey, where astrogeologists map celestial bodies.

For the great outdoors, head for the hills—Arizona's highest mountains begin at the northern outskirts of town. In summer, the mountains, hills, and meadows offer pleasant forest walks and challenging climbs. Winter snows transform the countryside into some of the state's best downhill and cross-country skiing areas. As a local guidebook, *Coconino County, the Wonderland of America,* put it in 1916, Flagstaff "offers you the advantages of any city of twice its size; it has, free for the taking, the healthiest and most invigorating

of climates; its surrounding scenic beauties will fill one season, from May–November, full to overflowing with enjoyment the life of any tourist, vacationist, camper or out doors man or woman who will but come to commune with nature."

SIGHTS

Flagstaff has many free parking spaces along the streets, by the Visitor Center, and in a few lots; these generally have a two-hour limit. A free all-day lot lies off Beaver St.; turn south

FLAGSTAFF'S FLAGPOLES

It's obvious that Flagstaff was named for a flagpole. The question is, which one? The first group of settlers to arrive from Boston claimed to have erected a flagpole in April or May of 1876, before the July 4th celebration held by the second Boston group later that year. The stripped pine tree left by the second group at their Antelope Spring camp may have been the pole that served as the town's namesake. Later travelers referred to the spot as the spring by the flag staff. As the first sheep ranchers settled nearby, the area became known as Flag Staff, then finally Flagstaff.

However some early settlers regarded a tall tree, trimmed of all branches, at the foot of McMillan Mesa as *the* flagstaff. Others disputed this idea, stating that Lieutenant Edward Beale had delimbed the tree in the 1850s or that it was the work of a later railroad-surveying party. No record actually exists of a flag ever flying from the tree.

At any rate, citizens gathered in the spring of 1881 and chose the name "Flagstaff" for the settlement.

FLAGSTAFF

To Snowbowl, Hart Prairie, and Grand Canyon South Rim

SHULTZ PASS RD.

ELDEN LOOKOUT RD.

180

★ MUSEUM OF NORTHERN ARIZONA

COCONINO CENTER FOR THE ARTS ★

PIONEER MUSEUM ★ ★ ART BARN

FORT VALLEY RD.

BUFFALO PARK ■

MCPHERSON PARK ■

GEMINI DR.

J. LIVELY ICE RINK ■

FOREST AVE.

FLAGSTAFF MEDICAL CENTER ■

FLAGSTAFF FIELD CENTER OF U.S.G.S. ■

FORT VALLEY SHOPPING CENTER ■

FLAGSTAFF HIGH SCHOOL ■

TURQUOISE DR.

THORPE PARK/ ADULT CENTER ■

LOWELL OBSERVATORY ★

ELM AVE.

CHERRY AVE.

TOLTEC

MARS HILL RD.

HUMPHREYS

LEROUX ST.

BEAVER ST.

SAN FRANCISCO ST.

SWITZER CANYON DR.

PUBLIC LIBRARY ■

CITY HALL ■

POST OFFICE (DOWNTOWN BRANCH) ■

GREYHOUND BUS ■

COTTAGE AVE.

CENTENNIAL BUILDING ★

AMTRAK/FLAGSTAFF VISITOR CENTER ■

66 180

RIORDAN RD.

CLINE LIBRARY ■ ★ OLD MAIN

BUTLER AVE.

ENTERPRISE RD.

I-40 EXIT 198

To I-40 Exit 191

PERFORMING AND FINE ARTS BUILDING ■

★ WALL AQUATIC CENTER

66

WOODY MOUNTAIN CAMPGROUND ⛺

KIT CARSON RV PARK ⛺

UNIVERSITY PLAZA SHOPPING CENTER ■

★ LUMBERJACK STADIUM

RIORDAN MANSION STATE HISTORIC PARK ●

THE INN AT NAU ■

WOODY MTN. RD.

To Williams

SHERWOOD FOREST SHOPPING CENTER ■

TARGET ■

KNOLES DR.

NORTHERN ARIZONA UNIVERSITY

40

GREEN TREE VILLAGE SHOPPING CENTER ■

SAN FRANCISCO ST.

FOREST MEADOWS ST.

MCCONNELL CIR.

To Arboretum

WOODLANDS VILLAGE BLVD.

40

MILTON RD.

WALKUP SKYDOME ★

WOODLANDS VILLAGE PLAZA AND WAL-MART ■

89A

I-40 EXIT 195, I-17 EXIT 340

17

To Airport, Fort Tuthill County Fairgrounds, and Sedona

To Verde Valley and Phoenix

To Lake Mary and Payson

LAKE MARY RD.

MOON

FLAGSTAFF

ELDEN PUEBLO ★

To Sunset and Wupatki
National Monuments,
Grand Canyon North and
South Rims, and Page

▲
Mt. Elden
(9,299 ft)

89

KOA CAMPGROUND ∧

ELDEN LOOKOUT TRAILHEAD ■

U.S. FOREST SERVICE
(PEAKS RANGER ■
STATION)

FLAGSTAFF MALL
(INDOORS)

CEDAR PLAZA
■ SHOPPING
CENTER

BUSHMASTER
PARK

CEDAR   AVE.   LOCKETT RD.   ■ PARK SANTA FE
                                    SHOPPING CENTER

GREENLAW LN.   MUSEUM
        U.S. FOREST SERVICE CLUB ■
        (SUPERVISOR'S OFFICE)

KACHINA SQUARE SHOPPING
CENTER

SEVENTH AVE.   LAKIN
                DR.
POST OFFICE (MAIN)

INDUSTRIAL DR.

40

I-40 EXIT 201

40

COUNTRY CLUB DR.

ELDEN HILLS
GOLF COURSE

OAKMONT DR.

To Walnut Canyon
National Monument
and Winslow

ROUTE 66/SANTA FE AVE.

FOURTH ST.

BUTLER

AVE.

EDGEWOOD ST.

BLACK BART'S
■ STEAK HOUSE
& RV PARK

■ LITTLE AMERICA

MT. PLEASANT DR.

0   2 mi

0   2 km

from Route 66, then right just after the railroad tracks; RVs can park in an adjacent lot by crossing the railroad tracks on Beaver St., turning right on Phoenix Ave., then right into the parking area.

Museum of Northern Arizona

This active museum features excellent displays of the geology, archaeology, anthropology, cultures, and fine art of the Colorado Plateau. A timeline of Native Americans illustrates their stages of development during prehistoric times with beautiful archaeological findings. A prehistoric kiva mural comes from an excavation of Awatovi on Hopi lands. Contemporary Native American exhibits illustrate the traditions of northern Arizona tribes and their basketry, pottery, weaving, kachina dolls, and ceremonies. Art galleries display changing exhibits of Native American and Southwestern works. The museum's attractive building has walls of dark volcanic stone and tile roofs; it encloses courtyards filled with native flora.

Popular museum-sponsored shows take place during the summer, exhibiting excellent arts and crafts: The Hispanic Festival runs the weekend before Memorial Day; the Hopi Marketplace runs on the weekend nearest July Fourth; Navajo Marketplace is on the first weekend in August; Zuni Marketplace is held in late August or early September, and the Festival of Pai Arts is in late September. Enduring Creations, a changing sales exhibition of the finest Native American, Hispanic, and Western artwork, runs through the summer. The museum shop sells high-quality Native American work, including Navajo blankets, jewelry (by Navajo, Hopi, and Zuni), Hopi kachina dolls and pottery by several tribes. A bookstore stocks an excellent selection of books and posters related to the region. Rio de Flag Nature Trail makes a half-mile loop in the little canyon behind the museum; borrow the trail booklet—both adult and children's versions available—from the ticket desk. You can use the museum's library—one of the most extensive for Southwest topics—across the highway in the Research Center; it's open Mon.–Fri. 9 A.M.–5 P.M.

A visit to the Museum of Northern Arizona is highly recommended for anyone planning to buy Native American crafts, to visit the reservations of northern Arizona, or to better understand the natural history of the area surrounding the Grand Canyon.

Set beside a little canyon in a pine forest, the museum is open daily 9 A.M.–5 P.M.; admission is $5 adults, $4 seniors, $3 students with I.D., $2 ages 7–17, tel. 928/774-5213; website: www.musnaz.org. From downtown Flagstaff, head three miles northwest on US 180; the museum is on the left.

Scenic Sky Ride

Arizona Snowbowl's chairlift will take you to 11,500 feet on the San Francisco Peaks for great panoramas. It's open daily 10 A.M.– 4 P.M. in summer (June 21–Labor Day weekend), then Fri.–Sun. from Labor Day– mid-October, weather permitting; tel. 928/779-1951. A restaurant serves lunch. The ride costs $9 adult, $6.50 seniors 65–69 (free age 70+), $5 kids 8–12. To reach the Snowbowl, drive northwest seven miles from downtown on US 180, then turn right at the sign and drive seven miles on a paved road.

Pioneer Museum

After completion in 1908, this venerable stone building served 30 years as the Coconino County Hospital for the Indigent. Townspeople also knew it as the "poor farm"—because stronger patients grew vegetables in the yard.

Today the building houses permanent and changing exhibits that illustrate many aspects of life in Flagstaff's pioneering days. Old photos and artifacts tell the stories of ranchers, timber men, scientists, explorers, and families. A giant stuffed bear greets visitors on the second floor; slip by the beast to see a restored hospital room and more galleries. Exhibits here may include memorabilia of Percival Lowell and his observatory and the camera gear and photos of Emery Kolb, who came to the Grand Canyon in 1902, set up a photo studio with his brother Ellsworth, and continued showing movies and stills until 1976.

Outside, you can peer into the restored 1908 Ben Doney Cabin, moved here from a site east of town. A working blacksmith shop, often in use in summer, and old farm machinery lie behind the museum. By the road stands a powerful 1929 steam locomotive used by the logging industry, with a log car and caboose. On the first weekend in June, the Wool Festival features shearing and other skills, and the Independence Day Festival demonstrates traditional crafts on the weekend nearest July Fourth. Playthings of the Past marks the winter holiday season. Pioneer Historical Museum, run by the Northern Division of the Arizona Historical Society, is open Mon.–Sat. 9 A.M.–5 P.M.; donation requested. There's a small gift shop; tel. 928/774-6272. From downtown, the museum lies on the right just past Sechrist School, about two miles northwest on US 180.

The Art Barn

Regional artists and art patrons have banded together to operate this large sales gallery. Here you'll find a great selection of works by both Native American and Anglo artisans, including paintings, sketches, photographs, pottery, jewelry, kachina dolls, Navajo rugs, sand paintings, rock art (petroglyph reproductions), and books. You can also purchase old pawn jewelry. The Art Barn has its own bronze foundry and a frame shop. Prices are right, too, since there's no distributor markup or big advertising budget. The Art Barn is open Tues.–Sat. 10 A.M.–5 P.M.; tel. 928/774-0822. It's conveniently located behind the Pioneer Museum.

Lowell Observatory

Percival Lowell (1855–1916) founded the observatory in 1894, using his personal fortune to fund a search for signs of intelligent life on Mars. The observatory's early contributions to astronomy included spectrographic photographs by V.M. Slipher that resulted in the discovery of the expanding universe, and Clyde Tombaugh's 1930 discovery of Pluto. Research continues with telescopes here, at Anderson Mesa 12 miles southeast of town, and at other locations.

In the Steele Visitor Center, you can explore the field of astronomy with interactive exhibits and see many examples of instruments used by astronomers over the years. Informative 90-minute tours begin with a multimedia program illustrating the history and work of the observatory; you'll then visit the 1896 24-inch Clark refractor telescope used to study Mars and the expanding universe and to map the Moon for lunar expeditions. The tour continues to the Rotunda, designed as a library by Lowell's wife but completed only in 1916—the year of Lowell's death. Inside you can see the spectrograph used in the discovery of the expanding universe and other historical exhibits, such as the Pluto photographic plates, with the same view Tombaugh enjoyed at the instant he found Pluto. The final stop on the tour visits the specially designed telescope used to discover Pluto. You're free to join and leave the tours as you wish and explore the grounds on your own, but guests can see interiors only with the tour guide. A solar viewing program takes place daily if the clouds cooperate; call for the time.

The visitor center is open daily 9 A.M.–5 P.M. April–Oct. and noon–5 P.M. the rest of the year, except closed Mon.–Tues. in January and February. A bookstore has good reading along with posters and videos. Admission is $4 adults, $3.50 seniors and university students,

FLAGSTAFF

PLANET X

The ancients recorded five bright star-like wandering bodies. Later generations figured out that these—and Earth as well—are planets. While conducting star surveys in 1781, William Herschel discovered a seventh planet, now known as Uranus, which had been plotted on sky charts at least two dozen times as a star. Astronomers used these positions to plot the planet's orbit, but Uranus was not moving according to Newton's mechanics. In the early 1820s it was moving too slowly, but by the end of that decade it was moving too fast.

British astronomer John Couch Adams and French astronomer Urbain Leverrier, working independently, performed laborious calculations based on the assumption that the gravitational pull of an undiscovered eighth planet was affecting Uranus' movement. Both men's predicted positions for the new planet were very close and a short telescopic search

soon revealed the "new" planet, which was named Neptune.

Neptune had also been plotted as a star on several charts before its 1846 discovery. Again, the planet did not seem to be following a perfect orbit. Several astronomers started calculations to find a ninth planet, which they dubbed "Planet X." Percival Lowell spent years figuring a position for Planet X but did not have suitable telescopes to search the sky for it. Since his main interest lay in finding signs of life on Mars, his instruments were powerful, but did not show wide-angle views, and they were so slow photographically that some exposures required guidance hour after hour—night after night in some cases—for a single photograph.

Lowell died before a suitable telescope could be built, and the sky search for Planet X did not begin again for more than a decade. Harvard president A. Lawrence Lowell (Percival's broth-

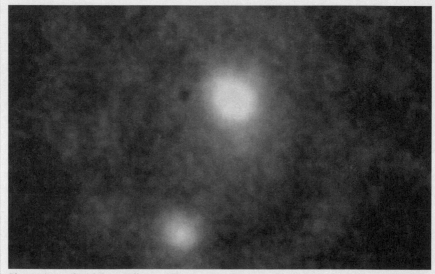

Pluto, pictured with its small moon Charon, remains the only planet in our solar system that has not been visited by a spacecraft.

er) donated money to build a small but wide-angled and photographically fast telescope. This instrument exposed plates 14 inches by 17 inches covering a field 12 by 14 degrees and required less than an hour of exposure.

Each plate showed between 40,000 and one million stars. Since the distant planet was too far away to be recognizable as one by any telescope, only its motion against the background of stars as it circled the Sun would reveal it as a planet. Thus, each plate would be duplicated several days later and then each star image would be compared from plate to plate until one of the "stars" was found to have moved a distance appropriate for a planet that far from the Sun.

Twenty-two-year-old Kansas farm boy and astronomy student Clyde Tombaugh set to work exposing the plates by night and using a blink comparator by day to conduct the search. The blink comparator would flash a view of part of one plate through a microscope eyepiece, then flash a view of the corresponding section of a second plate. If an object had moved, it would appear in the eyepiece as if it were jumping back and forth. That sounds easy, but Tombaugh examined hundreds of thousands of star images during a search of about nine months before finding one that moved an appropriate distance. He also discovered some asteroids and variable stars in the process.

Although Tombaugh discovered Pluto on February 18, 1930, using plates made on January 23 and January 29, Lowell Observatory cautiously waited to announce the new planet, studying its motion in the meantime to verify that it was truly the long-sought Planet X. The announcement was made on March 13, 1930—the 75th anniversary of Lowell's birth.

Many people wanted to name the new planet for Percival Lowell; others favored Clyde Tombaugh. An English schoolgirl sent in the winning suggestion "Pluto" in honor of the Greek god of the underworld, brother of Jupiter and Neptune. The planet's astronomical symbol became "P" with an "L" bottom stem. This abbreviation for Pluto also represented Percival Lowell's initials and honored his contribution.

and $2 ages 5–17. The entry fee includes the guided tours, which depart at 10 A.M., 1 P.M., and 3 P.M. April–Oct., but only at 1 P.M. and 3 P.M. Nov.–March.

At night, the visitor center reopens for Sky Tonight Programs and viewing through the historic Clark telescope, weather permitting; these run Mon.–Sat. in summer, then decrease to only Sat. in midwinter; call to check days and times. The cost is the same as for a daytime visit.

The observatory schedules many special events through the year, so it's worth calling or looking at the website to check times and see what's coming up; tel. 928/774-2096 (recording); website: www.lowell.edu. The observatory sits atop Mars Hill, one mile from downtown, and is well signed; head west on Route 66 and continue straight on Santa Fe Ave. where the highway curves left. In winter the steep road up Mars Hill requires caution and often snow chains.

Earth and Planetary Geologic Studies

Many of the scientists at the Flagstaff Field Center of the U.S. Geological Survey study and map Earth's moon, the planets, and other solid bodies of our solar system using data collected from space missions. They also investigate Earth's landforms such as volcanoes and sand dunes, formed by the same processes as those on extraterrestrial bodies. The Apollo astronauts received geologic training and tested their equipment here, and were later guided while on the Moon by geologists from this center. Other scientists at the center investigate and monitor many of Earth's geologic processes. Hydrologists monitor stream flows and geologists study rock layers, faults, and volcanoes. Geologic mapping helps define our landscape and what lies beneath it.

You're welcome to visit the Field Center and browse among exhibits throughout the buildings' hallways. Begin by picking up a self-guided tour brochure in the lobby of Buildings 3, 4, or 6. Giant maps and spectacular color images from spacecraft cover the walls in the hallways. Images include shots of Jupiter and Saturn and their moons, remote-sensing products showing the Earth's features, and views sent back by spacecraft landing on Mars and Venus. The geology of the Moon and most solid-surfaced planets and their satellites has been mapped in surprising detail. Even cloud-covered Venus gave up some of her secrets through radar images with computer-generated color. Building 4 displays additional planetary exhibits, while the hallways of Building 3 show maps and photos of geologic and hydrologic studies here on Earth. Building 6, the Eugene M. Shoemaker Center for Astrogeology, should be open by late 2002. You'll be able to step into the lobby to see the exhibit area with the stories of Shoemaker, Apollo astronauts, and others who have contributed to our knowledge of the Moon and beyond. Models and dioramas will show spacecraft. Building 6 will also feature "A Walk Through the Solar System," as well as a specialized library open to the public for reference use.

You may visit Mon.–Fri. 8 A.M.–4:30 P.M. Remember that the people working here are normally too busy to show visitors around. Also, don't enter offices or labs unless invited. To arrange tours for scientific or educational groups, call or write in advance to the U.S. Geological Survey, 2255 N. Gemini Dr., Flagstaff, AZ 86001, tel. 928/556-7000. The Flagstaff Field Center's website, www.flag.wr.usgs.gov, features some of the work done and products available. The Center lies atop McMillan Mesa off Forest Ave./Cedar Ave., 1.5 miles northeast of downtown. Nearby Buffalo Park is a good place to go for a walk or hike.

Riordan Mansion State Historic Park

The Riordan brothers, Timothy and Michael, arrived in Flagstaff during the mid-1880s and eventually took over the Arizona Lumber & Timber Company. Both became involved with the social, business, and political life of early Flagstaff. In 1904, they built a grand mansion just south of downtown. A "Rendezvous Room" connected the wings occupied by each brother's family. The architect Charles Whittlesey, who also designed El Tovar Hotel on the rim of the Grand Canyon, used a similar rustic style of logs and stonework for the mansion exterior. The brothers christened their joint home *Kinlichi,* Navajo for "Red House."

Tours of 50–60 minutes visit Timothy's side of the house and reveal how the wealthy lived in Flagstaff during the early 1900s. Guides offer history and comment on the furnishings and architectural features. Only the Riordans have lived here, and all the rooms still display their original furniture, most done in American Craftsman style. The wing occupied by Michael's family has recently opened to the public as well, with exhibits that you can see on your own. You can compare the two sides of the house, which mirror each other.

The park is open daily 8:30 A.M.–5 P.M. from May–October; tours depart on the hour with the first one at 9 A.M. and the last at 4 P.M. During the rest of the year, hours are 10:30 A.M.–5 P.M. daily with the first tour at 11 A.M. and the last at 4 P.M. There's no charge to see the exhibits in the visitor center or to take the self-guided tour of the grounds. Fees to go inside the mansion are $5 adults, $2.50 ages 7–13; tel. 928/779-4395. It's best to phone in advance for tour reservations. A video shown on request has interior views. Standard wheelchairs can access the lower floor. Picnic tables are near the parking area. You'll find this piece of historic Flagstaff between S. Milton Rd. and Northern Arizona University, about a half mile south of downtown; turn east on Riordan Road toward NAU from S. Milton, then turn right at the sign, opposite Ardrey Auditorium.

Northern Arizona University (NAU)

Flagstaff's character and population owe much to this school, just south of downtown. The university began in 1899 as Northern Arizona Normal School, housed in a vacant reformatory building. Four young women received their diplomas and teaching certificates two years later.

In 1925 the school began offering a four-year Bachelor of Education degree and took the name Northern Arizona State Teachers College. The program broadened over the years to include other degrees, a program in forestry, and graduate studies. In 1966 the institution became a university. NAU's sprawling campus now covers 686 acres, supplemented by the School of Forestry's 4,000-acre laboratory forest. The High Altitude Training Center's programs attract athletic teams from around the world to improve their performance in the thin mountain air.

The 1893 Old Main building, on McMullen Circle in the northern part of campus, houses changing exhibits of the **Old Main Art Gallery** on the first floor and a permanent collection of fine art and furniture in the

Marguerite Hettel Weiss Gallery on the second floor. Be ready for almost anything in the **Richard E. Beasley Gallery** upstairs in the Fine and Performing Arts Building, south on Knoles Dr., where 30-day shows feature contemporary art. Call 928/523-3471 or check website: www.nau.edu to find what's showing at the galleries; they're open Mon.–Sat. except between shows.

Northern Arizona University (NAU) Observatory, tel. 928/523-7170, built by the U.S. Air Force as an atmospheric research observatory in the early 1950s, is still used today for research, but it primarily serves as an educational tool for university students and the general public. Volunteers, mostly astronomy club members, hold an open house most clear Friday nights at 7:30 P.M. with special open nights for astronomical events such as eclipses and occultations. It's off S. San Francisco St. adjacent to a high-rise dormitory and practice field.

Wall Aquatic Center, tel. 928/523-4508, contains a large indoor swimming pool on Franklin Ave. between S. Beaver and S. San Francisco Sts.; it's open to the public. Call or check the Web for the schedule.

To learn about NAU services and events, call or visit the University Union Information Desk, tel. 928/523-4636, or call the switchboard, tel. 928/523-9011; website: www.nau.edu. **NAU Downtown** also offers information, event tickets, and parking permits in Heritage Square at Aspen Ave. and Leroux St., tel. 928/523-1628. A free shuttle bus makes a loop around the northern and southern parts of the main campus. Ask someone for the location of the stop nearest you. The service runs about every 15 minutes Mon.–Thurs. 7:35 A.M.–11 P.M. and Friday 7:35 A.M.–5 P.M. during the main school terms. To park on campus, pick up a visitor's permit from NAU Downtown (see above) or from the **Parking Services/Visitor Information** office, tel. 928/523-3591, in the Centennial

Building at the southwest corner of Dupont Ave. and S. Beaver St.; it's open Mon.–Fri. 7:30 A.M.–5 P.M. (4:30 P.M. in summer). After hours you can obtain a parking permit from the police office at Lumberjack Stadium off S. San Francisco Street.

The Arboretum

Plant enthusiasts here do research on native and nonnative flora that thrive in the cool climate of the Flagstaff area. More than 700 species of plants and trees grow on the 200-acre grounds, despite the short 75-day average growing season. At 7,150 feet elevation, the arboretum is the highest botanical garden in the United States doing horticultural research. You'll get a good introduction to the flora of the Colorado Plateau here. Northern Arizona residents can gain a wealth of landscaping and gardening information.

Tours of 45–60 minutes, which begin at 11 A.M. and 1 P.M., introduce ongoing projects and take you through the solar greenhouse and outdoor gardens. You'll see endangered species that the staff works to propagate. Exhibits, which you can also visit on your own, include gardens of native and adapted plants, wildflowers, herbs, and vegetables. The constructed wetlands area uses native plants to treat wastewater, which gets recycled for watering other plants. A nature trail through the ponderosa pine forest has a 0.6-mile inner loop and a one-mile outer loop. The visitor center has exhibits, including mounted specimens of many local species. A gift shop offers books, cards, a bird list, Extension Bulletins (gardening and tree advice), seeds, and gardening supplies. You can purchase plants at the Summer Plant Sale and Garden Fair on the third weekend of June and through the season, then again at the Holiday Plant Sale on the first Saturday in December.

Annual events include the two plant sales and an Open House on the second Saturday in July. The Arboretum is open daily 9 A.M.–5 P.M. from April 1–Dec. 15; admission is $4 adults, $3 age 6–12; tel. 928/774-1441; website: www.thearb.org. No pets permitted. Summer (June–Sept.) is the best time to visit. Picnic tables are available. From S. Milton Rd. in Flagstaff, head west 1.9 miles on Route 66, then turn south four miles on Woody Mountain Road.

Elden Pueblo

The resourceful Sinagua tribe lived at this site below Mt. Elden about A.D. 1150. Some of the pueblo, including a large community room, has been excavated. A leaflet explains and illustrates features of the ruin, open during daylight hours; there's no admission charge. It's on the northeast edge of town; head north on US 89 past the Flagstaff Mall and the Peaks Ranger Station to the signed turn on the left, just before the Camp Townsend-Winona Road.

RECREATION

City Parks

Drop in one of these for a picnic under the pines, a playground for the kids, or a game of tennis or basketball. You can reach Flagstaff Parks & Recreation at 211 W. Aspen Ave.; tel. 928/779-7690. **Thorpe Park** lies just west of downtown at 245 N. Thorpe Rd.; the adjacent Adult Center, tel. 928/774-1068, hosts many community activities and clubs. From downtown, head west on Route 66 and keep straight where the highway curves left, continue west on Santa Fe Ave. about 5 blocks, then turn right one block on Toltec Street. **McPherson Park** and the adjacent ice skating rink at **Jay Lively Activity Center,** tel. 928/774-1051, lie northeast of downtown at 1650 N. Turquoise Dr.; you can head north on San Francisco St. from downtown, turn right on Forest Ave., then left on Turquoise Drive. Over on the east side of town, **Bushmaster Park** is at Lockett Rd. and Alta Vista Dr. (turn south

© BILL WEIR

team roping at the Pine County Pro Rodeo

from Lockett Rd. at the sign); there's also a skate park here for skateboards, rollerskates, and rollerblades.

Flagstaff Urban Trail System
You don't have to go far for a hike, as this trail network goes right through town. It connects the Mt. Elden trails with the Arizona Trail, Walnut Canyon National Monument, and other areas surrounding Flagstaff. Mountain bikers, hikers, joggers, and cross-country skiers use the trails, which currently total about 20 miles. The City Planning Office in the Flagstaff City Hall at 211 W. Aspen has maps.

Horseback Riding
The Flagstaff area is great horse country. If you don't have your own steed, local riding stables can provide one; reservations are advised.

The Flying Heart Barn, tel. 928/526-2788, offers hour-long, half-day, and full-day rides year-round on and near the San Francisco Peaks; head 3.5 miles north on US 89 from I-40 Exit 201. **MacDonalds Ranch,** US 180 and Snowbowl Rd., tel. 928/774-4481, rides below the Peaks on one- and two-hour trips and hayrides between Memorial Day and Labor Day weekends.

Downhill Skiing
Arizona Snowbowl, on the San Francisco Peaks, has some of Arizona's best downhill action. Four chair lifts and a tow rope service 30 runs/trails ranging from novice to expert. From the top of Agassiz Chairlift, it's two miles and 2,300 feet down. With sufficient snow, the Snowbowl is open for skiing daily 9 A.M.–4 P.M. from mid-December–Easter. Lift tickets cost $33 ($27 afternoons on weekends and holidays; $20 afternoons on weekdays) for adults; $18 ($13 afternoons) for ages 8–12; $13 seniors 65–69; and free for kids seven and younger and for seniors over 70. Call 928/779-1951 for recorded information about lifts, rentals, and instruction and for weather and road conditions; website: www.arizonas-nowbowl.com.

Hart Prairie Lodge (elev. 9,200 feet) offers a ski school, rentals, repairs and a restaurant. **Ski Lift Lodge,** on US 180 opposite the Snow Bowl Road turnoff, tel. 928/774-0729 or 800/472-3599, has rooms and a restaurant. To reach the Snowbowl, drive northwest seven miles from downtown on US 180 to the sign, then turn right seven miles on a paved road, which sometimes requires chains and/or 4WD.

Cross-Country Skiing

Flagstaff Nordic Center, tel. 928/779-1951, offers more than 40 km of groomed trails ranging from beginner–advanced near Hart Prairie and the San Francisco Peaks. A five-km marked trail leads to the Hochderrfer Hills (maximum elevation 9,200 feet). The center provides ski lessons, a beginner package, a snowshoe-only trail, equipment rentals and sales, and a snack bar. Races, clinics, and moonlight tours highlight the calendar. It's open daily from about mid-November–mid-April, as weather permits. Trail passes run $10, free for kids seven and under and seniors 70 and over; snowshoers pay $5; website: www.arizonasnowbowl.com. Take US 180 northwest 16 miles from downtown to near Milepost 232.

Cross-country skiers also head to Hart Prairie and Wing Mountain, two undeveloped skiing areas near the San Francisco Peaks. The rolling meadow and forest country is ideal for ski touring. Reach Hart Prairie by driving 9.5 miles northwest of town on ·US 180, then turning right on the south end of Forest Road 151 and continuing as far as the road is clear. Parking on US 180 is prohibited, but there are some signed parking areas just off it. For Wing Mountain, continue on US 180 just past Hart Prairie Rd., then turn left onto Forest Road 222B. For road and skiing conditions near the Peaks, call the Forest Service's Peaks Ranger Station at 928/526-0866.

The groomed trails of Mormon Lake also attract cross-country skiers. **Mormon Lake Ski Center,** in the village of Mormon Lake, has 20 km of groomed diagonal and skating trails ranging from easy to challenging. It's open daily, snow permitting, with a trail fee of $5 per adult or $15 per family, rentals, and instruction; tel. 928/354-2240 (toll call from Flagstaff). Drive 20 miles southeast on Lake Mary Rd., then turn right eight miles on Mormon Lake Loop Road. **Mormon Lake Lodge** has rooms, cabins, and a cafe/steakhouse; tel. 928/774-0462 (Flagstaff) or 354-2227 (local). For Mormon Lake road and ski conditions, call the Forest Service's Mormon Lake Ranger Station at 928/556-7474.

Climbing

Vertical Relief Climbing Center, tel. 928/556-9909 or 877/265-5984, has indoor walls up to 40 feet high to challenge all ages and abilities. Staff also offer instruction, a store, and local climbing information. The center is open daily at 205 S. San Francisco St.

ACCOMMODATIONS

Accommodation costs fluctuate greatly with the number of visitors, the season, and the day of the week; summer weekends are the most expensive. Rates listed below apply in summer but go higher on holiday or special-event periods. Off-season, prices can drop substantially, especially at the more expensive establishments. Winter rates may rise a bit during the ski season and weekends, depending on demand.

Bed and Breakfasts

Birch Tree Inn Bed & Breakfast, 824 W. Birch Ave. tel. 928/774-1042 or 888/774-1042, offers comfortable rooms, some with private bath, and a hot tub in a 1917 house for $59–99 s and $69–119 d; website: www.birchtreeinn.com.

Dierker House Bed & Breakfast, 423 W. Cherry Ave., tel. 928/774-3249, has rooms with shared bath in a 1914 house decorated in antiques; rates start at $60 d with tax. **The Tree House Bed & Breakfast,** 615 W. Cherry Ave., tel. 928/214-8664 or 888/251-9390, features suites with private bath on the second floor of a 1915 house surrounded by large cottonwoods; a hot tub is outdoors; rates are $105 d. **Lynn's Inn,** 614 W. Santa Fe Ave., tel. 928/226-1488 or 800/530-9947, has beautifully restored early 20th-century furnishings in a ca. 1905 house; rooms and suite have private bath and run $85 d ($95 d rooms and $105 d suite Fri.–Sat.).

The Inn at 410, tel. 928/774-0088 or 800/774-2008, offers distinctive guest suites in a 1907 residence, a restored Craftsman-style bungalow at 410 N. Leroux St.; all have private bath, most have fireplaces, and some a Jacuzzi tub; rates run $135–190 d; website: www.inn410.com.

Jeanette's Bed & Breakfast, tel. 928/527-1912 or 800/752-1912, is furnished with early 20th-century antiques in a Princess Ann–style house at 3380 E. Lockett Rd.; each room has private bath at rates of $99–145 d including a gourmet breakfast; website: www.jeanettes-bb.com.

Lake Mary Bed & Breakfast, tel. 928/779-7054 or 888/241-9550, lies out in the country, three miles southeast of town on Lake Mary Rd., with many hiking, biking, and horse riding opportunities. The house was built in Jerome in the 1930s, then moved here and added to; the four guest rooms all have private bath and go for $80 d, $110 four people.

The Sled Dog Inn, tel. 928/525-6212 or 800/754-0664, is in the woods six miles south of town at 10155 Mountainaire Rd. (I-17 Exit 333). You can go dog sledding in winter. Rooms have private bath and range from $110 d for a regular room to $185 d for a two-bed

suite; website: www.sleddoginn.com.

Hostels

For a lively backpacker scene with an international crowd, head south across the tracks to the Grand Canyon or Du Beau hostels. Each offers free pickup at the Greyhound station, discounts for car rentals, and tours to the Grand Canyon and Sedona. Guests have use of a kitchen, common room, and Internet computers (small fee); both hostels are under the same management and on the Internet at website: www.grandcanyonhostel.com. There's no need for a hostel card or passport. Call ahead, if possible, to make the recommended reservations with a credit card; summer is the busiest time.

Grand Canyon International Hostel, 19 S. San Francisco St., tel. 928/779-9421 or 888/442-2696, offers dorm beds at $14 ($16 in summer) and double rooms at $28–31 d ($32–35 d in summer) including tax and breakfast.

The **Du Beau International Hostel,** nearby at 19 W. Phoenix Ave., tel. 928/774-6731 or 800/398-7112, has dorm spaces at $14 ($16 in summer) and motel rooms for $29–31 d ($32–35 d in summer) including tax and breakfast.

Historic Downtown Hotels

Both of Flagstaff's hotels here are registered historic landmarks. The **Weatherford Hotel,** 23 N. Leroux St., tel. 928/774-2731, is named for J.W. Weatherford, who came to Flagstaff in 1887 from Texas and stayed 47 years. He built the hotel, quite elegant in its day, in 1897. Zane Grey wrote *Call of the Canyon* while staying here, describing the hotel as it was in 1918. Weatherford's other projects included an opera house and the Weatherford Road (now a hiking trail) in the San Francisco Peaks. Rooms in this historic hotel cost $35–45 d ($55–65 d in summer), but expect some noise from the nightclub. **Charly's,** the hotel's restaurant and pub, serves food and brew downstairs. Musicians often perform foot-tapping bluegrass, jazz, blues, folk, or rock 'n' roll Friday and Saturday nights. Upstairs, the Zane Grey Bar has live music on special occasions.

Hotel Monte Vista, 100 N. San Francisco St., tel. 928/779-6971 or 800/545-3068, dates to 1927 and has seen a lot of history. This was Flagstaff's grand hotel where movie stars stayed to film in nearby locations. You can stay in rooms named for those guests, such as the John Wayne, Jane Russell, and Gary Cooper suites. The Monte Vista still has many businesses under its roof, including Hennessy's (breakfast, lunch, and dinner daily), a lounge, the Old Post Office Salon & Spa, and Gadfly's Gifts. Rooms with shared bath cost $50 d but are rarely available, rooms with private bath run $60–150 d and suites are $90–150 d; website: www.hotelmontevista.com.

Motels and Hotels

For a complete listing of Flagstaff motels and hotels, see the **More Accommodations in the Gateway Cities** Appendix.

Campgrounds

You really need your own vehicle to camp. The following places nestle in ponderosa pines; all have showers except as noted. **Fort Tuthill County Campground,** tel. 928/774-3464, is open May 1–Sept. 30 with $9 dry sites for tents or RVs and $13 sites with water and sewer (no electricity) plus a $5 reservation fee; the restroom/shower building may be closed during renovation but porta-johns will be available; there's a quarter-mile nature trail and the five-mile Soldiers Trail. The campground is five miles south of downtown off I-17 Exit 337.

Black Bart's RV Park, tel. 928/774-1912, is open all year, $20 tent (three-night limit) and $22 RV with hookups; there's a steak house on the premises. It's two miles east of downtown near I-40 Butler Ave. Exit 198.

Flagstaff KOA, 5803 N. Hwy. 89, tel. 928/526-9926 or 800/KOA-FLAG, is open all year, $21 tent or RV no hookups, $25 with water and electricity, $27 with full hookups, and $36 for a "kamping kabin"; it's five miles northeast of downtown on Route 66/US 89, 1.1 miles north from I-40 Exit 201.

Greer's Pine Shadows, 7101 N. Hwy. 89, tel. 928/526-4977, is an adult RV park for self-contained rigs (no restrooms or showers) open mid-April–mid-October. Sites cost $19 with hookups; it's 1.8 miles north of I-40.

J&H RV Park, 7901 N. Hwy. 89, tel. 928/526-1829, has sites for RVs only from early April–late October in an adult-oriented atmosphere three miles north of I-40 Exit 201. Rates are $23.50–29 with hookups; there's also a hot tub.

Kit Carson RV Park, 2101 W. Route 66, tel. 928/774-6993, is open year-round, $27 RV with hookups. You'll find it two miles west of downtown; take I-40 Exits 191 or 195.

Woody Mountain Campground, 2727 W. Route 66, tel. 928/774-7727, is a half mile farther west and open mid-March–October; rates are $17 tents or $23 RVs with hookups.

Munds Park RV Resort, tel. 928/286-1309, offers sites 17 miles south of Flagstaff near I-17 Exit 322; it's open April 1–Oct. 31. Rates are $19 tent, $19–23.50 RV with hookups.

Ponderosa Forest RV Park & Campground, tel. 928/635-0456 or 888/635-0456, has year-round sites in the woods for tents ($13) and RVs ($19 with hookups) with a nearby store. It's north of I-40 Parks Exit 178, 17 miles west of Flagstaff and about halfway to Williams.

Most established campgrounds on U.S. Forest Service land lie 14 or more miles outside Flagstaff—southeast off Lake Mary Road, south in Oak Creek Canyon, and north near Sunset Crater National Monument. For more information on these and other campgrounds in the Coconino National Forest near town, contact the Peaks

Ranger Station, 5075 N. Hwy. 89, Flagstaff, AZ 86004, tel. 928/526-0866; website: www.fs.fed.us/r3/coconino.

Dispersed camping on Forest Service lands surrounding town provides another option. The ponderosa pine forests offer lots of room but no facilities—just be sure you're well out of the city and not on private or state land. The Coconino National Forest map shows Forest Service land and the back roads. Carry water and be *very* careful with fire; in dry weather the Forest Service often prohibits fires in the woods and may even close some areas.

FOOD

Flagstaff, for its size, offers an amazing number of places to eat. But then, it has a lot of hungry tourists and students to feed. Most restaurants cater to the eat-and-run crowd. You'll find the well-known chains and fast-food places on the main roads, but with a little effort you can discover some unique restaurants and cafes. Come downtown for local atmosphere—old-fashioned home-style eateries abound.

You'll enjoy Flagstaff's clean mountain air while dining because of the city's nonsmoking ordinance. A few places, such as Granny's Closet and Fiddlers on S. Milton, have separate smoking and nonsmoking sections; bars that serve food may be all smoking.

Downtown (north of the tracks)

Chez Marc Bistro, 503 N. Humphreys St., tel. 928/774-1343, offers fine country French cuisine with indoor and outdoor seating at a historic 1911 residence; it's open Thurs.–Sun in summer for lunch and daily year-round for dinner. Most dinner entrees run about $30 and reservations are recommended. **Down Under,** 6 E. Aspen Ave. at Leroux St., tel. 928/774-6677, prepares creative New Zealand and other styles daily for lunch and dinner (reservations are recommended); may close Mon. evenings in winter.

Charly's Pub and Grill, in the old Weatherford Hotel at 23 N. Leroux St., tel. 928/779-1919, serves good American food daily for lunch and dinner. **Downtown Diner,** 7 E. Aspen Ave., tel. 928/774-3492, dishes out American food daily for breakfast and lunch and Mon.–Sat. for dinner, but don't expect much in the way of decor. **Mountain Oasis,** 11 E. Aspen Ave., tel. 928/214-9270, has a tasty mix of Mediterranean, Southwestern, and international flavors with many vegetarian options; open Sat.–Sun. for breakfast and daily for lunch and dinner. **Pasto,** 19 E. Aspen Ave., tel. 928/779-1937, serves Italian food, including vegetarian and wheat-free options, in a casual fine-dining atmosphere with seating indoors and in a courtyard; open nightly for dinner. **Alpine Pizza,** 7 N. Leroux St., tel. 928/779-4109, is open daily for lunch and dinner.

Café Espress, 16 N. San Francisco St., tel. 928/774-0541, serves homemade natural foods, including many vegetarian items, plus coffees from the espresso bar and baked goodies from the oven; it's open daily for breakfast and lunch, and Wed.–Sat. for dinner. **Kathy's,** 7 N. San Francisco St., tel. 928/774-1951, is a cozy cafe with American standbys and a few exotic items such as Aussie burgers and Navajo tacos; it's open daily for breakfast and lunch. The historic Monte Vista Hotel offers **Hennessey's,** 104 N. San Francisco St., tel. 928/779-3211, open daily with American food for breakfast, lunch, and dinner.

You'll find good Mexican food at bargain prices in **Martan's Burrito Palace,** 10 N. San Francisco St., tel. 928/773-4701, open Mon.–Sat. for breakfast and lunch. **El Metate,** 103 W. Birch and Beaver St., tel. 928/774-5527, offers Mexican dining daily for lunch and dinner. **Kachina Downtown,** 522 E Route 66, tel. 928/779-1944, presents Mexican food in a pleasant setting daily breakfast, lunch, and dinner.

FLAGSTAFF

If you're looking for inexpensive Chinese-American food and don't care about the decor, try the **Grand Canyon Cafe,** 110 E. Route 66, tel. 928/774-2252, or the **Hong Kong Cafe,** at 6 E. Route 66, tel. 928/774-9801; both are open Mon.–Sat. for breakfast, lunch, and dinner.

Downtown (south of the tracks)

Macy's European Coffee House and Bakery, 14 S. Beaver St., tel. 928/774-2243, offers a big selection of fresh-roasted coffee and a menu of pasta dishes, sandwiches, soups, salads, quiches, and home-baked goodies daily for breakfast, lunch, and dinner. **La Bellavia Sandwich Shoppe,** 18 S. Beaver St., tel. 928/774-8301, is a little cafe open daily for breakfast and lunch. **Beaver Street Brewery/Whistle Stop Cafe,** 11 S. Beaver St., tel. 928/779-0079, serves pizza, sandwiches, salads, and fondues along with a selection of local brews daily for lunch and dinner; there's a beer garden outside. **NiMarco's Pizza,** 101 S. Beaver St., tel. 928/779-2691, is open daily. **Cottage Place,** 126 W. Cottage Ave., tel. 928/774-8431, serves American and continental specialties in a romantic setting; open Tues.–Sun. for dinner in a 1909 bungalow; reservations are recommended.

Thai food devotees enjoy the **Dara Thai Restaurant,** 14 S. San Francisco St., tel. 928/774-0047, open Mon.–Sat. for lunch and dinner. **Pesto Brothers,** 34 S. San Francisco St., tel. 928/913-0775, offers a cafe and deli with antipasto, salads, pasta, fish, and meat dishes; open Mon.–Sat. for lunch and Tues.–Sat. for dinner. **Morning Glory Cafe,** 115 S. San Francisco St., tel. 928/774-3705, features a mostly vegetarian menu of homemade food including blue corn tamales, chicken pozolé, and a variety of salads and ̄oups for lunch. It's open Mon.–Fri. for lunch ̄d Sat. for breakfast.

̄afe Olé, 119 S. San Francisco St., tel. ̄74-8272, specializes in homemade Mex-ican dishes; it's open Tues.–Sat. for lunch and dinner. **Aladdin's,** 211 S. San Francisco St., tel. 928/213-0033, serves tasty Middle Eastern, Greek, and International specialties (takeout too) open Mon.–Sat. for lunch and daily for dinner. **El Charro,** 409 S. San Francisco St., tel. 928/779-0552, is a popular Mexican café open Mon.–Sat. for lunch and dinner.

Northern Arizona University

The Garden Terrace Dining Room, tel. 928/523-1616, at The Inn at NAU prepares a breakfast buffet daily, fine lunches Mon.–Fri., and dinners Tues.–Friday. The Friday dinners often feature a magnificent seven-course set menu; reservations are required. In summer, the dining room serves only breakfast and lunch. The Inn is off S. San Francisco Street.

University Union, in the north-central campus, offers a variety of fast-food eateries. **University Dining** is a large cafeteria in the central campus. **North Union** has fast-food establishments on the north edge of campus. **South Campus Dining** offers cafeteria fare and the **South Campus Student Union** contains **The Peaks,** serving food ready to go.

Other Areas

American Cuisine: Galaxy Diner, 931 W. Route 66, tel. 928/774-2466, features '50s music and movie-star decor with American classics such as sandwiches, platters, milkshakes, sodas, and sumptuous deserts; breakfasts are especially good and are served all day; open daily for breakfast, lunch, and dinner. **Woodlands Cafe,** 1175 W. Route 66, tel. 928/773-9118, serves American food daily for breakfast, lunch, and dinner in a Southwestern atmosphere at Radisson Woodlands Hotel. **Granny's Closet,** 218 S. Milton Rd. (just south of the railroad underpass), tel. 928/774-8331, fixes steak and other meat dishes, seafood, and Italian cuisine; open daily for lunch and dinner. **Mike and Ronda's,** 21

S. Milton Rd., tel. 928/774-7008, pulls in the crowds with generous servings of low-priced American café fare, open daily for breakfast and lunch. A second location at Park Santa Fe Shopping Center, 3518 E. Route 66, tel. 928/526-8138, is open daily for breakfast and lunch and Tues.–Sat. for dinner. Breakfasts are very popular.

Fiddlers Restaurant, 702 S. Milton Rd., tel. 928/774-6689, serves up ranch-style steaks, chicken, shrimp, and sandwiches daily for dinner. **Casa del Panzon,** 801 S. Milton Rd., tel. 928/556-0093, prepares South-western dishes with a choice of meat, seafood, and vegetarian; open daily except Mon. for lunch and dinner. **Furr's Family Dining,** 1200 S. Milton Rd., tel. 928/779-4104, offers buffets daily for lunch and dinner. **Souper!Salad!,** 1300 S. Milton Rd., tel. 928/774-8030, is open daily for lunch and dinner with a buffet of soups and salads. **Buster's,** 1800 S. Milton Rd., tel. 928/774-5155, features seafood and an oyster bar along with steak, ribs, chicken, veal, and sandwiches in Green Tree Village; open daily for lunch and dinner. The two **Sizzlers** offer good deals on meat and fish entrees plus a big salad bar at 2105 S. Milton Rd., tel. 928/779-3267, and at 3540 E. Route 66, tel. 928/526-3391. **Red Lobster,** 2500 S. Beulah Blvd. in the Woodlands Village area, tel. 928/556-9604, has the nautical decor of a Maine lobster house for fish, shrimp, crab, and of course lobster, along with steak and chicken; it's open daily for lunch and dinner. A model train circles the dining areas of **The Crown Railroad Cafe,** which does popular American standbys, including a choice of 66 omelets, at 2700 S. Woodlands Village Blvd. near Wal-Mart, tel. 928/774-6775, and at 3300 E. Route 66, tel. 928/522-9237.

Little America's Western Gold Dining Room, 2515 E. Butler Ave., tel. 928/779-7900, serves a big brunch on Sunday, a buffet lunch Mon.–Fri., and dinner nightly; the coffee shop is open daily for breakfast, lunch, and dinner. Also in the Butler Ave. area and just off I-40 Exit 198 are the **Country Host Restaurant** and **Kettle Restaurant,** both open daily for breakfast, lunch, and dinner.

Black Bart's Steak House, 2760 E. Butler Ave. near I-40 Exit 198, tel. 928/779-3142, serves up steak, seafood, and other American fare; it's open nightly for dinner with singing waiters and waitresses to entertain you. Many locals say you'll find the best steaks in town at **Lupo's Horsemen Lodge,** tel. 928/526-2655, which fixes steak, ribs, chicken, trout, and seafood; it's open for dinner nightly except Sunday (and Mon. in winter) on US 89, 3.6 miles north from I-40 Exit 201.

Italian Cuisine: Mamma Luisa, 2710 N. Steves Blvd., tel. 928/526-6809, has excellent Italian cuisine nightly for dinner at Kachina Square off E. Route 66; reservations are advised. The Olive Garden Italian Restaurant, 2550 Beulah Blvd. in the Woodlands Village area, tel. 928/779-3000, serves pasta, seafood, meats from the grill, and breadstick-style pizzas; there's a children's menu too; it's open daily for lunch and dinner. The nearby **Fazoli's,** 2675 S. Beulah Blvd., tel. 928/214-8220, offers "Italian food. . . fast" in an informal setting for pastas, pizza, and salads at; open daily for lunch and dinner. **Dan's Italian Kitchen,** 1850 N. Fort Valley Rd. (US 180), tel. 928/779-9349, is a small place open Mon.–Sat. for lunch and dinner on the route to the Grand Canyon.

Mexican Cuisine: Flagstaff's large Mexican-American population provides the town with some tasty food. In addition to the Mexican eateries listed under downtown, try **Jalapeño Lou's,** 3050 E. Route 66, tel. 928/526-1533, which specializes in New Mexico cuisine and will please chili lovers; open nightly for dinner. In the southern part of town there's **Chili's Grill & Bar,** 1500 S. Milton Rd., tel. 928/774-4546, open daily for lunch and dinner.

Asian Cuisines: Delhi Palace, 2700 S. Woodlands Village Blvd. near Wal-Mart, tel. 928/556-0019, offers fine north Indian food daily for lunch (buffet available) and dinner. It's the restaurant where you're most likely to spot the author!

Sakura Restaurant, 1175 W. Route 66, tel. 928/773-9118, prepares Japanese teppanyaki and sushi Mon.–Sat. for lunch and nightly for dinner in the Radisson Woodlands Hotel.

Chinese dining is always close at hand in Flagstaff. The following restaurants serve lunch and dinner daily except as noted. South of downtown, you can choose from **Hunan West** (closed Monday) in University Plaza off S. Milton Rd., tel. 928/779-2229; **August Moon,** 1300 S. Milton Rd., tel. 928/774-5280; and **Szechuan,** 1451 S. Milton Rd., tel. 928/774-8039. In east Flagstaff, **Asian Gourmet,** 1580 E. Route 66, tel. 928/773-7771, has an exceptionally long vegetarian menu as well as good selections of meat and seafood dishes in the Western Hills Motel; the dining room décor is an odd mix of cowboy and Chinese, but the food is authentic! Farther east, you'll find **China Star,** 1802 E. Route 66, tel. 928/8880, with buffets and ala carte; **Hunan East,** 2028 N. Fourth St., tel. 928/526-1009; **Golden Dragon Bowl,** 2730 Lakin Dr. across from Kachina Square, tel. 928/527-3238; and **Mandarin Gardens,** Park Santa Fe Shopping Center at 3518 E. Route 66, tel. 928/526-5033.

Groceries

Nearly every shopping center has a supermarket, and you can find **Fry's** and **Albertsons** at the corner of E. Route 66 and Switzer Canyon Drive. **Farmer's Market** specializes in fresh produce, often at bargain prices; it's at 1901 N. Fourth St., just off E. Route 66; tel. 928/774-4500. **New Frontiers,** 1000 S. Milton Rd., tel. 928/774-5747, ·ells natural foods and offers deli dining ʌd take-out.

ENTERTAINMENT AND EVENTS

The free weekly paper *Flagstaff Live!* details the local music scene, movies, arts, restaurants, events, sports, and hikes.

Sports and NAU Culture

Northern Arizona University presents theater, opera, dance, concerts, and a variety of sports events. For information and tickets, contact NAU Central Ticket Office, University Union, tel. 928/523-5661 or NAU Downtown, Heritage Square at Aspen Ave. and Leroux St., tel. 928/523-1628. During the summer, three professional teams hold training camps on NAU's campus: the **Arizona Cardinals** (football), the **Phoenix Suns** (basketball), and the **Phoenix Mercury** (women's basketball). Call the Flagstaff Visitor Center for fan information.

Nightlife

The **Museum Club,** 3404 E. Route 66, tel. 928/526-9434, began in 1931 as a museum and trading post with such taxidermy oddities as a two-headed calf and a one-eyed lamb along with more conventional animals, Native American artifacts, and a rifle collection. Curious motorists sputtering down early Route 66 dropped in to see the thousands of exhibits inside this huge log structure. Five years later another entrepreneur converted it into a nightclub to attract the growing crowds of motorists as well as local folk looking for some good music and dancing. Aspiring recording artists traveling cross-country stopped by to perform for appreciative audiences. The Museum Club continues the tradition of fine country music while introducing additional music styles popular with the younger crowd. It's also known as the "The Zoo" because stuffed animals still gaze down from the walls. *Car and Driver* magazine named it one of the top 10 roadhouses in the nation. Wandering through the rustic interior, you'll find photos and news clippings on the walls, a dance floor, and a magnificent late-19th century bar. Something's happening nightly in the Museum Club; call or check the Internet at website: www.museumclub.com.

You'll find most of the other nightlife downtown, where venues include **Charly's,** 23 N. Leroux St., tel. 928/779-1919; **Flagstaff Brewing Co.,** 16 E. Route 66, tel. 928/773-1442; **The Alley,** 22 E. Route 66, tel. 928/774-7929; **Mogollon Brewing Co.,** 15 N. Agassiz St., tel. 928/773-8950; and **Monte Visa Lounge,** 100 N. San Francisco St., tel. 928/774-2403.

Events

People in Flagstaff put on a variety of festivals, fairs, shows, and concerts during the year. The Flagstaff Visitor Center will tell you what's happening; tel. 928/774-9541 or 800/842-7293; website: www.flagstaff.az.us. Major annual events include **Flagstaff Winterfest** in February, featuring over 100 events such as skiing competitions, sled-dog races, snow games, and entertainment. In May, residents celebrate **Cinco de Mayo** with a parade and arts and crafts fair. June activities include **The Great Fiesta del Barrio & Fajita Cook-off** on the second Saturday and **Pine Country Rodeo and Parade** on the third weekend. Flagstaff's **Fabulous Fourth Festivities** commemorate the 4th of July and Flagstaff's founding with a parade, the Fair of Life arts and crafts show, a gem show, historic walks, horse racing, a pioneer festival, barbecue, and fireworks. Also in July, **Arizona Highland Celtic Festival** celebrates the people of Brittany, Cornwall, Ireland, Isle of Man, Scotland, and Wales with dancing, athletic demonstrations and, of course, bagpiping. **Summerfest** on the first weekend in August features top Southwestern artists for an arts and crafts show. Heritage Square downtown hosts ongoing summer events. Also, from May–September, the Museum of Northern Arizona's **Heritage Program** features Hispanic and Native American

marketplaces, entertainment, artists' demonstrations, and Enduring Creations, a sales exhibit. **Coconino County Fair** runs over Labor Day weekend in September as does an arts and crafts show. The **Festival of Science** presents talks, demonstrations, and open houses during a 10 day period in late September. The **Northern Lights Holiday Parade** and **Holiday Lights Festival** in December round out the year's activities.

SHOPPING AND SERVICES

Art Galleries and Native American Crafts

Shops in downtown Flagstaff display a wealth of regional arts and crafts. Native American artists create much of the distinctive work. You'll see paintings, jewelry, Navajo rugs, Hopi kachina dolls, pottery, and baskets. The **Museum of Northern Arizona's** gift shop and the **Art Barn,** both northwest of town on US 180, feature excellent selections of Native American arts and crafts.

Bookstores

McGaugh's Newsstand, 24 N. San Francisco St, tel. 928/774-2131, downtown has a good selection of newspapers, magazines, Arizona books, and general reading. **Barnes & Noble Booksellers,** 701 S. Milton Rd., tel. 928/226-8227, offers a spacious store with a cafe. **NAU Bookstore,** tel. 928/523-4041, includes many regional and general publications on the east side of campus. **Northland Publishing,** 2900 N. Fort Valley Rd./US 180, tel. 928/774-5251, produces outstanding regional and children's books plus some cookbooks and posters; the sales room often has discounted titles and is open Mon.–Fri. 8 A.M.–5 P.M.; website: www.northlandpub.com. The **Museum of Northern Arizona,** 3101 N. Fort Valley Rd./US 180, tel. 928/774-5213, sells excellent books on Southwestern Native American cultures, archaeology, and natural history; it's three miles northwest of downtown. **Waldenbooks,** in the Flagstaff Mall, tel. 928/526-5196, stocks good regional and general reading selections. **Crystal Magic,** 5 N. San Francisco St., tel. 928/779-2528, features spiritual and New Age titles downtown.

For used books, including many regional titles, drop by **Bookman's Used Books,** 1520 S. Riordan Ranch St., tel. 928/774-0005; it offers 250,000 used books and some new ones as well as music, videos, and games. A few doors south, **Hastings,** tel. 928/779-1880, sells discounted new books, music, and videos. **Dragon's Plunder,** 217 S. San Francisco and Butler Ave., tel. 928/774-1708, has about 80,000 used books. **Starlight Books,** 15 N. Leroux St., tel. 928/774-6813, has a smaller selection of mostly used books and specializes in modern first editions, rare and antique books, and does out-of-print orders.

Outdoor Equipment and Rentals

Babbitt's Backcountry Outfitters, 12 E. Aspen Ave., tel. 928/774-4775, carries an extensive selection of backpacking, climbing, and cross-country ski gear downtown. **Peace Surplus,** 14 W. Route 66, tel. 928/779-4521, offers hiking, camping, winter sports, and fishing gear downtown; website: www.peacesurplus.com. **Mountain Sports,** 1800 S. Milton Rd., tel. 928/779-5156, has mountain bikes as well as hiking, camping, and winter sports gear south of downtown.

Photo Equipment and Supplies

Wal-Mart and supermarkets carry print and a bit of slide film. For the best selection of slide, professional, and large format film, try **Photo Outfitter,** one block off Route 66 at 25 N. San Francisco St. downtown, tel. 928/779-5181 or 800/640-0224 (AZ only). **P.R. Camera Repair,** 111 E. Aspen Ave., tel. 928/779-5263 offers service.

Postal Services

The main **post office,** tel. 928/714-9302, is at 2400 N. Postal Blvd. off E. Route 66; General Delivery mail can be sent to you with a zip code of 86004-9998. There's a downtown branch at 104 N. Agassiz St.; tel. 928/779-3589, and another in the NAU Bookstore basement.

Medical Services

If you need medical attention, it's cheaper to go directly to a doctor's office or clinic than to the hospital. You'll find many offices along N. Beaver Street. **Concentra Medical Centers,** 120 W. Fine (west of Beaver), tel. 928/773-9695, welcomes walk-in patients daily. **Walk-in Medical Care,** near the Flagstaff Mall at 4215 N. Hwy. 89, tel. 928/527-1920, provides similar services. **Flagstaff Medical Center,** 1200 N. Beaver St., tel. 928/779-3366 is the local hospital. In **emergencies**—police, fire, and medical—dial 911.

INFORMATION

Visitor Center

The very helpful **Flagstaff Chamber of Commerce's Visitor Center** staff can answer your questions and tell you what's happening. The office, downtown in the Amtrak depot (1 E. Route 66, Flagstaff, AZ 86001), is open daily 8 A.M.–5 P.M. Literature in the lobby may be available after hours; tel. 928/774-9541 or 800/842-7293; fax 556-1308; email visitor@flagstaff.az.us.; website: www.flagstaff.az.us. Other useful websites include website: www.flagguide.com and website: www.flaglive.com.

Coconino National Forest

The **U.S. Forest Service** provides information and maps about camping, hiking, and road conditions in the Coconino National Forest surrounding Flagstaff. The **Supervisor's Of-**

fice, tel. 928/527-3600, is at 2323 E. Greenlaw Lane (Flagstaff, AZ 86004) behind Knoles Village Shopping Center; it's open Mon.–Fri. 7:30 A.M.–4:30 P.M. Staff have information sheets on recreation in all of the districts on the Coconino Forest. You can buy any of the National Forest maps for Arizona here or choose from a small selection of books. On the Web, visit the forest at website: www.fs.fed.us/r3/coconino.

For more detailed information on the Mt. Elden, Humphrey's Peak, and O'Leary Peak areas north of Flagstaff, contact the **Peaks Ranger Station,** 5075 N. Hwy. 89 (Flagstaff, AZ 86004), tel. 928/526-0866; it's open Mon.–Fri. 7:30 A.M.–4:30 P.M. For the lake and forest country south of town, check with the **Mormon Lake Ranger District** office, 4373 S. Lake Mary Rd. (Flagstaff, AZ 86001), tel. 928/774-1182; it's open Mon.–Fri. 7:30 A.M.–4:30 P.M. and Saturday during summer. Each of these two offices has information for both areas, so you can often get everything that you need with one visit.

Arizona Game and Fish Department

This office provides fishing and hunting licenses and information at 3500 S. Lake Mary Rd. (Flagstaff, AZ 86001); it's open Mon.–Fri. 8 A.M.–5 P.M.; tel. 928/774-5045; website: www.azgfd.com.

Libraries

Looking for a good place to read up on Arizona or to keep dry on a rainy day? The **Flagstaff City Library's** attractive ski-lodge architecture makes it an especially enjoyable spot downtown at the corner of 300 W. Aspen Ave. and Sitgreaves St.; tel. 928/779-7670. Hours are Mon.–Thurs. 10 A.M.–9 P.M., Friday 10 A.M.–7 P.M., Saturday 10 A.M.–6 P.M., and Sunday 11 A.M.–6 P.M.; website: www.flagstaffpubliclibrary.org. Many good regional books enrich the Arizona Collection. Art exhibits by local artists and photographers change monthly.

NAU's **Cline Library,** tel. 928/523-2171, carries many books and periodicals. It's also far easier to find an available Internet computer here than at the city library. Hikers can plan trips and copy maps in the Government Documents section. The library is open daily during regular school sessions and Mon.–Fri. between terms. Upstairs, the **Special Collections and Archives Department,** tel. 928/523-5551, contains an outstanding array of Arizona-related publications and photos; changing exhibits appear in the entranceway. It's open Mon.–Fri. 8 A.M.–6 P.M. (5 P.M. in summer). The library website, website: www.nau.edu/library, has the entire card catalog online, encyclopedias, plus a searchable database of about 7,000 images from Special Collections.

The **Museum of Northern Arizona,** tel. 928/774-5211, ext. 256, has an excellent regional library in the Research Center across the highway from the museum; it's normally open Mon.–Fri. 9 A.M.–5 P.M.

TRANSPORTATION

Tours

Nava-Hopi Tours (The Gray Line), tel. 928/774-5003 or 800/892-8687, operates bus tours to the Grand Canyon ($42), Oak Creek Canyon-Sedona-Jerome-Montezuma Castle ($40), Petrified Forest-Painted Desert-Meteor Crater ($58), Lake Powell/Glen Canyon float trip ($109), and Monument Valley ($74). Nava-Hopi requires at least 24 hours' advance notice; children 5–15 ride at half price on most trips. The last three itineraries don't operate in winter. Buses leave from the 114 W. Route 66 station; website: www.navahopitours.com.

Local taxi companies can arrange Flagstaff and northern Arizona tours. Other local tour operators have brochures at the Visitor Center.

Car Rental and Taxi

A rental car allows more extensive sightseeing than public transportation and costs less if several people get together. Rates fluctuate with supply and demand, competition, and the mood of the operators; call around for the best deals. See the Yellow Pages for agencies; you'll find offices in town and at the airport. For a taxi, call **Sun Taxi,** tel. 928/774-7400; **Arizona Taxi,** tel. 928/779-1111; or **A Friendly Cab,** tel. 928/774-4444.

Local Bus

Mountain Line, tel. 928/779-6624 (TDD number is 779-6635), serves most of the city with three routes Mon.–Fri. and two routes on Saturday. Pick up a schedule at the Flagstaff Visitor Center, public library, or at one of the Safeway stores in town.

Long-Distance Bus

Greyhound, 399 S. Malpais Lane, tel. 928/774-4573 or 800/231-2222, offers daily departures south to Phoenix and Sky Harbor Airport, east along I-40 to Winslow and Holbrook and west to Williams and Kingman. Services also continue to Tucson, Los Angeles, Las Vegas, Albuquerque, and other destinations. The station lies just south of downtown off S. Milton Rd.; it's open 24 hours; website: www.greyhound.com.

Nava-Hopi, 114 W. Route 66, tel. 928/774-5003 or 800/892-8687, buses head north to the Grand Canyon at least once daily ($14 each way) and south to Phoenix's Metrocenter and Sky Harbor Airport a few times daily ($24 each way) via Camp Verde; website: www.navahopitours.com.

Train

Amtrak, 1 E. Route 66, tel. 928/774-8679 or 800/872-7245, offers service on the Southwest Chief every evening for Los Angeles ($64–114 one way), and every morning for Albuquerque ($59–106 one way) and on to Chicago or Orlando. The price depends on availability—book ahead or travel off-season for the lowest rates; roundtrip tickets are double but there are also special All Aboard America and fly/train fares; website: www.amtrak.com.

Air

America West, tel. 800/235-9292, flies about six times daily to Phoenix for a stiff $195 each

This building served as Flagstaff's train depot from 1889 to 1926.

COURTESY OF AISLINN RACE

way, but a roundtrip with a 21-day advance purchase and a Sat. overnight costs little more; website: www.americawest.com. Pulliam Field, Flagstaff's airport, lies five miles south of town; take I-17 Exit 337.

Nava-Hopi and Greyhound offer ground transport to Sky Harbor Airport in Phoenix at much lower costs; see "Long-Distance Bus" above.

North of Flagstaff

Peaceful today, this 3,000-square-mile area of volcanic peaks, cinder cones, and lava flows presents some impressive landscapes and geology. The majestic San Francisco Peaks, highest of all Arizona mountains, soar 5,000 feet above the surrounding plateau. Eruptions beginning between one million and 400,000 years ago created this giant volcano whose center later collapsed, forming a caldera. During Pleistocene ice ages, glaciers then carved deep valleys on its slopes. Hundreds of small cinder cones, of which Sunset Crater is the youngest, surround the Peaks. There's no reason to assume the San Francisco Volcanic Field is finished, either. The area has experienced volcanic activity, with periods of calm, during its long history (but no eruptions in the past 700 years).

Tribes of northern Arizona regard the San Francisco Peaks as a sacred place. The Hopi believe the Peaks are the winter home of their kachina spirits and the source of clouds that bring rain for crops. The Peaks also occupy a prominent place in Navajo legends and ceremonies, representing one of the cardinal directions.

In 1984, the federal government set aside 18,963 acres of this venerable volcano for the Kachina Peaks Wilderness, selecting the name because of the importance of the site to the Hopi people. The Forest Service maintains a network of trails in the wilderness, and any of the peaks and hills make a good day-hike destination. Cyclists may not ride here, even on the former roads, because of the wilderness designation. Foresters at the **Peaks Ranger**

Station, 5075 N. Hwy. 89 (Flagstaff, AZ 86004), tel. 928/526-0866, offer maps and hiking information for this region. The book *Flagstaff Hikes* by Richard and Sherry Mangum lists many possibilities in the San Francisco Peaks area.

SUNSET CRATER VOLCANO NATIONAL MONUMENT

Sunset Crater, a beautiful black cinder cone tinged with yellows and oranges, rises 1,000 feet above jagged lava flows about 15 miles northeast of Flagstaff. Although more than 700 years have passed since the last eruptions, the landscape still presents a lunar-like appearance, with trees and plants struggling to grow.

Eruptions beginning in A.D. 1064 or 1065 sent indigenous people fleeing for safety. By 1110 activity had subsided enough to allow them to settle in the Wupatki Basin, 20 miles northeast of Sunset Crater. You can visit the remains of their communities and see a museum in Wupatki National Monument, reached via the Sunset Crater-Wupatki Loop Road, one of the prettiest scenic drives in Arizona. Lava flows and smaller ash eruptions continued from Sunset Crater possibly as recently as 1280.

In the late 1920s, some Hollywood filmmakers thought Sunset Crater would make a great movie set. They planned to use dynamite to simulate an avalanche, but local citizens put a stop to their plans. Sunset Crater became a national monument in 1930.

Visitor center exhibits illustrate the forces deep within the Earth and their fury during volcanic eruptions. You can watch a seismograph as it tracks the earth's movements. Film clips of Hawaiian volcanic eruptions show how Sunset Crater may have looked during its periods of activity. Rangers give varied programs, mainly during the summer, on geology, seismology, birds, and other topics. Check the bulletin board at the visitor center or call for times and places.

Lenox Crater (elev. 7,240 feet), one mile east of the visitor center at the first pullout on the left, provides a close look at a cinder cone with a crater. It's a short, steep climb, requiring 30–45 minutes to the rim and back; elevation change is 280 feet.

The self-guided **Lava Flow Trail,** which begins 1.5 miles east of the visitor center, loops across the Bonito Lava Flow at the base of Sunset Crater; allow 30–60 minutes for the one-mile walk, less for the paved quarter-mile inner loop that's wheelchair accessible. A trail leaflet, available at the start of the trail and at the visitor center, explains geologic features and ecology. You'll see fumaroles (gas vents), lava bubbles, squeeze-ups, and lava tubes that seem to have cooled only yesterday.

Before rangers prohibited climbing on Sunset Crater in 1973, hikers wore a deep gash in the soft cinder slopes. Most of the damage has been repaired, though you can still see faint scars.

Bonito Campground, across the road from the visitor center, is open from mid-May–mid-September; it costs $12 a site and offers drinking water and restrooms but no showers; groups can reserve sites; tel. 928/527-1474 (campground) or 526-0866 (Peaks Ranger Station). Campfire programs run on summer evenings. Dispersed camping is allowed in other areas of the national forest such as along Forest Roads 420, 552, and 418 west of US 89; Forest Road 776 (can be dusty from ATVs) south of Sunset Crater; and Forest Road 150 (hot in summer) south of the road through Wupatki. Visitor center staff can make suggestions and sell you the Coconino Forest map.

You'll find **picnic areas** near the visitor center, at the Lava Flow Trail, and at Painted Desert Vista between Sunset Crater and Wupatki National Monuments. The visitor center is open daily 9 A.M.–5 P.M. except Christmas with extended hours in summer; the road and trails stay open all day; tel. 928/526-0502; website: www.nps.gov/sucr. The admission fee of $3 per person age 17 and up includes entry to Wupatki National Monument. You can reach the visitor center by driving north 12 miles from the Flagstaff Mall on US 89, then turning east two miles on a signed road.

O'Leary Peak

Weather permitting, the summit of this 8,965-foot lava-dome volcano provides outstanding views into Sunset Crater. Forest Road 545A begins about a quarter mile west of Sunset Crater visitor center and climbs 5.5 miles to the fire lookout tower at the top. A gate about a quarter mile in blocks motor vehicles. You can hike or mountain bike up the scenic road and get a good workout. The summit provides the best view of the colors of Sunset Crater and the Painted Desert beyond in late afternoon; the San Francisco Peaks are best in the morning.

WUPATKI NATIONAL MONUMENT

Prehistoric farmers, identified as the Sinagua Culture by archaeologists, settled in small groups near the San Francisco Peaks in about A.D. 600. They lived in partly underground pithouses and tilled the soil in those few areas with sufficient moisture to support corn and other crops. The eruption of Sunset Crater in A.D. 1064 or 1065 forced many to flee, but it also improved the farming potential: volcanic ash, blown by winds over a large area, acted as a water-conserving mulch.

After about 1110, people returned and were joined by ancestral Puebloan people from northeastern Arizona. They settled 20 miles northeast of Sunset Crater in Wupatki Basin, which became the center of a group of cosmopolitan villages. A mix of cultural traits can be seen at Wupatki, including Kayenta Anasazi, Sinagua, Cohonina, and Hohokam. Large, multistoried pueblos replaced the brush shelters and pithouses of former times. Some villages seem defensively built; competition for scarce resources may have created friction or fostered cooperation.

During the 1200s, people began to leave the area. Archaeologists think the inhabitants migrated southward to the Verde Valley, eastward to Homolovi on the Little Colorado River, and northeastward to the Hopi mesas and Zuni villages. Hopi oral histories trace at least eight clans to the Wupatki area.

Seven of the best-preserved pueblos have road and trail access; all other sites and the monument's backcountry remain closed to visitors except for the seasonal ranger-guided hikes to Crack-in-Rock. Please stay on designated trails.

Wupatki Visitor Center

You'll see pottery, tools, jewelry, and other artifacts of early cultures on exhibit here. A Wupatki room reconstruction shows how the interior of a typical living chamber might have looked. You'll also learn a little about the present-day Navajo and Hopi tribes who live near the monument. You can buy books, posters, maps, and videos related to the region. Rangers may offer 15-minute orientation talks and provide demonstrations of prehistoric and modern crafts and activities at Wupatki Pueblo.

Wupatki Visitor Center, tel. 928/679-2365, is open daily 9 A.M.–5 P.M. with extended hours in summer; closed Dec. 25th; website: www.nps.gov/wupa. From Flagstaff, you can drive 12 miles north on US 89, then turn right and go 21 miles via Sunset Crater National Monument on a very scenic loop road. Or take the northern turnoff from US 89 for the loop road, 26 miles north of Flagstaff, and head east 14 miles. The nearest motels and restaurants are in Flagstaff and Gray Mountain. Hank's Trading Post offers groceries and snacks 1.2 miles north of the US 89-Wupatki junction. See Bonito Campground in the Sunset Crater section above for area camping possibilities.

Doney Picnic Area sits between cinder cones about four miles northwest of the visitor center on the loop road. **Doney Mountain Trail** climbs gradually to a saddle in the Little Doney Craters, from which you can turn left to a lower overlook or right to a higher one, each about 0.4 mile one way from the picnic area. Both forks pass small dwellings, probably used by the prehistoric people as field houses while tending nearby gardens. You'll enjoy a panorama of the Wupatki Basin, Painted Desert, and San Francisco Peaks. Interpretive signs explain area ecology and the exploits of prospector Ben Doney.

Wupatki Pueblo

At its peak, Wupatki contained nearly 100 rooms and towered multiple stories. The Hopi name refers to "something long that has been cut or divided." A self-guided trail, beginning behind the visitor center, explains many of the features of Wupatki; pick up a trail brochure at the start.

A community room, where village meetings and ceremonies may have taken place, lies to one side of Wupatki. The ballcourt at the far end of the village may have been used for games or religious functions. It's one of several found in northern Arizona, probably introduced by the Hohokam Culture of the southern deserts. Archaeologists reconstructed the masonry ballcourt from wall remnants; the rest of Wupatki Pueblo is stabilized. A

FLAGSTAFF

blowhole, 100 feet east of the ballcourt, may have had religious importance. A system of underground cracks connects to this natural surface opening; air blows out, rushes in, or does nothing at all, depending on atmospheric pressure. Researchers once tried to enter the system but couldn't get through the narrow passageways.

Wukoki Pueblo

Families lived in this small pueblo, the best-preserved structure in the park, for perhaps three generations. You can step inside the rooms for a closer look. From the Wupatki visitor center, drive a quarter mile toward Sunset Crater, then turn left 2.5 miles on a paved road.

Citadel Pueblo

This fortress-like pueblo, perched atop a small volcanic butte nine miles northwest of the Wupatki Visitor Center, stood one or two stories high and contained about 30 rooms. From the top, look for some of the more than 10 other residences nearby (most of these are not open to visits). On the path to the Citadel, you'll pass the pueblo of **Nalakihu,** Hopi for "House Standing Outside the Village." Nalakihu consisted of two stories with

13 or 14 rooms. You can visit both sites on a short self-guided trail.

Lomaki Pueblo

Lomaki, Hopi for "Beautiful House," sits along a small box canyon. Tree-ring dating of roof timbers indicates the occupants lived here from about A.D. 1190–1240. The small two-story pueblo contained nine rooms. A quarter-mile trail from the parking area also passes small dwellings beside Box Canyon. The turnoff for Lomaki lies northwest of Wupatki Visitor Center, 0.3 mile beyond Citadel on the opposite side of the road.

Crack-in-Rock Pueblo

Rangers lead overnight backpack trips to this area during April and October. Crack-in-Rock stands atop an easily defended mesa with sweeping views of the Little Colorado River and distant hills. You will see petroglyphs carved around the base of the mesa and on two nearby mesas, as well as many other pueblo sites. The 14-mile roundtrip hike is moderately difficult and costs $30. Call or write for information at least two months in advance; Wupatki National Monument, tel. 928/679-2365, HC 33, Box 444A #14, Flagstaff, AZ 86004.

East and West of Flagstaff

TO THE EAST: WALNUT CANYON NATIONAL MONUMENT

Sinagua made this pretty canyon their home more than 800 years ago. Ledges eroded out of the limestone cliffs provided shelter from rain and snow—the inhabitants merely had to build walls under the ready-made roofs. Good farmland, wild plant foods, and forests filled with game lay close by. Clear waters of Walnut Creek flowed seasonally in the canyon bottom.

After occupying Walnut Canyon from A.D. 1125–1250, the people moved on. Some Hopi clans trace their ancestors back to this site. More than 300 Sinagua cliff dwellings remain; you can see and enter some along a loop trail constructed by the National Park Service. Another loop trail on the rim passes a pithouse site and a small pueblo.

Visitor Center

A small museum displays pottery and other artifacts of the Sinagua Culture. Exhibits show how the people farmed and how they used wild plants for baskets, sandals, mats, soap, food, and medicine. A map illustrates trading routes to other indigenous cultures. Rangers will answer questions about the archaeology and natural history of Walnut Canyon. During the summer, they offer interpretive programs; call ahead for times and to make reservations for the hikes. Ranger-led trips include the Ledges Hike to cliff dwellings off the main trail and the Ranger Cabin Hike to a 1904 Forest Service that once served as a visitor center for Walnut Canyon. A bookstore sells a wide selection of books, maps, and videos related to the monument and region.

The self-guided 0.9-mile **Island Trail** begins behind the visitor center and winds past 25 cliff dwellings. You can get a feeling of what it was like to live here. The paved path descends 185 feet with 240 steps, which you'll have to climb on the way out; allow 45–60 minutes. Because of the high elevation (6,690 feet), the trail isn't recommended for people with mobility, respiratory, or cardiovascular problems. The easy **Rim Trail** visits two scenic viewpoints, a pithouse site, and a small pueblo, and signs describe the varied plants and wildlife found here. Allow 20–30 minutes for the three-quarter-mile loop, which is paved, level, and wheelchair accessible. Pets cannot go on trails.

Vegetation changes dramatically from the pinyon and juniper forests near the rim to the tall Douglas firs clinging to the canyon ledges. Black walnut and several other kinds of deciduous trees grow at the bottom. Rock layers will be familiar to Grand Canyon visitors. The lower 100 feet of Walnut Canyon belongs to the Coconino Sandstone, 265-million-year-old sand dunes that have turned to stone. The upper 300-foot layer of rock is Kaibab Limestone, formed in a sea about 255 million years ago.

Walnut Canyon National Monument remains open all year except Christmas, though snows can close the trails for short periods. The visitor center is open daily 9 A.M.–5 P.M. and hours may be extended in summer. Island Trail closes one hour before the visitor center does. The entrance fee is $3 per person age 17 and over. Vehicles pulling cars and large trailers may have trouble negotiating the turnaround loop at the visitor center. You'll find picnic areas near the visitor center and on the drive in. From Flagstaff, head east seven miles on I-40 to Walnut Canyon Exit 204, then turn south three miles on a paved road; tel. 928/526-3367; website: www.nps.gov/waca.

Arizona Trail near Walnut Canyon

Hikers and mountain bikers enjoy forests, canyon scenery, and views of the San Francisco Peaks along this section of trail. A sign 2.5 miles in on the Walnut Canyon National Monument road points the way to a trailhead 1.7 miles to the west along a graded dirt road. From here the path heads southwest, crossing a side canyon of Walnut and paralleling the rim before dropping down into upper Walnut Canyon just west of Fisher Point in about six miles. A branch of Flagstaff's Urban Trail System joins here. In another mile you'll reach the junction for Sandy's Canyon Trail, which climbs the canyon to a trailhead near Lake Mary Road in three-quarters of a mile. The Arizona Trail curves to the southeast and continues four miles to Marshall Lake. Mountain bikers may need to walk the steep sections at the side canyon and at the descent into Walnut Canyon. The monument visitor center may have a map.

TO THE WEST: WILLIAMS

Small and friendly, Williams (pop. 2,700) proudly proclaims itself "Gateway to the Grand Canyon." Arizona 64, on the east edge of town, is the shortest route—58 miles—between I-40 and the famous park. Williams, nestled among pine-forested hills and expansive meadows at an elevation of 6,780 feet, offers a better choice of accommodations and restaurants at lower prices than those at the Grand Canyon. Travelers also enjoy the old architecture downtown, Route 66 nostalgia, and staged gunfights. The popular Grand Canyon Railway puffs its way north to the Grand Canyon daily from the old station downtown. Even if you're not riding the rails, it's worth taking a look at the historic train, the museum, and morning Wild West show. Most travelers, in a hurry to get someplace else, miss the pretty country surrounding Williams—splendid Sycamore Canyon, small fishing lakes, high volcanoes, forest drives, and hiking trails. Route 66 fans can drive segments of the old highway east of Williams and mountain bike two loops on old alignments west of town; the Visitor Information Center and the Forest Service office have brochures with maps.

History

Charles Rodgers, the first white settler here, started a cattle operation in 1878. The railroad and lumber town founded several years later took its name from Bill Williams Mountain just to the south. The mountain in turn honored mountain man Bill Williams, who roamed the West from 1825 until his death at the hands of Utes in 1849. He earned reputations as a skilled marksman, trapper, trader, and guide—and, some say, as an accomplished horse thief, preacher of profane sermons, and prodigious drinker. An 8.5-foot statue of "Old Bill" stands in Monument Park at the west end of downtown.

Today the Bill Williams Mountain Men perpetuate his adventurous spirit. The group dons buckskin clothing and fur hats, stages a 180-mile horseback ride from Williams to Phoenix most years, and works to keep the history of the mountain men alive. The Buckskinners, a family-oriented group, puts on frontier-era garb for black-powder shoots.

A more recent period of Western history came to an end at Williams in October 1984, when I-40 bypassed the last section of old US Route 66. A sentimental ceremony, complete with songwriter Bobby Troup of "Route 66" fame, marked the transition. The famous highway from Chicago to Los Angeles carried many families to a new life in Arizona and California. Its replacement, I-40, now travels an unbroken 2,400-mile path from Durham, North Carolina, to Barstow, California. Local businesses suffered when traffic bypassed Williams, but I-40 signs attempt to lure Grand Canyon visitors through downtown even though the real exit for the park is just east of town!

Grand Canyon Railway

Passenger trains first steamed out of Williams to the Grand Canyon's scenic splendor in 1901, replacing an expensive and arduous stage ride. Railroad service ended with the last passenger train carrying just three customers in 1968, but it started anew after a 21-year hiatus. Once again, Canyon visitors can enjoy a relaxing ride through the forests and ranching country of northern Arizona to the historic log depot in Grand Canyon Village, just steps away from the rim. Grand Canyon Railway runs steam locomotives from Memorial Day weekend through September, then vintage diesels the rest of the year. (If the train is too long for the steam engine to pull by itself, a diesel will be slipped in, too.) Trains run roundtrip daily except December 24 and 25 from the 1908 Williams Depot downtown; the depot is half a mile south from I-40 Exit 163 on Grand Canyon Blvd., or it can be reached via either of the other two I-40 Williams exits to downtown. Wheelchair users can access the depot and some of the train.

Before the ride starts, you can take in the Grand Canyon Railway Museum (open daily 7:30 A.M.–5 P.M.), outdoor train exhibits, and a Wild West show; all these are free and open

Grand Canyon Railway train steaming north of Williams

to the public. The depot also has a gift shop. The restaurant Max and Thelma's serves meals.

Once underway, strolling musicians and Wild West characters on board entertain. Passengers on the return trip can expect a little excitement during a staged horseback chase and train robbery before "the law" catches up with the outlaws.

The restored 1923 Harriman coaches have reversible seats; roundtrip fare is $60 adults and $27 children ages 2–16. Passengers can also go Club Class (same as coach but with a bar and coffee, juice and pastries provided in the morning) for $82, First Class (reclining chairs and continental breakfast plus appetizers and champagne or sparkling cider on the afternoon journey) for $120, Deluxe Observation Class (First Class with dome views; ages 11 and up only) for $142, and the Luxury Parlor Car (First Class with seating in overstuffed divans and an open-air rear platform) for $153; children get discounts on all of these. One-way fares are available too. If you have a national park pass, let reservations staff know so that you won't be charged for park admission. The Grand Canyon Railway also offers

packages with train tickets, a room at the Fray Marcos Hotel, and some meals, with options for Grand Canyon tours and accommodations; tel. 800/843-8724 (800/THE-TRAIN); website: www.thetrain.com.

Recommended check-in is 8 A.M. or earlier, in time to have breakfast, see the museum and Wild West show, and board the train for its 9:30 A.M. departure. The train arrives at Grand Canyon, across the street from El Tovar Hotel and canyon rim, about 11:45 A.M. Boarding time for the return trip is 3 P.M. for a 3:15 P.M. departure and 5:30 P.M. return to Williams. South Rim tours within this time period are available at extra cost when you make reservations. The three hours at the Grand Canyon is enough for only a quick look, so you may wish to arrange to stay and ride back another day.

Recreation

Mountain Ranch Stables, behind the Quality Inn, tel. 928/635-0706, offers a variety of trail rides from half an hour to overnight during the April–Oct. season; it's just south of I-40 Pittman Valley Exit 171, six miles east of Williams. **Stable in the Pines,** beside the Circle Pines KOA, tel. 928/635-1930, has summer horseback riding; it's three miles east at I-40 Exit 167, then east 0.4 mile on the north frontage road. Play golf in the pines at the 18-hole **Elephant Rocks Golf Course,** tel. 928/635-4936, during the roughly mid-March–mid-Nov. season. Go west on Railroad Ave. across I-40 (or take I-40 Exit 161 and head north) and drive a mile and a half.

Downhill-ski in winter at the small **Williams Ski Area,** four miles south of town on Bill Williams Mountain, tel. 928/635-9330. It offers a 2,000-foot poma lift (600 vertical feet), 700-foot rope tow for the beginners' slope, lessons, snack bar, rental shop, and ski shop. Full-day weekend lift tickets cost $25 for adults and $20 for children and seniors; rates are lower for weekdays and half days. Cross-country skiers have marked trails. The ski season lasts from about mid-December to the end of March; turn south 2.2 miles on Fourth St., then right at the sign.

Spring Valley Cross-Country Ski Trail has three loop possibilities of 6.5–8 miles each, rated easy–moderate; the season at the 7,480-foot-plus elevations runs winter to early spring. Spring Valley is 14 miles east on I-40 to Parks Exit 178, then north six miles on Forest Road 141; Forest Service offices have a ski trail map. Undeveloped cross-country ski areas include Sevier Flat and Barney Flat on the way to Williams Ski Area and the White Horse Lake area.

Oak Hill Snowplay Area is eight miles east of town on I-40 to the Pittman Valley Rd./Deer Farm Exit 171, then east 2.4 miles on Route 66 on the north side of I-40. Only inner tubes and flexible materials may be used. Separate runs accommodate tubers and skiers.

Motels and Hotels

Business Route I-40, between Exits 161 and 165, divides downtown into one-way streets—Route 66 eastbound and Railroad Avenue

westbound. Grand Canyon Boulevard from I-40 Exit 163 joins these streets in the center of downtown. Most of the town's motels and restaurants lie along Route 66, formerly known as Bill Williams Avenue. Downtown offers the most atmosphere and the convenience of being able to walk to many places. The older places can be bargains, though it's a good idea to check the rooms first. Don't believe the old sign that still advertises rooms "from $3.50" on the 1892 Grand Canyon Hotel on Route 66—the hotel has been closed for a while! For a listing of Williams motels and hotels, see the More Accommodations in the Gateway Cities Appendix at the back of the book.

Bed and Breakfasts

For a real sense of history, it would be hard to beat the **Red Garter Bed and Bakery,** 137 W. Railroad Ave., tel. 928/635-1484 or 800/328-1484, a restored 1897 Victorian Romanesque building. The upstairs rooms of the former brothel all have private bath and include the Parlor ($75 d), Madam's Room ($90 d), Big Bertha's Room ($110 d), and Best Gal's Room ($110 d). Guests awaken to fresh-baked pastries for breakfast in the downstairs bakery, once a rowdy saloon. The establishment at one time had a Chinese chop house and opium den out back. Innkeeper John Holst has photos of the building, saloonkeeper, madam, and customers of the old days. It closes mid-Dec.–mid-Feb.; website: www.redgarter.com.

Sheridan House Inn, 460 E. Sheridan, tel. 928/635-9441 or 888/635-9345, features suites with a gourmet breakfast, casual dinner, private bath, and many extras. Suites go for $135–195 d; website: www.grandcanyonbbinn.com.

Canyon Country Inn, 442 W. Route 66, tel. 928/635-2349 or 877/405-3280, offers homey rooms with private bath and continental breakfast downtown for $77.50 d, $120 family.

Terry Ranch Bed & Breakfast, 701 Quarterhorse off Rodeo Drive, tel. 928/635-4171 or 800/210-5908, is a Country Victorian log house with a veranda and rocking chairs; rooms have private bath, $110–155 d; website: www.terryranchbnb.com.

Campgrounds

Railside RV Ranch, 877 Rodeo Rd., tel. 928/635-4077 or 888/635-4077, is the closest campground to downtown; it has showers and a store, but lacks shade trees. Rates run $16 tents (just a few sites available) and $19–23 RVs with hookups. From I-40 Exit 165, take the business route west toward town, then turn right on Rodeo Rd.; or from downtown, go north on Grand Canyon Blvd., right on Edison Ave., left on Airport Rd., then right on Rodeo Road.

Red Lake Campground and Hostel, 10 miles north on AZ 64 from I-40 Exit 165, tel. 928/635-4753, is open all year with coin-operated showers, limited cooking facilities, a store, and tour booking. Rates are $12–14 tents and $18 RVs with hookups; the hostel facilities cost $11 per person or $33 d for a private room.

Circle Pines KOA, tel. 928/635-2626 or 800/562-9379, is open year-round in the ponderosa pines; head three miles east to I-40 Exit 167, then go east 0.4 mile on the north frontage road. Rates are $18 tents, $24–27 RVs with hookups, $35 "kamping kabins"; amenities include volleyball, badminton, basketball, game room, and an indoor pool and hot tub. In summer, there's a snack bar and you can take in evening movies, van tours to the Grand Canyon, and horseback riding.

Grand Canyon KOA, tel. 928/635-2307 or 800/562-5771, lies five miles north of Williams on AZ 64 (I-40 Exit 165) on the way to the Grand Canyon; it offers tent ($18.50) and RV ($25–29 with hookups) sites and cabins ($36–42) with indoor pool,

hot tub, store, game room, laundry, and showers from March–October.

Ponderosa Forest RV Park & Campground, tel. 928/635-0456 or 888/635-0456, has year-round sites in the woods for tents ($13) and RVs ($19 with hookups) with showers and a nearby store. It's north of I-40 Parks Exit 178, 14 miles east of Williams and about halfway to Flagstaff.

The Forest Service maintains four campgrounds, all on small fishing lakes (trout and catfish) with drinking water, interpretive programs, and camp hosts, but no showers. They're open from early May to about mid-October at elevations of 6,600–7,100 feet. Kaibab, Dogtown, and White Horse Lake may stay open off-season without drinking water, fee, or camp host. Dispersed camping is allowed throughout most of the forest except within half a mile of developed campgrounds, one-quarter mile of surface water, or where signed "No Camping." Boaters can use motors up to eight hp on Cataract and Kaibab lakes, but only electric motors are allowed on the other lakes.

Cataract Campground lies two miles northwest of town; head west on Railroad Ave. across I-40 to Country Club Dr. (or take I-40 Exit 161 and go north), then turn right one mile immediately after going under railroad tracks and look for the entrance on the left. Sites cost $10.

Kaibab Campground is four miles northeast of town; drive east on Route 66 across I-40 (or turn north from I-40 Exit 165), go north two miles on AZ 64, then left one mile at the sign. Sites are $12.

Dogtown Campground and several trails lie 7.5 miles southeast of town; drive 3.5 miles south on Fourth St. (South Rd./Perkinsville Rd.), turn left three miles on Forest Road 140, then left 1.2 miles at the sign. Campsites go for $12.

White Horse Lake Campground lies miles southeast near Sycamore Canyon eight miles south on Fourth St., turn left on Forest Road 110, and follow signs. Sites are $12. A trail goes around the lake. Winter visitors to the White Horse Lake area enjoy ice fishing, cross-country skiing, and snowmobiling.

Food

Max and Thelma's, next to the depot, tel. 928/635-8970, serves American food daily for breakfast, lunch, and dinner, including steak, barbecue, seafood, and pasta. The restaurant has Southwestern and railroad décor. It's named after the couple who brought the Grand Canyon Railway back to life. **Rod's Steak House,** 301 E. Route 66, tel. 928/635-2671, is a Western-style restaurant serving good steak, seafood, and sandwiches daily for lunch and dinner. **Miss Kitty's Steakhouse and Saloon,** 642 E. Route 66, tel. 928/635-9161, serves up cowboy steak, ribs, seafood, and sandwiches in a spacious hall; musicians perform most evenings. Miss Kitty's is open daily for breakfast (buffet available) and dinner.

For Route 66 atmosphere, you can't beat **Cruisers Cafe 66,** 233 W. Route 66, tel. 928/635-2445, with meat and vegetarian fajitas, steak, chicken, ribs, seafood, pasta dishes, and sandwiches; it's open Sat.–Sun. for lunch (summer only) and daily for dinner.

The **Red Garter Bakery,** 137 W. Railroad Ave., tel. 928/635-1484, is open mornings and evenings for baked goodies. **Grand Canyon Coffee & Cafe,** 125 W. Route 66, tel. 928/635-1255, fixes coffees, sandwiches, and cakes daily for breakfast and lunch and Mon.–Sat. for dinner. For good American cafe food—and non-smoking despite the name!—try **Old Smokeys,** 624 W. Route 66, tel. 928/635-1915, open daily for breakfast and lunch. **Pine Country Restaurant,** 07 N. Grand Canyon Blvd., tel. 928/635-18, is another cafe and serves breakfast, 'h, and dinner daily.

Pancho McGillicuddy's Mexican Cantina, 141 W. Railroad Ave., tel. 928/635-4150, serves Mexican cuisine and a few American items daily for lunch (summer only) and dinner in the 1893 Cabinet Saloon building. Musicians perform daily on summer evenings and some weekends off season. **Rosa's Cantina,** 411 N. Grand Canyon Blvd., tel. 928/635-0708, offers traditional Mexican food daily (may close Mon.) for lunch and dinner. **Pizza Factory,** 214 W. Route 66, tel. 928/635-3009, turns out pizza, pasta, calzones, and sandwiches and has a small salad bar. It's open daily for lunch and dinner. **Safeway** supermarket is at 637 W. Route 66.

Events

Downtown rings to the sound of gunfire as cowboys stage shootouts every morning year-round at the train depot; gunfights also break out on the streets every evening during summer. Working cowboys show their skills in the **Summer Rodeo Series** on Fri. and Sat. nights. **Bill Williams Rendezvous** on Memorial Day weekend attracts the Buckskinners and Mountain Men to town for a black powder shoot, Saturday parade, street dance, and arts and crafts. **Festival in the Pines** on the last weekend of June is a juried arts and crafts show with food and entertainment. Townsfolk celebrate **July 4th** with a parade and fireworks. Working cowboys show what they've learned in the **Cowpuncher's Reunion Rodeo** on the first weekend in August. Top rodeo cowboys compete in the **PRCA Rodeo** on Labor Day weekend. **Old Route 66 "Cruisin' the Loop" Day** brings back the classic cars and memories of the '50s on the second weekend of October. **Mountain Village Holiday** runs from Thanksgiving–New Year's Day with arts and crafts and, on the second Saturday in December, a parade of lights.

Information

The **Visitor Information Center,** 200 W.

Railroad Ave. (Williams, AZ 86046), tel. 928/635-4061 or 800/863-0546, has staff from both the Williams-Grand Canyon Chamber of Commerce and the Kaibab National Forest to help you explore and enjoy the region. The office serves so many travelers headed for the Grand Canyon that it stocks brochures and sells maps and books for that area too, as well as the rest of Arizona. It's open daily 8 A.M.–5 P.M. (to 6:30 P.M. in summer) in the heart of downtown in a 1901 passenger train depot; website: www.visitwilliams.com and website: www.thegrandcanyon.com. The *Williams Guidebook* by Richard and Sherry Mangum covers local history, walks, hikes, mountain bike trips, and scenic drives.

Kaibab National Forest staff can tell you about backcountry drives, hiking, camping, fishing, and road conditions in the Williams area. Stop by the Visitor Information Center downtown at 200 W. Railroad Ave. or visit the **Williams Ranger District** office, tel. 928/635-2633, open Mon.–Fri. 7:30 A.M.–4 P.M. The office is 1.5 miles west from downtown at 742 S. Clover Rd. (Williams, AZ 86046); head west on Railroad Ave. and turn left at the sign before I-40 onto the frontage road; website: www.fs.fed.us/r3/kai.

The **public library,** 113 S. First St. (just south of Route 66), tel. 928/635-2263, is open Tues.–Saturday.

Tours and Transportation

To tour the Grand Canyon, try **Grand Canyon Van Tours** (summer only) at Circle Pines KOA, tel. 928/635-2626 or **Marvelous Marv's Tours,** tel. 928/635-4948 or 800/655-4948; marvelousmarv.com.

Canyon Dreams, 135 W. Route 66, tel. 520/635-9434 or 888/731-4680, has a tiny backpacking shop and offers day and overnight hiking tours in the Grand Canyon; website: www.canyondreams.com.

Greyhound, 1050 Grand Canyon Blvd., tel. 928/635-0870 or 800/231-2222, offers several east- and westbound departures daily from the stop at the Chevron station just north of I-40 Exit 163. **Amtrak** trains stop at Williams Junction, three miles east of town; tel. 800/872-7245 or website: www.amtrak.com; the Fray Marcos Hotel offers a shuttle.

VICINITY OF WILLIAMS

Grand Canyon Deer Farm

Visitors enjoy walking among tame deer and hand feeding them at this well-run petting zoo. Llamas, miniature donkeys, pronghorn, wallabies, and talking birds like the attention, too. The farm also has a buffalo, reindeer, exotic goats, a potbellied pig, and other familiar creatures. Peacocks strut across the grounds. The Deer Farm is open daily year-round except Thanksgiving and Christmas; the hours are 8 A.M.–7 P.M. in June–Aug., 9 A.M.–6 P.M. in March–May and Sept.–Oct, and 10 A.M.–5 P.M. Nov.–Feb. (weather permitting). Admission is $5.50 adults, $4.50 seniors 62 and over, $3 children 3–13; tel. 928/635-4073 or 800/926-3337. It's on Deer Farm Rd., eight miles east of Williams off I-40 Pittman Valley/Deer Farm Exit 171. Or from Flagstaff, head west 24 miles on I-40 to Exit 171.

Get Your Bikes on Route 66!

Abandoned sections of historic Route 66 have become two mountain bike trails west of Williams. You can make loops on both by following the unpaved 1922 and partly paved 1932 alignments. Devil Dog Bicycle Tour makes a five-mile loop in ponderosa pines south of I-40 Devil Dog Exit 157; it can be done in 30 minutes. Ash Fork Hill Bicycle Tour is a six-mile loop farther west in pinyon-juniper woodlands and takes about an hour; the ride begins just north of I-40 Welch Exit 151. Stop by the Visitor Information Center or Forest Service office in Williams for a brochure with maps.

Bill Williams Mountain

You can reach the summit of this 9,256-foot peak by any of three hiking trails or by road. Pine, oak, and juniper trees cover the lower slopes, and dense forests of aspen, fir, and spruce grow in protected valleys and at higher elevations. On a clear day, you'll enjoy views of the Grand Canyon to the north, San Francisco Peaks and many smaller volcanoes to the east, Sycamore Canyon and parts of the Verde Valley to the south, and vast rangelands to the west. If it's open, climb up the Forest Service lookout tower at the top for the best views. Hiking season lasts from about June–September; you should always carry water. With a car shuttle, you can go up one trail and down another, or hike a trail just in one direction.

The eight-mile roundtrip **Bill Williams Mountain Trail** climbs the north face of the mountain. You'll reach the road about a half mile from the summit; either continue on the trail across the road or turn up the road itself. The trailhead (elev. 6,900 feet) is near the Williams Ranger District office, 1.5 miles west of town; from I-40, take Exit 161 toward Williams, then turn right (west) 0.7 mile on the frontage road.

The nine-mile roundtrip **Benham Trail** climbs the south and east slopes, crossing the road to the lookout tower several times. To reach the Benham Trailhead (elev. 7,265 feet) from Williams, go south 3.5 miles on Fourth St., then turn right about 0.3 mile on Benham Ranch Road. The gentler grade of this trail makes it good for horseback riders as well as hikers; the trailhead has a corral.

The **Bixler Saddle Trail** starts at Bixler Saddle on the west side of Bill Williams Mountain and climbs past majestic rock formations and good viewpoints. It joins the Bill Williams Mountain Trail fairly close to the top, five miles roundtrip; the summit is another half mile or so. For the trailhead, take I-40 west from Williams to Devil Dog Road Exit 157, head south on Forest Road 108 about a mile,

then turn left 3.6 miles on Forest Rd. 45/Bixler Saddle Road to its end. The last bit may require a high-clearance vehicle. The Kaibab National Forest map (Williams District) will help to navigate the forest roads.

You can also drive up with a high-clearance vehicle; from Williams head 4.7 miles south on Fourth St., then turn right seven miles on Forest Road 111. The road closes in winter.

Keyhole Sink Trail

A pleasant stroll, also marked for cross-country skiers, leads through ponderosa pines to a seasonal pool in a little box canyon. Aspen, wildflowers, and lush grass thrive here; you're likely to see some birds, too. Prehistoric people left petroglyphs, estimated to be 1,000 years old, on the dark basaltic rock. The easy walk is about 1.2 miles roundtrip with little elevation gain. To reach the trailhead, drive east on I-40 from Williams to Pittman Valley Exit 171, exit north, then head east 2.4 miles on Historic Route 66; parking is on the right at Oak Hill Snowplay Area, which features picnic tables, a warming shed, and toilets. The trailhead is north across the road. Coming from Flagstaff, you can take I-40 Parks Road Exit 178, turn north, then west 4.3 miles on Route 66; you'll pass **Garland Prairie Vista Picnic Area** 1.1 miles before reaching Oak Hill Snowplay Area.

Dogtown Trails

Dogtown Lake (elev. 7,100 feet) offers a campground, picnic area, and good hiking. **Dogtown Lake Trail** makes a pleasant 1.8-mile stroll around the lake from the picnic area. **Davenport Hill Trail** begins near the boat ramp on the east side of the lake, follows Dogtown Wash, climbs to a bench, then switchbacks to the 7,805-foot summit. You'll pass through ponderosa pine, Douglas fir, white fir, and aspen forests with some good views. The trail is five miles roundtrip and has an elevation gain of 700 feet. **Ponderosa Nature Trail** is an easy, level, three-quarter-mile loop that branches off the Davenport Hill Trail; a brochure describes the forest environment at stops along the way. Dogtown Lake, named for the prairie dogs common in the Williams area, is 7.5 miles southeast of town; drive 3.5 miles south on Fourth St. (South Rd./Perkinsville Rd.), turn left three miles on Forest Road 140, then left 1.2 miles at the sign.

Sycamore Canyon Point

Sycamore Canyon remains wild and rugged, without any roads or facilities. Elk, deer, black bears, and other animals find food and shelter on the canyon's rim and within its depths. Hikers and horseback riders can use a network of trails. Sycamore Canyon Point, 23 miles southeast of Williams, offers a breathtaking panorama. From town, drive eight miles south on Fourth St. (South Rd./Perkinsville Rd.), then turn left on Forest Road 110 and travel to its end, approximately 15 miles farther. The last five miles are single lane and may be signed "Not For Low-Clearance Vehicles," but careful drivers may make it. Road signs may direct you left on Forest Roads 109 and 12, then back to 110, but you should be able to get through staying on 110. No trails enter the canyon from this side, though you can spot a path going down the opposite side.

Sycamore Rim Trail

This 11-mile loop overlooks parts of upper Sycamore Canyon and travels past seasonal waterfalls, lumber mill and railroad sites, lily ponds (good swimming), and pretty forest country. Stone cairns mark the trail, shown on both the Kaibab and Coconino Forest maps. Trailheads lie southeast of Williams near the junction of Forest Routes 13 and 56, at the end of Forest Road 56, at Pomeroy Tanks off Forest Road 109, and at Sycamore Falls off Forest Road 109; see the Kaibab or Coconino Forest maps.

If you're in the mood for only a short hike, walk 0.3 mile south from the end of Forest Road 56 to an overlook of Sycamore Canyon. The Visitor Information Center downtown at 200 W. Railroad Ave. and the Williams Ranger District office have a map and trail description.

Sycamore Falls

You can easily reach two waterfalls near White Horse Lake. The spectacle, however, occurs only during spring runoff and after heavy rains. From White Horse Lake, turn right two miles (north) on Forest Road 109 to the Sycamore Falls Trailhead, about two miles south of the junction with Forest Road 13. A small waterfall is visible in a canyon just to the right, but walk ahead and a bit to the left to see a larger one, 80–100 feet high.

Perkinsville Road

Beginning as Fourth Street in downtown Williams, Perkinsville Road heads south through the pine forests of the Mogollon Rim, drops down to the high-desert lands of the Verde Valley, crosses the Verde River at historic Perkinsville Ranch, then climbs rugged hills to the old mining town of Jerome. The first 25 miles is paved, followed by 27 miles of dirt. Though dusty and bumpy in spots, the route is usually okay in dry weather. No vehicle

pronghorn

BOB RACE

should attempt the unpaved section after winter snowstorms or heavy summer rains. Allow three hours for a one-way drive, more if you'd like to stop to admire the views. Stock up on gas and water before heading down this lonely road. The Prescott National Forest map covers the entire route.

ASH FORK

Declaring itself the "Flagstone Capital of the USA," Ash Fork occupies high-desert grasslands 19 miles west of Williams and 50 miles north of Prescott. Its location at the junction of I-40 and AZ 89 makes this small community a handy stopping place for travelers. The town grew up around a railroad siding built near Ash Creek in 1882, where passengers and freight transferred to stagecoaches or wagons for Prescott and Phoenix. Ash Fork (pop. 650) now serves as a highway stop and center for livestock raising and sandstone quarrying.

Accommodations

As in Williams, most of the businesses lie along two parallel one-way streets—Lewis Ave. for westbound traffic and Park Ave. for eastbound. Take I-40 Exits 144 or 146. **Ashfork Inn,** west of downtown near I-40 Exit 144, tel. 928/637-2514, is the best choice; $22 s, $29 d.

Ash Fork KOA includes a pool, store, and laundry at 783 Old Route 66, tel. 928/637-2521; rates run $16.50 tents, $19.50–21.50 RV with hookups, and $27 d for cabins. **Cauthen's Hillside RV Park** is on the south frontage road near I-40 Exit 144, tel. 928/637-2300; rates are $7 tents or RVs without hookups, $14 with hookups. Both campgrounds stay open all year and have showers.

Food

Ruby's 8th Street Deli, 823 Park Ave., tel. 928/637-0066, serves up Mexican food,

pizza, and subs. **Picadilly Pizza & Subs** is next to the Chevron station, just south of the west I-40 Exit 144. A park on Lewis Ave. has picnic tables.

SELIGMAN

Another old railroad town, Seligman (pop. 900) now relies more on ranching and tourists. The first residents arrived in 1886 and called the place Prescott Junction, because a rail line branched south to Prescott. Though the Prescott line was later abandoned, the town survived. The present name honors brothers who owned the Hash Knife Cattle Company. Modern travelers on I-40 can take Exits 121 or 123 for the motels and restaurants in town or head northwest on old Route 66. This former transcontinental highway is a longer route to Kingman than I-40, but it offers a change of pace and a glimpse of America's motoring past. It also provides access to the Havasupai and Hualapai reservations (see "Western Grand Canyon and The Arizona Strip"). You'll also find food and lodging at the Grand Canyon Caverns Inn northwest of Seligman, Hualapai Lodge in Peach Springs, and Frontier Motel in Truxton. There's also a 17.5-mile segment of Route 66 east of town that turns southeast just east of downtown; if approaching Seligman from Ash Fork, you can drive it by turning off I-40 at Crookton Rd., Exit 139.

Accommodations

Nearly all businesses lie along Route 66: **Stagecoach 66 Motel,** 639 E. Route 66, tel. 928/422-3470, $30 s, $34 d; **Deluxe Inn,** 203 E. Route 66, tel. 928/422-3244, $28 s, $31 d; **Canyon Lodge,** 114 E. Route 66, tel. 928/422-3255, $37 s, $40 d; **Romney Motel,** 122 W. Route 66, tel. 928/422-7666, $35 d; and **Historic Route 66 Motel,** 500 W. Route 66, tel. 928/422-3204, $47 s, $57 d.

Seligman **Route 66 KOA** is open year-round just east of town with a swimming pool and showers; rates are $17 tent, $21–23 RV with hookups; tel. 928/422-3358. **Historic Route 66 General Store and Campground,** on the west end of town, is open all year with showers; it costs $12.68 for tents or RVs without hookups and $16–19 with hookups including tax; tel. 928/422-3549.

Food

Get your malts, sodas, fast food, and maybe a joke or two at the colorful **Delgadillo's Snow Cap,** 301 E. Route 66, tel. 928/422-3291. **Countryside Cafe,** at the Stagecoach Motel just east of town, tel. 928/422-3470, serves breakfast, lunch, and dinner daily. **Patty's Home Cookin',** 223 E. Route 66, tel. 928/422-0014, has Thai-American food daily for breakfast and lunch and Mon.–Sat. for dinner. Patty's also offers a couple of bed and breakfast rooms and a small grocery. The **Copper Cart Restaurant,** 103 W. Route 66, tel. 928/422-3241, offers a varied American menu daily for breakfast, lunch, and dinner. The steak house and cafe on the west end of downtown lack smoke-free sections. A small park downtown has picnic tables.

GRAND CANYON CAVERNS

Vast underground chambers and some pretty cave formations attract travelers on old Route 66. The caverns lie 25 miles northwest of Seligman, then one mile off the highway. A giant dinosaur stands guard in front. On 45-minute guided tours, you descend 21 stories by elevator to the caverns and walk about a quarter mile with some steps and inclines. Tours operate daily 8 A.M.–6 P.M. from Memorial Day–October 16, then 9 A.M.–5 P.M. in winter (closed Christmas Day); admission is $9.50 adults, $6.75 children 4–12. A gift shop at the entrance has some cave exhibits and photos from the early days, when visitors were lowered 150 feet at the end of a rope.

Grand Canyon Caverns Inn offers year-round accommodations near the turnoff on Route 66; rates are $45 s, $50 d, lower in winter. Self-contained RVs only may park in a campground with drinking water but no showers or hookups for $6.50. The cavern restaurant is open about the same hours as the tours. For information on cave tours or motel reservations, call 928/422-3223.

Resources

More Accommodations in the Gateway Cities

Flagstaff Motels and Hotels

Light sleepers should be aware that many accommodations lie near the railroad tracks. For quieter nights, try the motels on S. Milton Rd. and adjacent Beulah Blvd. and Woodlands Village Blvd.—all well away from trains.

Rates listed below apply in summer but can be higher on holidays or during special events. Lodgings are grouped by weekend rates, often substantially above those during the week. For other types of accommodations, see pages 206–209.

Motels: Under $50

Although hostels offer the cheapest places for solo travelers, a party of two or more can often do better in a motel. Drive along East Route 66 to look for the bargain places; the "strip" extends three miles. Most motels post prices except on summer weekends, when no bargains exist. The low-priced places usually have satisfactory rooms, but always check them first to make sure they're clean.

Downtown

Townhouse Motel, 122 W. Route 66, tel. 928/774-5081, offers a very central, though noisy, location for $27 d ($30–32 d Fri.–Sat.).

South and West of Downtown

Family Inn, 121 S. Milton Rd., tel. 928/774-8820, costs $30 d ($32 d and up Fri.–Sat.).

Arizonan Motel, 910 S. Milton Rd., tel. 928/774-7171, is near NAU, $29 s, $32 d ($36 d Fri.–Sat.).

Autolodge, 1313 S. Milton Rd., tel. 928/774-6621, is a good value in this part of town at $35 d ($39 d Fri.–Sat.).

Hidden Village Motel, 822 W. Route 66, tel. 928/774-1443, has an indoor pool at $35–38 s, 40 d ($48 d Fri.–Sat.).

East of Downtown

"Budget Row" features the best selection in town of bargain places. You can try:

Snowbowl Motel, 618 E. Route 66, tel. 928/773-4818, is basic at $25 s, $30 d ($27 s, $32 d Fri.–Sat.).

Whispering Winds Motel, 922 E. Route 66, tel. 928/774-7391, has mostly kitchenettes from $30 s, $35 d ($40 s, $45 d Fri.–Sat.).

Relax Inn Motel, 1500 E. Route 66, tel. 928/779-4469, runs $25 s, $30 d ($30 s, $35 d Fri.–Sat.).

Western Hills Motel, 1580 E. Route 66, tel. 928/774-6633, has a pool and the Asian Gourmet Restaurant, $30 s, $35 d ($40 s, $45 d Fri.–Sat.).

Chalet Lodge, 1990 E. Route 66, tel. 928/774-2779, costs $25 s, $29 d ($29 s, $35 d Fri.–Sat.).

Wonderland Motel, 2000 E. Route 66, tel. 928/779-6119, is $26 s, $28 d ($35 d Fri.–Sat.).

Twilite Motel, 2010 E. Route 66, tel. 928/774-3364, runs $28 s, $32 d ($32 s, $35 d Fri.–Sat.).

66 Motel, 2100 E. Route 66, tel. 928/774-6403, has some kitchenettes from $22 s, $25 d ($32 d Fri.–Sat.).

Royal Inn, 2140 E. Route 66, tel. 928/774-7308, costs $28 s ($35 d Fri.–Sat.).

Pinecrest Motel, 2818 E. Route 66, tel. 928/526-1950, has some kitchenettes from $25 s, $35 d ($30 s, $40 d Fri.–Sat.).

Carousel Inn, 2918 E. Route 66, tel. 928/526-3595, charges $22–38 d

($35–60 d Fri.–Sat.).

Geronimo Inn, 3100 E. Route 66, tel. 928/527-3377, runs about $30 s, $40 d ($36 s, $46 d Fri.–Sat.).

Butler Avenue Area (I-40 Exit 198)

Motel 6, 2440 E. Lucky Lane, tel. 928/774-8756 or 800/4MOTEL6, has a pool at $30 s, $36 d ($34 s, $40 d Fri.–Sat.).

Motels and Hotels: $50–100
South and West of Downtown

The Inn at NAU, tel. 928/523-1616, puts you in the heart of campus with large rooms and fine dining; students operate the facilities under the School of Hotel and Restaurant Management at a cost of $79 d ($99 d Fri.–Sat.) including breakfast; there's no tax; www.hrm.nau.edu.

University TraveLodge, 801 W. Route 66, tel. 928/774-3381 or 888/259-4404, features a Jacuzzi, hot tub, sauna, and family suites at $70 d ($80 d Fri.–Sat.).

Economy Inn, 224 S. Mikes Pike, tel. 928/774-8888, is near NAU and runs $35–45 d ($49–69 d Fri.–Sat.).

Highland Country Inn, 223 S. Milton Rd., tel. 928/774-5041 or 877/470-6626, sits near NAU and goes for $32–49 d ($32–69 d Fri.–Sat.).

Canyon Inn, 500 S. Milton Rd., tel. 928/774-7301, has a location near NAU, $30 s, $37 d ($90 s, $100 d Fri.–Sat.).

Crystal Inn, 602 W. Route 66, tel. 928/774-4581 or 800/654-4667, features an indoor pool and a hot tub near NAU, $45–55 d ($50–70 d Fri.–Sat.).

Saga Budget Host, 820 W. Route 66, tel. 928/779-3631 or 800/BUD-HOST, has a pool for $35–39 s, $49–59 d ($49 s, $59–69 d Fri.–Sat.).

Days Inn, 1000 W. Route 66, tel. 928/774-5221 or 800/329-7466, offers a pool, $50–99 d ($59–119 d Fri.–Sat.).

Budget Inn, 913 S. Milton Rd., tel. 928/774-5038, offers a pool and hot tub near NAU, $49 d ($89 d Fri.–Sat.).

Comfort Inn, 914 S. Milton Rd., tel. 928/774-7326 or 800/221-2222, has a pool near NAU, $69 d ($94–99 d Fri.–Sat.).

Quality Inn, 2000 S. Milton Rd., tel. 928/774-8771 or 800/228-5151, offers a pool for $69–89 d ($79–120 d Fri.–Sat.).

Fairfield Inn by Marriott, 2005 S. Milton Rd., tel. 928/773-1300, 800/574-6395, or 800/228-2800, has a pool at $59–65 d ($75–79 d Fri.–Sat.).

Motel 6 Woodlands Village, 2745 S. Woodlands Village Blvd., tel. 928/779-3757 or 800/4MOTEL6, has a pool, $40 s, $46 d ($52 s, $58 d Fri.–Sat.).

Sleep Inn, 2765 S. Woodlands Village Blvd., tel. 928/556-3000, features an indoor pool and hot tub at $75–80 d, $85–90 d for a mini-suite; add $5 on weekends.

Econo Lodge West, 2355 S. Beulah Blvd., tel. 928/774-2225, 800/490-6562, or 800/553-2666, has a pool and two hot tubs at $60–80 d ($70–90 d Fri.–Sat.).

Ramada Ltd. West, 2755 S. Woodlands Village Blvd., tel. 928/773-1111, 877/703-0291, or 800/2-RAMADA, offers mini-suites with microwaves and refrigerators plus a pool, sauna, and exercise room at $50–80 d ($70–100 d Fri.–Sat.).

North of Downtown

Ski Lift Lodge, on US 180 opposite the Snow Bowl Road turnoff, tel. 928/774-0729 or 800/472-3599, is open year-round and has a restaurant and winter ski packages, $75 d ($85 d Fri.–Sat.).

East of Downtown

Inn Suites, 1008 E. Route 66, tel. 928/774-7356 or 800/898-9124, features a pool and rooms with microwave and refrigerator (the most expensive rooms also have a Jacuzzi tub and kitchenette), $70–130 d ($90–150 d Fri.–Sat.).

King's House Motel (Best Western), 1560 E. Route 66, tel. 928/774-7186 or 800/528-1234, offers a pool at $69 d ($79 d Fri.–Sat.).

Flagstaff Motel, 2204 E. Route 66, tel. 928/774-0280, runs $27 s, $29 d ($49 s, $59 d Fri.–Sat.).

Rodeway Inn, 2650 E. Route 66, tel. 928/526-2200 or 800/228-2000, costs $30–60 d ($50–70 d Fri.–Sat.).

Pony Soldier Motel (Best Western), 3030 E. Route 66, tel. 928/526-2388 or 800/356-4143, includes an indoor pool, hot tub, and restaurant at $69–89 d ($79–99 Fri.–Sat.).

Howard Johnson Inn, 3300 E. Route 66, tel. 928/526-1826 or 800/437-7137, has the Crown Railroad Restaurant, $39 d ($50 Fri.–Sat.).

Hampton Inn, 3501 E. Lockett Rd., tel. 928/526-1885 or 800/HAMPTON, offers an indoor pool and hot tub for $69 d ($75–79 d Fri.–Sat.).

Days Inn East, 3601 E. Lockett Rd., tel. 928/527-1477 or 800/446-6900, has an indoor pool and hot tub at $80 d ($100 d Fri.–Sat.).

Super 8, 3725 N. Kaspar Ave., tel. 928/526-0818 or 888/324-9131, costs $49 s, $54 d ($54 s, $59 d Fri.–Sat.).

Butler Avenue Area (I-40 Exit 198)

Motel 6 Butler Avenue, 2010 E. Butler Ave., tel. 928/774-1801 or 800/4MOTEL6, has a pool for $38 s, $44 d ($52 s, $58 d Fri.–Sat.).

Continental Inn & Suites, 2200 E. Butler Ave., tel. 928/779-6944, features an indoor pool and hot tub in an atrium and a game room at $35 s, $59 d ($35 s, $69 d Fri.–Sat.), fireplace suites run $89 d ($99 Fri.–Sat.).

Super 8, 2285 E. Butler Ave., tel. 928/774-1821 or 800/800-8000, has a pool and sauna at $45 s, $52 d ($79–89 d Fri.–Sat.).

Holiday Inn, 2320 E. Lucky Lane, tel. 928/526-1150 or 800/465-4329, has an indoor/outdoor pool and a hot tub at $99 d every day.

Econo Lodge Lucky Lane, 2480 E. Lucky Lane, tel. 928/774-7701 or 888/349-2523, includes an indoor pool and hot tub for $60 d ($79–99 d Fri.–Sat.).

Aspen Country Inn, 2500 E. Lucky Lane, tel. 928/226-7111, offers a pool at $35 s, $45 d ($40 s, $50 d Fri.–Sat.).

Red Roof Inn, 2520 E. Lucky Lane, tel. 928/779-5121 or 800/545-5525, includes a pool and hot tub at $48–58 d ($67–80 d Fri.–Sat.).

Motels and Hotels: $100–150 and up
Downtown

Comfi Cottages of Flagstaff, tel. 928/774-0731 or 888/774-0731, have kitchens and provide a full breakfast at various locations, $110–145 d or $220–250 for up to 6–8 guests; www.comficottages.com.

South and West of Downtown

Radisson Woodlands Hotel, 1175 W. Route 66, tel. 928/773-8888 or 800/333-3333, offers a pool, indoor and outdoor hot tubs, sauna, and exercise room at $109–149 d every day.

Embassy Suites Hotel, 706 S. Milton Rd., tel. 928/774-4333 or 800/EMBASSY, has a pool and hot tub near NAU for $119–129 s, $129–139 d ($129–139 s, $139–159 d Fri.–Sat.).

Hampton Inn & Suites, 2400 S. Beulah Blvd., tel. 928/913-0900 or 800/HAMP-TON, features an indoor pool and hot tub at $99 d ($101–129 d Fri.–Sat.), Jacuzzi rooms cost $109–139.

AmeriSuites, 2455 S. Beulah Blvd., tel. 928/774-8042 or 800/833-1516, includes an indoor pool, hot tub and rooms with microwave and refrigerator for $99–149 d ($129–149 d Fri.–Sat.).

Arizona Mountain Inn, 4200 Lake Mary Rd., tel. 928/774-8959 or 800/239-5236, nestles in the pines about three miles southeast of downtown; rooms (including breakfast) and rustic cabins are $80 d ($110 d Fri.–Sat.); www.arizonamountaininn.com.

East of Downtown

Residence Inn by Marriott, 3440 N. Country Club Dr., tel. 928/526-5555 or 800/331-3131, has kitchens in all units and fireplaces in some and includes a pool, hot tub, and nearby golf at $99–170 d studio or $170–209 two-bedroom every day.

Mountain Country Management & Realty, 2380 N. Oakmont Dr. (office), tel. 928/526-4287 or 800/424-7748, has furnished condos of 1–3 bedrooms in the Continental Country Club area, $110–200 per day or you can arrange weekly or monthly stays.

Butler Avenue Area (I-40 Exit 198)

Little America, 2515 E. Butler Ave., tel. 928/779-2741 or 800/352-4386, offers a pool, restaurants, and coffee shop for $119–129 d rooms and $150–275 d suites every day.

Ramada Limited, 2350 E. Lucky Lane, tel. 928/779-3614 or 800/2RAMADA, has a pool at $69–95 d suites ($125–150 d suites Fri.–Sat.).

Williams Motels and Hotels

Summer is also peak season for Williams. Prices at most places tend to stay the same through the week, though they rise on holidays or if the town gets busy. Listings run from west to east. For other types of accommodations, see pages 224–226.

Under $50

Budget Host Inn, 620 W. Route 66, tel. 928/635-4415 or 800/745-4415, charges $40–60 s, $45–69 d.

Westerner Motel, 530 W. Route 66, tel. 928/635-4312 or 800/385-8608, costs $48 d.

9 Arizona, 315 W. Route 66, tel. 928/635-4552, is $25–35 d.

Arizona Welcome Inn & Suites, 750 N. Grand Canyon Blvd. off I-40 Exit 163, tel. 928/635-9127 or 888/895-0997, is $45–59 d, $69–130 d suites.

Route 66 Inn, 128 E. Route 66, tel. 928/635-4791 or 888/786-6956, runs about $40 s, $40–48 d.

American Inn, 134 E. Route 66, tel. 928/635-4591, is $28–48 d.

The Downtowner Motel, 201 E. Route 66, tel. 928/635-4041, costs $35 s, $40 d.

Grand Motel/Gateway Motel, 219 and 234 E. Route 66, tel. 928/635-4601, runs $40–50 d.

Courtesy Inn, 344 E. Route 66, tel. 928/635-2619, is $45 d.

$50–100

Days Inn, 2488 W. Route 66 near I-40 Exit 161, tel. 928/635-4051 or 800/329-7466, costs $62–120 d.

Norris Motel, 1001 W. Route 66, tel. 928/635-2202 or 800/341-8000, offers a pool and hot tub, $55 s, $55–59 d.

Super 8, 911 W. Route 66, tel. 928/635-4045 or 800/800-8000, runs $59–69 d.

Motel 6, 831 W. Route 66, tel. 928/635-9000 or 800/466-8356, is $46 s, $52 d ($56 s, $62 d Fri.–Sat.).

Motel 6, 710 W. Route 66, tel. 928/635-4464 or 800/466-8356, costs $42 s, $48 d ($52 s, $58 d Fri.–Sat.).

Highlander Motel, 533 W. Route 66, tel. 928/635-2541 or 800/800-8288, charges $48 s, $52 d.

Mountain Country Lodge, 437 W. Route 66, tel. 928/635-4341 or 800/973-6210, is $69 d.

Howard Johnson Express Inn, 511 N. Grand Canyon Blvd. off I-40 Exit 163, tel. 928/635-9561 or 800/720-6614, has an indoor pool and hot tub at $35–59 s, $49–89 d.

Holiday Inn, 950 N. Grand Canyon Blvd. near I-40 Exit 163, tel. 928/635-4114 or 800/HOLIDAY, features a restaurant, indoor pool, hot tub, and sauna at $89–119 d or $119–159 d for a suite.

Fairfield Inn by Marriott, 1029 N. Grand Canyon Blvd. north of I-40 Exit 163, tel. 928/635-9888 or 800/228-2800, has a

Accommodations

pool and hot tub for $79 d.

Econo Lodge, 302 E. Route 66, tel. 92/635-4085 or 800/553-2666, runs $55–65 d.

TraveLodge, 430 E. Route 66, tel. 928/635-2651 or 800/578-7878, costs $50–59 d.

El Rancho Motel, 617 E. Route 66, tel. 928/635-2552 or 800/228-2370, is $57–63 s, $63–73 d.

Mountain Side Inn, 642 E. Route 66, tel. 928/635-4431 or 800/462-9381, has a steak house, pool, and hot tub for $86 d.

Super 8, 2001 E. Route 66 near I-40 Exit 165, tel. 928/635-4700 or 800/800-8000, costs $50–60 s, $55–65 d.

Quality Inn Mountain Ranch, seven miles east, just south of I-40 Exit 171, tel. 928/635-2693 or 800/228-5151, features a meadow and forest setting, two restaurants, pool, tennis, and summer horseback riding, $89 d.

$100–150

Best Western Inn of Williams, 2600 W. Route 66 near I-40 Exit 161, tel. 928/635-4400 or 800/635-4445, offers a pool and hot tub at $99–109 d, $119 d for a suite.

Fray Marcos Hotel, downtown at Grand Canyon Railway Depot, tel. 928/635-4010 or 800/843-8724, has a pub and a nearby restaurant, $119 d.

Suggested Reading

Description and Travel

Annerino, John. *Adventuring in Arizona.* San Francisco: Sierra Club Books, 1996. True to its name, this excellent guide lists backroad driving tours, hiking trails, river trips, and climbing routes through the state's most spectacular country. Includes history and travel tips.

Arizona Highways. 2039 W. Lewis Ave., Phoenix, AZ 85009, tel. 602/712-2000 or 800/543-5432; www.arizonahighways.com. Published monthly, this outstanding magazine features superb color photography with articles on the state's history, people, places, wildlife, back roads, hiking, and humor. Arizona Highways also publishes many books on these themes plus some large-format photography titles.

Casey, Robert L. *Journey to the High Southwest.* Chester, CT: Globe Pequot Press, 2000. The author presents travel experiences and advice for southern Utah and adjacent Arizona, New Mexico, and Colorado.

Fishbein, Seymour L. *Grand Canyon Country: Its Majesty and Its Lore.* (National Geographic Park Profiles) New York City: Random House, 1997. Incredible color photography illustrates fine text.

Halper, Evan, and Paul Karr. *Hostels U.S.A.* Old Saybrook, CT: The Globe Pequot Press, 2000. A comprehensive guide to hostelling with an introduction and listings; it also covers some of Canada. Descriptions give a feel for the atmosphere of each place.

Houk, Rose. *The Peaks.* Phoenix: Arizona Highways, 1994. Text and photos capture the beauty and character of the San Fran-cisco Peaks and the land and towns that surround them.

Kosik, Fran. *Native Roads: The Complete Motoring Guide to the Navajo and Hopi Nations.* Tucson: Treasure Chest Publications, 1999. Many historic photos illustrate this guide to the Navajo and Hopi lands and the surrounding area.

Mangum, Richard K., and Sherry G. Mangum. *Flagstaff Historic Walk; A Stroll Through Old Downtown.* Flagstaff: Hexagon Press, 1993. This handy pocket-sized book tells the story of early Flagstaff with many old photos. The authors lead occasional tours of downtown too; ask at the Flagstaff Visitor Center.

Rees, Lucy. *The Maze, A Desert Journey.* Tucson: The University of Arizona Press, 1996. A contemporary Welsh woman explores the wilderness of Arizona on horseback from the Verde Valley to the Hopi mesas.

Story Behind the Scenery series: *Grand Canyon; Grand Canyon-North Rim; Glen Canyon-Lake Powell; Rainbow Bridge; and Canyon de Chelly.* Las Vegas: KC Publications. Beautiful color photos highlight the text in each of these magazine-format titles.

Hiking and Bicycling

Adkison, Ron. *Hiking the Grand Canyon National Park.* Helena, MT: Falcon Publishing, 1997. Detailed descriptions, elevation profiles, and maps cover the most popular trails, along with a good introduction.

Annerino, John. *Hiking the Grand Canyon.* A Sierra Club Totebook. San Francisco: Sierra Club Books, 1993. Easily the most comprehensive guide to trails and routes within the canyon. A long introduction provides background on geology, natural history, Indians, and hike planning. The large fold-out topo map clearly shows trails and routes. River-runners will be pleased to find a section of trail descriptions beginning at the water's edge.

Butchart, Harvey. *Grand Canyon Treks.* Bishop, CA: Spotted Dog Press, 1998. This book combines the texts of legendary Grand Canyon hiker and explorer Harvey Butchart's three earlier guides, originally published in the 1970s and 1980s by La Siesta Press. It's a great source of ideas for off-trail hikes and climbs.

Fletcher, Colin. *The Man Who Walked through Time.* New York City: Random House, 1989. Well-written adventure tale of Fletcher's two-month solo hike through the Grand Canyon. Fletcher was the first to travel its length within the park on foot.

Green, J.D., and Jim Ohlman. *Hiking in the Grand Canyon Backcountry.* Kissimmee, FL: Tower of Ra Publishing, 1995. With this book, you can discover many of the lesser known trails and routes in the Canyon. Some of the more popular trails are described too.

Kals, W.S. *Land Navigation Handbook.* San Francisco: Sierra Club Books, 1983. After reading this book you'll be able to explore Arizona's vast backcountry with confidence. This handy pocket-guide not only offers details on using map and compass, but tells how to navigate using the sun, the stars, and an altimeter.

Kelsey, Michael R. *Canyon Hiking Guide to the Colorado Plateau.* Provo, UT: Kelsey Publishing, 1999. One of the best guides to hiking in the canyon country, with descriptions and maps for destinations in Arizona, Utah, and Colorado. Geologic cross-sections show the formations you'll walk through. The au-

thor uses the metric system, but the book is otherwise easy to follow.

Kelsey, Michael R. *Hiking and Exploring the Paria River.* Provo, UT: Kelsey Publishing, 1997. The classic Paria Canyon hike, with information on nearby Bryce Canyon and other geologically colorful areas. Includes histories of John D. Lee, ghost towns, ranches, and mining.

Mangum, Richard K., and Sherry G. Mangum. *Flagstaff Hikes.* Flagstaff: Hexagon Press, 2001. This comprehensive guide, now in its fifth edition, describes hiking trails surrounding Flagstaff.

Mangum, Richard K., and Sherry G. Mangum. *Williams Guidebook.* Flagstaff: Hexagon Press, 1998. Not many people know about the beautiful country surrounding this town south of the Grand Canyon. Most of the book has been devoted to hikes, but you'll also find local history and visitors' information.

Martin, Tom. *Day Hikes from the River: A Guide to 75 Hikes from Camps on the Colorado River in Grand Canyon National Park.* Flagstaff: Vishnu Temple Press, 1999. If you're lucky enough to be able to do a river trip through the Grand Canyon, this book will help you explore the wonderful canyon worlds here.

Ray, Cosmic. *Fat Tire Tales and Trails.* Flagstaff: self-published, 2000. "Lots of way cool mountain-bike rides around Arizona . . . both summer and winter fun."

Steck, George. *Grand Canyon Loop Hikes I.* Evergreen, CO: Chockstone Press, 1989. These long trips all involve extensive off-trail hiking with difficult route finding, cliffs, and major changes in elevation. Experienced Grand Canyon hikers who are well-conditioned and mentally prepared can plan adventurous outings with the detailed descriptions.

Steck, George. *Grand Canyon Loop Hikes II.* Evergreen, CO: Chockstone Press, 1997. This newer and larger book offers additional challenging loops.

Thybony, Scott. *Official Guide to Hiking the Grand Canyon.* Grand Canyon: Grand Canyon Association, 1997. Introduction and guide to the best-known trails of the Grand Canyon.

Tighe, Kelly and Susan Moran. *On the Arizona Trail: A Guide for Hikers, Cyclists, & Equestrians.* Boulder, CO: Pruett Publishing, 1998. The first guidebook to the Arizona Trail takes you all the way from Mexico to Utah with detailed descriptions. New trail sections continue to be constructed, so you'll need to check for the latest conditions, yet this book makes a great place to start planning your trip.

Warren, Scott S. *Exploring Arizona's Wild Areas; A Guide for Hikers, Backpackers, Climbers, X-C Skiers, & Paddlers.* Seattle: The Mountaineers, 1996. Although the author covers only the designated wildernesses, the 87 described will keep you busy for a long time.

Waterman, Laura, and Guy Waterman. *Backwoods Ethics: Environmental Issues for Hikers and Campers.* Woodstock, VT: Countryman Press, 1994. Thoughtful commentaries on how hikers can explore the wilderness with minimal impact. Case histories dramatize the need to protect the environment.

River-Running and Boating

Abbey, Edward. *Down the River.* New York City: E.P. Dutton, 1991. Abbey expresses joy and concern in a series of thoughtful, witty, and wide-ranging essays on the American West.

Belknap, Buzz. *Grand Canyon River Guide.* Evergreen, CO: Westwater Books, 1990. Covers the 288 miles of Colorado River through Marble and Grand Canyons between Lees Ferry and Lake Mead.

Crumbo, Kim. *A River Runner's Guide to the History of the Grand Canyon.* Boulder: Johnson Books, 1981. Highly readable guide with a foreword by Edward Abbey.

Kelsey, Michael R. *Boater's Guide to Lake Powell.* Provo, UT: Kelsey Publishing, 1996. This comprehensive guide will help you explore the lake, whether traveling in a small inflatable raft, as the author did, or a more luxurious craft. Includes many maps, photos, and hiking descriptions.

Ryan, Kathleen Jo (photographer and producer). *Writing Down the River: Into the Heart of the Grand Canyon.* Flagstaff: Northland Publishing, 1998. Fifteen of today's best female writers tell of their experiences in the Grand Canyon. Impressive color photos illustrate the pages.

Stephens, Hal G., and Eugene M. Shoemaker. *In the Footsteps of John Wesley Powell: An Album of Comparative Photographs of the Green and Colorado Rivers, 1871–72 and 1968.* Boulder: Johnson Books and The Powell Society, 1987. Fascinating photo album of identical river views snapped nearly 100 years apart. Photos show how little—and how much—the forces of erosion, plants, and human beings have changed the Green and Colorado River Canyons. The text describes geologic features of each of the 110 pairs of photos. Maps show locations of camera stations.

Stevens, Larry. *The Colorado River in Grand Canyon: A Comprehensive Guide to Its Natural and Human History.* Flagstaff: Red Lake Books, 1998. The introduction and maps guide you from Lees Ferry to Lake Mead with descriptions of geology, Indian history, exploration, flora, and fauna.

History

Cline, Platt. *They Came to the Mountain: The Story of Flagstaff's Beginnings.* Flagstaff: Northern Arizona University with Northland Publishing, 1976. A highly readable account of Flagstaff's founding and early years. The author has completed his trilogy on the area that began with *Mountain Town: Flagstaff's First Century* (1994) and *Mountain Campus: The Story of Northern Arizona University* (1983).

Crampton, C. Gregory. *Standing Up Country.* Tucson: Rio Nuevo Publishers, 2000. Illustrated historical account of the people who came to the canyon lands of Arizona and Utah—Indians, explorers, outlaws, miners, settlers, and scientists.

Dellenbaugh, Frederick S. *A Canyon Voyage: A Narrative of the Second Powell Expedition Down the Green-Colorado River from Wyoming, and the Expeditions on Land, in the Years 1871 and 1872.* Tucson: University of Arizona Press, reprinted 1984. Dellenbaugh served as artist and assistant topographer on the expedition.

Dimock, Brad. *Sunk Without a Sound.* Flagstaff: Fretwater Press, 2001. The tragic honeymoon of Glen and Bessie Hyde, who disappeared on a river trip in the Grand Canyon in 1928, remains one of the Canyon's most haunting mysteries. Here is the story of their disappearance along with possible reappearances. The author not only extensively researched the facts and theories, but recreated the Hyde's trip with a replica of their crude Idaho sweep scow that proved nearly uncontrollable in the rapids.

Howard, Kathleen L. and Diana F. Pardu. *Inventing the Southwest: The Fred Harvey Company and Native American Art.* Flagstaff: Northland Publishing, 1996. Illustrated history of how the partnership of the Santa Fe Railroad and Fred Harvey Company brought America and the Southwest Indians together.

Hughes, J. Donald. *In the House of Stone and Light.* Grand Canyon: Grand Canyon Association, 1978. A well-illustrated history of the Grand Canyon from the early Indians to the modern park.

Lee, Katie. *All My Rivers Are Gone; A Journey of Discovery Through Glen Canyon.* Boulder: Johnson Books, 1998. The author describes traveling through and falling in love with this canyon and the subsequent loss of it under the waters of Lake Powell. Some of her songs accompany the text.

Lummis, Charles F. *Some Strange Corners of Our Country.* Tucson: University of Arizona Press, 1891, 1892, reprinted in 1989. Step back a century to visit the Southwest's Indian country, Grand Canyon, Petrified Forest, and Montezuma Castle.

Pattie, James Ohio. *The Personal Narrative of James O. Pattie.* Missoula, MT: Mountain Press Publishing Co., 1988. Reprint of 1831 edition. An early fur trapper, who claimed to be the first white American to see the Grand Canyon, tells of his experiences in the wild lands of the West during the 1820s.

Powell, J.W. *The Exploration of the Colorado River and Its Canyons.* Mineola, NY: Dover Publications, reprinted 1961 and Penguin USA, reprinted 1997. Powell relates the story of his epic 1869 expedition—the first running of the Colorado River through the Grand Canyon—along with a description of the Grand Canyon and travels in the region. His encounters with Indian cultures provide a glimpse of their traditional ways.

Suggested Reading

Rusho, W.L., and C. Gregory Crampton. *Lees Ferry: Desert River Crossing.* Salt Lake City: Tower Productions, 2001. An historical study of Lees Ferry, with over 135 rare and unusual photographs.

Warner, Ted J., editor, and Fray Angelico Chavez, translator. *The Dominguez-Escalante Journal; Their Expedition Through Colorado, Utah, Arizona, and New Mexico in 1776.* Salt Lake City: University of Utah Press. Although unsuccessful in their goal of crossing from Santa Fe to California, the expedition's journal provides an early look at the land and native peoples of the Four Corners region, including the Arizona Strip, Lees Ferry area, and the Hopi Mesas.

Archaeology

Grant, Campbell. *Canyon de Chelly: Its People and Rock Art.* Tucson: University of Arizona Press, 1978. The author describes the geology, archaeology, and history of the canyons. Nearly half the well-illustrated text is devoted to a discussion of the wealth of petroglyphs and pictographs left by the ancestral Puebloan people, Hopi, and Navajo.

Lister, Robert, and Florence Lister. *Those Who Came Before: Southwestern Archaeology in the National Park System.* Tucson: Southwest Parks & Monuments Assoc., 1993. A well-illustrated guide to the history, artifacts, and ruins of prehistoric Indian cultures in the Southwest. Includes descriptions of the parks and monuments that contain these sites today.

Noble, David Grant. *Ancient Ruins of the Southwest.* Flagstaff: Northland Publishing, 2000. A well-illustrated guide to the prehistoric ruins of Arizona, New Mexico, Colorado, and Utah.

Patterson, Alex. *A Field Guide to Rock Art Symbols of the Greater Southwest.* Boulder: Johnson Books, 1992. A dictionary-style guide to petroglyphs and pictographs grouped by subject with many illustrations.

Roberts, David. *In Search of the Old Ones; Exploring the Anasazi World of the Southwest.* New York City: Touchstone Press, 1997. In his quest to understand prehistoric people, the author relates stories of early archaeological discoveries along with his own explorations in the Southwest. The book is unusual in that it's told from a perspective of a writer, not an archaeologist.

Arizona's Tribes of Today

Courlander, Harold. *The Fourth World of the Hopis: The Epic Story of the Hopi Indians as Preserved in Their Legends & Traditions.* Albuquerque: University of New Mexico Press, 1987.

Courlander, Harold. *Hopi Voices: Recollections, Traditions, and Narratives of the Hopi Indians.* Albuquerque: University of New Mexico Press, 1982. A selection of 74 Hopi narratives explaining their mythology, history, exploits, games, and animal stories. One of the best books on Hopi culture.

Day, Jonathan S. *Traditional Hopi Kachinas: A New Generation of Carvers.* Flagstaff: Northland Publishing, 2000. Jonathan Day provides a look into Hopi culture with cultural background, interviews with carvers, and 90 color photos. You'll learn the differences between kachina dolls made for collectors and traditional ones for ceremonial use.

Dedera, Don. *Navajo Rugs: How to Find, Evaluate, Buy and Care for Them.* Flagstaff: Northland Publishing, 1996. A history of Navajo weaving, including regional styles and practical advice.

Dittert, Alfred, Jr., and Fred Plog. *Generations in Clay: Pueblo Pottery of the American Southwest.* Flagstaff: Northland Publishing, 1980. An introduction to the pottery of the Pueblo Indians, both prehistoric and modern. Well-illustrated with black-and-white and color photos.

Dozier, Edward P. *Hano, A Tewa Indian Community in Arizona.* Orlando: Holt, Rinehart and Winston, 1966. A study of Tewa history, society, religion, and livelihood.

Dyk, Walter (recorded by). *Left Handed Son of Old Man Hat: A Navajo Autobiography.* Lincoln: University of Nebraska Press, 1995, original copyright 1938. This Navajo relates his story of growing up in the late 1800s.

Gillmore, Frances, and Louisa Wetherill. *Traders to the Navajos.* Albuquerque: University of New Mexico Press, 1934, 1983. The Wetherills lived in and explored the Monument Valley region, trading with the Navajo. The authors tell stories about lost mines, early travelers, and the Navajo people.

Gilpin, Laura. *The Enduring Navajo.* Austin: University of Texas Press, 1994. An excellent book of photographs of the Navajo people, their homes, land, ceremonies, crafts, tribal government, and trading posts.

Jacka, Lois Essary, and Jerry Jacka. *Art of the Hopi, Contemporary Journeys on Ancient Pathways.* Flagstaff: Northland Publishing, 1998. Beautiful color photos on almost every page of this large-format book show the skills, versatility, and variety of Hopi artists.

Jacka, Lois Essary, and Jerry Jacka. *Navajo Jewelry: A Legacy of Silver and Stone.* Flagstaff: Northland Publishing, 1995. Text and color photography introduce the Navajo people, then show more than 250 examples of jewelry from the late 1800s to the present, with descriptions of materials and techniques used.

James, Harry C. *Pages from Hopi History.* Tucson: University of Arizona Press, 1974. Beginning with the tribe's mythical entrance into this world, the author traces Hopi history through early migrations, encounters with the Spanish, difficulties with Mexicans and Navajo, resistance to U.S. authority, to their lives today.

Kawano, Kenji. *Warriors: Navajo Code Talkers.* Flagstaff: Northland Publishing, 1990. The story of how a small group of Navajo Marines in the Pacific during World War II used their language to create a code that could not be broken by the Japanese. The book portrays 75 of the surviving Navajo code talkers.

Locke, Raymond F. *The Book of the Navajo.* Los Angeles: Holloway House Publishing, 1992. Navajo legends, art, culture, and history, from early to modern times.

Luckert, Karl W. *Coyoteway: A Navajo Holyway Healing Ceremonial.* Tucson: The University of Arizona Press and Flagstaff: Museum of Northern Arizona Press, 1979. A rare look at an important Navajo ceremony. It requires nine days and involves chanting, firemaking, sand painting, and other rituals. Photos and chant translations provide a peek into intricate Navajo beliefs.

Page, Susanne, and Jake Page. *Hopi.* New York City: Harry N. Abrams, Inc., 1982 and Abradale Press, 1994. The authors record Hopi spiritual life in text and large color photos, revealing aspects of everyday living, ceremonies, and sacred places rarely seen by outsiders.

Simmons, Leo, ed. *Sun Chief: The Autobiography of a Hopi Indian.* New Haven: Yale University Press, 1963. A Hopi tells of his experiences growing up in both the Hopi and Anglo worlds, then returning to traditional ways.

Teiwes, Helga. *Hopi Basket Weaving; Artistry in Natural Fibers.* Tucson: University of Arizona Press, 1996. The author tells about Hopi women and why they weave. You'll learn of the origins of basketry, techniques, and use in ceremonies.

Titiev, Mischa. *Old Oraibi: A Study of the Hopi Indians of Third Mesa.* Albuquerque: University of New Mexico Native American Studies, 1992. Detailed account of Hopi society and ceremonies.

Wright, Barton. *Clowns of the Hopi.* Flagstaff: Northland Publishing, 1994. These characters amuse audiences while protecting traditions. The book provides explanations, including the deeper meanings of the clown's antics, with drawings and historic and modern photos.

Wright, Barton. *Hopi Kachinas: The Complete Guide to Collecting Kachina Dolls.* Flagstaff: Northland Publishing, 1985. The author explains and illustrates the wide variety of dolls—from clowns to ogres.

Wright, Margaret. *Hopi Silver.* Flagstaff: Northland Publishing, 1998. History and examples of Hopi silversmithing.

Yava, Albert. *Big Falling Snow.* Albuquerque: University of New Mexico Press, 1992. A Tewa-Hopi discusses the history and traditions of the Tewa and Hopi, including conflicts with missionaries and government officials who tried to Americanize the tribes.

Zolbrod, Paul G. *Diné bahane': The Navajo Creation Story.* Albuquerque: University of New Mexico Press, 1988. Deities, people, and animals come to life in this translation of Navajo mythology.

Natural Sciences

Arnberger, Leslie P., and Jeanne R. Janish. *Flowers of the Southwest Mountains.* Tucson: Southwest Parks & Monuments Assoc., 1982. Descriptions and illustrations of flowers and common trees found above 7,000 feet.

Barnes, F.A. *Canyon Country Geology.* Thompson Spring, UT: Arch Hunter Books, 2000. Geologic history and guide to rockhounding with an emphasis on southeastern Utah and adjacent Arizona.

Bowers, Janice Emily. *100 Desert Wildflowers of the Southwest.* Tucson: Southwest Parks & Monuments Assoc., 1989. A general introduction with brief descriptions, including a color photo of each flower.

Bowers, Janice Emily. *100 Roadside Wildflowers of Southwest Woodlands.* Tucson: Southwest Parks & Monuments Assoc., 1989. Brief descriptions and color photos of 100 flowers found above 4,500 feet.

Cunningham, Richard L. *50 Common Birds of the Southwest.* Tucson: Southwest Parks & Monuments Assoc., 1999. Each bird is represented by a color photo and description of migration, feeding, and nesting habits; the text includes Spanish and Latin names.

Desert Botanical Garden staff, and others. *Desert Wildflowers; A Guide for Identifying, Locating, and Enjoying Arizona Wildflowers and Cactus Blossoms.* Phoenix: Arizona Highways, 1997. Text and color photos take you through the seasons in the different desert regions of the state and provide practical advice for growing your own at home.

Dodge, Natt N., and Jeanne R. Janish. *Flowers of the Southwest Deserts.* Tucson: Southwest Parks and Monuments Assoc., 1985. Desert plant and flower guide for elevations under 4,500 feet.

Elmore, Francis H., and Jeanne R. Janish. *Shrubs and Trees of the Southwest Uplands.* Tucson: Southwest Parks & Monuments Assoc., 1976. Color-coded pages help locate plants and trees found above 4,500 feet.

Fischer, Pierre C. *70 Common Cacti of the Southwest.* Tucson: Southwest Parks & Monuments Assoc., 1989. Each cactus is represented by a color photo and description.

Gray, Mary Taylor. *Watchable Birds of the Southwest.* Missoula: Mountain Press Publishing, 1995. Color pictures reveal 68 species in wetlands, open-country, and high-country habitats.

Halfpenny, James, and Elizabeth Biesiot. *A Field Guide to Mammal Tracking in North America.* Boulder: Johnson Books, 1988. No need to guess what animal just passed by. This well-illustrated guide shows how to read the prints of creatures large and small. More determined detectives can peruse the intriguing scatology chapter.

Hare, Trevor. *Poisonous Dwellers of the Desert.* Tucson: Southwest Parks & Monuments Assoc., 1995. The text describes creatures to watch out for—poisonous insects, snakes, and the Gila monster—with advice on insecticides and bite treatment. Also listed are some nonvenomous animals often mistakenly believed to be poisonous.

McKee, Edwin D. *Ancient Landscapes of the Grand Canyon Region.* Flagstaff: Northland Publishing, 1982. Brief account of the geologic history of the Grand Canyon.

Olin, George, and Dale Thompson. *Mammals of the Southwest Deserts.* Tucson: South-

west Parks & Monuments Assoc., 1982. Well-illustrated with black-and-white and color drawings.

Peterson, Roger Tory. *A Field Guide to Western Birds.* Boston: Houghton Mifflin Co., 1998. Well-illustrated with drawings.

Smith, Robert L. *Venomous Animals of Arizona.* Tucson: University of Arizona Press, 1982. Ever wonder about a scorpion's love life? Good descriptions of poisonous insects and animals, with medical notes.

Whitney, Stephen. *A Field Guide to the Grand Canyon.* Seattle: Mountaineers Books, 1996. Excellent, well-illustrated guide to the Canyon's geology, early Indians, flowers, trees, birds, and animals. Most of the information also applies to other canyons on the Colorado Plateau. Includes practical advice for visiting and hiking in the Grand Canyon.

Onward Travel

Barnes, F.A. *Utah Canyon Country.* Utah Geographic Series, Inc. no. 1; 1994. Stunning color photos illustrate this book about the land, people, and natural history of southern Utah. The text also describes parks, monuments, and practicalities of travel.

Metzger, Stephen. *Moon Handbooks: Colorado.* Emeryville, CA: Avalon Travel Publishing, 1999. Colorado calls you to Mesa Verde National Park, beautiful canyon country, the heart of the magnificent Rocky Mountains, and other fascinating areas.

Metzger, Stephen. *Moon Handbooks: New Mexico.* Emeryville, CA: Avalon Travel Publishing, 2000. Explore the landscapes, ancient pueblos, Spanish sites, wilderness areas, art, and cities of New Mexico with this informative guide.

Weir, Bill. *Moon Handbooks: Arizona.* Emeryville, CA: Avalon Travel Publishing, 2002. The most comprehensive guide to the Grand Canyon state has all you need to get started on journeys to the backcountry and city lights.

Weir, Bill, and W.C. McRae. *Moon Handbooks: Utah.* Emeryville, CA: Avalon Travel Publishing, 2001. Explore the magical canyon country north of Arizona with this handy and comprehensive guide. It reveals Utah's unique history, city sights, mountains, and deserts.

Weir, Bill. *The National Geographic Traveler Arizona.* Washington D.C.: National Geographic, 2001. Beautiful color photos illustrate the introduction and highlights of the state.

Reference

Arizona Atlas & Gazetteer. Freeport, ME: Delorme, 2001. Topographic maps at 1:250,000 scale show great detail along with grids for GPS (Global Positioning System) use, but they are difficult to read.

Arizona Road & Recreation Atlas. Berkeley: Benchmark Maps, 1998. Exceptionally easy-to-read maps at 1:400,000 scale with GPS grids and both shaded landscape and color-coded land-ownership maps.

Cheek, Lawrence W., and others. *Photographing Arizona; Practical Techniques to Improve Your Pictures.* Phoenix: Arizona Highways, 1992. How do the Arizona Highways photographers get such spectacular results? Find out in this well-illustrated book!

Comeaux, Malcolm L. *Arizona: A Geography.* Geographies of the United States series. Boulder: Westview Press, 1981. A 336-page volume full of information on Arizona geography, settlement, population, resources, and agriculture.

Walker, Henry P., and Don Bufkin. *Historical Atlas of Arizona.* Norman, OK: University of Oklahoma Press, 1986. Clear maps and concise text cover the geography, Indian tribes, exploration, and development of Arizona.

Accommodations Index

Accommodations Index

Restaurant Index

Restaurant Index

General Index

Acknowledgments

Many thanks go to the hundreds of people who assisted in making *Moon Handbooks: Grand Canyon* as complete and accurate as it is! I am especially indebted to my mother, Doris Weir, for editing the entire book—diligently rearranging words and commas to make the text easier and clearer to read. I've been fortunate also to have a top-notch editor at Avalon Travel Publishing, Angelique Clarke, who helped polish and fit all the sentences into this book. The rest of the Avalon Travel Publishing crew—see copyright page for credits—updated the maps, laid out the pages, and helped the book on its way into your hands.

Staff of the National Park Service at the Grand Canyon took time out from their busy schedules to assist in many ways. Just a few of those who aided the author in the park are Clair Roberts (Tuweep Ranger), who offered ideas and updates for the Toroweap area; and Colleen Hyde (photo archives), who led the author into the park's huge collection of historic photos. Many other National Park Service people helped with research and fact checking at the region's national monuments and at Glen Canyon National Recreation Area. Foresters with the U.S. Forest Service provided many helpful ideas for their forests on both sides of the Grand Canyon. Staff at offices of the Bureau of Land Management gave me valuable advice on exploring the remote and beautiful Arizona Strip. Chambers of commerce supplied valuable ideas, travel tips, and maps.

The friendly crews of Grand Canyon Dories and Canyon Explorations introduced the author to the Grand Canyon from river level with skill and style.

Acknowledgments

U.S.~Metric Conversion

1 inch	=	2.54 centimeters (cm)
1 foot	=	.304 meters (m)
1 yard	=	0.914 meters
1 mile	=	1.6093 kilometers (km)
1 km	=	.6214 miles
1 fathom	=	1.8288 m
1 chain	=	20.1168 m
1 furlong	=	201.168 m
1 acre	=	.4047 hectares
1 sq km	=	100 hectares
1 sq mile	=	2.59 square km
1 ounce	=	28.35 grams
1 pound	=	.4536 kilograms
1 short ton	=	.90718 metric ton
1 short ton	=	2000 pounds
1 long ton	=	1.016 metric tons
1 long ton	=	2240 pounds
1 metric ton	=	1000 kilograms
1 quart	=	.94635 liters
1 US gallon	=	3.7854 liters
1 Imperial gallon	=	4.5459 liters
1 nautical mile	=	1.852 km

To compute celsius temperatures, subtract 32 from Fahrenheit and divide by 1.8. To go the other way, multiply celsius by 1.8 and add 32.

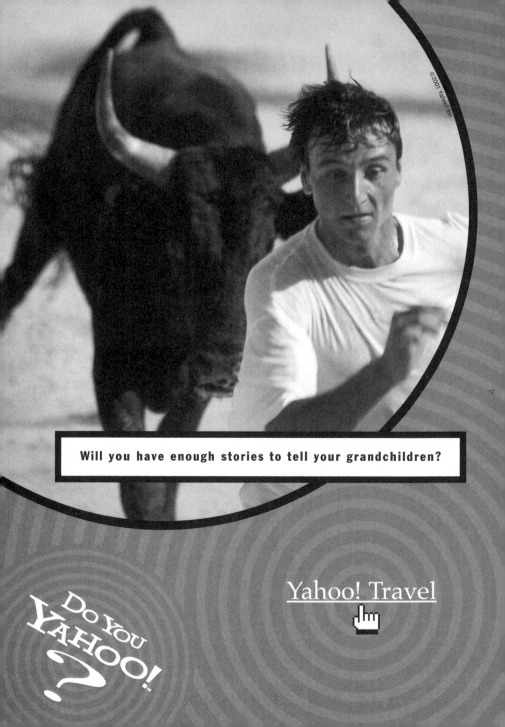

Will you have enough stories to tell your grandchildren?